LEGAL ASPECTS OF CRIMINAL EVIDENCE

Julian R. Hanley

County Judge, Wyoming County, New York

Wayne W. Schmidt

Operating Director of
Americans for Effective Law Enforcement, Inc.

Former Director of the Legal Center,
International Association of Chiefs of Police

McCutchan Publishing Corporation
2526 Grove Street
Berkeley, California 94704

ISBN 0-8211-0758-5
Library of Congress Catalog Card Number 76-28825

To Betty
       —J.R.H.

To Jody
       —W.W.S.

Preface

Knowledge in the field of criminal evidence is of ancient background joined with the modern development of decisions and statutes. This book will inform the law enforcement officer and students of the rules of evidence that guide the enforcement of criminal law in its two most important stages—investigation and trial.

The two authors here uniquely combine a wealth of experience: lawyer, legal writer, appellate advocate, county prosecutor, and judge of a court of record hearing all types of criminal cases. The material is set forth in a clear, comprehensive, and forceful manner.

Much of the work of the investigative law enforcement officer is concerned with the gathering of evidence that is admissible in court. His success in doing this depends upon a thorough knowledge of court decisions and the rules of evidence. The collection and presentation of such evidence is the foundation of justice. The way it is done may seriously affect the life, liberty, and property of others, as well as the reputation of the officer and the law enforcement agency for which he works. The officer's responsibility is to collect all available evidence, but this must be done in a legally accepted manner. His duty is to secure conviction of the guilty and exoneration of the innocent.

It is hoped that this book will open new avenues of knowledge that will assist the law enforcement officer as he carries out his role in the administration of justice. It is dedicated to law enforcement officers, students, and teachers of the subject. All are involved in that most commendable and satisfying of human endeavors—service to their fellow men.

Paul Howard, Bakersfield College
Project Curriculum Adviser

Contents

3. Detention and Arrest in General   45

4. Search and Seizure Generally   69

5. Arrest and Search Warrants   99

9. Questions, Answers, Impeachment, and Cross-Examination of Witnesses   183

13. Physical and Scientific Evidence: Preservation
and Custody   267

14. Special Problems of Proof   295

15. Grand Juries, Suppression Hearings, Appeals, and Forfeiture Proceedings   323

C. APPELLATE ADVOCACY

D. FORFEITURE PROCEEDINGS

1

Introduction to Evidence

(1.1) Scope of Text

Once a person is suspected of having committed a crime, how is he arrested, tried, and convicted? We are not concerned here with the court procedure running from arrest to conviction, but, rather, with the legal proof that is required along the way. The only evidence that can be used against the suspect is legal evidence, that is, evidence that is allowed in court. This chapter is, therefore, devoted to a discussion of legal evidence.

The standards of legal evidence are not the same in all stages of criminal procedure. Evidence may vary in some respects according to whether one is involved in a matter preliminary to trial or the actual trial itself. It is necessary, therefore, for anyone interested in the field of criminal law and criminal evidence to have some understanding of the normal legal processing of a criminal case. The legal processing begins, of course, with an arrest. But what proof is needed to make the arrest in the first place? Suppose, for example, that you are a patrolman on the street, and a tipster whispers to you from a dark alley that there is a heroin sale taking place in a nearby apartment. Is this sufficient evidence to justify your pounding up the stairs, breaking down the door, and arresting the drug dealers? Again, suppose you stop a car for a traffic violation, and the occupants arouse your suspicion. Do you need a search warrant to open the trunk of the car? If so, what proof must you supply the judge in order for him to issue a search warrant? In both cases, in order to answer the questions, you must know the law of evidence.

After the alleged felon has been arrested, a number of preliminary steps are normally taken before he is brought to trial. First, he is entitled to a preliminary hearing before a magistrate to determine if there is enough legal evidence to hold him on the charge. Perhaps you, as the arresting officer, intended to be on vacation at the time of this hearing. Could you sign an affidavit and leave it with the judge instead of testifying in person?

If the magistrate finds that the man should be held for prosecution, the next step may be a hearing before a grand jury. A grand jury is a pretrial investigative body that screens felony cases.

After all the necessary preliminary steps have been completed, the day finally arrives when the actual trial begins. The trial can assume one of two forms. Occasionally a person waives his right to trial by jury and will be tried by the judge without a jury. The normal criminal case, however, requires a jury of twelve people. These people are selected by a procedure whereby the judge and the attorneys for both sides question prospective jurors. A certain number of the prospective jurors may be discharged for cause. This means that there is some reason why they could not be fair and impartial in making a judgment in the case. The court thus excuses them. Others may be excused by either side for no reason at all; this is known as peremptory challenges. The law of the particular jurisdiction states the number of such challenges that can be used by the lawyers for both sides. When the jury is finally selected and sworn in, the search for truth, known as a trial, is ready to begin.

The prosecutor first makes an opening statement in which he outlines what he intends to prove. When these remarks are concluded, the defense counsel may or may not make an opening statement, depending upon his strategy. Some defense lawyers almost never make an opening statement, but let the case develop.

The prosecution is the first side to present its evidence, which consists of testimony from witnesses and of exhibits that are placed in evidence. When the prosecution completes its presentation, the defense normally moves to dismiss the charge on the ground that it has not been proven. If the court overrules this motion, the defense offers whatever evidence it has to disprove the charge. When all the evidence has been introduced, both sides "rest." The defense usually renews its motion for dismissal at this point. If the court overrules this motion, the defense counsel and the prosecuting attorney make their closing argument (summation) to the jury.

The judge next "charges" the jury. That is, he explains to them the law that is involved in the case they have been hearing. The jury then retires to deliberate. As soon as they arrive at a verdict, they return to the courtroom to disclose it.

The sequence of events described above can be interrupted by a "mistrial." Among the reasons for which a mistrial can be declared are an emergency, such as an illness of one of the participants, the commission of a grave legal error during the trial, or a "hung" jury (one that is unable to reach a verdict). If a mistrial is properly declared by the judge, then the entire case must be retried. The preliminary steps, however, do not have to be repeated.

If the jury finds the suspect guilty, he may make an appeal to a higher court. The only way the conviction can withstand the scrutiny of the appellate court is if sufficient legal evidence is produced against the defendant to prove guilt beyond a reasonable doubt.

We have now arrived at the primary question in this chapter: what is evidence? Simply stated, evidence is anything offered in court to prove the truth or falsity of a fact in issue.

As we have said, arrest is one thing, but conviction is something else. The police may have much information about a suspect—a tip from an informer, an intercepted phone call, physical evidence from the scene of the crime. All of these, however, may not be used in court. The accused cannot be convicted by *any* proof, but only by *legal* proof (evidence that is admissible in court).

What are the usual court rules that admit one type of proof in a criminal case, but disallow another? It is really not as difficult to determine this as some lawyers and judges would have you believe. The rules of criminal evidence are, in fact, exact, but it takes judgment and knowledge to apply them to the facts at hand. And anyone involved in law enforcement must include a knowledge of these rules among his basic working tools.

(1.2) Definitions

"Evidence" is anything offered in court to prove the truth or falsity of a fact in issue. "Testimony" is the spoken evidence given by a witness in court. "Real evidence" refers to a tangible object or to exhibits offered in evidence, such as a murder weapon, burglar's tools, or illegal drugs involved in a crime. "Demonstrative evidence" is in the form of a model, an illustration, a chart, or an experiment offered as proof.

There are two general classes of evidence—direct and circumstantial. "Direct evidence" comes from any of a witness' five senses and is, *in itself*, proof or disproof of a fact in issue. For example, if a witness saw and identified the murderer or heard the shooting, he would be giving direct evidence, that is, something he observed that directly proves the crime.

"Circumstantial evidence" is indirect proof showing surrounding circumstances *from which the main fact is inferred*. Typical of circumstantial evidence would be a detective's description of the track of something's having been dragged across the lawn at the scene of the murder or bloodstains found in the trunk of a car belonging to the husband of the victim.

"Admissibility of evidence" concerns the question of whether evidence will be allowed to be used in court. "Weight of evidence" refers to its believability. Though evidence may be technically legal and, thus, admissible in court, the question remains as to whether or not it should be given any real value or "weight."

(1.3) Development of the Rules of Evidence

Every society evolves its own court system to resolve individual disputes or to settle the claim that one of the rules of the group has been broken. We classify the first (disputes between individuals) as a civil action. This type of suit usually concerns property or money. The second (violating the rules of the group) is a criminal case.

We have come a long way from settling matters by trial by combat or trial by ordeal. Neither have the English-speaking peoples adopted trial by inquisition, in which the accused himself must supply much of the proof by answering questions. In the United States we employ the adversary trial system. This system is based on the idea that the truth will more nearly come out if it is tested by the giving of testimony in open court under the questioning and cross-questioning of opposing lawyers.

In order that everyone who is accused of a crime might receive the same treatment, the courts of England, on which our system is based, gradually developed rules defining what matters would be allowed as proof in criminal cases and how trials should proceed. Without such rules, one person's case might be tried in one way and another person's in another way. That is, without such court-approved consistency, we could never hope to approach a system of equal justice.

The gradual development of our law of evidence traces back to early English court decisions. Even today judges will occasionally use an old English case as a guide in deciding a question of evidence. Through the years they have had to decide what proof would be received in individual court cases and what would be rejected. Many of these judicial decisions are written down and then collectively printed in book-form court reports. The federal government and every state publish their own court reports throughout the year. These reports are available to bench, bar, and public as guides to past judicial rulings.

The law ever seeks stability. Thus each court tries to follow the precedent of earlier cases within its jurisdiction that have been decided on the same issue. This adherence to legal precedent is known by the Latin phrase "stare decisis."

Another basis for legal stability is the fact that the lower courts are bound by the decisions of the higher, appellate courts in their state. If, for example, the highest court in California rules that bookmaker slips can be used as evidence in a gambling case, then every lower court in that state must do the same thing.

The body of law found in court decisions is generally referred to as being part of the "common law," as opposed to the statutes enacted by legislatures. Legislative bodies do pass laws concerning evidence, and we must often consult both sources to determine what is legal evidence in our area.

Thus, the rules of evidence, whether common law or statutory, are not the same in every state; nor are they identical with those in the federal courts. The similarities, though, are much greater than the differences. In general, all American courts follow the same basic rules of criminal evidence. A detective from Chicago testifying in a murder case in Ohio would find himself very much at home.

Though we depend heavily on legal precedent, our law is not stagnant. With the passage of time, the courts themselves gradually modify, change, and sometimes overrule prior decisions. In the past fifteen years, for example, largely because of federal court decisions, there have been more changes in the American law of criminal evidence than in twice the number of years preceding. Times change, and so do the courts. For example, rules governing the use of letters and documents as evidence in court have evolved to include the use of tape recordings, moving pictures, and closed-circuit television. Just over the judicial horizon is coming the use of lie detectors and voiceprint analyzers.

We are protected by the law's slowness, but nurtured as well by its change. To know the law of evidence requires the learning of its rules of yesterday, but prudence dictates that we also anticipate its changes of tomorrow.

(1.4) Enactment of Evidentiary Codes

Some foreign countries are code states and do not have a common-law system. From the time of Hammurabi to that of Napoleon, governments have attempted to put all their law into statute form. The strength of the system of legal codes is that all the law is in one place, the statutes. The weakness of it is its rigidity because human affairs are never constant.

As has been said, the United States combines the two systems, mixing the rigidity of the statutes with the flexibility of the common-law court decisions.

All states and the national government have statutes on the law of evidence. Some states, among them California (California Evidence Code), have complete evidentiary codes. The Congress of the United States by Public Law 93-595 (Federal Rules of Evidence, effective July 1, 1975) has also enacted a complete evidentiary code. It covers a broad spectrum, from defining what evidence is relevant to the use of documents and expert testimony and the method of hearing witnesses.

Laws affecting the use of evidence are also often found in many individual state statutes that are not included in an evidentiary code as such. They may range from a motor vehicle statute governing the use of blood alcohol tests in traffic arrests to the use of official laboratory reports before grand juries and the use of police and business records in criminal trials.

All of the above brings us back to the same point. In order to be certain of any specific rule of criminal evidence, you must consult your area's evidentiary code, if there is one, its statutes, and its court decisions on the subject.

(1.5) Burden of Proof in General

There is a common saying among prosecutors that it is easy to indict but hard to convict. This is true. Before the indictment and arrest of a suspect the advantage is with the state, with its paid professional staff of investigators, its laboratory technicians, and its police and prosecutors—all supported by public funds. Once the suspect is arrested, he becomes the defendant, and the advantage is with him. His greatest advantage is that the prosecution has the entire burden of proving his guilt. The prosecution must, in fact, not only prove the defendant's guilt, but must prove it beyond a reasonable doubt. It is not necessary for the defendant to prove a thing. Unless he chooses to do so, he need not even take the stand to testify and to answer the accusation against him.

Many thoughtful people question the wisdom of this system because it so favors the defendant, but the majority feel that it is preferable to have a guilty person go free than to have an innocent person be convicted.

The roots of the idea that the prosecutor must prove everything go back to the days of the king's hangmen, the rack, and the torture chamber. Confessions were extorted by literally stretching men's bones, and the axman's block was almost a relief. Hence, the Fifth Amendment to the Constitution, which manifests our suspicion of tyrannical oppression, provides that no man may be compelled to testify against himself. Thus, the People must not only prove guilt beyond a reasonable doubt, but they must do it without taking any testimony from the defendant. In fact, the right against self-incrimination is so carefully guarded that it "forbids either comment by the prosecution on the accused's silence or instructions by the court that such silence is evidence of guilt," as was stated in *Griffin v. California*, 380 U.S. 609 (1965).

Certain information may, however, be obtained from a non-testifying defendant: a handwriting sample, a mental examination, or observation of the defendant in court (*21 Am Jur 2d*, Secs. 360-365).

An additional factor, adding still more to the prosecution's burden of proof, is the presumption of the defendant's innocence. From the moment he steps into the courtroom, the jury must presume he is innocent. This presumption stays with him throughout the entire trial until, and if, it is overcome by the People's proof of guilt beyond a reasonable doubt. The presumption of innocence applies to every element of the crime with which the defendant is charged. It is not intended to shield the guilty but to prevent the conviction of the innocent.

Reynolds v. *U.S.*, 238 F. 2d 460 (1956) stated: "The presumption of innocence is predicated not upon any express provision of the federal constitution, but upon ancient concepts antedating the development of the common law." Legal historians trace the idea to Deuteronomy and the laws of Sparta and Athens. In *Coffin* v. *U.S.*, 156 U.S. 432 (1894), it is said to be not so much a rule of law as a substantial right of a citizen.

And so, in summary, the burden of criminal proof is completely on the People, the defendant is protected by the Fifth Amendment, and the trial commences with the presumption that he is innocent. The prosecution's burden, and, by extension, law enforcement's, is a heavy burden of proof indeed, and this burden never shifts.

(1.6) Prima Facie Case

When the prosecution rests, having presented all of its proof, the defense counsel usually asks the judge to dismiss the charge on the ground that the People have failed to prove a "prima facie" case. Sometimes the motion is granted.

Prima facie literally means "first view." Prima facie proof in a criminal case is evidence that on its surface is sufficient to prove the charge. It is not necessary that the evidence be conclusive. The defense may always rebut it by contradictory or explanatory evidence, if it has any.

The prosecutor has the burden of producing enough evidence that, at first view, standing alone, is sufficient beyond a reasonable doubt. For example, the prosecution proves the identity of an accused rapist by the testimony of a passerby who saw the suspect leave the building in which the rape took place or by the victim's hair sample on the defendant's clothing. The victim herself can only give a general description. Though the defendant may have an alibi . . . . other defense, the state at this point has proved a prima facie case.

(1.7) Corpus Delicti

The prosecution must always prove the "corpus delicti," the fact that a crime has been committed. A jury cannot deliberate as to who committed it, unless the state first proves that there has been a criminal act (*People* v. *Beltowski*, 162 P. 2d 59 [1945]; *People* v. *Battle*, 10 Cal. Rptr. 627). The jimmied store door and the blown safe inside is the corpus delicti of a burglary, that is, proof that there was a criminal act of breaking in to steal. The half-burned house with evidence of the gasoline used by the arsonist to start the fire would be the corpus delicti of arson.

Because the phrase "corpus delicti" literally means "body of the crime," people often mistakenly think it only refers to the body in a homicide. A popular misconception has grown up that the police cannot prove a murder unless they find the body. This is not so. Producing the corpse only proves a death, not a crime. Murder has been proven many times by circumstantial evidence of the crime even though the body was lost forever.

In the days of sailing ships an English murder case (*Rex* v. *Hindmarsh*, 2 Leach C.C. 569) established a rule that is still followed today. There was an indictment for two counts of murder, one for killing by beating and the other for killing by drowning. The alleged crime occurred at sea. A witness testified that he was awakened at midnight by a violent noise, that on reaching the deck he saw the accused murderer pick the captain up and throw him overboard, and that the captain was not heard from again. Another witness stated that he had earlier heard the prisoner threaten to kill the captain. Near where the captain had been seen a large piece of wood was found, and the deck and part of the accused's clothing were stained with blood. The defense counsel called for an acquittal because the body was never found, arguing that the captain might have been picked up at sea by a passing ship. The court found sufficient proof of corpus delicti, however, and sent the case to the jury. The jury found the defendant guilty, and he was executed.

The problem of corpus delicti in a murder case still exists today, and the courts often disagree as to the required measure of proof. Today's killing in a backyard barbecue pit has the same problem of corpus delicti as yesterday's killing at sea.

Pendleton was indicted for murder on August 26, 1972, in that, "With intent to cause [the] death" of his wife, he struck her with his hands and burned her body in their barbecue pit (*People* v. *Pendleton*, 42 A.D. 2d 144 [1973]). The state based its case on the following facts: One afternoon Pendleton and his wife Virginia had a backyard clambake to which they invited ten guests. Pendleton dug a pit over four feet long; in it a fire was burning throughout the day. In the early morning hours the beer ran out, and the guests left for a club to get more to drink.

Pendleton, his wife, and two guests returned home and sat around the fire. The others left the backyard at about 4:00 a.m., leaving Pendleton and his wife sleeping in the lounge chairs. The next morning Pendleton went into the house and said something about Virginia's being missing. Some of the guests looked for her later in the day, but were unable to find her. One person scratched around in the barbecue pit and turned up something that appeared to be a bone, but someone else said it was a log, and so they pursued the matter no further.

Still later in the day Ronald, the son, poked around in the pit and found bones. When the police arrived they raked out Virginia's skull, which was adhering to a partially burned log. Evidence presented at the trial showed that logs and the mattress from a chaise lounge were found on top of the bones. Pendleton had given conflicting statements and in effect admitted that he had hit his wife with his hands, but denied that he had killed her. The witnesses who described the events of the day said that Virginia was unsteady when she drank and that she had fallen down several times.

At the close of the prosecution's case, the trial judge dismissed the charge on the ground that the prosecution had failed to prove the corpus delicti. He said that there was proof of death but not of a crime, since Virginia might have fallen into the pit by accident. On appeal, the higher court disagreed with the decision of the lower court, holding that there was sufficient proof of a slaying as opposed to an accident. The appellate court pointed out particularly that, since logs and a mattress were on top of the body, it was incredible, if she had fallen into the pit and Pendleton had found her there, that he would have put this material over her simply to get rid of the corpse.

Years ago an English judge, in discussing the proof required for the corpus delicti, supposed a situation in which a man was seen to enter the London docks quite sober, only to come out later quite drunk, staggering from the door of a wine cellar where millions of gallons of wine were stored. "I think," said the judge, "that this would be reasonable evidence that the man had stolen some of the wine, though no proof be given that any particular vat had been broached."

Larceny can be proved without recovering the stolen jewels, kidnapping without finding the victim, England's great train robbery without the million pounds—just as long as the prosecution can prove by other evidence that a crime was committed, that is, the corpus delicti.

And so, today as yesterday, evidence proving the corpus delicti is always a part of the prosecution's burden of proof.

(1.8) Shifting of the Burden of Proof

Appellate courts everywhere have wrestled with the legal theory of whether or not the burden of proof ever shifts from the prosecution to the defense. What happens when the defendant offers to explain the crime in some way, such as presenting an alibi? Does the defendant also have to give proof beyond a reasonable doubt and assume all the other responsibilities that are normally those of the prosecution? Though the legal theory of shifting the burden of proof is mainly a problem to be discussed by court and counsel, men's necks have, nonetheless, often been stretched over legal points finer than this one.

The generally accepted answer to the question above is that the accused is not required to explain anything, although he may do so if he wishes. After the state has made a prima facie case of guilt, the task of showing any contrary evidence is up to the defendant. The accused must come forward with any defense he may have. Thus it is said that he has the "burden of explanation" (*State* v. *Buckley*, 133 A. 433 [1926]).

Evidence offered to explain or excuse the charge that is peculiar to the defendant's own knowledge or that is more readily available to him is always his responsibility to initiate. From that point on, courts have split on who has the burden of proof. Some authorities have ruled that, when such a positive defense is raised by the defendant, the burden immediately shifts to the People, who are then required to prove the negative beyond a reasonable doubt (*People* v. *Kelly*, 302 N.Y. 512 [1951]; *People* v. *Sandgren*, 302 N.Y. 331, 334 [1951]).

A variation of this is found in N.Y. Penal Law, Sec. 2500 (2), which holds that when the defendant has offered such a defense, he must prove it by a preponderance of the evidence. The constitutionality of this contention has been questioned in some cases, among them *Stump* v. *Bennett*, 398 F. 2d III (1968), cert. den. 393 U.S. 1001; *People* v. *Balogun*, 372 N.Y. 2d 384 (Misc. 1975).

The most generally accepted rule is that, once the defendant introduces this type of explanatory evidence, the burden of proof rests with the prosecution, but the jury must consider all the evidence and find guilt only if it is convinced beyond a reasonable doubt (*People* v. *Egnor*, 175 N.Y. 419 [1903]).

Another problem of burden of proof arises when the criminal charge rests on a negative. Some examples of this are a charge of operating a business without a permit or a criminal charge of carrying a pistol without a license. The state does not have to prove an absence of a permit or a license in these cases because knowledge concerning the charges rests solely within the defendant. If the defendant has such a permit or license, he can easily offer it in evidence (*29 Am Jur 2d*, Sec. 153, but see *Johnson* v. *Wright*, 509 F. 2d 828 [5th Cir. 1975]). The state is only required to prove a negative matter if it is something not peculiarly known to the accused.

(1.9) Affirmative Defenses

In criminal cases there are a variety of explanatory defenses that the law labels "affirmative defenses." When one of these is used, the defense in effect may be saying "Yes, I do not deny the crime occurred, but I am not guilty because . . . ." The burden of proving such matters and the way they affect the state's case may vary with the nature of the defense.

a. Alibi

The dictionary defines "alibi" as a plea of having been elsewhere "at the time of the commission of an act." Since the law uses the same definition, an alibi goes farther than a denial that the defendant was at the scene of the crime. An alibi is evidence that the defendant was at another place at the time the crime was committed, thus making it impossible for him to have been guilty. It is a complete, legitimate defense.

Legal authorities have quibbled over whether or not an alibi is technically an affirmative defense, which could result in a shifting of the burden of proof to the defendant. A federal court finally cleared up this point in a decision emanating from a murder case in Iowa (*Stump* v. *Bennett*, supra). The defendant, a man named Stump, was convicted in the Iowa courts of murder and was sentenced to seventy-five years in jail. The prosecution had produced an eyewitness who identified Stump as the assailant at the time and place of the murder. Stump's defense witnesses swore that he was driving on the highway between Des Moines and Knoxville at the time of the crime.

The Iowa evidentiary code put the burden on the defendant of proving his alibi by a preponderance of the evidence. The federal court reasoned that placing the defendant at the scene of the crime was an essential element of the crime and had to be a part of the state's proof. Therefore, the decision continued, the Iowa code was an unconstitutional violation of due process because it attempted to shift the burden of proof to the defendant.

No matter how it is defined, the accepted rule now is that if there is to be an alibi defense the defendant must take the initiative in introducing such evidence. The accused is not held, however, to any measure of proof on the subject of alibi. The burden of proving guilt in a case where an alibi is introduced never shifts from the state. The jury considers the alibi evidence along with everything else in arriving at a verdict. The prosecution in these cases never loses its burden of proving guilt beyond a reasonable doubt.

b. Capacity and Insanity

The law assumes that everyone has ordinary intelligence and is, therefore, capable of committing criminal acts. Though there was an old common-law provision that infants under seven were incapable of committing crime and that those between seven and fourteen were presumed to be incapable, this has largely become obsolete as each state has enacted its own laws defining juvenile delinquents.

Since normality is presumed, the state does not have to prove it and, therefore, does not have to prove criminal capacity in general. This is simply a practical matter. If the prosecution had to prove every defendant was normal, conviction would be impossible. Hence, this is the basis for the assumption that every person has ordinary intelligence and the capacity to commit criminal acts, with the exception of certain matters involving infants that have been referred to previously.

By the same reasoning, the law also presumes that everyone is sane. In most jurisdictions insanity is considered an affirmative defense to be proven by the accused. The measure of proof required of the defendant to prove insanity can be set by statute (*People* v. *Brown*, 37 A.D. 2d 685 [1971]). Requiring the defense to prove insanity by measurable proof is constitutional because it does not actually shift the burden of proving one of the elements of the crime, there being a presumption of sanity (*Leland* v. *Oregon*, 343 U.S. 790 [1952]).

c. Statute of Limitations

In the absence of a law setting a time limit on bringing criminal charges, prosecution could be started at any time. Most jurisdictions, however, have statutes of limitations listing the time when various criminal prosecutions must begin. In general, all misdemeanors and most felonies have time limits; murder usually does not.

The prosecution has the burden of showing that the crime was committed within the proper time. Some statutes state that the time limit is suspended when the defendant is out of the state. If so, the defendant must prove he was not absent all of the time, as this would be something that would be peculiarly within his knowledge.

d. Duress

Sometimes the accused claims that he was coerced or forced to commit a crime. The is the affirmative defense of duress. Suppose, for example, a banker was taken at gunpoint from his home, with his wife held there as a hostage, was driven to his bank, and was directed to remove $200,000.00 from the vault. He would have a good defense of duress were he charged with grand larceny.

Since the affirmative defense of duress does not remove any element of proof from the prosecution, the defendant has the burden of proving it. As with the proof of insanity, the measure of the defendant's proof of duress may also be set by the jurisdiction, such as in N.Y. Penal Law, Sec. 25 (2), 40.00.

e. Entrapment

Entrapment is inducing a person to commit a crime that he would not otherwise have committed. It is recognized everywhere as an affirmative defense. On the question of the burden of proof, entrapment also does not negate any essential legal element. Thus the defendant has the burden of proving it.

Illustrative of entrapment is a New York case in which one Laietta was tried for theft by extortion for attempting to shake down an employer named Friedman (*People* v. *Laietta*, 30 N.Y. 2d 68 [1972], cert. den. 407 U.S. 923). Friedman had fired a worker named Frank for disloyalty and had paid him $500.00 for a signed general release. When Friedman received a threatening telephone call about the matter, he contacted the police, who installed a tape recorder in his car. The defendant unwittingly did his negotiating in the car. Recorded on the tapes was a conversation in which the defendant said: "We're not threatening you remember [but] look, you are going to get hurt if you don't pay. That's it . . . . This idiot [Frank] called some ginzo in . . . Italian families are closely knit."

Laietta claimed entrapment, saying that Friedman was actually a police agent and that he had induced him to commit the crime. Found guilty in the lower court, the defendant appealed the decision. In reviewing the case, the appellate courts held that while entrapment is an affirmative defense, it does not require any less proof in the People's prima facie case. Therefore, the New York statute calling for proof of entrapment by a preponderance of the evidence was held to be constitutional.

f. Miscellaneous Defenses

There are other affirmative defenses that the defendant must raise and prove if he is going to use them. Among them are a claim of double jeopardy (being tried more than once for the same crime); immunity from prosecution granted by a prior court in return for testimony incriminating another defendant; consent of the victim; and self-defense.

In many cases statutes (for example, N.Y. Penal Law, Secs. 150.05-150.10, 190.15, 155.15) define other affirmative defenses, such as the claim in an arson case that a fire was set for a legal purpose; in the defense in a bad check case that the loss was paid back in a specified time; or in a larceny case that the property was appropriated under a good faith claim of right. This type of defense also does not shift the burden of proof in any way, and the People must still prove a prima facie case beyond a reasonable doubt.

(1.10) The Burden of Going Forward

When courts are concerned with the technical problems involved in the burden of proof, they are careful to distinguish between the burden of going forward—introducing the proof of the explanatory defense—and the burden of proving such a defense.

In all cases of positive defense, where the crime is not denied but the defendant offers proof to explain or justify himself, the courts are unanimous in saying that such a defendant has "the burden of going forward." That is, the defendant, not the state, first has to introduce the evidence of avoidance of guilt. If it is an accepted affirmative defense, the defendant may be required to prove it by a preponderance of the evidence. The courts insist, however, that, in the end, the real burden of the proof of guilt, regardless of the type of positive defense, never shifts from the state. And the state must still prove guilt beyond a reasonable doubt.

(1.11) Proof Beyond a Reasonable Doubt

In a civil case, such as a suit for money or property, all that is required of the plaintiff is that he prove his case by a "fair preponderance of the evidence," enough simply to tip the scales of justice. But in a criminal trial, as we have emphasized, much more evidence is needed, since proof of guilt must be beyond a reasonable doubt.

This ancient precept of English justice, which applies to everyone accused of a criminal act, means exactly what it says: a doubt based on reason and arising out of all the evidence or the lack of it. A reasonable doubt is not just any doubt that a person might have.

It is a doubt to which one can assign a reason. The prosecution is not, of course, required to prove guilt to a mathematical certainty. If that were so, it would be useless to prosecute anyone. It is possible, however, to prove guilt to a reasonable certainty, and the People are held to that standard only. This, then, is the measure of evidence that law enforcement personnel must gather and produce in legal form in order to convict a suspect—proof beyond a reasonable doubt.

(1.12) Stipulations

An entirely different way of admitting proof is by stipulation, that is, agreement of the attorneys. Opposing lawyers sometimes agree to let certain evidence be used. Evidentiary matters can then be settled by a stipulation in open court by both the prosecution and the defense. They may stipulate, for example, that a certain state of facts exists or that if a named witness were called he would testify in a certain manner. A counsel will occasionally stipulate that something be introduced as evidence that the court would ordinarily reject; polygraph test results are sometimes used in this way. Usually, however, stipulations as to evidence are employed by counsel for noncontroversial matters, and they are made to expedite the trial of cases.

(1.13) Summary

Much that the police gather as "evidence" cannot legally be used in court. It is necessary, therefore, that every law enforcement officer have a basic knowledge of the law of criminal evidence.

Evidence is any matter offered in court to prove the truth or falsity of a fact in issue. There are two general classes of evidence—direct and circumstantial. Direct evidence is proof from a witness's five senses that in itself is proof of the fact in issue. Circumstantial evidence is indirect proof from which one can logically infer the ultimate facts in issue.

There are two sources of the law of evidence. One is the common law, which is based on past court decisions. The other is found in individual statutes or in evidentiary codes. Both must be consulted in order to learn the laws in any one jurisdiction. Though the law of evidence varies from state to state, the basic rules are the same in all of our courts.

The defendant in every criminal case is presumed to be innocent. Because the accused is protected by the Fifth Amendment, he cannot be made to testify. And he is not required to prove anything. The prosecution must overcome this presumption of innocence by proving the guilt of the defendant beyond a reasonable doubt.

The state attempts to prove initially a prima facie case, that is, proof of guilt "at first view." It has the burden in every criminal trial of proving the corpus delicti—the fact that a crime was committed. If some affirmative defense is to be used, such as insanity, alibi, or duress, the accused must introduce this proof. Even if the accused employs an affirmative defense, however, it is generally accepted that the state must still prove guilt beyond a reasonable doubt. This burden, in fact, never shifts.

2

Admissibility of Evidence

(2.1) General Rules

No evidence has any practical value unless the judge allows it to be used in court, that is, admits it as evidence. To be legally usable, the proof offered must first pass a series of tests. And, of course, any evidence to which an objection is made must properly pass the test of legality.

Initially the evidence must be "relevant." A stock objection the opposing counsel may use is that evidence is "incompetent, irrelevant, and immaterial." This broad attempt to block the admissibility of evidence covers all possibilities, but will normally be rejected as not being specific enough. Yet there are occasions when the evidence is so obviously inappropriate that just the word "objection" will be sufficient to have it excluded.

(2.2) Relevance and Materiality

Many a legal hair has been split by judges, attorneys, and writers of textbooks in an attempt to decide whether an evidentiary item was relevant or material. For all practical purposes, any theoretical difference between the two terms may be disregarded. Strictly speaking, evidence is relevant if it tends to prove a fact in issue before the court. But relevant evidence must also be material; that is, it must be important. If immaterial evidence were admissible, trials could drag on for months. Evidence that is only remotely connected to the crime is said to be immaterial. If, on the other hand, the evidence proves something, but what it proves is not in issue in a particular trial, it is said to be irrelevant.

The problem of relevancy of evidence is the same for both the law enforcement officer and the judge. Does the item of evidence tend to prove the guilt or innocence of the accused? Does it have a bearing on the issue? If it does, is it a direct or remote bearing?

Relevance is really not susceptible to a legal definition, but rests on common sense. As one authority put it, "The only test of relevancy is logic. With this simple statement we must be content. Nothing could be gained in a code of rules making it a thesis on the subject . . . ."

When evidence is offered and an objection is raised, the trial judge must decide whether the item really tends to prove or disprove the issue before the court. If it does, it is relevant and thus passes the first test of legal usefulness.

(2.3) Exclusion of Relevant Evidence

Evidence may be considered relevant, and yet it may not be admitted for some other reason. That is, another rule may exclude it. This means that the law of evidence is largely a study of the rules of exclusion.

A relevant matter may be excluded, for example, simply at the discretion of the judge. He may exercise this discretion if he feels that the evidence to be presented, though otherwise material, might lead to undue hostility, sympathy, or prejudice on the part of a jury. Uncommonly gory police photographs are often not admitted as evidence because they might influence the jury excessively.

Another reason for exclusion is the possibility that the proof might unfairly surprise an opponent. Sometimes relevant evidence is excluded because it could confuse the jury or cause them to argue about a matter that is not part of the issue in question. Relevant evidence may also be rejected simply because it is cumulative. Thus, if a matter has been proven once, it need not be proven a second, a third, or a fourth time.

It is the general rule that evidence will not be excluded unless one of the sides states an objection. Though the judge may reject it on his own motion, he is not likely to do so. The opponent must take the initiative in excluding evidence. If he makes no objection to what the other side introduces, he waives the rule, and any evidence can be used.

(2.4) Evidence of Other Crimes

At this point we are not dealing with the use of evidence of other crimes to discredit a witness or as rebuttal evidence. What happens when the prosecution offers proof of other crimes committed by the defendant as direct proof of guilt in the present situation? Great caution must be exercised when this type of evidence is allowed, since the commission of one crime is not proof that an individual would commit a second. Thus, evidence of other crimes is objectionable, not because it has no probative value, but because it has too much. "The natural tendency of the tribunal . . . is to give excessive weight to the vicious record of crime thus exhibited and either to allow it to bear too strongly on the present charge or to take the proof of it as justifying a condemnation, irrespective of the guilt of the present charge" (*Wigmore on Evidence*, v. 2, Sec. 193). Even a habitual criminal may well be innocent of the crime with which he is charged (*State* v. *Rand*, 238 Iowa 250 [1947]).

In non-English-speaking countries the entire past criminal record of the accused is an important part of the prosecutor's case. So it was in England before 1680. Eventually the English changed this and barred the use of such proof by the crown. In 1692 there was an English murder case known as Harrison's Trial, *12 How. St. Tr.* 833, in which a witness for the crown was asked about a felony committed by the accused three years before. The judge stopped the testimony, saying: "Hold, hold. What are you doing now? Are you going to arraign his whole life? How can he defense himself against charges of which he has no notice? And how many issues are to be raised to perplex me and the jury? Away! Away! That ought not to be: that is nothing to the matter."

Like so much of the law of evidence, this rule of exclusion is subject to several exceptions. Three hundred years after the judge's cry of "Away! Away!" in Harrison's trial, New York's highest court had to deal with the same problem. In so doing, it enumerated and explained the exceptions that do allow the state to include additional crimes as part of its case.

The case in New York was concerned with a society murder that was a sensation in its day. On December 24, 1898, Henry Cornish received a package in the mail containing a blue bottle labeled "Bromo Seltzer." Thinking it a Christmas gift, he passed it on to one of the women of the household. A day or two later he saw another one of the women (Mrs. Adams) in the kitchen with her head resting on her hands, suffering from a headache. At his suggestion she took some of the medicine from the blue bottle to alleviate the pain. When she complained about the taste, Cornish took some of the medicine, saying "Why that stuff is all right." Mrs. Adams started for the kitchen and collapsed. Her face turned blue, and she was dead before the doctor arrived. Meanwhile, Cornish had become ill and, after visiting the police, left for the Knickerbocker Athletic Club, "the journey being marked by frequent interruptions necessitated by the condition of his stomach and bowels."

The "Bromo Seltzer" was found to contain cyanide of mercury. Molineaux, an athletic director of the Knickerbocker Athletic Club, had had a dispute with Cornish, had sent him the bottle of poison, and was thus tried for Mrs. Adams's murder. The prosecutor was not content simply to prove the murder at hand, although he had ample evidence, including proof of Molineaux's handwriting on the package. The state proved, in addition, all the details of a prior murder, claiming that Molineaux had once poisoned a man named Barnet by mailing him a packet of "Kutnow" powder containing cyanide of mercury. It seems that Molineaux was jealous of Barnet's attentions to the woman with whom the defendant was in love.

The court explained the rule on this type of additional criminal proof: "Evidence of other crimes is competent to prove this specific crime charged when it tends to establish (1) motive (2) intent (3) the absence of mistake or accident (4) a common scheme or plan ... (5) the identity [of the accused] ...." The court thus reversed Molineaux's first-degree murder conviction, pointing out that proof of the Barnet murder did not come within any of the exceptions that would allow evidence of one crime to prove another (*People* v. *Molineaux*, 168 N.Y. 264 [1901]).

Though the Molineaux trial occurred many years ago, its rule still applies today. The five exceptions allowing evidence of additional crimes as proof of the crime charged are detailed below.

a. Motive

When motive is an issue, evidence of other of the defendant's acts is admissible, if the acts are not too remote. Proof that a police officer charged with bribery had previously received hush money from other houses of prostitution has been allowed. In cases of adultery, statutory rape, or incest, sexual acts subsequent to the act charged are relevant to show a lascivious disposition on the part of the accused. In cases involving assault, previous similar acts of the defendant against the victim are allowed as proof of motive. In cases concerned with gambling, previous possession of betting slips or proof of prior gambling convictions is allowable. Examples of actual cases include *People* v. *Duffy*, 212 N.Y. 57 (1914); *People* v. *Thompson*, 212 N.Y. 249 (1914); *People* v. *Thau*, 219 N.Y. 39 (1916); *People* v. *Goldstein*, 295 N.Y. 61 (1945); *People* v. *Formato*, 286 A.D. 357, affd. 309 N.Y. 979 (1956).

A less obvious illustration than the above involved the robbery-murder of a sixty-six-year-old upstate New York chicken farmer named Charles Bower. The victim was found shot dead, lying in front of his garage. The evidence showed that he customarily carried money in a wallet in his left shirtfront pocket. When the body was found, the wallet was missing, the shirt pocket was torn, and the button from his overalls' strap was discovered nearby. One, Delorio, was accused of the murder. At his trial the judge allowed the state to prove that Delorio had only three cents in his pocket when he was released from jail on another charge three days before the killing. The jury found him guilty, and he appealed the conviction. The appellate court approved of the use of this evidence as showing that Delorio had a motive to steal, even though it involved proof of another crime (*People* v. *Delorio*, 33 A.D. 2d 350 [1970]).

b. Intent

Motive and intent are often thought of as being the same, but there is a clear legal distinction between them. Motive is the moving power, the reason for doing something. Intent is the mental purpose to do a specific thing to bring about such a result. The jealous husband may well have had a good reason (motive) to kill his wife's lover, but probably did not have the intent to kill him, since he stated: "I only meant to scare him away. The gun went off by accident."

Sometimes guilty knowledge as bearing on intent may be proven separately, often by evidence of other crimes. For example, in a homicide case the state would be allowed to prove that the defendant stole a pistol the day before the killing and used it in the crime (*Stone* v. *State*, 210 Miss. 218 [1950]). Other illustrations might include proof of previous occasions of passing counterfeit money to show this was an intentional act in the present case; earlier receipt of stolen property as evidence of a similar present offense; prior offenses of forgery as proof of possessing forged checks; former fraudulent thefts to demonstrate larceny by false pretenses.

c. Absence of Mistake

Where guilty knowledge is an issue, evidence of other offenses by the accused can properly be used to show that his act was not done by mistake. Illustrations used previously allowing evidence of other crimes to prove intent apply equally here.

d. Common Scheme or Plan

Evidence of other crimes is admissible when it is closely connected with the crime charged and tends to prove a common scheme. It is relevant, however, only if it is offered as circumstantial proof of the present charge. Often one crime may be closely connected with another so that proof of crimes A and B can be introduced as good evidence of crime C. Proof of a series of treatments might be offered to show one event of practicing medicine without a license. Mail fraud or embezzlement cases might involve evidence of a series of these acts to establish the one being charged.

e. Identity

Frequently evidence of other crimes is used to prove the defendant's identity. This can only be done, however, where identity is an issue in the case. There must be a connection between the two offenses to show that whoever committed the first crime also committed the second (*People* v. *Mazza*, 135 C.A. 2d 587 [1955]). This connection can usually be made where an unusual method (modus operandi) was used. If the same method was employed in both crimes, proof of the earlier one would be allowed as tending to identify the accused as the guilty party in the present offense.

In a federal fraud case one Fernandez was charged with defrauding a bank with a supposed timber sale that was part of a swindle. The bank received telephone calls about the timber deal from a man calling himself Belcher and from a timber cruiser supposedly named Rotschy. The government claimed that Fernandez made all these calls. A bookkeeper who had formerly worked for Fernandez was allowed to testify that on various occasions, not connected with this case, Fernandez made other telephone calls in which he misrepresented himself. One of the counts of the indictment in the crime being charged against Fernandez involved a forged deed. The bookkeeper told how Fernandez had used the duplicating machine and cellophane tape to add unauthorized signatures to other papers.

The court approved the use of all of this testimony as showing a particular modus operandi. It ruled that this was circumstantial proof that Fernandez was the guilty person in this case, even though the testimony involved proof of other crimes (*Fernandez* v. *U.S.*, 329 F. 2d 899 [1964], cert. den. 379 U.S. 832).

f. Use of Confessions Involving Other Crimes

An entirely different problem arises when the accused makes a confession in which he also admits to other crimes. The police are not going to stop his recital since it could be very useful. But what happens at the trial when the prosecutor attempts to offer this confession in evidence?

The defense counsel will, of course, object to the use of a confession that mentions crimes other than that for which the defendant is being tried. As we have seen, this is normally a valid objection. If possible, the confession will be redacted (which is the legal term for edited), and any mention of other crimes will be removed. Should the confession containing references to other crimes be allowed as evidence, the conviction will probably be set aside on appeal.

A murder case in Washington, D.C., involved just such a situation. Davis was found murdered in the hallway of a tourist home, having been shot in the chest. A witness had seen a man wearing dark trousers and a blue jacket with gold buttons near the premises. A detective noticed the similarity of dress on a man named Wiggins, who had been arrested later on another charge. He interrogated Wiggins at the station house, later in an unmarked police car, and in various locations around the city, asking him about the Davis murder. When they were riding in the police car, Wiggins began to talk. At the murder trial the officer testified about this conversation:

"I don't know what you are going to think, but I killed Frank, and I don't know what you are going to think, but I killed Davis." He continued to talk and he told me there was a contract out for Davis' life and that he took it . . . that killing Davis didn't bother him but the fact that . . . he was looking at Davis face to face when he shot him bothered him . . . the contract was worth fifteen hundred dollars. He got five hundred dollars and was supposed to get the other one thousand. He mentioned that this wasn't the first time he had killed someone. He had killed three other people. He looked at me and said "You want to know their names don't you?" and I said "No." Then he stated "Well I'm not crazy. I kill only on contract."

The appeals court, noting the prejudicial effect of allowing proof of the other killings, pointed out that this material could have been excised without impairing the confession. Wiggins's murder conviction was reversed, and the case was sent back for retrial (*U.S.* v. *Wiggins*, 509 F. 2d 454 [1975]).

The law enforcement officer should always keep the Wiggins case in mind. If a suspect's confession includes references to other crimes he has committed, be sure that if the confession is put in writing, the additional crimes are included in one paragraph. That portion can then be omitted when the defendant comes to trial.

g. Confessions of Codefendants

There is an additional problem involving the use of confessions. When there are codefendants, the confession of one may implicate the other. But confessions can only be used to incriminate the person who has made the confession and not his accomplice.

If A and B are tried jointly, and the prosecution uses A's confession, which implicates both, B has no chance to defend himself against the accusation unless A testifies. If A does take the stand, then B's lawyer can cross-examine him concerning the matter that was in the confession. There is, however, no guarantee in most cases that A will testify in his own behalf. Therefore, unless the references to B can be omitted from A's confession, there will have to be separate trials for each defendant in order that the court can be certain that A's confession will be used only against A. At B's trial A's confession could not, of course, be used (*Bruton* v. *U.S.*, 391 U.S. 123 [1968]).

(2.5) Weight of Evidence

During the course of a trial an objection may be made regarding the "weight of evidence," as opposed to its admissibility. For example, in a case of drunk driving the defense might object to the acceptability of the blood alcohol test as evidence because the blood sample was kept in the arresting officer's home overnight. The defense might claim that the sample was contaminated. A judge could well admit the test results in evidence for whatever they might be worth, holding that the irregular custody did not preclude the legal admissibility, but could only affect the "weight of the evidence," that is, its accuracy and believability.

Though courts and attorneys sometimes confuse the two terms, as long as evidence is legally admissible, it should be allowed for whatever value or weight the jury might assign to it.

(2.6) Circumstantial Evidence

Circumstantial evidence is indirect proof of a fact, that is, proof from which one can logically infer that a fact exists. The defendant's fingerprints from a burglarized store, bloodstains from the trunk of a murder suspect's car, and the sudden wealth of a bank teller suspected of theft are all examples of circumstantial evidence. None is direct proof of the crime, but each provides strong circumstantial evidence of guilt.

There is a popular misconception that circumstantial evidence should not be believed. All courts, in fact, carefully circumscribe its use. First of all, it cannot be too remote, and it must be logical and not mere conjecture. Circumstantial evidence cannot be used to draw "an inference from an inference," and it must be "clear and convincing." Accepted with these limitations, circumstantial evidence is often the most convincing type of proof there is.

We commonly use circumstantial evidence in our daily lives. Suppose, for example, Mother goes into the kitchen and finds Junior with crumbs on his face and the lid off the cookie jar. Junior, perceiving the danger, says, "I didn't do anything!" Whom is she going to believe—Junior or the circumstantial evidence? The evidence in our cookie case can be classified like that of any crime. If the mother were called on to testify, her recitation about the cookie crumbs would be direct evidence that her son had a dirty face, but it would be circumstantial evidence that he had taken the cookies from the jar and had eaten them.

Usually the only way to demonstrate a state of mind, intent, motive, or malice is by circumstantial evidence. Intoxication normally falls into this category since the proof may largely be a description of the individual's unsteady walk, slurred speech, or erratic driving.

A typical example of a crime proved entirely by circumstantial evidence was the conviction of one Wachowicz for attempted burglary. A tavern manager locked his doors and left the premises at 3:30 a.m. Sometime later a prowl car observed Wachowicz and another man near the tavern. As the police got out of the car, the defendant "made three or four quick steps" while his companion stuck something in his shirt that proved to be a pinch bar. Examination of the tavern showed one door partly pried open with the inside hooks pulled loose. There were jimmy marks on all the doors, and the pinch bar fitted the marks on the wood. Upon being questioned, neither man would admit a thing. Thus circumstantial evidence constituted the entire case against Wachowicz.

The defendant was convicted and appealed the decision. The appellate courts upheld the conviction, saying that the only reasonable conclusion that could be drawn from the evidence was that when the police arrived the defendant had just attempted to break into the tavern (*People* v. *Wachowicz*, 22 N.Y. 2d 369 [1968]).

The lesson a police officer should learn from this type of case is never give up just because your proof is entirely circumstantial. If logic is on your side, the jury and the court usually will be also.

It is plain, then, that both kinds of evidence—direct and circumstantial—are acceptable in court. There is no reason for anyone to refuse to accept circumstantial evidence in a criminal case as long as there are proper instructions from the court concerning its use.

(2.7) General Presumptions

What if the prosecutor had to prove that the judge was qualified and was legally elected or appointed, that the criminal statute involved had been properly passed by the legislature and signed by the governor, and that every defendant was sane? If the state were required to do all this, it might never get around to proving the crime itself. But all this and much more are eliminated by a variety of presumptions applicable to criminal cases. Some are presumptions of law and others of fact, but both materially affect the burden of proof.

Legal scholars argue whether something from which a jury can draw a conclusion is a "presumption" or an "inference." Though the modern trend is to use the latter term, the legal result is largely the same regardless of which is used.

Some presumptions are said to be "conclusive" and others "rebuttable." Strictly speaking, there cannot be a "conclusive presumption" in the sense that an opponent is precluded from showing any evidence to rebut it. A conclusive presumption is usually a rule of law. Examples might include the presumption that a child under a stated age cannot commit a felony or that a boy under fourteen is incapable of rape (*Wigmore on Evidence*, v. 9, Sec. 2492; *Farnsworth v. Hazlett*, 197 Iowa 1367 [1924]). It must be remembered that in the jurisdictions that have these rules they are actually laws. You cannot rebut them, and you must accept them.

Several classes of genuine presumptions are recognized everywhere. They are discussed below.

a. Presumptions of Fact and Law

These presumptions generally are regarded as being the same as an inference. To be legally valid, however, there must be a reasonable connection between the fact proven and the ultimate conclusion inferred from it. The inference must flow naturally and logically from it. Otherwise the presumption will be ruled unconstitutional because it lacks due process of law. There have been a number of court decisions on this precise point.

One of the earliest landmark cases in the U.S. was *Yee Hem* v. *U.S.*, 268 U.S. 178 (1925). The federal law stated that illegal possession of opium gave rise to the presumption that it had been unlawfully imported. The court held that the statutory presumption was logical and therefore valid, on the ground that it was highly improbable that there could be a legitimate possession of opium outside the medical field. Thus, any possessor must know that the opium was illegally imported.

In 1969 the same court had to deal with a federal marijuana charge against Timothy Leary (*Timothy Leary* v. *U.S.*, 395 U.S. 6 [1969]). Customs agents found marijuana in Leary's car when he tried to cross from Mexico on the international bridge. The drug was on the person of his teenage daughter. A federal statute authorized a jury to infer from a defendant's possession of marijuana that it was illegally imported. The courts struck down this statute as unconstitutional, saying that since marijuana is grown in this country, there is no logical basis for stating that because a person has it he must "know" that it was imported.

The Supreme Court met the problem again in a case involving heroin and cocaine (*Turner* v. *U.S.*, 396 U.S. 398 [1970]). Turner and two other men were stopped by federal agents in New Jersey just as their car emerged from the Lincoln Tunnel. The agents saw Turner throw a package on top of a wall. It proved to be a foil-wrapped package of 1.468 grams mixture of cocaine. Under the car seat they discovered a tinfoil package of heroin. At the trial the government introduced both packages in evidence, but gave no other proof of where they came from.

A similar federal statute was involved. It stated that the possession of heroin and cocaine created a presumption that the possessor knew that the drugs were illegally imported. The court upheld the presumption concerning heroin, since it is not produced in this country, but struck down the law making the same presumption regarding cocaine. Because cocaine is manufactured here, a possessor cannot "know" that the drug was illegally imported.

The courts must deal with problems concerning presumption in areas other than drugs. An example was a federal statute involving the possession of a gun or ammunition by any person who had been convicted of a crime of violence or who was a fugitive from justice. It stated that if such an individual was found in possession of a gun or ammunition he could be presumed to have transported it in violation of the federal law governing interstate shipment of firearms. The decision was that there was no reasonable inference between such possession and illegal interstate transportation of guns. The statutory presumption was thus held to be unconstitutional (*Tot* v. *U.S.*, 319 U.S. 463 [1943]).

A New Jersey statute at one time provided that, if a person could not give a good account of himself, this was prima facie evidence that he was in New Jersey for an unlawful purpose. Further, anyone in the state for an unlawful purpose was guilty of disorderly conduct. The federal courts also struck down this law as being an illogical presumption. The fact that a person cannot give a good account of himself might conceivably mean that he is up to no particular good, but it is not reasonable to say that what he is up to must be "unlawful" (*U.S.* v. *Margeson*, 259 F. Supp. 2566 [1966]).

The state of Washington passed what might be considered a very convenient statute. It stated that, if a defendant charged with a violent crime is armed with an unlicensed weapon, it is prima facie proof of his intent to commit such a crime of violence. A defendant named Odom left the state employment office, returned with a .44 caliber magnum (unlicensed), and shot the supervisor twice, leaving him permanently paralyzed. The appellate court, in reversing Odom's conviction, pointed out that a presumption created by statute must follow beyond a reasonable doubt from the first fact. You cannot conclude that because a man has an unlicensed weapon he intends to do violence with it. The statute therefore lacked constitutional due process of law (*State* v. *Odom*, Wash. 519 P. 2d 152 [1974]).

A teacher's oath case from Oklahoma involved a different type of presumption that was found to be unconstitutional. The statute required teachers to take an oath that they had never belonged to any organization listed by the U.S. attorney general as being subversive. The court ruled that under this statute the mere fact of membership would be a conclusive presumption of disloyalty. This, the court said, would be a violation of due process as set forth in the Fourteenth Amendment since membership in a Communist front organization might be innocent (*Wieman* v. *Updegraff*, 344 U.S. 183 [1953]).

b. Presumption of Innocence

The presumption of innocence (discussed in Chapter 1) is perhaps the best-known presumption in English criminal law. Here, the jury must assume that the accused is innocent from the moment he enters the courtroom. This presumption stays with him through the entire trial and remains until, and only if, the prosecution overcomes the presumption by proof of guilt beyond a reasonable doubt. This presumption is surely the strongest we have that favors the defendant.

c. Presumption of Intent

Intent is a material element that the prosecution must prove in the majority of criminal cases. Did the youth really intend to steal the car, or did he simply take a joyride? When the janitor picked up the wallet from the washstand shelf in the airport men's room, did he intend to steal it, or are we to believe his story that he was going to turn it in at the airline desk? Intent is a mental operation. One cannot open a person's head, look inside, and determine his intentions. The law must, therefore, give the prosecution some practical assistance if it is ever going to get a conviction.

The law provides this assistance in the form of a well-recognized presumption: a person is presumed to intend the logical consequences of his act. His intent may be inferred from what he does. If a man points a gun he knows to be loaded at you and pulls the trigger, the law presumes that he intended to shoot you. Either by statute or by general rule, every person is presumed to intend the natural and probable consequences of his voluntary acts (*31-A C.J.S.*, "Evidence," Sec. 15, p. 243).

d. Knowledge of the Law

A general belief exists that everyone "is presumed to know the law." A more accurate way of putting it is that an accused may not claim ignorance of the law as a defense in order to escape punishment.

A common illustration of this concerns possession of a gun. A man from a state where a license is not required may drive into one where it is. He has a pistol on the seat of his car, which is perfectly legal in his home state but which is a serious crime in the new state. Even though he was completely ignorant of the requirement of a special license, this is no defense.

e. Failure to Testify

There is no presumption against an accused who fails to take the stand in his own defense. He is protected by the Fifth Amendment, and the Constitution "forbids either comment by the prosecution on the accused's silence or instructions by the court that such silence is evidence of guilt" (*Griffin* v. *California*, 380 U.S. 609 [1965]). On the contrary, where the defendant does take the stand (except in some limited situations such as pretrial hearings), he waives this constitutional privilege and may be completely cross-examined on any pertinent matter, the same as any other witness.

f. Nonproduction of Evidence

It may be inferred from the unexplained failure of a defendant to call an available witness who has a particular knowledge or to produce evidence within his control that the evidence would be unfavorable to the accused. There are, however, at least three conditions under which this inference will not be made: if the witness is equally available to both sides; if the witness has been subpoenaed, but fails to appear; or if the witness is hostile.

Even when the above conditions are met, the courts are cautious in allowing the inference and may give a narrow interpretation as to whether the witness is "available" or "under the control" of the party or whether he actually has a "particular knowledge" of the facts.

g. Character or Reputation

In criminal cases "character evidence" is a recognized and often effective defense. The most widely accepted view, however, is that there is no presumption one way or another as to whether the accused is of good or bad character (*Greer* v. *U.S.*, 245 U.S. 559 [1918]).

Some jurisdictions do maintain that there is a presumption of good character. Whether the court rules that there is or is not such a presumption, the practical result at the trial is the same. First of all, the term character evidence is a misnomer. The prosecution cannot prove that the accused is a nasty character by demonstrating that he pulled wings off butterflies when he was a child and now runs nefarious errands for the Mafia. Neither can the defense show what a good character he is by having his minister testify that he goes to church every Sunday, gives generously to the United Fund, and is fond of dogs and little children.

Character evidence is, actually, the rankest kind of hearsay. It reflects the reputation one has in his community, and it depends on the reputation for truthfulness of the person who is testifying.

Should the defense offer evidence of good character, the state may, in rebuttal, offer evidence of bad character if it has any (*People* v. *Lingley*, 207 N.Y. 396 [1913]).

(2.8) Official Presumptions

There are many official presumptions. They presume that official acts were performed properly, and they are rebuttable.

a. Legality of Proceedings

It is presumed that all past legal proceedings have been legally and properly carried out. The rule applies to courts, commissions, and all other legal bodies (60 A.L.R. 2d 780; *Permian Basin Area Rate Cases*, 390 U.S. 747 [1968]).

The state commonly uses this rule in prosecutions where the offense or punishment is more severe because of a prior conviction for a felony. The prosecution simply introduces the certificate of prior criminal conviction, and it is presumed to be legal. If the accused claims that the old conviction was improper, he has the burden to come forward and prove it.

A court hearing a criminal case is presumed to have been regularly constituted and to have jurisdiction over the defendant concerning the crime for which he is being tried. It is also presumed that the court's records and its warrants are correct (*People* v. *Wissenfeld*, 169 C.A. 2d 59 [1959]).

An even wider application is involved where the accused claims a conviction or court judgment was unconstitutional under either the state or federal Constitution. Here, too, it is presumed that the judicial proceeding was constitutional. The objector has the burden of overcoming this presumption.

b. Acts of Officers and Officials

Similarly the acts of officers and officials in the performance of their duties are presumed to have been done legally and within the realm of their authority (*Vitelli* v. *U.S.*, 250 U.S. 355 [1919]). Unless there is proof to the contrary, the acts of officers making court-authorized searches and seizures or in executing warrants are presumably legal. The same is true of arrests.

It is presumed that information on which an arrest and indictment are based has been legally secured by the officials involved.

This presumption of official legality applies to all officers and agents of the government. Included among them are the governor who forwards extradition papers, the postman who mails the requisition, the sheriff who serves the governor's warrant, the district attorney who conducts the hearing, and the officers who return the wanted man to the state demanding him.

There is also a presumption of the regularity of a judicial record, which includes the fact that the signature is genuine on a document having an official seal.

Even the posting of signs in municipal speed zones has been done regularly (*People* v. *Love*, 306 N.Y. 18 [1953]).

c. Legislative Acts

All laws, ordinances, and other legislative acts are presumed to have been validly adopted. Were this not so, the prosecution would have the ridiculous burden of proving the validity of every law involved in every criminal case, from the murder statute down to the evidentiary code. Thus, all federal, state, and local laws are presumed to be valid and binding.

d. Foreign Laws

In some criminal cases the law of a sister state or a foreign nation is involved. Proof can always be presented by testimony from a legal expert knowledgeable in the field or by the introduction of reference material. If such proof is absent, the court may presume that the foreign law involved is the same as that of the local jurisdiction. In some situations, however, the court may take official notice of what the foreign law may be.

(2.9) Presumptions Concerning Particular Acts

A variety of acts, which are discussed below, do not require special proof.

a. Use of the Mails

In the ordinary course of postal service any letter that has been properly addressed and mailed is presumed to have been received (California Evidence Code, Sec. 641; *People* v. *Rosenbloom*, 119 C.A. 759 [1931]). This practical rule is universally adopted, not because the courts have some unwarranted confidence in the U.S. mail, but because the sender is not in a position to prove that the letter was received. The recipient must overcome the presumption of delivery, if he can.

b. Identity

Identity will ordinarily be presumed from the same name. The more unusual the name, the stronger the inference of identity (*Wigmore on Evidence*, v. 2, Sec. 411). Thus, a record of conviction in the same name will be sufficient in some jurisdictions to establish the defendant's criminal history. In other courts it is taken as prima facie proof, but not enough standing alone to establish the record.

c. Continuing Fact or Condition

It is often difficult to prove the exact conditions that existed at the time of the crime. This is, for example, a common problem in cases of drunk driving. Witnesses may describe the individual's condition an hour before the arrest. A blood test may be taken a half hour after the accident, but what was the driver's actual condition at the time of the crash?

The victim of a rape or an assault may not be examined until the day following the crime. A sanity test may take place a week or many months after the offense occurred. Mental or physical condition at the time of the crime can be a vital issue.

The same is true of many other facts related to physical conditions. Police photographs may show road signs, highways, bridges, or buildings months or days before or after the event.

Medical testimony will often help to relate physical or mental conditions back to the time of the crime. Sometimes, however, there will only be evidence of a condition before or after the crime. In this situation the law of evidence comes up with a presumption: once a fact has been proven, the condition continues until proven otherwise.

A few states restrict the use of the rule when it is applied to criminal cases (*Sokolic* v. *State*, 228 Ga. 788 [1972]). As a general rule, however, evidence of a condition before or after the event is accepted on the common-sense ground that it was the same at the time of the crime. Once a thing has been proven, its existence is presumed to continue where that would normally happen in human experience.

The use of such evidence is largely left to the discretion of the trial judge. Its admissibility, and, of course, its weight, will be affected by how closely it is connected in time with the crime itself.

d. Sobriety, Normality, and Sanity

As has been said, the law assumes that everyone is sober, competent, and sane, unless, of course, there is evidence to the contrary.

To begin with, it is presumed that every accused is sober, since that is the normal course of human events. The presumption is refuted by evidence of intoxication.

The law further generalizes by presuming that individuals are normal, both physically and mentally. If a sex offender claims that he is mentally retarded, he must produce evidence of low intelligence.

Finally, the law presumes sanity. The definition of criminal insanity varies somewhat from state to state as modern psychiatry seeks to modify the law's relatively narrow view. The usual rule has been that if the accused was aware of his act and knew it was wrong, he was criminally responsible, regardless of any label of mental illness that the medical profession might attach to him. If insanity is a defense, the accused must offer proof of his insanity and thereby overcome the presumption that he is sane. In actual practice the presumption usually leads to a battle between opposing psychiatrists. This simply means that the psychiatrists for the defense testify first, they are contradicted by the prosecution's mental experts, and the jury makes up its own mind.

These factors relating to the defendant's mental and physical condition are peculiarly within his own knowledge. Thus it is only fair that he be the one required initially to offer proof of any abnormal condition where it is pertinent.

e. Suicide

Suicide is a most abnormal event, and so there is a legal presumption against it (*Byers* v. *Pacific Mutual*, 133 C.A. 632 [1933]). Should suicide be a defense in a murder case, for example, the defendant, to overcome this presumption against suicide, must do so by offering what evidence he can to show that the victim did in fact kill himself.

f. Legitimacy

This is one of the strongest presumptions known to the law. The husband is presumed to be the father of any child born in wedlock. It occasionally is involved in criminal matters where the relationship is material. Family offenses or incest are examples that come to mind.

This presumption of legitimacy sometimes produces harsh results, but it is necessary. Otherwise, a husband could escape responsibility for his children simply by denying his parentage.

(2.10) Presumptions Indicating Guilt

If the evidence plausibly points toward guilt, it may be accepted. Such proof is, strictly speaking, not a presumption. It is circumstantial evidence from which an inference of guilt may be drawn (*People* v. *Stewart*, 74 Ill. App. 407 [1966]).

a. Flight or Concealment

Suppose, for example, there is a bank robbery, and the police catch a suspect running down the street away from the bank. One might consider his flight as strong evidence of guilt. Or suppose the the police find a man hiding in a closet in an apartment where drugs have recently been purchased. Again, one could assume from the suspect's concealment that at least an inference could be made concerning evidence of guilt.

Though all courts desire to protect the accused from false charges, they differ somewhat on the value to be given evidence of flight or concealment before an arrest. Most courts, however, hold that neither raises a presumption or inference of guilt (*Starr* v. *U.S.*, 164 U.S. 627 [1897]; *People* v. *Davis*, 29 Ill. 2d 127 [1963]).

Courts will accept proof of flight or concealment, such as that of a suspect fleeing the city soon after a crime has been committed and then hiding out. These actions will be taken as some proof of guilt, although other reasons may be introduced to explain them (*People* v. *Hoyt*, 20 C. 2d 306 [1942]).

If you, as a police officer, ever become involved in prosecuting a charge with this type of circumstantial evidence, you should remember one rule. Proof of flight or concealment may be shown, but it is up to the jury to determine what value it has, without benefit of any presumption or inference. Juries have more common sense than they are often given credit for, and they are quite likely to take either of these actions as a strong indication of guilt.

b. False Statements

The prosecution can prove occasionally that the accused gave false statements, either in oral or written form. They may have evidence at other times that the defendant obtained false statements from third parties to support his defense. In either case an inference of guilt results.

c. Malice

In some cases actual malice is an element. The only possible way to prove this is by evidence of the facts and circumstances. The very nature of the crime itself may create a presumption that it was done maliciously, that is, with a deliberate attempt to harm or destroy. Assault with a deadly weapon is often cited as an example of this.

d. Possession of Fruits of Crime

The possession of the fruits of crime is by itself proof from which an inference of guilt may be drawn. Though the possession of stolen goods soon after a crime has been committed is not conclusive proof, that fact alone gives rise to a strong inference of guilt (*Wilson* v. *U.S.*, 162 U.S. 613 [1896]; *People* v. *Volpe*, 20 N.Y. 2d 9 [1967]). Once the crime has been proven, the unexplained or falsely explained possession of stolen property, such as from burglary, robbery, or larceny, is generally said to give rise to a presumption of guilt (*People* v. *Russell*, 34 C.A. 2d 665 [1939]; *People* v. *Kulig*, 373 Ill. 102 [1939]).

When this type of proof is offered, defense counsel may argue that such a presumption has the effect of violating the defendant's rights under the Fifth Amendment. By giving this legal result to his possession, one is, in effect, making the defendant testify against himself. The defense made this claim in a recent case where one, Barnes, was accused of forging government checks. The government also offered evidence that he was found to possess recently stolen government checks payable to third persons. The court held that such evidence was proper. It ruled that one could presume from the unexplained possession of these checks that the defendant knew they were stolen. This was proven and was thus offered as circumstantial evidence of the forgery. The court said, furthermore, that this did not violate his Fifth Amendment right not to testify (*Barnes* v. *U.S.*, 412 U.S. 837, 93 S. Ct. 2357 [1973]).

e. Possession and Ownership

Some presumptions regarding possession and ownership are widely accepted in civil law and occasionally come into play in some criminal cases. The general rule is that whatever is found in a person's possession is presumed to be his. Also, if a person exercises acts of ownership over property, there is a similar presumption that it is his.

f. Statutory Presumptions

The state and federal governments all have various statutes containing presumptions that arise from certain situations. Illustrations of this type were discussed in the cases listed earlier under "General Presumptions." Some other examples are statutes that presume that a pawnbroker has knowingly accepted stolen goods if he has made no reasonable inquiry as to the legal ownership; that presume that the presence of a weapon in an automobile is the possession of everyone in the car; and that presume that the presence of illegal drugs in a car or in a room in clear view is evidence of possession by all the occupants (N.Y. Penal Law, Secs. 165.55, 220.25).

(2.11) Judicial Notice

There are some things that a court will accept as true without any proof. The judge does this by taking "judicial notice" of them without any introduction of evidence. Though this is an inherent power in all courts, in some jurisdictions its use may be somewhat restricted by statute (for example, California Evidence Code, Sec. 453). In addition, different judges have different ideas on the subject. Thus the wise police officer will find out in advance what the judge's attitude is on taking judicial notice. He will then know, for example, whether the court will take judicial notice that La Salle Street runs into Green Street or whether he will be required to testify to this fact.

It must be remembered that a judge can take judicial notice of matters of general knowledge, not of something that he may be acquainted with. He may, for instance, be personally aware of the fact that there is a stoplight in front of a certain station house, but cannot, without proof, take judicial notice of it at a trial (California Evidence Code, Sec. 450).

a. Judicial Notice of Facts

Facts that are so universally known that they cannot reasonably be the subject of dispute will generally be recognized by judicial notice. When this is the case, it is not necessary to introduce an almanac or an encyclopedia in evidence. Matters of common knowledge, natural phenomena, history, language, and geography fall into this category. No one, for example, has to offer proof that water freezes or objects fall.

Scientific phenomena are often recognized by judicial notice. In recent years, for instance, courts have taken judicial notice of the validity and accuracy of radar. It is only necessary to prove the accuracy of the particular apparatus used in the case (*People* v. *MacLaird*, 264 C.A. 2d 972 [1968]).

Matters of geography are commonly accepted in this way. As an illustration, one court took judicial notice the tide affects the San Joaquin River past the port of Stockton (*Colberg* v. *California*, 67 C. 2d 408 [1967]).

In the realm of language even "street talk" has been judicially noticed. Thus, in a drug case in California the court took judicial notice that the term "reds" means capsules of Seconal®(*People* v. *Hubard*, 9 C.A. 3d 827 [1970]).

One judge aptly stated the rule concerning the judicial notice of facts in *AhKow* v. *Nunan*, 5 Sawy. 552: "We cannot shut our eyes to matters of public notoriety and general cognizance. When we take our seats on the bench, we are not struck with blindness and forbidden to know as judges what we all see as men."

b. Judicial Notice of Laws

Without exception, every court takes judicial notice of treaties between the United States and foreign countries, including official interpretation of these treaties. Courts even take judicial notice of the absence of treaties such as those concerned with extradition.

They also take judicial notice of the laws within their jurisdiction, even if the attorneys forget to mention one. Courts above the municipal level are sometimes fussy about taking judicial notice of municipal ordinances. They may require proof of their existence, but will allow the presumption that they were validly enacted. In addition, official regulations, such as sanitary codes and rules governing the income tax, are judicially recognized since they have the force of law.

Courts generally do not take judicial notice of foreign laws since they are beyond their field of knowledge. A number of states, however, judicially recognize the laws of sister states.

In regard to judicial records, a court always takes judicial notice of its proceedings, but not of other courts. Official records of the latter must be introduced in evidence.

(2.12) Summary

Evidence is of no value unless it can be used in court. To be admissible it must be relevant, and even then it must pass a variety of other tests.

Evidence of other crimes committed by the accused may be offered by the prosecution. Courts restrict its use, however, because of possible undue prejudice toward the defendant. Such proof is limited to proving motive, intent, identity, absence of mistake, or a common scheme or plan.

Motive and intent are terms that are easily confused. Motive is the reason for the crime. Intent is the conscious purpose to commit the criminal act.

Confessions containing reference to other crimes raise difficulties in the trial. Often the only way such a confession can be admitted in evidence is if the recitals of other crimes can be removed.

There are a number of legal presumptions or inferences. Some of the well-recognized ones are the presumption of innocence; the presumption that a person intends the normal consequences of his actions; and the negative presumption against a litigant resulting from the nonproduction of evidence that is within his control.

In order for a presumption to be constitutionally valid, there must be a logical connection between the initial fact proven and the conclusion drawn therefrom.

There exist several official presumptions: that past legal proceedings are valid; that officials have acted legally in performing their duties; that laws were properly adopted.

Some presumptions apply to particular situations—that mail has been received; that a proven fact has continued to exist; that persons with the same name are the same. Sanity, normality, and sobriety are presumed. There is a strong presumption against suicide. Finally, the husband is the presumed father of children born in wedlock.

There are presumptions of guilt. The giving of false statements or possession of the fruits of crime are examples. Flight or concealment, while not labeled a presumption of guilt by many courts, is accepted as circumstantial evidence against the accused.

Courts will often take judicial notice of generally known facts of geography, history, or science, thus bypassing the necessity of proof. Judicial notice will also be taken of the laws of the forum or of a court's own proceedings.

3

Detention and Arrest

(3.1) Detention in General

A detention is not an arrest and is a lesser intrusion on an individual's rights. It is a temporary curtailment of personal freedoms and is justified for limited purposes. The most common form of temporary detentions are those associated with "stop-and-frisk" practices.

For many years conscientious police officers have stopped suspicious individuals to ask them questions about their conduct. These stops are frequently accompanied by frisks, a limited form of searching the person's outer clothing. In 1968 the Supreme Court, in an eight-to-one decision, upheld the right of police officers to detain suspicious individuals temporarily and to frisk those who appear to be dangerous. The landmark case was *Terry* v. *Ohio*, 392 U.S. 1 (1968).

Terry was one of three men who was pacing back and forth in front of a jewelry store in downtown Cleveland. Police Detective McFadden, who was highly experienced in foot patrol surveillances, believed they were casing the store in contemplation of an armed robbery. He confronted the men and asked them their names, but their reply was not understandable. He grabbed Terry, turned him around, patted his overcoat, and removed a pistol he found there. A companion had a bulge in his coat that also turned out to be a weapon. Terry was convicted of carrying a concealed weapon, and he appealed.

The question was whether McFadden had probable cause to believe Terry was armed. The Supreme Court agreed with Terry that McFadden's actions constituted a "search." In justifying a temporary detention and pat-down, a lesser standard of proof is required for a determination of probable cause. The Supreme Court enunciated for the first time the existence of a sliding scale: the greater (or lesser) the physical intrusion, the greater (or lesser) the amount of proof necessary to sustain police action under the Fourth Amendment.

The Supreme Court clearly acknowledged the duty of police officers to investigate suspicious conduct and to attempt to question persons acting in a peculiar fashion. Once a legitimate detention is made, an officer may have the right, on the basis of the particular circumstances, to pat down a suspect for a weapon. The court, with Justice Douglas dissenting, felt it could not "blind" itself to the increasing dangers to police officers from armed assault. Weapons confiscated during a properly conducted stop and frisk would, therefore, be admissible in evidence against the accused.

(3.2) Evidentiary Facts Justifying Stops

Police officers have a sworn duty to investigate crimes that have been committed, to investigate crimes that are in the process of being committed, and to prevent crimes that are about to be committed. The *Terry* case involved a crime that was about to take place—a robbery. Though an officer has probable cause to believe a crime is about to take place, if no offense has occurred he cannot arrest anyone at this stage. Nevertheless, as a peace officer, he must use whatever constitutional powers he has to prevent the forthcoming occurrence. This is the power of temporary detention and questioning.

To justify a valid stop, an officer need only show that he suspected an individual of criminal conduct and that his suspicion was reasonable. These are two separate criteria, one subjective and the other objective. The *subjective* test is the officer's belief, in good faith, that the suspect is involved in criminal activity: past, present, or future. The *objective* test is that the officer's belief, which is based on commonly accepted standards of conduct, was reasonable under all the circumstances. Many factors alone, or in conjunction with other factors, will satisfy the objective test. Some of them are listed below.

1. Does the suspect resemble a person who is wanted for a past offense?

2. Does the officer know the suspect, and does the latter have a record or reputation for criminal conduct?

3. Is the suspect behaving peculiarly, under all of the circumstances? Is he running, sneaking down an alley, hiding in bushes, or carrying a flashlight and bag?

4. Did the suspect attempt to conceal himself or to avoid contact with the officer when the latter came into view? Is he trying to conceal or discard something?

5. Is the suspect's clothing unusual? Examples would include denims in the parking lot used by opera patrons or a deliveryman with neither merchandise nor a delivery truck. The combination of neighborhood, sex, race, and age of the person might provide sufficient reason to justify a stop.

6. Is the suspect in a peculiar place, such as on the roof, near the delivery entrance of a store at an unusual hour, or under a car in a parking lot?

It is impossible to give a comprehensive list of such factors since circumstances alone will justify or excuse "suspicious" activity. The Supreme Court made clear, however, that in determining the objective test of reasonableness an officer's training and experience may enter into the record. Thus, it is not relevant if a judge, defense lawyer, or ordinary citizen thinks a suspect's behavior is or is not peculiar. An officer, such as McFadden who had thirty-nine years of experience, may draw on his specialized knowledge of criminal behavior in deciding whether to stop and question a person. The court must respect an officer's training and experience, but the burden remains with the prosecution to elicit this information. An example follows.

In justifying a stop and frisk, Officer Jones testifies that the suspect looked "suspicious." He explains that he has patrolled the particular neighborhood—an upper-class, white, residential area—for three years. While many residents employ members of minority groups as maids, gardeners, or handymen, none of them live in their employers' homes, and, to the officer's knowledge, none work at night except as butlers and cooks. The suspect is black. He was dressed in a leather jacket, motorcycle boots, and jeans. Officer Jones states that in three years he has never seen a black man walking the streets at this time of night, dressed in this manner. In all likelihood, an appellate court would rule that the officer's subjective belief of suspicion was reasonable. And while the race and clothing of the suspect might not seem peculiar to the average citizen, Officer Jones's three years of experience in patrolling the neighborhood must be taken into account in justification of his actions in stopping and frisking the suspect.

(3.3) Evidentiary Facts Justifying Frisks

The power to stop is not the power to frisk. Each activity must be justified on separate and distinct bases. To be specific, officers must reasonably suspect that the person they are dealing with is armed and dangerous in order to frisk him. The Supreme Court made clear that an officer "need not be absolutely certain that the individual is armed" because his suspicion is enough, if his suspicion is reasonable. Again, it is a two-fold test of subjective and objective belief. Not certainty, not probable cause, but reasonable suspicion is the critical test.

The suspected danger need not be imminent. It can be a future danger (after the officer leaves the scene). It can be a danger to others—potential victims of violence. As the court said, the power to frisk is justified upon the need to protect the safety of officers "or that of others." For example, four armed officers might approach a suspicious person with their guns drawn. The fact that there are four officers and a single suspect is not the test. If the officers depart without frisking the suspect, he would be free to accost unarmed citizens.

Thus, at a suppression hearing, cross-examination of officers as to their "degree" of apprehension is simply not relevant to the proof at issue. An officer is not required to testify that he was "afraid" or that the defendant posed an actual or imminent threat to him. It is sufficient for the officer to express a belief that he suspected the defendant of being armed and to articulate sufficient facts to indicate that his belief was reasonable under the circumstances.

Below are some of the factors that would be relevant in determining whether a frisk is appropriate.

1. Is the suspected offense one that is associated with weapons?

2. Does the suspect have a reputation for violence or use of weapons?

3. Does the suspect have adequate identification? Does he present a plausible explanation for his whereabouts and actions?

4. Is the suspect overly "nervous" or overly nonchalant about the confrontation?

5. Is there a noticeable bulge in his clothing?

6. If the suspect is in a vehicle, does he make any "furtive" movements prior to the stop?

Valid stop-and-frisk procedures are not, of course, restricted to pedestrians. Suspicious persons are often encountered in automobiles. A gun is just as dangerous when hidden under the seat, in an unlocked glove compartment, above a visor, or under papers on the seat as when it is in the suspect's pocket. An officer who has the right to conduct a pat-down of the suspect's clothing may also check these areas in the vehicle for a secreted weapon. The frisk normally cannot be extended to a locked glove compartment or a trunk. It would make no difference if the suspect jumped out of his car just prior to the encounter. An officer would still have the right to make a preliminary check of the vehicle for weapons. If this were not so, the suspect could get back into the car, and the law would be frustrated.

There has been much discussion over what is an acceptable pat-down. The frisk is usually restricted to outer clothing. But, in winter, when heavy overgarments are worn, an officer may not be able to detect a bulge, and the coat may have to be unbuttoned to frisk sweaters or work clothing worn underneath. In the absence of secretive movements, an officer may not reach into a suspect's pockets without first feeling a bulge. If it appears that the suspect is stashing a gun when he sees the officer, the gun should, of course, be immediately retrieved. Nothing in the Fourth Amendment requires an officer to jeopardize his safety while performing a ritualistic ceremony, if it can be assumed there is adequate reason to believe the suspect is armed. As an example, a citizen approached Officer Connolly in a high-crime area and told him that Williams, who was seated in an auto, was carrying a firearm. Connolly knew the citizen, and the citizen knew the suspect. Connolly walked over to Williams's car and asked him to open the door. Instead, Williams rolled down the window. Connolly immediately reached through the window and pulled a loaded revolver from Williams's waistband. The Supreme Court affirmed the legality of the immediate frisk in a six-to-three decision (*Adams* v. *Williams*, 407 U.S. 143 [1972]).

In the above case, it would have been dangerous for Connolly to interrogate Williams, forcibly pull him from the car, conduct a pat-down, then remove the weapon. It is clear that, under certain circumstances, the stop and frisk may be coterminous. In unusual cases, such as *Adams* v. *Williams*, supra, the officer may have enough information—coupled with the suspect's conduct—to justify a frisk without any formalities.

Two presidential assassination attempts by women in 1975 should make it clear that females are not exempt from stop-and-frisk procedures. In addition to an examination of their outer clothing, their handbags may be squeezed and opened if they are firm. Discretion should, of course, be used in pat-down procedures executed by male officers.

Stop-and-frisk procedures cannot be used to prevent the destruction of evidence or to escalate a minimum number of facts into a situation of probable cause. The crinkle of cellophane in the pockets of a known narcotics peddler is a prime example.

In every case where the frisk results in an arrest, the officer must be prepared to document his activity step by step in his report. The report should include why he stopped the suspect, why he frisked him, and why he reached into his clothing or pockets. These progressive steps must be elicited one by one by the prosecutor during the suppression hearing. If this is not meticulously done, the court will conclude that the search was illegal.

There should be no mistake about it. The stop-and-frisk procedure constitutes a search and is judged by the Fourth Amendment. The standard is, however, less rigid. It is reasonable suspicion, as opposed to probable cause.

There is nothing consensual about stop-and-frisk procedures.

It should be remembered that the suspect is not under arrest, but the power to detain him is, nevertheless, a fact of law. Reasonable force, but never deadly force, may be used to detain and frisk a suspect. Suspicious persons cannot be compelled to answer questions, and, unless a statute or ordinance provides otherwise, they are not legally compelled to produce identification. California, for example, has a provision in its penal code requiring that identification be produced, on demand of police officers, when the citizen is encountered under suspicious circumstances.

The length of detention is not an arbitrary standard. Some states and cities set a maximum time limit for detention under stop-and-frisk laws. Such codes merely implement an inherent right of police officers. But the length of detention must not be unreasonable under any circumstances. Factors that might increase the length of detention include:

1. a check with headquarters for information concerning criminal history and outstanding warrants;
2. verification of the identification that has been produced;
3. ascertainment of the security of nearby premises or vehicles;
4. reasonable delay to await the arrival of nearby witnesses.

(3.4) Collateral Evidence Found

Although the stop-and-frisk procedure is justified on the basis of the need to protect investigating officers and others from assaults with weapons, anything found in a *properly conducted* frisk is admissible as evidence against the accused. Many suppression hearings based on frisks do not involve weapons; narcotics are often located by this procedure. The scope of the frisk determines whether narcotics will be admissible. If the frisk was restricted to a pat-down for hard objects, and the object turns out to be narcotics or paraphernalia, the confiscation will, in all likelihood, be upheld. Tightly wrapped tinfoil packets and hypodermic needles may feel like a switchblade knife, which is, of course, a concealed weapon. Glassine or cellophane packets would, on the other hand, crinkle and not feel like a gun or knife; it is likely that these items would be suppressed.

(3.5) Elements of an Arrest

A person is arrested when he is taken into custody for the purpose of answering to a court. In criminal cases, arrests can be made with or without an arrest warrant. In civil cases, the warrant is always used. There are a number of views concerning arrest. One holds that a person is "arrested" whenever his freedom is significantly curtailed in some manner. The rationale for this view is that the act of arrest is part of an "imprisonment." Imprisonments, of course, can result from natural as well as human causes and may be accidentally, negligently, or intentionally caused. A person who is kidnapped, for example, has been wrongfully imprisoned, but not falsely arrested.

It is generally agreed that there are four elements to every arrest: authority, intent, custody, and knowledge. The first assumes that the "officer" must be acting under real or assumed authority. There must be either a right to make the arrest or a claim of right on the part of the officer or the person acting in place of the officer. It may be that the person making the arrest has not qualified as a peace officer, that the warrant he holds is defective on its face, or that the law being enforced has been repealed or held unconstitutional. In each of these instances there has been an arrest, albeit an illegal one.

For the second element, intent, there must be a bona fide intention to take the person into actual custody for the purpose of his appearance in court. Thus, if a person is temporarily stopped for the purpose of investigation or is issued a notice to appear in court, he has not been arrested since there was no intent to take him into custody. While the purpose of an arrest is to take a person before a judicial body (or to an executive agency upon judicial order), peace officers can suspend the process and release the person in custody. Though, in terms of paperwork, a person can be "unarrested," in fact, there have been an arrest and a release.

The third element of an arrest—custody—requires actual or constructive restraint of the person arrested. Needless to say, it is not necessary to handcuff or otherwise physically restrain a person to arrest him. Physical contact is not needed if the arrestee voluntarily submits to the arresting officer. It is said that the slightest touching of a person satisfies the requirement of custody. But physical contact alone will not make an act an arrest, without the additional factor of knowledge.

To satisfy the fourth element of an arrest, a person must know—recognize or understand—that he is being arrested. It is usually sufficient to tell an individual he is under arrest. Other words and other acts, however, have the same effect. Thus, the suspect is told to put his hands up, he is handcuffed by a uniformed officer, and he is led away. Knowledge of the arrest is only important when there is no physical contact by the officer, that is, no actual custody. Voluntary submission, as mentioned, constitutes constructive custody. One's knowledge that he has been arrested need not be simultaneous with the act of custody, and there can still be a lawful arrest. Otherwise there could not be a valid search, incidental to an arrest, of an unconscious person. (See "Searches Incident to Arrest" in Chapter 4.)

Most arrests take place when an officer informs a person of his intention to take him into custody, coupled with the voluntary submission of the arrestee. But words alone will not constitute an arrest, unless physical force or voluntary submission follows.

(3.6) Probable Cause

The Fourth Amendment states that "no warrants shall issue, but upon probable cause . . . ." The standard for arrests, without warrant, is the same. State, county, and municipal law enforcement officers are bound to enforce the U.S. Constitution. Their arrests are judged by the same criteria as those applying to federal officers. This is because the Fourth Amendment is made applicable to the states through the Fourteenth Amendment.

To state the matter simply, an officer must have knowledge of sufficient facts and circumstances to form the belief that, first, a crime *probably* was committed and that, second, the arrestee *probably* perpetrated the acts constituting the suspected offense. The test is both subjective and objective. In the subjective realm, the officer must believe the supportive facts and conclude the existence of probable cause. In the objective realm, the court must agree that a man of reasonable caution would also conclude that probable cause, in the constitutional sense, in fact existed.

The question of probable cause is normally one of law, not of fact, and is to be decided by the judge, not the jury. The question is occasionally one of mixed law and fact, and thus a judge—sitting as a trier of fact—would decide whether to believe the officer. The determination of probable cause is made at a preliminary or suppression hearing, preceding a full trial. There is no jury at this phase of the criminal justice system. In a civil case alleging false arrest, the judge decides whether the facts upon which the officer relied constituted probable cause, which is a question of law. If, however, the officer's credibility is at issue, a question of fact arises, and that is decided by a civil jury. (For a complete discussion of suppression hearings, see Chapter 15.)

Common law requires that a misdemeanor must take place in the "presence" of the officer in order to justify a warrantless arrest. In the case of felonies, an officer may act on "information and belief." Many states have abolished the distinction by statute and permit arrests on information and belief in both categories of offenses. Other states, on the basis of judicial interpretation, have enlarged on what constitutes an officer's presence. For example, the continuation of hostile or threatening conduct would justify an arrest for simple battery that preceded the officer's appearance on the scene. These are sometimes called "on view" arrests. An officer can, however, rely on his other senses in justifying his presence. First, he might hear words that indicate the existence of the offense. Second, he might smell marijuana or spirits. Third, he might feel a concealed knife or blackjack on a suspect. Fourth, he might taste a liquid that seems to be liquor.

Many courts have held that an officer is justified in making a warrantless misdemeanor arrest in a common-law state when the suspect admits he is committing a continuous offense, such as wrongful possession. It is usually true, on the other hand, that an officer cannot later make an on view arrest for acts committed in his presence earlier, if he was unaware of the criminal activity at the time; he must obtain a warrant.

In common-law states, an arrest warrant charging a misdemeanor will be necessary when the offense did not occur in the presence of the officer or when the officer saw the offense but delayed apprehension. An example of an offense that occurred outside the presence of an officer follows. A local grocer summons officers to report that Smith gave him a worthless check. In a common-law state, the grocer must swear out a warrant charging Smith with petty fraud. As an example of delayed apprehension, a vice officer observes various forms of illegal gambling taking place. In the hope of catching the owners of the operation, he continues his surveillance long after the games cease, finally determining who the operators are.

Arrest warrants should be obtained charging the keeper and the patrons when their apprehensions are later effected.

As implied in the phrase itself, "probable cause" is a question of probabilities. Officers need not be legal specialists, and the courts ordinarily will not require precise legal analysis from them. Each arrest will be judged on the facts and circumstances known to the officer at the time a warrantless arrest is made or when an affidavit for an arrest warrant is written. Some of the factors that may lead an officer to conclude that he has probable cause are the same as those that would also justify a stop. (See "Evidentiary Facts Justifying Stops," above.) The amount of proof needed to justify an arrest is, of course, necessarily higher than that required to justify a temporary detention. Such elements as knowledge that a crime was recently committed and a complete description of the offender and his car will normally support a conclusion of probable cause. Less information, which will justify a temporary detention, may be used to build probable cause, such as admissions made during questioning or the finding of a weapon during a frisk.

In determining the existence of probable cause, an officer may use evidence that is legally inadmissible in the trial of the accused, but is admissible at the suppression hearing. Common among this type of evidence are statements obtained from a confidential informant that implicate the accused. Other factors of restricted admissibility include flight, furtive movements, evasive answers, records of arrest or of conviction, lack of identification, known criminal associations, and otherwise "suspicious" conduct. Factors that establish probable cause and that are admissible in the actual trial include knowledge the crime was recently committed, coupled with the location of the accused at the time of his apprehension; the time of the day or night; the clothing worn; the vehicle used (if it has been identified); evidence seized as the result of a lawful frisk; inculpatory (incriminating) statements made prior to custody of the accused.

The degree of proof necessary might be depicted schematically on a scale from 0 to 100. A slight amount of proof indicating guilt would be evident when it appears that an officer has a "mere hunch" (MH) that a suspect is guilty. This occurs when the officer subjectively knows something is "wrong," but cannot adequately particularize his suspicions. It is sometimes called "police intuition." At the next level is the standard required to justify a valid stop and frisk, a "reasonable suspicion" (RS). This is based on facts that the officer can articulate, but that, admittedly, do not fall into the category of probable cause. Probable cause (PC) is that amount of proof necessary to justify a warrantless arrest (or search) and to obtain an arrest warrant (or search warrant). At this stage an arrest (or search) becomes reasonable and lawful. It is still not sufficient for a conviction, however, since in criminal cases proof must be shown beyond a reasonable doubt (BRD), which is represented near the far end of the spectrum.

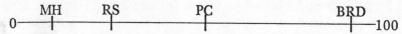

Because officers can initiate an arrest at the stage of probable cause, they may be able to obtain the additional evidence necessary to support a conviction through their efforts in the postarrest period. It may be that physical evidence is found at the time an officer makes a search incident to a custodial arrest. The subject may respond to lawful questioning and admit his culpability. A witness may identify the suspect after his apprehension. In such cases the amount of proof will escalate from probable cause to proof beyond a reasonable doubt.

A number of factors can invalidate an otherwise lawful arrest. For instance, an officer cannot obtain the necessary probable cause by illegally secreting himself on someone's property or by making a forcible entrance. If an officer is lawfully on the premises for another reason, anything seen may be used to formulate probable cause. Thus, an officer responds to a fire alarm and sees smoke inside a building. He makes a forcible entry to determine if anyone needs aid. When he gets inside, he observes a burglar on the premises. He would be justified in apprehending the burglar. Alternatively, if he had observed illicit activity on the premises, such as contraband in plain sight, he could later charge the owner or occupant with illegal possession.

(3.7) Collective Information and Radio Broadcasts

Officers may rely upon information that they give to each other. It is presumed to be valid until proven otherwise. For example, one officer may obtain statements from a confidential informant, another may make a surveillance, a third may obtain a records check, and a fourth may actually investigate the scene of the crime. Any officer, after discussing these things with each of the other officers, may swear out an arrest warrant or make a warrantless arrest, if there are no additional legal barriers.

One of the principal applications of the rule relates to serving arrest warrants. If probable cause exists for the issuance of an arrest warrant, the apprehension will be valid regardless of who serves the warrant. The arresting officer does not need to learn the particulars of the offense and investigation. If, however, the warrant was issued on less than probable cause, the arrest would not be lawful. Moreover, anything found incident to an unlawful arrest cannot be used in evidence later on.

Suspects are often apprehended on the basis of information relayed in an all points bulletin (APB) or a "be on look out" (BOLO) message. Once again, the transmission of information, like the existence of an arrest warrant, must be buttressed by probable cause. If the evidence supporting the broadcast does not rise to the level of probable cause, the arrest will be unlawful.

In 1971 the Supreme Court decided the case of *Whiteley* v. *Warden*, 401 U.S. 560 (1971). A local sheriff, investigating a burglary, swore out a warrant on the defendant. The sheriff was acting on information received from a confidential informant. The affidavit in support of the arrest warrant was conclusory and did not incorporate the informant's information, upon which the sheriff had relied. Whiteley was subsequently arrested in another town by an officer who was aware of the outstanding warrant. Tools and coins taken in a burglary were found in his possession. The Supreme Court ruled, however, that this evidence had to be suppressed.

The following rules apply in an analysis of the *Whiteley* case.

1. Assuming the underlying reliability of the confidential information, the sheriff could have arrested Whiteley without a warrant. The actual knowledge that an offense occurred, coupled with information from a reliable informant, could furnish the basis for a reasonable person to conclude the existence of probable cause.

2. Even though the sheriff had probable cause to make a warrantless arrest, he chose to have a warrant issued. The warrant was defective, however, because the affidavit upon which it was

based did not recite enough facts to conclude the existence of probable cause.

3. The officer who arrested Whiteley had a legal right to rely on the legitimacy of the arrest warrant. The existence of the warrant, though it was defective, protected that officer from civil claims for false arrest, but it did not furnish him with probable cause. The sheriff had such knowledge. The arresting officer did not. Because the affidavit upon which the warrant was issued was defective, the warrant should not have been issued by the magistrate.

4. If the sheriff, in addition to broadcasting information concerning the issuance of the warrant, had also added facts that would have constituted probable cause, the subsequent arrest would have been lawful. Such an arrest would not be based on the defective warrant alone, but would be a warrantless arrest using the facts and circumstances relayed to the arresting officer by the sheriff.

The rule is a rather simple one. If an officer has probable cause to make an arrest and swears out a valid warrant, anyone can make a valid arrest in the constitutional sense. But if the warrant is defective because of an insufficient affidavit, only the officer who swore out the warrant can make a lawful arrest; the legality of that arrest would be the underlying probable cause that would justify a warrantless arrest. Finally, should the arresting officer in a distant location learn additional information supporting a conclusion of probable cause, the subsequent apprehension would be a valid warrantless arrest. The additional information could come from either of two sources: the original officer, or facts learned by the arresting officer. The following example demonstrates the point.

A radio bulletin alerts city officers to be on the lookout for Smith, who is wanted for the burglary of a TV repair shop. A full description of Smith's station wagon is included by the sheriff of a nearby county where the alleged crime took place. Officer Jones, on seeing the vehicle, pulls it over and asks the driver for his license. In the back of the wagon Officer Jones sees six TV sets.

In this example we simply do not have enough information to know whether the local sheriff had probable cause to order the arrest of Smith. A warrant, based on an affidavit indicating the existence of probable cause, was not obtained. A warrant issued on a conclusory affidavit would have the same effect. Officer Jones did, however, sufficiently corroborate the information he received, which would lead a reasonable man to conclude that Smith had, indeed, taken the TV sets in the reported burglary. On the other hand, if the TV sets were located in a locked trunk that was opened on the demand of Officer Jones, the arrest and seizure would have been defective.

The principal exception to the *Whiteley* rationale is that officers are lawfully furnished with an excuse to investigate the accused and to make good use of anything seen or of statements made to them in the course of the investigation. If these factors, added to an insufficient radio broadcast, add up to a finding of probable cause, the subsequent arrest and search incident to arrest would be valid.

There are two major exceptions to the rule in *Whiteley*: exigent circumstances and fresh pursuit. Thus, if several officers appear on the scene, and one officer asks the others to assist him in making the apprehension, the legality of the arrest will be based on the information known to the officer requesting assistance. This would be true even if, for example, the officer who apprehends the suspect is in a back alley while the officer who requested assistance is in the front. Courts will not require officers who locate and take custody of a suspect at or near the scene of the crime to explain laboriously why they concluded the existence of probable cause.

Officers may lawfully assist each other in the apprehension of a fleeing suspect who is being pursued by another officer. Since time is of the essence, the law does not require the officer, in the heat of chase, to confide fully in all those assisting him in the capture.

(3.8) Federal Offenses and Immunity

State and local officers are sworn to uphold the Constitution and the laws of the United States. They frequently make arrests for offenses that are both state and federal in nature, such as bank robbery, possession of narcotics, interstate theft, and certain crimes concerned with weapons. Either the federal or state government may decide to prosecute the crime involved. If a county prosecutor refuses to charge the suspect, the U.S. attorney can act instead, and vice versa. Selection of the forum is a matter of comity between sovereigns.

Some offenses are solely federal in nature. Many involve the postal service, the Internal Revenue Service, or crimes committed on federal reservations. Pursuant to 18 U.S. Code, Sec. 3041, a state or local officer may swear out a warrant in either state or federal court for individuals suspected of federal offenses. While a state court judge cannot try the offense charged, he can order the defendant held for trial or discharge him from custody. A state or local officer may arrest, without warrant, a person who commits a purely federal offense if a warrantless arrest is permitted by state law.

Certain classes of persons are, by federal law, immune from arrest. Ambassadors, foreign ministers, their families, members of their official households, civil and military attachés, personal servants, and personal secretaries have full diplomatic immunity. Delegates to the United Nations, the Organization of American States, and the North Atlantic Treaty Organization also have official immunity. Foreign nationals and U.S. citizens employed as clerical staff, as well as all ranks of consuls, do not have diplomatic immunity except when they are on official foreign business. To ascertain whether a person has full or partial immunity, the chief of protocol of the U.S. Department of State should be contacted.

Law enforcement officers should, as a matter of courtesy among friendly nations, notify the closest embassy, consulate, or legation of the arrest of any foreign national. The imprisonment or assault of a foreign ambassador or minister is a federal crime punishable by up to ten years of imprisonment in accord with 18 U.S. Code 112.

The Constitution prohibits the arrest of all U.S. senators and representatives, except for treason, felonies, and breach of the peace, during their attendance at a session of Congress and while they are traveling to and from such sessions. Thus, they are immune from arrests for misdemeanors and traffic violations during the entire time Congress is in session, and not just during their working hours.

Many state senators and representatives have immunity from state misdemeanors and traffic offenses, similar to members of the U.S. Congress. Members of the state militia who are on duty, judges, lawyers, and jurors attending court, and other classes of persons may be given limited immunity under state law.

(3.9) Particular Types of Arrests

Not every arrest is for a criminal offense. Persons may be arrested on civil process, issued by a court of competent jurisdiction.

For example, bench warrants may be issued for contempt of court, as when a witness fails to appear on a subpoena that has been served in a civil case. The ancient writ of *capias* is a civil arrest process and is sometimes used to bring in a person for a mental examination. The writ of *ne exeat*, which is rarely used, orders the detention of a person until he posts an appearance bond in a civil case; this will "guarantee" his appearance. According to common law, an officer may not use deadly force or forcibly enter a dwelling to execute a civil arrest. Other degrees of reasonable force are permissible.

Citizens are authorized to make arrests in criminal cases, without warrant, when the offense is committed in their presence. This power does not normally extend to offenses concerned with municipal ordinances, but is reserved for felonies and breach of the peace. Citizens may also be "deputized" to assist officers in making an arrest. This is not a new procedure. The *posse comitatus* is of ancient origin, and no one who has seen a Western can fail to have witnessed posses in action. The common law recognizes that it is the duty of all male adults to come to the aid of officers who request it; recent statutes have included women when the rule has been codified. As a matter of fact, in some cases it is a criminal offense to refuse to assist law enforcement officers in the execution of their office.

Under statutes existing in most states, merchants are given powers of arrest or detention with respect to shoplifting offenses. They may, if they have sufficient information and belief, detain and sometimes arrest suspected shoplifters. Under such laws police officers need not view misdemeanors committed only in the presence of shopkeepers and security personnel hired by the store.

An individual who is on parole does not enjoy the civil rights of ordinary citizens. He may be apprehended, without warrant, for parole violations. He may be searched without warrant, without probable cause, and without first being placed under valid arrest. This is because he is still *legally* confined under the conditions of parole.

Bondsmen, under common law, have an absolute right to retake those for whom they have posted bond should those individuals attempt to skip town or otherwise impair the conditions of their appearance in court. They may cross state lines and, without warrant or other legal process, capture and return the accused to the jail from which he was released on bond.

Police officers may arrest and detain a person who is wanted, on warrant or bulletin, to answer for the commission of an offense in another state. This power is granted by the U.S. Constitution, which requires that each state give "full faith and credit" to the legal processes of sister states. Except in exigent circumstances, however, resident police officers should not apprehend suspects on a bulletin alone, unless the request indicates a warrant has been issued. In situations where the suspect is fleeing, an officer can, of course, detain him until a warrant has been obtained. Officers may promptly pursue a fleeing suspect across state lines to make the apprehension, but the offender may not be returned to the state in which he is supposed to have committed the crime without due process of law. Nearly all states have adopted the Uniform Fresh Pursuit Act and the Uniform Extradition Act. These statutes give an accused the right to a hearing before the governor of the state to which he has fled before he can be returned to the state that issued the warrant.

(3.10) Use of Force

Police officers may use reasonable and necessary force to apprehend a criminal suspect. They are not required to retreat from an assault, as is an ordinary citizen in most cases. They are not required to time their arrest so that it can be effected with the least amount of resistance. They are not bound to use psychology or to wait for hours or days before flushing out an armed suspect who offers resistance. What is good police policy and what is good law may surely differ. Thus, an officer may be fired for escalating or not defusing a situation, but ordinarily he cannot be sued or prosecuted for immediately apprehending a suspect who is resisting arrest.

If the offense is a misdemeanor, an arresting officer may not use deadly force to apprehend a fleeing suspect. In every state an officer may—as a last resort—use deadly force to apprehend a suspect who is believed to have committed a dangerous felony. In most states this applies to all grades of felonies. It makes no difference that the offense is minor. To state the matter simply, the law will not permit felons to flee from justice.

What constitutes a "last resort" is open to question. An officer does not have to assume that the suspect probably will be captured by other officers or that he may give himself up. If it can be shown, however, that the chase was too short or that the officer was too lazy to give chase, a jury will probably conclude that the officer was not justified in killing the suspect.

Regardless of whether the offense is serious or whether the suspect's arrest is attempted or not, a police officer may use deadly force to defend himself against the use of deadly force. This principle does not escalate in degrees. An attacker with a knife, with a broken beer bottle, with a fireplace poker, or with an automobile that he is using as a weapon may be shot dead with an elephant gun. Even though there may be twenty-five armed officers against one armed suspect, any officer may return the fire as though the suspect were taking aim against him individually.

Most cases where excessive force has been alleged do not involve the use of deadly force. An officer is not only privileged to use a reasonable and necessary amount of force to make an apprehension; he is obligated to use more force than the person resisting arrest. Here, then, the law will examine the degrees of responsive force. There are no ready answers, and the progression is not necessarily from pebbles to boulders or from table lighters to chairs.

Entry of dwellings and other premises by force in order to effect an arrest is limited to two situations. The first occurs when officers are in hot pursuit or the criminal acts are of a continuous nature. The second takes place when officers who are armed with an arrest or search warrant have first requested consensual entry, which is refused. (This aspect of law is more fully discussed in Chapter 5.)

Handcuffs may be used to restrain or transport arrested persons who are suspected of felonies, breach of the peace, or minor offenses when it is thought that they might escape or assault the arresting officers. Some departments use them routinely on all offenders.

(3.11) False Arrest

Civil action may be taken against a police officer, and in most cases the unit of government that employs him, for false arrest, false imprisonment, and malicious prosecution. The gist of a suit for false arrest is that the officer arrested the civil plaintiff without probable cause. It is of no consequence whether the officers acted maliciously, recklessly, or for personal gain. While such factors might subject an officer to punitive damages if the plaintiff prevails, they have nothing to do with liability. In a suit for false arrest a complete defense is that there was probable cause for the arrest to be made. If a felon is bound over in a preliminary hearing in criminal court, or if the civil court determines the existence of probable cause, the judgment will be in favor of the officer, who is the defendant.

In most cases the existence of probable cause is a question of law for the judge. There is, consequently, little a sympathetic jury can do for the officer other than limit the amount of damages. Recently, however, many federal courts and several state courts have adopted the doctrine of "good faith." When it is viewed schematically on the diagram appearing in the section on "Probable Cause," above, good faith is to the left of probable cause and to the right of reasonable suspicion. If an officer makes an arrest without probable cause, but *reasonably* believes in good faith that he has probable cause and that the arrest is lawful, he will be immune from any damages.

Good faith is thus an objective and subjective test. First, the officer must in honest good faith believe in the legality of his actions. Second, this belief must be reasonable under the circumstances. The jury answers these questions, which provide added protection to officers. A foolish officer, for example, might honestly believe he can arrest blue-eyed, blond-haired males only because they have those characteristics. His belief would not be reasonable and would fail the objective part of the two-part test.

False imprisonment is the unlawful incarceration of a person. Though it often follows a false arrest automatically, it could arise because of a failure to release someone after his bond was posted, after the charges were dropped, or after he served his term. This charge can be used to sue officers who detain persons *without* justification in a stop-and-frisk situation at the scene of a crime or the place where a raid has taken place. Good faith is normally not a defense in an action alleging false imprisonment when the plaintiff is held in jail beyond the proper time.

Malicious prosecution is the actual prosecution of criminal charges against the accused when probable cause is absent and when the charges were brought for malicious reasons. The circumstances prompting this action usually arise when police officers learn that the accused is no longer a good suspect, but fail to notify the court or prosecutor of the person's innocence or his ironclad defense.

Civil claims of excessive force often accompany arrests. These allegations are, in reality, for civil assault and civil battery. They are common-law claims. Since a lawful arrest may be accompanied by excessive force, the existence of probable cause or proof of guilt beyond a reasonable doubt is not involved in the claims or their defense.

Plaintiffs who prevail in personal injury litigation are generally entitled to compensatory damages, both special and general. Special damages are those capable of setting a dollar figure: loss of earnings, cost of bond, attorneys' fees, and medical expenses, if any. General damages are those assessed for the pain or suffering, humiliation, and defamation of the plaintiff. A jury has wide discretion in imposing damages for general purposes. In cases of flagrant police misbehavior, a jury can award punitive damages to "teach and punish" the civil defendant. In most jurisdictions neither cities nor insurance companies will indemnify an officer for punitive damages, and they cannot be discharged through the bankruptcy courts. Thus an officer may have to pay such damages for the rest of his life.

An officer who merely serves a regular arrest warrant is immune from liability for false arrest. He can rely absolutely on the determinations made by the court that issued the warrant and the regularity of the proceedings upon which it is based.

(3.12) Entrapment

Entrapment has been defined as the procurement of a person to commit a crime that he did not contemplate or would not have committed, for the sole purpose of prosecuting that person. Though it is not recognized as a defense against prosecution at common law, most states acknowledge it as a defense in their codes of criminal law and procedure.

In *U.S.* v. *Russell*, 411 U.S. 423 (1973), the Supreme Court affirmed the conviction of a manufacturer of methamphetamine (speed). An undercover agent delivered a necessary component to the suspect and agreed to split the profits. After the drug was produced, the federal agents raided the laboratory and arrested the suspect. The Supreme Court held that:

1. the defense of entrapment is not a constitutionally protected right;
2. in the absence of "shocking" conduct on the part of law

enforcement officers, a conviction would not be set aside merely because the government participated in the crime;

3. a predisposition to commit the crime, on the part of the defendant, precludes the defense of entrapment.

States are free to adopt their own rules concerning the entrapment defense, and the rules may be more rigorous in some jurisdictions than others. At the local level, entrapment is often raised in vice cases. In some jurisdictions, for example, a plainclothes police officer can offer to purchase the services of a prostitute, but cannot set the price, which must be fixed by the suspect.

Entrapment poses problems of enforcement when officers deal with first offenders. As noted, a predisposition to commit the offense will usually prevent a successful defense based on entrapment. To ensure a conviction, officers frequently do not make an arrest immediately after the commission of the first crime, but wait until a second offense has taken place. This usually establishes predisposition. In cases charging the sale of narcotics by first offenders, however, it may not be necessary to wait for a second transaction before making an arrest. If, for example, a large quantity of narcotics is seized, a jury would probably believe that the defendant intended to engage in narcotics transactions as a business. In any event, the crime of possession of narcotics would not be subject to the defense of entrapment, and a conviction for this less serious offense would usually follow.

It is not improper for a police officer to give a suspect marked money, to misrepresent his true identity, or to pose as an addict or hoodlum. In *Sherman* v. *U.S.*, 356 U.S. 369 (1958), however, the Supreme Court found "shocking" police conduct. Federal agents had persuaded an addict, who was in the process of breaking himself of the habit, to obtain heroin and to readdict himself. The defense has also been successfully raised when prior to the commission of a planned crime, police officers have discouraged a participant from withdrawing.

Though entrapment as a defense must be raised by the defendant, in some cases a judge will rule as a matter of law that officers encouraged the defendant's participation in the offense. In most cases, however, it will also be a question for the jury because of variances in testimony between the officer and the defendant.

(3.13) Summary

Not every time a police officer deprives a citizen of his freedom is there an arrest in the legal sense. The Supreme Court has made clear that a temporary detention, although it constitutes a seizure within the meaning of the Fourth Amendment, is not an arrest. Police officers may stop citizens, forcibly if necessary, to conduct a preliminary investigation in order to determine whether a crime has taken place, is in progress, or is about to take place.

To justify a stop, a police officer must be able to articulate facts that would lead a prudent person to believe that the officer reasonably suspects a person of criminal activity. This detention is incident to his power to investigate. Moreover, if the officer reasonably suspects that the person with whom he is dealing might be armed, a limited search can be conducted. This search, called a frisk, is restricted to a pat-down of the suspect's outer clothing for weapons. If the frisk is properly conducted and is not a generalized search of the person, evidence fortuitously found is admissible in a criminal trial.

To consummate an arrest, an officer must have the authority to make an arrest and the intention to arrest the suspect. There must be some restraint of the suspect, either physical or mental, and the suspect must understand that he has been arrested. The Fourth Amendment requires that police officers have probable cause before a lawful arrest can be made. This means that an officer must reasonably believe that a crime has been committed and that the suspect is the perpetrator.

The law recognizes that police officers have unique experience and specialized training that make them more proficient in their field than the normal citizen. They may use this combination of education and experience in determining whether there are sufficient grounds to justify a stop or an arrest. They must, however, be able to recount fully the underlying facts and circumstances in court, or the detention or arrest will be found unlawful.

4

Search and Seizure Generally

(4.1) The Fourth and Fourteenth Amendments

Two phrases of the Fourth Amendment to the U.S. Constitution contain the real substance of its protections. The first is the prohibition against "unreasonable" searches. The second is the requirement of "probable cause." In regard to the first prohibition the amendment states that the people have the right to be secure in their persons, houses, papers, and effects from unreasonable searches and seizures. Thus, the amendment protects people, not corporations, animals, or inanimate objects. Although it specifies "houses," the word has been interpreted to include barns, warehouses, offices, and other structures. No mention was made of boats, which, of course, existed in the eighteenth century, or of automobiles, trucks, and aircraft, which did not. Nevertheless, the protections of the Fourth Amendment have been extended, by interpretation, to these forms of personal property. Thus, the gist of the amendment is that people are protected from unreasonable searches, regardless of what is searched.

Only a few types of searches can be considered unreasonable. If a search is reasonable, other things being equal, the search is constitutional. It is sometimes claimed that a warrantless search is unreasonable and therefore illegal because there was ample time to procure a warrant. That is not, however, the proper test. The real question is whether it was reasonable to require a warrant under the circumstances of the case.

The second major prohibition of the amendment states that no warrants shall be issued except on "probable cause." This requirement has also been extended to warrantless searches, warrantless arrests, and arrest warrants, as was discussed in Chapter 3. The specific requirements to be met in determining the existence of probable cause are discussed in Chapter 5 under the heading "Probable Cause."

The Fourth Amendment also requires that warrants be based on an oath or affirmation, which particularly describes the place to be searched and the persons or things to be seized. For a discussion of these matters, see Chapter 5 under the heading "Grounds for Issuance."

The Fourteenth Amendment is important in constitutional history because it was originally thought that the first eight amendments only applied to congressional enactments and to federal officers. But the "due process clause" of this amendment makes it clear that these amendments also apply to state enactments and to locally constituted law enforcement officers.

(4.2) The Exclusionary Rule

The single most important rule of evidence is the one that suppresses and rejects otherwise admissible evidence because it was obtained in an "illegal" manner, in this case, in violation of the Fourth Amendment. In earlier times it made no legal difference to the courts how physical evidence was obtained. But in 1914 the U.S. Supreme Court changed that. In *Weeks* v. *U.S.*, 232 U.S. 383 (1914), it ruled that evidence gathered by federal officers to be introduced in a federal criminal trial was subject to exclusion if it was obtained in violation of the Fourth Amendment.

The *Weeks* decision stated that courts should not sanction convictions obtained by "unlawful seizures and forced confessions." In order to force the police to comply with the Fourth and Fifth Amendments, it was necessary to exclude "tainted" evidence from the criminal trial itself. Thus, a "guilty" man might go free because, as one jurist has said, the "constable has blundered." The rule applies equally to intentional abuses and negligent omissions. A number of people feel that the rule has had unfortunate results. They believe that it detracts from the main purpose of a criminal trial—the search for the truth and the determination of the guilt or innocence of an accused. Further, they see it as encouraging police officers to commit perjury in order to secure the admission of probative evidence. Finally, they think that it causes considerable delays in the prosecution of offenses and an enormous expense, particularly at the appellate stage.

Many states followed the federal courts in adopting the exclusionary rule. But for over thirty years nearly half of the states did not recognize it. This gave rise to the "silver platter doctrine." Thus, if a federal agent uncovered evidence through an illegal search, the evidence could be admitted in a state court that did not have an exclusionary rule. Moreover, during one period of time, even states that recognized the rule applied it only to state searches and still admitted evidence that had been illegally seized by federal agents. So, too, the federal courts admitted evidence illegally seized by state officers. The "illegal evidence" was thus "served up" on a "silver platter."

The Supreme Court addressed itself to the issue in the famous case of *Mapp* v. *Ohio*, 367 U.S. 643, decided in 1961, by which time twenty-six states had fashioned some form of an exclusionary rule. That decision marks the beginning of what is known as "The Criminal Law Revolution." The Ohio courts had sustained the conviction of Mrs. Mapp for possession of obscene matter. The evidence brought forth to prove her guilt was seized during an unlawful search of her home. In reversing the conviction and ordering the suppression of that evidence, the Supreme Court relied on the Fourteenth Amendment. It felt that a citizen had a right to be "free from unreasonable state intrusion." The failure of a state to observe its own laws, said the court, would eventually destroy the government itself.

The exclusion of tainted evidence is not automatic. The defendant must affirmatively raise the issue before the court in a "motion to suppress." It is normal for the motion to be made before the actual trial begins. In some cases, in fact, a person can institute an action to suppress evidence that might be used to procure an indictment against him. Even if an accused fails to raise the motion before the trial, he can still object to the admissibility of the evidence at the time of trial. Most courts have held, however, that the issue cannot be first raised at the time of an appeal, unless good cause can be shown for not doing so previously.

Evidence that is suppressed is not necessarily returned to the accused. Things that are not returnable include the following:

1. contraband per se, which, by its nature, is illegal to possess, such as narcotics;
2. derivative contraband, which a statute has outlawed, such as automatic firearms;
3. evidence held pending an appeal, since a court of appeals can overrule a motion to dismiss that was granted below and order a new trial;
4. stolen property, which the rightful owner can obtain by a court order;
5. forfeitures, to which the exclusionary rule may not apply and which can be forfeited to the state, such as money gained from illegal activities, a weapon used to commit a crime, or a vehicle used to transport contraband.

It should be noted that the exclusionary rule also applies to "derivative evidence." This extension of the rule is called the "Fruit of the Poisoned Tree Doctrine." For example, through an illegal search of a suspect, officers find a key to a storage locker in a bus station. They open the locker, hoping to find evidence of the offense under investigation. The purpose of the rule would be defeated if it did not apply to evidence *derived* from an illegal search as well as to evidence seized from an illegal search. Thus, the exclusionary rule applies to direct and derivative evidence, seized as the result of an illegal arrest or search.

An exception to the Poisoned Tree rationale is operable when the police can show that they would have found the evidence anyway, and in a lawful manner. We can demonstrate this by returning to the example of the storage locker. If the officers already knew that the suspect had secreted evidence in a certain locker, but they did not have the key, they could have obtained a search warrant for the locker and forcibly opened it. Thus, the use of the illegally seized key would not have affected the outcome of the subsequent search, and the evidence should be admitted in spite of the use of the key.

The Supreme Court, under the leadership of Chief Justice Warren Burger, has carved out limited exceptions to the exclusionary rule.

Many objections to the impact of the rule on law enforcement have been raised. A few of these objections are set forth below. The first four were mentioned above, but are elaborated on here.

1. *It punishes all transgressions alike.* Police misconduct is a nebulous term that embraces a broad range of acts and omissions. It can be an affirmative act of substantial injury, such as kicking in the front doors of every home in a subdivision, without cause. Or it can be a minimal intrusion, such as a pat-down that goes beyond the suspect's outer clothing. It could be an omission, such as the failure to date a search warrant affidavit. It might be an intentional wrong-doing, such as the strip search of an innocent female suspect by a male officer; it could be negligence, such as mixing up warrants and their affidavits. Whatever the "misconduct" charged, all mistakes suffer the same penalty: the exclusion of probative evidence.

2. *The rule runs counter to the basic purpose of a trial, which is the search for truth.* Every trial, whether civil or criminal, has as its purpose the goal of determining the truth of the matter in dispute. In criminal trials, it is the guilt or innocence of the accused that should be determined. All of the rules of evidence are supposedly fashioned to facilitate that goal. Thus evidence is excluded when it is irrelevant, immaterial, or, by rule of law, incompetent. Evidence that suffers no inherent disability and is probative in nature is normally admissible, and it should be. Yet the exclusionary rule discards evidence that is probative and otherwise competent, but is not based on a desire to give an accused a fair trial; it is fashioned to deter police misconduct.

3. *The exclusionary rule encourages perjury by the police.* Few police officers would seriously consider framing an innocent defendant by giving false testimony on the issue of guilt or innocence. Testimony given at an evidence suppression hearing, however, relates to the method used to gather physical or testimonial evidence, and not to the presence or absence of evidence. Thus, perjury at a suppression hearing will not make a truly innocent suspect seem guilty; it will only decide whether a factually guilty suspect should be tried on the merits of the evidence. Simple misstatements of fact, such as whether an officer knocked before forcing open a door or whether he limited his pat-down to the suspect's outer garments, are examples of police perjury that do not affect the guilt or innocence in the nonlegal sense. Officers are therefore pressured, by the

nature of their assignments, to misstate these events. This is, of course, perjury.

4. *The exclusionary rule causes significant delays in the process of punishment.* Many criminologists and behavioral psychologists believe that the certainty and alacrity of punishment create a stronger deterrent effect than the severity of punishment. The pretrial suppression hearing causes but another delay in the process from arrest to incarceration. It is followed, in many instances, by a further delay at the trial stage. The introduction of physical or testimonial evidence often forms the exclusive basis for an appeal to an intermediate court of appeals, then to the state's supreme court. The usual methods of appeal are exhausted when the Supreme Court refuses to hear the case. But that does not end the appellate process. A collateral attack on the judgment may be made, in some instances, through a writ of habeas corpus at the U.S. district court. This writ is appealable to the U.S. circuit court, in a three-judge panel, followed by an en banc appeal before the entire circuit bench, and, once again, to the Supreme Court. It is not unusual for a defendant who was convicted ten years before to continue to file appeals based on illegal search and seizure.

5. *The rule causes an added expense to society.* Each appeal and each collateral attack brought by a defendant must be briefed and argued. In addition to the time spent in researching each point of law that is appealed, sufficient copies of the final brief must be reproduced (and often printed) at considerable expense. Lawyers for the state must prepare their oral arguments, travel to the court that is hearing the matter (often in a distant city), and present their arguments. A certified copy of the transcript, purchased from court reporters, must accompany the briefs at the first levels of appeal.

In many cases the appealing defendant is indigent. He must, therefore, be provided with a free copy of the transcript, free legal counsel in preparing his appeal, free printing of the briefs concerning his case, and free representation before the appellate court. "Free" to an indigent means paid for by the state. It is not unusual for the entire cost of processing numerous appeals to exceed the total cost of confining that defendant in a correctional institution for his entire life. It has been estimated that an appeal to the Supreme Court can cost as much as $50,000. And that is but one stage of the appellate process.

6. *Application of the rule does not prevent many types of police "misconduct."* There are many areas of enforcement activity where the time necessary to conduct a foolproof investigation prior to a raid or an arrest is so excessive compared to the punishments imposed by the penal code that there is no incentive to make the investigation. For example, to corroborate properly an informant's disclosures might require three surveillances utilizing three officers and two cars. Coupled with the cost of conducting a raid, the total expenditures would probably exceed $1,000. The maximum fine for keeping a bawdy house, running a gambling house, engaging in lewd behavior, possessing dangerous drugs, or participating in disorderly conduct may be $200. In many cases the maximum fine is not imposed, or the fine is suspended. If a jail term is possible, it may not be imposed, or it, too, may be suspended. Besides the factor of expense, a limited number of vice officers can raid four times as many people by dispensing with legally sufficient surveillances.

In one city it was learned that vice officers made arrests with no intention of prosecuting the offenders. These officers were pressured to "clean up" the city. A raid would result in the closing of a place where illegal activity was being carried out, the identification of suspects, the posting of bonds, the employment of legal counsel, and the investigation of reported crimes. Such activity gets narcotics, pornography, and gambling paraphernalia off the street and makes them unavailable for sale. It drives the cost of these goods up, makes trading in them less profitable, and creates additional expenses for "doing business." These factors may impose more dissuasion than the sanctions of fines and potential incarcerations. The exclusionary rule will not deter police officers who find that nonjudicial sanctions are equal to or more effective than judicial ones.

Police officers also know that they must exceed the bounds of permissible searches if they are to confiscate the maximum number of concealed weapons. Only a few convicted defendants are ever incarcerated for this offense in major cities, and yet the number of shootings continues to rise because of the legal difficulties encountered in properly seizing handguns. Again, the number of guns confiscated dramatically increases when the protections of the Fourth Amendment are relaxed. Those found with weapons are arrested, are identified in the records systems, and are required to post bond and employ legal counsel. The nonjudicial sanctions may be more effective when broadly applied than are judicial sanctions selectively applied. Thus, there are fewer guns in the community when the exclusionary rule does not serve as a deterrent to patrol officers.

7. *The exclusionary rule punishes society, not a misbehaving officer.* Society suffers every time a dope peddler or an armed robber is turned loose because of the exclusionary rule. The defendant is free to continue his illegal activity, to make sport of the system of criminal justice, and to harm society. But when, if ever, is a policeman demoted, suspended, or otherwise punished because he lacked probable cause to make an arrest or conduct a search? Even in those few cases where a defendant subsequently sues a police officer for false arrest or illegal search, the officer escapes punishment. In the first place, less than 4 percent of such suits are successful (Schmidt, *Survey of Police Misconduct Litigation, 1967-1971* [Evanston, Ill.: Americans for Effective Law Enforcement, Inc., 1974], 6). In the second place, the police department employs an attorney for the officer in 99.6 percent of the cases. In the third place, the city almost always pays a judgment in behalf of the officer. On the other hand, it is common knowledge that if an officer leaves his post, becomes intoxicated while on duty, or wears an improper uniform he will suffer disciplinary suspension and, sometimes, dismissal. But in our larger cities a vice squad can serve over 5,000 search warrants a year that are later thrown out as lacking probable cause, and not a single instance of police misconduct will be administratively prosecuted.

Alternatives to the exclusionary rule that would probably be more effective include:

1. mandatory civil liability for improper police conduct;
2. use of contempt of court procedures by the courts against errant officers;
3. implementation of an effective system of discipline, internally administered against police misconduct.

(4.3) Searches, Distinguished from Plain View

In one sense a "search" is, at least in the layman's terms, the examination of things for the purpose of finding something. To the courts, it is something quite different. A search is the seeking of something that is not in plain sight, in places where the object (or person) sought might be concealed. As stated by the Supreme Court in *Harris* v. *U.S.* (390 U.S. 234 [1968]), "It has long been settled that objects falling in the plain view of an officer who has a right to be in the position to have that view are subject to seizure and may be introduced in evidence." Simply stated, the "plain view rule" holds that readily observable things, seen by an officer (in a place where he has a right to be) are not the product of a "search" and are not subject to exclusion from evidence.

The plain view rule frequently arises in the course of police duties. Every time a police officer talks with a pedestrian, stops a motorist, or questions a suspicious person, the rule applies. For example, a patrol officer stops a motorist for speeding. While writing a notice for the motorist to appear in court, the officer observes the barrel of a gun protruding from under a newspaper on the seat of the car. Noticing the barrel is not a search, and the officer has probable cause to remove the newspaper and seize the weapon.

Observations within the rule are not limited to sightings with an unaided eye. Flashlights and vehicular spotlights may be used at night or in dark places. Thus, a foot patrolman, walking down the sidewalk at night, might routinely shine his flashlight into parked cars. If he observes narcotics paraphernalia on the backseat of an unoccupied sedan, he would have probable cause to seize the vehicle and arrest the driver on his return.

a. Open Fields

The "open fields doctrine" is an integral part of the plain view rule. Officers may enter private outdoor property to look for evidence, without a warrant or other justification, and anything seen in the course of their expedition falls within the plain view exception. A typical example of the application of the doctrine occurs in the pursuit of the growing of marijuana. An anonymous telephone call, a story told by hikers, a rumor—each could be the impetus for surveying hills and meadows. None of these, standing alone, would constitute probable cause. Yet, since a walk through fields and woodlands is not a "search," no violations of the Fourth Amendment arise because police officers are looking for marijuana that is being grown in open fields.

Though the doctrine appears to run counter to the concepts of private property and trespass, which are firmly rooted in Anglo-American law, such observations are, nevertheless, lawful. Even the

presence of a fence is not determinative. Is the fence designed to
keep animals in or people out? Unless the fence is obviously designed
to keep out intruders and that fact is clearly indicated, occupants of
the land do not have a consititutionally protected right to be free
from police invasion of property.

Numerous cases affirming the open fields doctrine arose during
Prohibition, when federal revenue agents sought out and destroyed
illegal stills.

Recent case law has added a new dimension to the open fields
doctrine. If the occupant or landowner has an "expectation of
privacy" over the fields, the search might be unlawful. The question
for the courts to determine is whether, under all the circumstances,
the occupant's expectation of privacy was reasonable. Thus, a farmer
would not have a reasonable expectation that his plowed fields near
a state highway are private. Conversely, a homeowner might reasonably expect that his fenced backyard would not be spied upon from
the roof of a nearby building.

b. Curtilage

Another concept of the law of property is that of curtilage.
It includes the area immediately surrounding a person's home and
has the same protections as the actual home. Trespass onto the
curtilage is not within the exception of the open fields doctrine.
It violates the Fourth Amendment and thus requires the issuance of a
search warrant, absent exigent circumstances. It is difficult to define
a building's curtilage. It is often considered the area that is a part of
the "domestic economy" of the household. It always covers the
immediate area surrounding a home and all attached structures.
Though it may include a nearby barn, it probably will not include a
distant outbuilding. There is no hard-and-fast rule that defines precisely the number of feet that the curtilage is from the home. Each
case is decided on its own facts and circumstances.

The use of telescopes and binoculars, by themselves, does not
render an observation unlawful. Police officers can, therefore, position
themselves in a location where it is lawful for them to be and observe
suspicious activities using magnifying lenses, except in Hawaii.

Police officers are not free, however, to accomplish illegal
searches with the use of mechanical devices and stand on technical
concepts of trespass. For example, an officer cannot stand outside

the bedroom window of a suspect and peer inside, because this is a violation of the curtilage. He could stand across the street on a sidewalk and look through an open window, as could any citizen. He could not climb to the roof of a nearby office structure and, with the aid of binoculars, look down into an apartment bedroom, if the only other way to look through the window was by standing just outside the window, within the curtilage. There is no "expectation of privacy" that a neighbor will not look out his window, but there is a reasonable expectation that one will not be spied upon from a nearby roof.

Thus, officers, by sitting in a parked car on the street, would be able to look into the front window of a home and see illegal activity because the occupants had carelessly left the drapes open. If the neighborhood is predominantly black and the officers are white, they may feel it prudent to park in an alley away from but in the line of sight of the windows. Anything they would see with the aid of binoculars is lawful because anyone parked on the street could see the same activities. There is no "search," and the events observed fall within the plain view rule.

c. Semiprivate Places

Another area of considerable litigation is the definition of a public place. If an officer sees incriminating evidence or actions in a public place, no search is involved, and the observations are admissible as evidence against an accused. If, however, an officer is in a private place without consent or without a warrant, his observations are not admissible against the accused.

Not every place is clearly public or private. Many are semiprivate. If, for example, a police officer walks through a department store during business hours, he is in a public place. This is because the store by implication invites the public to enter the premises, and the public has ready access to the store through unlocked doors facing a street or parking lot. When the officer enters an unlocked rest room, he is still in a public place. But if he enters a commode stall, stands on the plumbing, and looks over into another stall, he is conducting a search of a semiprivate area. It is easy to see the reason for this. First, if the stall has doors, the occupant has a reasonable expectation of privacy from intrusions. Second, a locked rest room stall does not provide the general public with ready access. If, therefore, an officer observes an addict taking a fix under these conditions, the observations will be excluded at the trial. To illustrate further the principle involved, suppose the activity is conducted in a doorless commode stall or in front of a urinal. In this case anyone who enters the rest room, including a police officer, could see the activity. It would make no difference if the officer had concealed himself behind a false air vent in order to observe the illegal actions since they were performed in plain view of anyone who entered the room.

d. Execution of Search Warrants

The plain view exception often takes effect during the course of searches conducted pursuant to a warrant. Thus, a warrant might command an officer to search for stolen goods. In the course of the search he finds narcotics. The contraband, although not named in the warrant, is admissible and should be seized because it was observed in plain view, within the course and scope of a lawfully conducted search. Officers executing a search warrant are in a place where they lawfully have a right to be. Anything they see of an evidentiary nature, therefore, can later be related in the courtroom. To state the matter simply, the officers do not have to close their eyes to contraband, weapons, instrumentalities of a crime, or fruits of other crimes.

Similarly, officers who enter a home or business to serve an arrest warrant need not blind themselves to the contents of the premises during the course of apprehending the defendant. As an example, officers enter a person's home to arrest him for failure to appear in court for a traffic violation. While in his living room, they see twelve television sets bearing a bill of lading stacked in a corner. The officers are free to investigate the circumstances of the defendant's possession of the sets, including tracing them to determine if they were stolen.

e. Inventories

Pursuant to departmental regulations or standing custom, officers usually check the contents of impounded vehicles. The routine taking of an inventory is not a search as defined by the Fourth Amendment. It is conducted for the purpose of safeguarding any valuables found in the vehicle, and it protects the officers from false claims of theft or from liability from mysterious disappearance.

Police officers would be derelict in their duties if they failed to remove weapons or valuable property from vehicles that are impounded, stored in an unprotected lot, or left parked beside a roadway.

Except in California, any items found in the course of conducting an inventory of a vehicle are admissible in court (*South Dakota* v. *Opperman*, 96 S. Ct. 3092 [1976]). This is because an inventory is not a search, and items found inadvertently come within the plain view exception. The courts in California have rejected this philosophy and thus exclude items found during the course of an inventory (*Mozetti* v. *Superior Court*, 4 Cal. 3d 699, 484 P. 2d 84 [1971]). In spite of this interpretation, it would be wise for officers in California to continue to conduct inventories in order to reduce losses by theft. While evidence fortuitously found would be inadmissible, officers can protect themselves against civil claims for negligent custody of personal property.

(4.4) Abandoned Property Rule

Property that has been abandoned belongs to no one. It has been defined as the voluntary relinquishment of possession, right, title, and claim to something, accompanied by an apparent intention of not reclaiming it. Law enforcement officers have occasion to use the rule of abandonment in four contexts.

First, objects that are thrown away by a pedestrian or a motorist may be picked up by an officer. Thus, an officer might not have probable cause to stop a suspect and search him for contraband, but he can legally retrieve the contraband if the suspect discards it. These are the so-called "dropsie cases," which are often encountered by uniformed officers who see known narcotics users in public. Defense attorneys commonly engage in vigorous cross-examination of arresting officers, seeking to prove that the narcotics were recovered by an illegal search rather than by abandonment.

Second, officers are sometimes called by the management to such places as hotels or motels when the housekeeping staff finds contraband or a weapon in a rented room. If the occupant has abandoned the premises, the search is lawful. If, on the other hand, the "abandonment" was temporary (that is, the occupant intended to return), the search is unlawful. Serious problems arise when the management has asked the occupant to leave for nonpayment of rent and later takes possession of the premises. The law cannot presume an occupant has abandoned the premises simply because he has been asked to leave for this reason.

Third, abandoned homes and apartment houses are frequently found in larger communities, often having been condemned for redevelopment purposes. They may be inhabited by drug addicts, criminals seeking refuge, and others. Police officers may enter these places without the consent of the occupants and without a search warrant. Occupants do not have a reasonable expectation of privacy and lack standing to object to the search on the grounds of the Fourth Amendment. This aspect of the rule also applies to abandoned automobiles.

Finally, officers working on cases related to narcotics and intelligence sometimes sift through trash and garbage deposited in refuse cans. If this can be accomplished without a physical trespass on the property of the occupant, the search is lawful. Officers may also enter into community-occupied space in an apartment building to search commonly used trash barrels. California alone has refused to recognize the validity of these searches and holds that they violate the occupants' expectation of privacy (*People* v. *Krivda*, 486 P. 2d 1262 [1971]).

(4.5) Searches Incident to Arrest

One of the most important exceptions to the requirement that officers have probable cause to search suspects is the incident to a legal arrest exception. In the past police officers would search an entire house or automobile when they placed an occupant under arrest. No further showing of cause was necessary.

In one of the most revolutionary cases decided by the Supreme Court under Chief Justice Earl Warren, the scope of searches incident to a legal arrest was dramatically curtailed. In *Chimel* v. *California*, 395 U.S. 752 (1969), the court announced that, thereafter, officers could only search the arrestee and the area immediately around him. The court said:

It is reasonable for the arresting officer to search the person arrested in order to remove any weapons that [might be used] to resist arrest or effect his escape. Otherwise, the officer's safety might well be endangered, and the arrest itself frustrated. In addition, it is entirely reasonable for the arresting officer to search for and seize any evidence on the arrestee's person in order to prevent its concealment or destruction. And the area into which an arrestee might reach in order to grab a weapon or evidentiary items must, of course, be guided by a like rule. A gun on a table or in a drawer in front of the one who is arrested can be as dangerous to the arresting officer as one concealed in the clothing of the person arrested. There is ample justification, therefore, for a search of the arrestee's person and the area "within his immediate control" —construing that phrase to mean the area from within which he might gain possession of a weapon or destructible evidence.

There is no comparable justification, however, for routinely searching rooms other than in which an arrest occurs, —or, for that matter, for searching through all the desk drawers or other closed or concealed areas in that room itself. Such searches, in the absence of well-recognized exceptions, may be made only under the authority of a search warrant.

The *Chimel* rule initially gave rise to the "arm's reach" doctrine. Most courts have more liberally construed the case and have adopted variants of the "lunge" doctrine. In its simplest analysis, the case restricts searches to those areas of a room where the arrestee can reach or jump over to.

Chimel also applies to arrests made when the suspect is apprehended in a motor vehicle. Officers may search the seat tops, under the front seats, the floorboard, above the visor, and an unlocked glove compartment. They may not extend the search to the trunk, a locked glove compartment, or under the hood.

A more serious question arises over whether an otherwise acceptable search can be continued after the suspect has been restrained or removed from the area where he was arrested. If the search of the room or the car is contemporaneous with the arrest, the search is proper. If the suspect has been placed in a transport vehicle or has been physically removed from the premises, the searching process must be discontinued. Inquisitive officers might think it wise to permit an arrestee freedom to move around unrestrained as long as possible. Not only is this dangerous to the officers, but the courts would find it a sham to avoid the restrictive consequences of the *Chimel* ruling.

No justification need be shown for a search of the clothing and accessories of the arrestee. They may be thoroughly searched if the search is conducted contemporaneous with the arrest and transport of the accused. Courts have disagreed over whether an officer can search a suitcase that an accused was carrying at the time of the arrest. Such inspections can often be justified on the theory that its contents are being inventoried, particularly when the accused was apprehended on the street or in a car.

Two qualifications of the *Chimel* ruling must be made. First, officers may, in many cases, walk into adjacent rooms, open closets, or peek under beds. This is to ensure that cohorts of the arrestee are not hiding in wait. These individuals might assault the arresting officers and prevent the arrest. Even stronger justification arises when accomplices in the crime are still at large, and their whereabouts are unknown. Second, under the plain view exception, officers need not ignore contraband, weapons, and evidence observed in open places while they are apprehending the accused and ensuring themselves against attack by concealed cohorts.

Finally, it must be noted that, long before the *Chimel* case was decided, courts condemned the so-called timed arrest. That is, officers may not unreasonably delay the apprehension of an accused merely to invade his home in the hope of extending their search to the premises he had occupied. If, however, a residential arrest is justified on the basis of other factors, the delay is reasonable. Thus, officers, armed with an arrest warrant for Smith, observe him walking home. Smith is part of a suspected drug ring, and his arrest on the streets would alert his accomplices. If the officers delay apprehension until he is inside his residence, the delay is reasonable and justified. Anything seen in plain view, once the officers are inside, is admissible as evidence. Items within Smith's reach, in the room where he is apprehended, can be lawfully searched.

Tensions in a community, which sometimes result in civil disturbances, can often be avoided by inconspicuous apprehensions. If hostile attitudes are prevalent in a neighborhood, delayed residential arrest of a local resident would be justified.

(4.6) Searches of Vehicles

Vehicular searches are, in most cases, an exception to the rule requiring issuance of a search warrant. This is because vehicles can be easily moved and concealed. Only on rare occasions, which are discussed below, are warrants necessary. Instances in which a vehicular search may be justified, without a warrant, include the following:

1. The officer has probable cause to search the vehicle.

2. The officer has probable cause to arrest the driver for a custodial offense of an evidentiary nature. That is, the offender must be booked, not released on citation, and the offense is one when physical evidence may be present.

3. The officer has probable cause to arrest the driver for a custodial offense of a nonevidentiary nature. Here, the scope of the vehicle search is limited by the *Chimel* ruling (see p. 83).

a. Probable Cause

When a police officer has probable cause to search a vehicle, he may normally do so without first obtaining a search warrant. The principal case in point is *Chambers* v. *Maroney*, 399 U.S. 42 (1970). In *Chambers* the officers had probable cause to search a vehicle they had stopped on the roadway for the proceeds from an armed robbery. They apprehended the occupants and returned to their station house, taking the car with them. At the station house they searched the car, finding the guns that had been used and the money that had been stolen.

The Supreme Court permitted the warrantless search because of the impracticability of obtaining a warrant for a movable object. The search was distinguished from the "incident to arrest," upon which the *Chimel* decision imposed limitations. In *Chambers* the officers had probable cause to look for the money and guns. And, unlike searches incident to arrest, the search did not have to be immediately contemporaneous with the arrest. The officers properly removed the vehicle to their station where they could complete the search with relative efficiency and safety.

Though a vehicle should normally be searched immediately, the existence of one or more of the following factors would justify removal and delay:

1. inclement weather;
2. hazardous traffic conditions;
3. poor lighting;
4. the gathering of a hostile crowd or the possibility that this might occur;
5. the need for a "technical" search, such as the use of ultraviolet or infrared rays, vacuum sweepings, and paint scrapings.

A later case, *Coolidge* v. *New Hampshire*, 403 U.S. 443 (1971), restricted somewhat the *Chambers* doctrine and is, therefore, an exception to the warrantless search rule. If officers who seek to conduct the search plan their actions in advance and have time to procure a warrant, they must do so. As an example, vice officers watch a runner pick up gambling proceeds every Friday for three weeks. On the fourth Friday they plan to stop him and search his car. A warrant is required under these circumstances.

Similarly, if the officers in the *Chambers* case had removed the suspects' automobile, impounded it, and delayed searching it promptly, a warrant would have been needed to justify a later search of the vehicle. No absolute time limit is imposed in such situations. Though a delay of a few minutes would not be unreasonable, a delay of a few hours would be.

The essential point of the decision is that a warrant is not required because a motor vehicle is movable. Courts have extended this ruling to situations where the auto has been rendered immobile, and when it has been parked and the driver is not present (*U.S.* v. *Bozada*, 473 F. 2d 389 [8th Cir. 1973], and cases therein cited). In either of these circumstances the safest course for an officer to follow is to obtain a warrant when the contents can be guarded (such as would occur during an impoundment). The mere fact that the car has been wrecked alongside the road would not mandate a warrant. Though it is true that the vehicle is immobilized, its contents could be easily removed and then destroyed or concealed elsewhere.

The scope of a warrantless search of a vehicle is the same as in situations when a search warrant has been procured.

b. Custodial and Evidentiary Offenses

When an officer makes a custodial arrest for a crime of an evidentiary nature, it is possible that the fruits of or the evidence of the offense, such as weapons or contraband, will be in the car. No special proof of the existence of these items is necessary to justify a complete warrantless search of the vehicle.

When a custodial arrest is made for a nonevidentiary offense, however, the scope of the permissible search is limited by the *Chimel* decision to the area immediately around the arrestee. Thus, officers see Smith, who is wanted on an outstanding warrant for nonsupport, driving a car. At the time the officers apprehend him, they may search the area around the front seat. This is done for their own safety since Smith could have secreted a weapon in the vehicle. But, because Smith is not being charged with an evidentiary offense, the officers cannot open his trunk or a locked glove compartment.

A custodial arrest is occasionally made for a traffic offense. They are normally of a nonevidentiary nature. If, however, the apprehension is for drunk driving, the arresting officers may search for intoxicants.

Most traffic offenses are handled by the issuance of a citation, and a custodial arrest is not involved. In these cases a search "incident to arrest" is not justified. If, however, the officer issuing the citation reasonably suspects that the driver may be armed and dangerous, he may frisk the occupant. Though the scope of the frisk of someone occupying a vehicle is broader than that permitted of a pedestrian, it parallels that allowed in searches incident to arrest. A gun kept under the driver's seat is just as accessible and as dangerous to the officer as one concealed in the driver's clothing—perhaps more so.

(4.7) Hot Pursuit and Exigent Circumstances

Two exceptional situations make a search warrant unnecessary. The first is the so-called hot pursuit exception. An officer who chases a fugitive, or is in fresh pursuit, does not need a search warrant to continue his chase into homes or offices, and anything found in the course of the pursuit and is incident to it is an admissible item. In order for the incident to qualify as this type of exception, the officer must have legal grounds to make an arrest, the suspect must be fleeing to avoid imminent capture, and the pursuit must be promptly started and continuously maintained. It is not necessary that the fugitive be constantly in sight of the officer or, for that matter, in sight at all. Certain interruptions are justified, such as calling for assistance, temporarily resting, if the pursuit is on foot, or stopping for gas or directions, if it is in a car.

Since fresh pursuit, in the absence of a statute, is a common-law rule, an officer must stop at the territorial limits of his jurisdiction. If, during the course of the pursuit, the officer finds incriminating evidence, contraband, or weapons, he may seize these items without a warrant.

The second exception is exigent circumstances. If a true

emergency exists, or is reasonably believed to exist, officers may enter the premises without a warrant. The most common example is the situation in which there is the threat of a bomb. Another is when officers believe a person may be in need of aid. The urgency of the incident justifies entry without a warrant, and, in most jurisdictions, anything seen inside in plain view may be seized without a warrant. In a few states the officer must return with a warrant for the actual seizure, but the entry and search without a warrant are lawful when they occur. The Supreme Court has made it clear that police officers cannot create their own exigent circumstances. These circumstances must exist independently. The following is an example of this. Officers had an arrest warrant for Vale and knew where he lived. Outside his home they witnessed him conduct an apparent narcotics transaction. They arrested Vale and searched his house. The search could not be justified on exigent circumstances since the police themselves created the circumstances (*Vale* v. *Louisiana*, 399 U.S. 30 [1970]).

(4.8) Consensual Searches

Nothing in the Fourth Amendment requires the issuance of a warrant when the party in possession of that which is to be searched validly consents to the search. There is nothing immoral or unethical about asking a suspect to give his consent. As a matter of fact, the majority of police searches are made on this basis. The "waiver" is simply the voluntary relinquishment of a known right—the right to demand a search warrant. Consensual searches are convenient because of several factors.

1. The search need not be based on probable cause or a lesser amount of proof.

2. The search does not have to be related to a valid arrest.

3. The officer does not have to name or particularly describe the property sought.

4. The search may be commenced long after the leads have become stale.

5. The premises to be searched do not have to be particularly described.

6. Extensive paperwork and judicial approval are unnecessary.

7. The search may be conducted outside the officer's jurisdiction.

a. Voluntariness

The consent must be freely given, without coercion or deceit. Once incriminating evidence or contraband is found, the suspect's only realistic defense is to challenge the legality of the consent itself. It is important, therefore, that officers document facts surrounding the giving of consent. It may not be enough simply to warn a suspect that he has the right to refuse to give his consent. Below are some factors that tend to prove the voluntariness of the consent.

1. The suspect actively assists the officers in conducting the search.

2. The suspect verbally incriminates himself.

3. The suspect expresses a belief that nothing incriminating will be found.

4. The suspect is the first to suggest that a search be made.

5. The suspect is well educated or holds a responsible position.

Factors that tend to prove a consent was not given voluntarily include the following.

1. The suspect is an alien or is semiliterate.

2. The original entry into the premises was illegal.

3. The consent was taken while the subject was at gunpoint and was handcuffed.

4. The officers made "implied threats" such as "You'll be better off if you cooperate."

5. The suspect was forcibly arrested and suffered minor injury, such as lacerations.

Exculpatory statements expressing belief that nothing will be found tend to support a finding of voluntariness. This is so because of the recognition that many suspects use affirmative means to suggest their innocence. Similarly, a suspect might believe that the items sought are well hidden and will not be discovered. The courts have also recognized that denials of ownership or a stated lack of authority to give consent are simply efforts to use an alternative defense.

The Supreme Court has held that an officer may not falsely state that he possesses a search warrant in the hope that he will obtain consent. Such action constitutes coercion and would invalidate the consent as "freely given." Officers may state that if consent is not given they will apply for a search warrant. They may also express the belief, if it is reasonable, that a warrant will be issued at their request. They can, moreover, advise the suspect that, unless he voluntarily consents to an immediate search, his premises will be placed under surveillance while they attempt to secure a search warrant. As stated in *U.S.* v. *Faruolo*, 506 F. 2d 490 (2d Cir. 1974), "In our view . . . the well founded advice of a law enforcement agent that, absent a consent to search, a warrant can be obtained does not constitute coercion. There is an admission by the officer that he has no right to proceed unless the defendant consents." This situation must be distinguished from a consent obtained by deceit, which would just as surely invalidate a consensual search as coercion. If a detective posed as a building inspector and sought to search a place for "building code vioations," the search would be illegal.

Deceit differs from "infiltration," which rests on another theory. If an officer works undercover or poses as a criminal, such action does not legally constitute deceit. Although deception is necessary, it is the "misplaced trust" put in the officer that leads to the finding of evidence or contraband. The officer is actually *invited* onto the premises. In the incident of the building inspector he is *permitted* to enter the place to be searched. As an example, officers, posing as customers, enter a pawnshop and ask to see "better buys." The owner takes them into the back room and displays stolen wares. The officers were invitees the owner mistakenly believed were genuine customers. The items observed in plain view are thus admissible.

The simplest method of ensuring that a suspect knows he has the right to refuse his consent is to tell him so. It is not essential that this be done. The Supreme Court has stated (*Schneckloth* v. *Busta-monte*, 93 S. Ct. 2041, 2059 [1973]) that the "prosecution is not required to demonstrate such knowledge as a prerequisite to obtaining a voluntary consent." A distinction should be made when the suspect is under arrest and in custody. At that stage a suspect is entitled to a recital of the *Miranda* warnings because of the "inherently coercive atmosphere" associated with custodial questioning. It is recommended that officers obtain written consents to search from suspects who have been arrested. Such waivers indicate that the suspect knows he has the right to refuse his consent. (See the appendix for typical authorizations in English and in Spanish.)

The burden of showing that a consent was involuntary rests on the defense. Nothing in the *Miranda* decision applies to consensual search cases. Some courts have, nevertheless, enlarged on a suspect's rights under the Fourth and Fifth Amendments as they are embodied in their respective state constitutions.

b. Scope and Capacity

Officers frequently assume that once consent is given it applies to all of their subsequent actions. This is untrue, and the courts will limit the areas of permissible search to the scope of the given consent. Authority to look in a glove compartment does not extend to a locked trunk. Consent to frisk a suspect does not include the right to rummage through his wallet. A suspect may limit the places that can be searched, define the time limits, direct the numbers or classes of searching officers, and revoke his consent at any time.

Consent may be given by juveniles as well as adults. Courts often hold, however, that a person lacks the capacity to give his consent when he is drunk, high on drugs, very youthful, mentally retarded, injured or in pain, illiterate, or hysterical.

Consensual searches are not limited to goods and chattels. A suspect can lawfully consent to the taking of his fingerprints or footprints; urinalysis; hair, blood, and seminal samples; handwriting and voice exemplars; paraffin and other skin tests; breath and pupillary examinations; and nalorphine injections (the nalline addiction test).

c. Third-Party Consent

At common law, a husband, as head of the household, could consent to a search of the family residence. Over half of the states have ruled that the wife can also consent to a search of the family residence. Five states (Arizona, Florida, Mississippi, North Carolina, and Oklahoma) have ruled, however, that wives lack the authority to allow police officers to enter the family's premises to search for evidence (see *Annotation*, 31 A.L.R. 2d 1078, Sec. 10). It is generally felt that one spouse has as much right as the other to control the household, in the absence of the partner. The Supreme Court has recently held that a wife may consent to the search of the family home under the Fourth Amendment, but states are free to fashion a more restrictive rule based on their state constitutions.

Some courts have examined the subject's marital situation to see if it was harmonious or antagonistic. Most courts have upheld the legitimacy of the consent if both parties live on the premises, since they have equal control or right of control over the property. It may be another situation when the spouse has moved out of the suspected home. If the vacating party has retained a key and has lawful access to the home, the consent is probably valid. On the other hand, if the vacating party returned the key to the other spouse on separation, a forcible entry based on the consent of the vacating spouse is of dubious validity.

So-called common-law marriages and temporary liaisons often result in relationships of convenience. The test of the validity of a consent is control and access. It is unnecessary to prove that one person authorized another to give his or her consent to a search. The following serves as an example. William Matlock lived with a woman in a large home. Officers who were investigating a bank robbery asked the woman for her consent to search Matlock's room, which she shared with him. Matlock was in custody, and his consent was not sought. The woman pointed out Matlock's room, and the officers confiscated a large quantity of money. The Supreme Court upheld the woman's consent and the subsequent seizure. Although the woman's statements were hearsay, the court found them inherently believable, made against her interests because she could have involved herself, and were thus admissible in a suppression hearing (*U.S.* v. *Matlock*, 415 U.S. 443 [1971]).

It is possible that one spouse may not have access and control over some property of the other, regardless of the length of time they have been married and cohabiting. Examples include a safe, a safe-deposit box, or a file cabinet that is locked and exclusively used by one spouse.

Regardless of the age of a child, his room may be searched with the consent of a parent who owns or leases the premises. Even if the child pays his parents something for support, the room he uses does not, in most cases, take on the context of separately rented property. When, however, a child lives with his spouse in separate quarters over which the parents have voluntarily relinquished control, the situation is different. The situation is similar when a parent moves in with an emancipated child. In that case the parent can only give consent to the search of his room and jointly occupied rooms. On the other hand, if the child owns or leases the home, he can usually grant consent to officers to search the entire premises, including rooms occupied by a parent, brother, or sister. Normally a brother or sister could not consent to the search of a sibling's private room, only to shared and commonly occupied rooms.

Roommates can give consent for the search of their own rooms and those occupied in common, such as the kitchen, bathroom, basement, garage, and hallways. This situation frequently arises in college towns and in communes.

Hosts may normally consent to the search of rooms occupied by visitors. If, however, the houseguest has a reasonable expectation of privacy, the consent will not be binding. Things left on the dresser of an unlocked bedroom are not within the zone of privacy. Things put in drawers or left in suitcases normally would be. Jointly used drawers, closets, and storage space do not create an expectation of privacy.

The concept of the expectation of privacy is a limited one. The expectation is not that a roommate, host, or cotenant will not consent to a police search. The expectation must be that this person will not have access to these places. Thus, the question is an expectation from an intrusion by the other party, not an expectation that his consent will not be given the police.

Landlords do not have the right to consent to a search of occupied property they have leased to another person, even if the tenant is in arrears. Once the tenant has vacated or given up occupancy, the landlord may consent to a search. Although a landlord might have a right to enter a tenant's premises to make repairs, to inspect for damage or hazards, and to show the premises to future tenants, this right is a limited one, and it cannot be extended to police officers for another purpose.

Hotel rooms that are occupied by guests, even past checkout time, are treated no differently than premises leased for longer durations. If a maid, bellhop, valet, or any other employee sees contraband or weapons in a room and notifies the police, the police should refrain from entering the room until a search warrant is obtained. If the officers responding to a call reasonably believe that evidence or contraband will be destroyed or removed, they may, of course, act immediately because of the exigent circumstances surrounding the event. Courts do not lightly uphold exigent searches and will often demand strict compliance with the warrant requirement.

Employers normally have the right to inspect lockers and work areas that are assigned to employees for the mutual convenience of workers and employers. Employees usually cannot expect immunity from employer-instituted searches of company property, including desks, file cabinets, and company-owned vehicles.

Employees do not have an unrestricted right to consent to the search of an employer's property. A manager, of course, has broader discretion in authorizing a search than a clerk. Partners, who at law are joint owners, may consent to the search of the company's premises, files, books, and other property. Silent partners in a limited partnership ordinarily do not have unlimited access and authority and cannot authorize such a search.

Schools, which are somewhere between employers and parents, have the power to authorize a search by police of lockers and other areas that are used by or assigned to a student. Dormitory rooms occupied by college-age students do not fall within this exception, and the school is relegated to the status of a landlord in these situations.

Parolees are released from prison on the condition that they, their automobiles, and their homes may be searched without further consent, and even against their will. Because parolees remain in "constructive custody" of the state, correctional officials and probationary and parole officers may conduct such searches over the objection of the former convict. This right may not be delegated to police officers investigating a crime. These officers may, however, instigate such a search and accompany correctional or parole officers at the time the search is made (*People* v. *Bason*, 97 Cal. Rptr. 302, 5 Cal. 3d 759 [1971]; *People* v. *Murgia*, 62 Cal. Rptr. 100, 103 [App. 1964]).

(4.9) Border Searches

Several federal statutes authorize searches at our nation's borders. It is unnecessary to demonstrate the existence of probable cause to justify such searches. This does not mean, however, that the border patrol and customs and immigration officers have complete freedom to conduct warrantless searches. They still must comply with the test of reasonableness as set down in the Fourth Amendment.

The mere fact that a person crosses a border is justification for a customs search. Officers may not subject an individual to indignities and intrusions on human privacy unless there is a reasonable suspicion that he is smuggling contraband or items subject to duty.

Recent court decisions have restricted the right of federal agents to conduct random searches at some distance from the actual border. For example, the occupants of a vehicle seen near but not crossing the Mexican border may appear to be Mexican nationals. This is not sufficient reason for federal agents to stop them to determine whether they are actually aliens. Probable cause is not necessary, however, at a fixed checkpoint some distance from the border.

(4.10) "Shocking" Searches

Some types of searches may "shock" the conscience of the reviewing court and are therefore illegal. The landmark case is *Rochin* v. *California*, 342 U.S. 165 (1952), where the Supreme Court invalidated the use of a stomach pump to retrieve narcotics the suspect had swallowed. The use of an emetic, given by medical personnel, has, however, been upheld. This is particularly true when the suspect swallows a balloon filled with narcotics, the contents of which could have fatal effects.

The Supreme Court also allowed, in *Schmerber* v. *California*, 384 U.S. 757 (1966), the extraction of blood from a suspect, under medically supervised conditions. Another case in California, *People* v. *Kraft*, 84 Cal. Rptr. 280 (App. 1970), held that the application of a scissors lock on the suspect's leg and holding his arm immobile constituted excessive force and was, therefore, an impermissible search.

Several courts have maintained that a successful attempt to prevent a suspect from swallowing apparent contraband is not an illegal search. This includes choking the suspect or inserting fingers into his mouth.

Searches of a suspect's rectum or vagina have been upheld, when they are done in a "dignified" manner, and when the officers have reasonable grounds to believe contraband has been concealed in these body cavities. Routine inspections of these areas are not permissible.

(4.11) Standing

Standing refers to the legality of a person's status to raise a motion or to seek other relief. The Federal Rules of Criminal Procedure provide that a "person aggrieved" by an allegedly illegal search and seizure may move that the court suppress an item from consideration in a criminal case and require its return to the owner. The rule was originally intended to afford relief to the party against whom the search and seizure was directed. The interpretation of the rule in recent years affords relief to anyone against whom there might be prejudice brought about by the seizure.

Prior to 1960, if a defendant denied possession or ownership of the item seized, he could not move that the court suppress it. This was considered an inconsistent defense, requiring a choice on the part of the defendant. It is no longer necessary to choose between inconsistent defenses. A defendant may deny possession and still move for suppression.

The genesis of the rules governing standing was the law of property. Thus, some courts ruled that a defendant could not move to suppress contraband that had been illegally seized, since the law provides that contraband cannot be legally owned or possessed. The Supreme Court has since ruled that Congress had merely intended to facilitate the forfeiture of contraband, not deny standing to move for its suppression in the criminal courts.

Many courts have ruled that if evidence is found in a stolen car the driver cannot complain of an illegal search of the vehicle and seizure of the evidence. Only the lawful owner of the car could assert that claim, and he is not an aggrieved party to the illegal search. There is a trend toward abolishing the concept of standing in suppression cases. California abolished the rule in 1955 (*People* v. *Martin*, 290 P. 2d 855 [Cal. 1955]), and other states have followed suit. Even in California a defendant may not move to suppress evidence seized from a vacant building or found abandoned on the street.

(4.12) Summary

The Fourth Amendment, made applicable to the states by the Fourteenth Amendment, applies to people, not to things or places. It has been continuously interpreted in light of modern phenomena, such as motor vehicles. Aside from its literal meanings, it prohibits unreasonable searches and allows those that are reasonable. There is no absolute warrant requirement, for example, and the test of reasonableness applies. The amendment is enforced by the most important of evidence in criminal cases: the exclusionary rule. It is an absolute rule. There are no gradations in sanctions based on the gravity of the unlawful character of a policeman's acts. The rule does not consider either the good faith of an officer or its total absence. It only theoretically deters police "misconduct."

Not every act that uncovers evidence, contraband, or other seizable items is a "search." Open lands are quite different from homes. Moreover, an officer does not have to close his eyes to things he observes in plain view, in a place he has a lawful right to be. He may use technical aids, such as field glasses, in his surveillances and accomplish lawfully what he could not do directly through trespass.

Decisions related to the Fourth Amendment no longer follow strict concepts of property. If a person has a reasonable expectation of privacy, any warrantless intrusion upon this right will give rise to the exclusion of evidence. Again, the test is the reasonableness of an individual's expectation of privacy, and no absolute lines are drawn. Officers can no longer justify their actions on the basis that they had a legal right to be where they could observe illegal activity.

Concepts of property are still important when they involve abandonment or consent. The Supreme Court has relaxed many of the technical aspects surrounding consent searches and has imposed the overall standard of reasonableness.

Vehicles are still treated differently than homes. Because they are movable and because their contents are more readily subject to removal, concealment, and destruction, a warrant is usually unnecessary. Though the Fourth Amendment still protects people without regard to the place searched, the rule of reasonableness recognizes the exigent circumstances that surround a vehicular search. Two types of searches are covered by distinct rules. Border searches do not require evidence of suspicious conduct unless the suspect is asked to disrobe or other significant intrusions are attempted. Inventory inspections are not really searches at all, at least in the criminal sense; they are justified by the duty of officers to safeguard property in their keeping.

Standing is an important, but not always the final, factor in determining the application of the exclusionary rule. It is of prime relevance when consent searches are sought, but should not be used to subvert the rights of a suspect.

5

Arrest and Search Warrants

As mentioned in Chapter 4, physical evidence is not admissible unless it has been lawfully collected. In many cases, the defendant goes free because of a faulty seizure of evidence. To avoid the consequences of the exclusionary rule, officers must be expert in the law of arrest, search, and seizure.

The subject of arrest and search warrants has never received more attention than now. In recent years the U.S. Supreme Court has emphasized the importance of interposing the determinations of a "neutral and detached magistrate" between the police officer and the citizen. Early in 1976 the California Supreme Court said that, unless there are exigent circumstances, police officers must obtain a warrant before arresting a person in his home; failure to do so will result in the suppression of evidence seized incident to the arrest (*People* v. *Ramey*, 127 Cal. Rptr. 629 [Cal. 1976]). Though this strict interpretation is not followed in other jurisdictions, it demonstrates, nevertheless, the judicial preference for warrants (*U.S.* v. *Watson*, 96 S. Ct. 820 [1976]).

The standards for a warrantless arrest or search are, moreover, the same for the issuance of an arrest or search warrant. There is one important difference between warrantless arrests and searches and those authorized by a magistrate, and it is this difference that ties warrant requirements into the substantive law of criminal evidence. A police officer must demonstrate the existence of probable cause at the time he applies for an arrest or search warrant. This demonstration must be full and unequivocal. All the supporting facts and circumstances must be set forth in the affidavit itself, which means the facts must be in writing or otherwise recorded.

In cases where a warrant was issued, the prosecution is bound by the contents of the affidavit. This is the so-called four corners rule (*U.S.* v. *Damitz*, 495 F. 2d 50 [9th Cir., 1974]), which means the demonstration of probable cause must be contained within the four corners of the piece of paper given to the magistrate. Something forgotten or unintentionally omitted is lost forever. No matter what evidence of guilt a police officer may have had at the time the warrant was sought, only the facts set forth in the affidavit will be considered when the motion to suppress is introduced. Deficient affidavits cannot be cured later by facts that the officer possessed but did not articulate at the time the warrant was issued. In many jurisdictions, oral statements made under oath cannot be considered by the issuing magistrate, who must consider only the written statements of the officer (*U.S.* v. *Anderson*, 453 F. 2d 174 [9th Cir., 1971]).

In the case of warrantless arrests and searches, an officer need not establish the existence of probable cause until the preliminary hearing stage (or trial, if the crime is a misdemeanor). This gives him additional time to gather the facts that point to the guilt of the accused. He cannot, of course, use after-acquired information (that is, information acquired after an arrest or search), but he is under less pressure once the arrest has been consummated.

(5.1) Probable Cause

Although arrest and search warrants require a judicial finding of probable cause, they involve different probabilities. Both warrants necessitate demonstration that a crime has taken place. An arrest warrant, however, requires an identification of the probable perpetrator; a search warrant does not. A search warrant presumes the existence of tangible evidence of the offense; an arrest warrant does not. The search warrant affidavit must go still further and demonstrate the likelihood that the things sought will be at a stated location during an identifiable time. Table 5-1 graphically illustrates the different probabilities.

As has been said, the first probability, common to both warrants, is that an offense has taken place. The existence of an offense report will, in routine cases, establish this fact. It is not necessary that the officer who swears out the warrant be the same one who completed the offense report. In larger departments a patrol officer completes the preliminary report of the theft, burglary, robbery, or other crime; a detective is then assigned to follow up the investigation and obtain necessary warrants. The individual who swears out the warrant (the affiant) need not communicate directly with the patrol officer for he is entitled to accept the written report at face value and to presume its correctness. A conscientious detective will, of course, call the victim, witnesses, and the uniformed officer who took the initial report, verifying all relevant details. In drafting the affidavit, the affiant should state the existence of the initial report, summarize its details, and indicate that he is swearing out the affidavit "on information and belief."

Specialized enforcement units usually do not receive citizen complaints; they produce their own reports to demonstrate the existence of an offense. This is usually true in the so-called inspectional services units, such as narcotics, gambling, and other vice squads. Reports of informants' interviews, surveillance reports, and undercover

Table 5-1
Probabilities in arrest warrants and search warrants

Prerequisite judicial findings	Arrest warrants	Search warrants
A crime was probably committed.	Yes	Yes
An identified suspect probably committed the act.	Yes	No
Tangible evidence of the offense exists.	No	Yes
Such evidence will be found at or in a described place.	No	Yes
Such evidence will be found at a certain time.	No	Yes

operational accounts furnish the necessary presumption of criminal activity. In the affidavit these documents are referred to in the same manner as offense reports.

In some states by statute and also under the federal rules, a search warrant may be issued for a crime in progress, but not yet committed. This is true of certain possessory offenses.

Only arrest warrants need identify a suspect. This is usually by name, but John Doe warrants, coupled with a description, are permissible. The affidavit must show that the suspect is the person who committed an act that is alleged to be illegal. As mentioned, a search warrant may be issued for a home, business, auto, boat, or airplane without naming a suspect. Nearly all states provide, however, that a search warrant may be issued for a described person. The affidavit must show why there is probable cause to believe that evidence will be found on him.

Search warrants require a demonstration that what is sought probably exists. This is simple when officers seek to recover stolen television sets, a murder weapon, or other specifically identifiable items. In addition, certain offenses, by their nature, employ tangible items describable by their generic nature. For example, bookmakers keep written records, narcotics dealers keep an inventory, addicts keep paraphernalia, and burglars keep tools.

The affiant should state his belief, which is based on stated facts, that the things sought will be found in the location to be searched. *People* v. *Prall*, 145 N.E. 610, 612 (Ill. 1924), described below, is an example.

The defendant, Prall, was arrested by a deputy sheriff for possession of automobile tires taken from a railroad siding. A search warrant for Prall's home was defective, because it was necessary for the deputy sheriff to allege that more tires were taken than had been recovered.

In general, the longer the time between the crime and the search, the greater is the likelihood that the items sought have been destroyed, sold, concealed, or otherwise disposed of. The nature of the offense, the type of item sought, and the individual who seems to be involved must, however, always be considered. If a professional burglar took six television sets, it is unlikely that he will have any of them after several months. If, however, the suspect is a rather young, nonprofessional criminal, he might keep one set for his personal use.

It is not necessary to assume that particularly described goods will exist if the crime, by its nature, involves a turnover of items, and these items are of the same generic class. Surveillances may indicate, for example, that a suspect has taken bets on horses over a period of several weeks. Officers do not have to assume that records of older transactions still exist; they need only allege that the crime requires the keeping of records. They have probable cause to believe, therefore, that recent entries are kept at a named location and that the newer records have replaced the older ones.

It is important in cases where there is a turnover of the items sought that the affiant demonstrate the continuing nature of the offense. This may be done in one of two ways: by two or more surveillances conducted on different days, or by disclosures from a reliable informant that the activity is continuing.

Though staleness is always a significant factor in search warrants, it is not in arrest warrants. Subject only to the statute of limitations, officers may possess probable cause for an indefinite period of time before seeking the issuance of an arrest warrant. Delays can, on the other hand, imperil the validity of search warrants unless continuity is shown.

(5.2) Grounds for Issuance

Search warrants are not among the warrants, writs, and other processes recognized by common law; they are wholly statutory. The Fourth Amendment requires that all warrants must be supported by probable cause, under oath, and they must particularly describe the person or things sought and the person or place to be searched. Most states require the request to be written, but transcribed testimony is constitutionally acceptable if it is allowed by statute. It is imperative that the affiant, sometimes called a complainant, state that he has been placed on his oath or affirmation. (At common law it was thought that a person would be reluctant to risk hell by swearing falsely with God as his witness.)

Although the oath is normally administered before an officer presents his facts, it may follow unless a state law forbids this practice. It is also customary to sign a form affidavit without raising one's hand and stating aloud, "I swear the truth of these matters so help me God." It is not an unforgivable error to do so, but it is important for officers to comply with formalities (see Edward C. Fisher, *Search and Seizure* [Evanston, Ill.: Northwestern University Traffic Institute, 1970], Sec. 71).

Search warrants can only be secured for enumerated offenses, whereas arrest warrants can be issued for any crime unless a statute demands issuance of a summons or citation. Only the things listed in the statute can be named in the warrant. Recent legislation tends to simplify the list to include the following:

1. contraband, the possession of which is unlawful;
2. instrumentalities used to commit any crime;
3. fruits of a crime;
4. items that are evidence of the commission of a crime or the identity of the perpetrator.

Prior to 1967 some states did not allow the issuing of search warrants that sought "mere evidence," which might be a blood-stained undershirt, mud scrapings from shoes, a diary or plans, powder burns on a cuff, or innumerable other things that could only be listed in a statute by category. These things could only be seized incidental to a valid arrest. A serious problem arose because of the restrictions imposed on the scope of searches incident to arrest in the *Chimel* case. The Supreme Court made clear in *Warden* v. *Hayden*, 387 U.S. 294 (1967), that "mere evidence" could be seized by warrant, assuming there was a statute authorizing such searches. Unfortunately, not all states acted promptly after the *Hayden* case and relied on pre-*Chimel* standards.

(5.3) Particular Description

The requirement that an item be particularly described is flexible. It means the best-known description of the thing sought, not necessarily a unique description. Officers should mention the specific things sought plus the generic name so as to authorize seizure of similar items found but not named in the warrant. For example, contraband can be loosely described as narcotics, illegal weapons, or counterfeit currency, but it is preferable to state heroin, cocaine, and other narcotics, a sawed-off shotgun, automatic rifle, and other illegal firearms, or counterfeit twenty-dollar notes and other U.S. tender.

Some courts have permitted a vague description in the warrant if a more precise description appeared in the affidavit and vice versa.

Ordinarily, however, care should be used to repeat the descriptions exactly.

Many of the cases with suppressed warrants involve misdescribed premises to be searched. A street address is sufficient where a single-family residence is involved, but it is preferable to state that the premises are a one- or two-storied single-family residence and to describe the home. One might state, for example, "a red brick structure with a front and rear entrance, green front door, and pitched roof covered by gray shingles." Rural property must be so clearly described that there can be no doubt about which place was meant, such as "a two-storied white frame farmhouse on Route 31, approximately 400 yards south of the intersection with Highway 7, on the west side of the road, surrounded by a white picket fence and behind a rural mailbox marked 'The Smiths.'" Some rooming houses do not number floors, much less rooms, and so they must be described in a way similar to the following: "past the front door and up two landings, south thirty feet and up one landing, south down the hallway to the third door on the left (east side of hall)." At least one court decision (*Morales* v. *State*, 170 N.W. 2d 684 [Wis. 1969]) has approved of the inclusion of a photograph of the premises, attached to the affidavit, and referred to in the warrant. A minor defect in the description will not invalidate the search unless it means that two or more places fit the description. Even in that case, if the affiant or other officer who conducted the surveillances also serves the warrant, the search will be upheld in most jurisdictions.

It is important that the affidavit and warrant list the parts of the building to be searched, unless there is probable cause to believe the things sought could be anywhere in it. This becomes critical when two or more unrelated persons or families share a residence. Only ingenuity can identify which person or family lives in the back, the basement, or the attic. If the officers learn they have named the wrong portion of the building once they have entered it, they should seal the exits and obtain a new warrant quickly.

As mentioned previously, search and arrest warrants may be obtained for persons as well as places. A name is ordinarily sufficient for an arrest warrant, and the name and address for a search warrant. If a physical description is known, however, it is preferable to include it in the warrant and the supporting affidavit. A physical description, photograph, or other method of identifying the individual must be part of a John Doe warrant. For example, a search warrant could be issued for the following: "a negro male, dark complected, balding, middle aged, who accompanies [name] on Monday mornings when money is picked up, and sits on the right side, front seat, of the red over white 1976 Mustang Lic. ASD-701."

The affiant should be described in such a manner as a police officer, victim, or eyewitness. In cases where only circumstantial evidence is present, it is essential that the affiant's background be set forth in detail. It is one thing for a priest or postman to see two people conversing; it is quite another for an experienced narcotics officer to observe this same conversation. Police officers may rely on their specialized training and experience when they are interpreting their surveillances and disclosures by informants. Chief Justice Warren Burger, speaking for two other justices in *U.S.* v. *Harris*, 403 U.S. 584 (1971), stated: "We cannot conclude that a policeman's knowledge of a suspect's reputation—something that policemen frequently know and a factor that impressed such a 'legal technician' as Mr. Justice Frankfurter—is not a 'practical consideration of everday life' upon which an officer (or magistrate) may properly rely in assessing the reliability of an informant's tip."

The following are typical recitations of expertise. They include the kind of information that officers should keep in their memo books, such as number of arrests, raids, and other law enforcement activities. The numbers in parentheses should always be kept up to date.

"I have been a police officer for (47) months and have been assigned to the gambling unit for (13) months; during this period I have made (74) arrests for gambling, (12) of which were for possession of gambling paraphernalia. I have participated in (53) gambling raids and have testified in (28) trials or suppression hearings involving gambling charges."

"I have been a police officer for (19) months and have been assigned to the narcotics unit for (3) months. I attended a five-day school for narcotics enforcement officers conducted by the Drug Enforcement Administration; I also attended a fourteen-hour in-service seminar on narcotics enforcement sponsored by the Metro Enforcement Group (MEG). I have participated in (28) narcotics arrests, (14) of which followed (8) narcotics raids."

An officer does not have to compile an impressive arrest record personally; it is sufficient that he participated in arrests or raids in order to gain the necessary expertise to give an opinion in a search or arrest warrant affidavit. Certain activities give important clues to the individual with expertise. The following examples illustrate what such a person might ascertain.

1. A gambling detective observes a suspected bookmaker carrying sheets of an off-white colored paper into an apartment. This could be nitrocellulose fibered rag, known as "flash paper," which instantly burns without residue; it is frequently used by wire room operators.

2. A gambling detective observes a suspected bookmaker carrying a plastic bucket, wooden salad fork, and bottle of liquid drain opener into an apartment. Gelatin paper, which is used extensively by wire room operators, rapidly dissolves in water. Decomposition is assisted by liquid drain openers. A large wooden fork quickens destruction in a plastic bucket.

3. A narcotics detective observes a suspected pusher giving tin-foil packets to a suspected addict and receiving money. Heroin and cocaine are often sold in aluminum foil or cellophane packets.

4. A narcotics detective observes a suspected pusher buy a large bottle of sleeping capsules at a drugstore. These capsules can be easily taken apart, filled with cut heroin, and recapped.

Burglars are known by their tools; gamblers and addicts are known by their associates; prostitutes and some homosexuals are known by the parts of town they frequent. Even if an officer-affiant is not personally acquainted with such facts, he can include them in his affidavit. The collective wisdom of the entire police department can be referred to in supporting pleadings. To reiterate, the important point to remember is that an officer's background should be particularized in the affidavit.

(5.4) Use of Informants

Generally speaking, there are three motives of informants. Television dramas highlight the underworld informer who implicates others for financial gain, revenge, the elimination of competition, or in the hope that his illegal activity will be overlooked. "Stoolies" are typically portrayed as disreputable characters. The motive of the second type of confidential informant is to be a good citizen. Someone who is not involved in criminal activities, but is motivated by a sense of right and wrong, falls into this category. Citizens often report neighbors, acquaintances, business contacts, or friends, and, therefore, they desire total anonymity. The third type of informant is a police officer, federal agent, or other law enforcement employee, and his motive is to perform his duty. Because of their dealings with certain groups or individuals, they are reluctant to take forthright action or to complain about suspects. Law enforcement officers are sometimes called "automatic informants" because they are automatically supposed to report criminal behavior.

All three types of informants may demand confidentiality. The underworld character may fear death, assault, or a lesser form of retaliation. A citizen may fear social ostracism, ridicule, or contempt. An officer may fear impairment of his efficiency or credibility.

Police agencies should keep careful records on confidential informants. For reasons of security, records of identity are normally kept in safe custody, accessible to only a few senior officers, and informants are customarily referred to in reports by number only. Each time an informant furnishes information, a report should be written, and an attempt should be made to verify the substance of the disclosures. A running record should be kept on all criminal informants because their tips cannot furnish the basis for probable cause unless prior reliability is demonstrated. This credibility is important because a confidential informant cannot be cross-examined like other witnesses. His information constitutes, therefore, hearsay evidence and is admissible at a suppression hearing, but not at a trial.

Proving an informant's reliability can be accomplished in a number of ways. The usual method is to allege that the informant has provided information in the past and that he has proved himself trustworthy. A single arrest that results from prior information can provide the necessary reliability, if one of two conditions are met: First, a conviction resulted from the arrest. Second, evidence was seized at the time of the arrest even though a conviction was not obtained for some reason or the prosecution is still pending.

Multiple arrests, regardless of whether evidence was seized and although the prosecution of the cases is still pending, also demonstrate reliability. Surveillances provide another way of verifying an informant's disclosures. If independent observations by police officers corroborate the information, reliability is established, as it is when a second informant independently corroborates the facts of the first informant.

A preeminent case on disclosures by an informant is *Spinelli* v. *U.S.*, 393 U.S. 410 (1969). The Supreme Court affirmed prior decisions that held that a police officer may obtain a warrant, based on the word of a confidential underworld informant, if, first, the affidavit states how the informant obtained his information, and, second, the word of the informant is sufficiently corroborated from past instances of reliability, surveillances, or other supporting sources. The problem is particularly acute when an informant who does not qualify for good citizen status is being used for the first time.

Courts abhor "hearsay on hearsay." Even if an informant has provided good leads a hundred times, the investigating officers must determine whether the latest disclosure is based on personal knowledge. Without such assurances, the information will not in itself support a conclusion that probable cause exists. The problem facing law enforcement officers is that an informant cannot always permit this information to be written into an affidavit without jeopardizing his anonymity. If, for example, an informant was the only person who saw a suspect in possession of stolen goods, the affidavit might as well give the informant's name to indicate how he knows the suspect to be in possession of the goods. There is no problem if several individuals saw the suspect in possession of the goods, unless, of course, the exact time was stated.

An affidavit can be intentionally vague concerning the way an informant obtained his information if the facts disclosed are in sufficient detail that a court can presume the knowledge is firsthand. The following is an example of such a statement. "A confidential informant told me that Jones has a quantity of heroin in his apartment at 234 Main, suite B. He said that the heroin is kept in red balloons and is concealed in a green vase. The vase is on a walnut bookshelf on the east side of the living room of said apartment. The informant has personal knowledge of the truth of this information."

Informants usually provide information in a particular area such as gambling, narcotics, or hijacking, but if they are reliable in one area they are usually reliable in another. It is not necessary that the informant's reliability be based on past experience in the activity under investigation.

The so-called good citizen informant receives greater respect from the courts. Thus, it is not necessary for the police to establish tested reliability, and the person's disclosures do not need independent corroboration. The Supreme Court concluded in *U.S.* v. *Harris*, supra, that a person who lacks experience as an informer and is not part of the criminal community can furnish probable cause to law enforcement officers. As with the *Spinelli* case, he would have to disclose how he learned of the suspected activity. The affidavit, in such cases, must affirmatively establish that the citizen is not a part of the scheme, does not have a criminal record, fears for his safety, and witnessed evidence of the offense. Statements from witnesses that they participated in an illicit act are also entitled to credibility since, in the words of the Supreme Court, "people do not lightly admit a crime . . . ." In the *Harris* case, which involved bootlegging, the citizen informant stated that he had recently purchased moonshine from the suspect.

The courts preserve the confidentiality of informants. To do otherwise would jeopardize their lives, their safety, and their privacy. In 1967 the Supreme Court clearly held that confidential, nonparticipating informants may establish probable cause for the police to make an arrest or to conduct a search. Their identities should not be disclosed as a matter of public policy. Though their disclosures may furnish underlying probable cause to support the search or arrest upon which the prosecution is predicated, they may not be used against an accused at his trial. In limited cases, however, courts will order production of an informant or revelation of his identity. Should this situation arise, the prosecution can either comply or drop the charges. The informant's confidentiality will not be breached unless disclosure is necessary to a fair trial or the informant actually participated in the offense being prosecuted. (For further elaboration of this subject, see Chapter 8.)

Confidential information received from other police officers is intrinsically reliable. It is unnecessary to establish a history of tested disclosures or to corroborate the information through surveillances. The knowledge of one officer, at law, is the knowledge of the whole police department, and officers are presumed, at law, to be truthful and to have a duty to exchange information. They are more likely to use care in repeating things overheard, and their hearsay is more likely to be valid. Information furnished among officers does not lose any credibility because of repetition; such exchanges are merely conduits of "official" knowledge. Though police officers normally want to testify against a suspect, there are valid reasons for preserving confidentiality. Undercover agents might be identified, working relationships with other informants might be impaired, and other unpleasant consequences might result.

The law distinguishes between named and confidential informants. This is because a named informant may be subpoenaed to a deposition, and he can be called to testify at the trial by either side and can be cross-examined. Most victims of and witnesses to a crime are named informants. They may, however, be treated as confidential informants. If they are credible public citizens, no showing of prior reliability is necessary, particularly when the victim or witness will be produced at the trial or when the information will only be used to develop probable cause for a search warrant.

In larger communities an anonymous informer may occasionally give information to police officers through the mails or over the telephone. Such informants cannot be accorded the good citizen presumption, and prior reliability must be shown. Reliability can be established where, in repeated instances, the anonymous informant is recognized by his handwriting, his voice, or through the use of a code name (*People* v. *Cain*, 15 Cal. App. 3d 687 [1971]).

(5.5) Surveillances

Surveillances are conducted by the police for a variety of purposes. They often provide the tactical information necessary to conduct an efficient and safe raid. Sometimes they are strategic, as when they are conducted to keep tabs on a known criminal or terrorist. They may explain motives of suspects or ensure that no other persons are involved. In addition, they may be necessary to aid in developing probable cause preparatory to the issuance of a search or arrest warrant. Surveillances standing alone, if sufficient, can, in fact, furnish the sole basis for a conclusion that probable cause exists. They are also necessary to corroborate information obtained from an underworld informant being used for the first time or informants who may have provided untrustworthy information in the past.

Police officers may lawfully follow a criminal suspect in public areas and make still or motion pictures of his activities (see Chapter 4 for a discussion of "Searches"). Binoculars, telescopes, and infrared scopes may be used to observe criminal suspects in public and semi-public places. Fluorescein powder, which is excited and becomes visible under ultraviolet light, may be employed. Electronic tracking devices (such as bumper beepers) can be attached to a private car; some courts have found, however, that a suspect's reasonable expectation of privacy may be invaded by their use, and so they should be employed only with the advice of counsel. Surveillances conducted by helicopters and covert rest room observations may, by their nature, be a violation of a suspect's reasonable expectation of privacy.

Police may enter open fields to observe property, and a fence designed to keep animals in or erected for apparently aesthetic reasons will not change an open place into a closed one. Areas in multiple-unit dwellings, such as common garages, hallways, and jointly used trash containers may be lawfully observed without a warrant.

A person living on the ground floor in a populous area who leaves his shades up and drapes open does not have a reasonable expectation of privacy. Officers may not peer into windows if doing so involves trespassing. It is also illegal for them to look from a rooftop, use a fire department snorkel truck, or utilize a telescope from a distant building. An officer should not completely rely on these generalized guidelines; he should, rather, seek the advice of a prosecutor in all important investigations.

Nothing prevents an officer from assuming the identity of an addict or other criminal, a salesman or customer, or ordinary citizen and from visiting a criminal suspect. A person who carelessly places his trust in another does so at his own peril. Deceptive pretenses, including the furnishing of the motive, opportunity, and means to commit a crime, are all lawful police activities.

A famous case, decided by the Supreme Court, involved former Teamster's Union official James Hoffa (*Hoffa* v. *U.S.*, 385 U.S. 293 [1966]). A government informant named Partin was invited into Hoffa's hotel suite and heard conversations that led to the latter's conviction for jury tampering. On appeal, Hoffa claimed that Partin's misrepresentations vitiated the invitation and consent. Mr. Justice Stewart, writing the court's opinion, stated: "Neither this court nor any member of it has ever expressed the view that the Fourth Amendment protects a wrongdoer's misplaced belief that a person to whom he voluntarily confides his wrongdoing will not reveal it."

The court went on to say that the Fifth and Sixth Amendments also were not violated by this practice. "The police are not required to guess at their peril the precise moment at which they have probable cause to arrest a suspect, risking a violation of the Fourth Amendment if they act too soon, and violation of the Sixth Amendment if they wait too long." In the same term of court, Chief Justice Warren, writing for the majority, upheld the practice of using an undercover agent who concealed his identity and misrepresented his true purpose.

Most surveillances do not involve police participation in an offense or overt observations. They usually consist of a list of names, addresses, and license plate numbers, information that is, on the surface, neutral. Once such observations have been completed, corroborative detail must be added by checking available records. Occupancy of a premise can be established through subscription records to telephone, newspaper, water, trash, electric, or gas services, tax rolls, licenses, and building permits. Vehicle registrations are available from the department of motor vehicles, secretary of state, or department of public safety. The identification of persons as "known" gamblers, narcotics users or peddlers, burglars or fences can be made through checks of criminal history with the FBI and state law enforcement agencies. Arrest records of suspects or their associates can assist in the development of probable cause, even though such information is hearsay and is inadmissible in a subsequent trial. Expert opinion of police officers can be used to interpret otherwise innocent facts.

In 1968 in Chicago police detectives had information that a named parking garage was used as a place for high-stakes crap games, policy ticket sales (numbers racket), and narcotics transactions. Surveillances showed that numerous persons entered and left the premises. A substantial number of these individuals, however, walked in and walked out or drove in and drove out. This activity is inconsistent with parking operations where customers walk in and drive out or vice versa. Many of the license plates were traced to persons with long records for gambling offenses. Some of the vehicles were traced to women. Records of marriage licenses, tax rolls, or subscriber services showed that these women were the wives of men who had similar criminal records. This case vividly demonstrated the importance of surveillances that corroborated informant disclosures of unknown reliability. The information acquired through surveillances was, by itself, insufficient. Extensive checks of records and experienced police

interpretations were necessary to demonstrate the existence of probable cause.

Post-Watergate morality has had its effects on surveillance practices. There is a growing tendency for courts to expand concepts
concerning privacy. As noted earlier, if a person has a reasonable
expectation of privacy, the surveillance is illegal under the *Katz*
decision (*Katz* v. *U.S.*, 389 U.S. 347 [1967]). Efforts to corroborate
or add to visual surveillance methods have also been changed. A
banker's association has recently challenged unsuccessfully the right
of federal agents to inspect customers' bank records without legal
process. Certain telephone companies and other utilities systematically
refuse to divulge information to local police departments. The Buckley
Amendment to the General Education Provisions Act, 45 U.S. Code,
Sec. 438, passed in 1974, forbids access to students' records by law
enforcement personnel unless they possess a court order.

(5.6) Administrative Search Warrants

A search warrant may be necessary for the enforcement of
public safety laws. In its 1966 term, the U.S. Supreme Court forbade
warrantless, nonconsensual searches of commercial places to enforce
building and fire codes. Probable cause in the usual sense is, however,
unnecessary. If the officers are acting pursuant to a reasonable legislative or administrative standard, if the search is necessary for the
protection of the public, and if the occupant has refused admission,
a warrant can be issued. A form affidavit could be used for this
purpose, leaving only the address to be filled in. This procedure
seems to cheapen the prestige of warrants. Six members of the
Supreme Court made clear, however, that the Fourth Amendment
protects people and places from unreasonable searches, regardless of
the purpose for which they are made.

Not all administrative searches are unreasonable without a warrant. Establishments that serve alcoholic beverages and other licensed
premises may, for example, be inspected as a condition of the special
privilege license.

(5.7) Execution and Use of Force

Arrest and search warrants are limited to a class of officers
named in the statutes. There is no inherent right of a municipal or

state police officer to serve all classes of criminal process, and, in some jurisdictions, only the sheriff and his deputies can serve warrants. A warrantless arrest can be made, using an arrest warrant as the basis for believing probable cause exists for the apprehension. Evidence seized incident to that arrest would be admissible in another case. Serving a search warrant, without legal authority to do so, would nullify the warrant.

Statutes or rules of court set the durational limits on serving search warrants, usually 72 to 240 hours. There is no similar restriction on arrest warrants. Some jurisdictions forbid serving any warrant at night unless it is so specified by the court on the warrant.

A warrant does not have to be promptly served, if there are good reasons for delay. A search warrant, for example, is normally served when an individual, usually the suspect, is on the premises. This makes it easier for the prosecution to prove a possessory offense, if contraband or fruits of a crime are located. On the other hand, officers may want to delay serving a search warrant until the suspect leaves, if they believe this would lessen the possibility of resistance. It is not improper to delay serving an arrest or search warrant so that more suspects will be present or so that other evidence will be found. Gambling detectives, for example, could legitimately delay the timing of a raid on an accounting station until all runners had turned in their collections.

A police officer is required to identify himself, announce his purpose, and request entry into the premises, unless those acts would be futile or dangerous. If his knock is unheeded or if entrance is refused, he may forcibly enter the premises. If the officer has a search warrant, it makes no difference whether or not the items sought are dangerous, whether or not they are feloniously possessed, or whether or not the offense under investigation is a misdemeanor or a felony. In the case of an arrest warrant, the crime can be of any magnitude, and it is not necessary to obtain a search warrant to enter the residence of the accused.

Occasionally a defendant, named in an arrest warrant, is believed to be staying at or hiding in the home of a third party. If officers have reasonable grounds to believe this to be the case, they may enter that home without procuring a search warrant.

Under the laws of some states, an elaborate procedure has been established for the procurement of "no-knock" warrants. Once the requirements are complied with, a warrant so endorsed can be served by an unannounced forcible entry into the premises.

(5.8) Scope of Search

The scope of a search incident to an arrest is the same in warrant situations as in warrantless arrests. (See Chapter 4 for discussion of the *Chimel* rule.) Search warrants specify the rooms, floors, and areas that may be searched. Officers must restrict themselves to the items sought, even though they suspect other evidence might be found. This does not mean that they must close their eyes to the obvious. If they are lawfully in a place looking for one class of goods or contraband and they see in plain view another class of seizable goods or contraband, the search is lawful. It is advisable in cases where "mere evidence" of an offense is fortuitously seen to secure the premises and to obtain a second search warrant. Contraband, weapons, and fruits of a crime can be immediately seized. This type of seizure is not by authority of the warrant, however; it is due to necessity.

A wise officer will always list small items to be sought with a search warrant. For example, currency is the fruit of many crimes; in possessory offenses, evidence of occupancy, such as rent receipts and mail addressed to the occupant, can be sought. Inclusion of these items will authorize officers to search desks, files, and storage boxes in minute detail. Once, however, officers have located the principal items sought and have established occupancy, the search must cease.

An officer would not ordinarily be authorized to remove paneling, rip up carpeting, or tear open chair cushions, but when he is dealing with experienced drug dealers, extreme measures may be called for. In one case, federal agents removed outer shingles, parts of the roof, and dug trenches in the yard of a house worth $65,000. They found nothing and were later sued; the Justice Department paid $160,000 to the owner for physical and mental damages.

It is important that all items seized be properly inventoried on the search warrant, which is returned to the clerk of the court that issued it. A copy of the warrant, together with a receipt for all items taken, must be given to the owner or party in possession of the premises.

(5.9) Electronic Surveillance Warrants

Title III of the Omnibus Crime and Safe Streets Act of 1968 regulates the issuance of warrants authorizing wiretapping and bugging. Most serious offenses are mentioned in the statute, including kidnapping, murder, sabotage, extortion, bribery of public officials, and certain other federal offenses. State attorneys general and district attorneys may personally apply for intercept orders, or authority to wiretap or to bug, in state court.

Not all eavesdropping situations require an intercept order. A person can unilaterally permit police officers to overhear conversations on his telephone, either on an extension or by an alligator clip receiver. A citizen or an officer can wear a concealed radio transmitter or tape recorder without an intercept order. Normal conversations can be taped in this fashion.

Courts have split as to whether a pen register (a device that records the numbers called on a telephone) intercepts a conversation.

Whenever police officers or federal agents have bugged or tapped a defendant in a criminal case without legal sanction, neither the conversations nor derivative evidence obtained by listening to the conversations can be admitted into evidence. A defendant is entitled to discover the tapes or transcripts and to have a hearing to determine whether any evidence presented against him was tainted by the illegal surveillances. *Kolod* v. *U.S.*, 390 U.S. 136 [1968], mandates an adversary hearing, and a dismissal will be granted if the prosecution fails to produce the transcripts.

Motions to suppress evidence obtained by electronic surveillance are handled in the same manner as motions to suppress physical evidence. An overheard party has standing to challenge the evidence if he can show a violation of *his* rights under the Fourth Amendment. A defendant could not usually challenge with any success the illegal interception of another's home or telephone.

(5.10) Summary

Although warrantless arrests and searches are judged by the same standards as those conducted pursuant to warrants, the courts have always expressed a preference for the latter. The procedure requires a police officer to seek out a neutral and detached judicial officer, usually a lawyer, and establish a prima facie case against a suspect.

Warrants are issued upon a statement made under oath, usually a written affidavit. Most courts have adopted the four corners rule, which requires that all elements that comprise the underlying probable cause be within the four corners of the written affidavit. Once a warrant is issued, it is too late for an officer to add additional facts he mistakenly overlooked. The warrant process forces police officers to arrange their facts and arguments carefully.

The Fourth Amendment requires "particular descriptions" of the person to be seized or searched, the place to be searched, and the things that are sought. The supporting investigations must be complete, and skill in verbal expression is demanded.

Informants and surveillances are often needed to come to the conclusion that probable cause exists. Often the two are intertwined, since neither an informant's disclosures nor a raw surveillance may alone be sufficient.

Care must be used in the execution of warrants, and statutory procedures cannot be avoided. Even a search warrant is a limited authority to intrude upon a suspect's rights. The scope of a search warrant is restricted to the items named and the nature of the offense under investigation.

6

Interrogations, Confessions, and Nontestimonial Evidence

A. INTERROGATIONS AND CONFESSIONS

(6.1) The Exclusionary Rule in General

In 1964 the U.S. Supreme Court revolutionized the law of confessions and interrogations, with the famous case of *Escobedo* v. *Illinois*, 378 U.S. 478 (1964). Danny Escobedo was a murder suspect who was being held in custody by the Chicago police. He had an attorney, but the officers concerned with the case refused the attorney access to his client. Escobedo made damaging admissions, which were later used at his trial. He was thus convicted of the crime. In reversing his conviction, the Warren Court ruled that once an investigation had "focused" on a particular suspect, he was entitled to specific warnings before he could be interrogated.

Two years later, in *Miranda* v. *Arizona*, 384 U.S. 436 (1966), the court ordered an addition to the warning. The "focus" test was all but abolished. Instead, the court adopted the concept of "custodial interrogation." This means that a defendant's pretrial statements are not admissible in evidence to prove his guilt if those statements were obtained by state officers during an interrogation and while the defendant was in custody, *unless* he was warned of his rights under the Fifth Amendment and properly waived them.

The penalty for failure to comply with the requirements of the *Escobedo* and *Miranda* decisions is the exclusion of the statements from the trial, which could prove the guilt of the accused. In the past, trustworthy statements were always admissible, regardless of the ignorance of the accused, his ability to pay for a lawyer, or the hopelessness of his custody.

(6.2) Voluntariness of Statements

As was indicated above, prior to the *Escobedo* case, trustworthy statements voluntarily given were always admissible. Needless to say, if a confession was beaten out of a suspect, or if he was coerced into confessing under the duress of a threatened beating, lynching, or other violence, the confession was tainted. Some of the circumstances that would always invalidate a confession include the following:

1. brutality or threatened brutality;
2. promises to drop the charges or to forgo prosecution of other suspected crimes;
3. threats to arrest members of the suspect's family or to cut off welfare assistance to them;
4. threats to contact the suspect's employer and have him fired should he not cooperate;
5. holding the suspect on false charges;
6. refusing the suspect the right to make bail;
7. using false or illegally seized evidence to induce a confession.

Sometimes there is a fine line between "clever tactics" and coercion. Police officers are not required to be "friendly" with a suspect. They may ask questions in an indignant or hostile manner. They may express belief that the suspect is lying. They can interrogate a suspect using teams of officers, some friendly, some antagonistic. They can play on the suspect's conscience. Officers may act confident that the suspect is guilty and suggest reasons why they believe him to be lying. They may sometimes even express sympathy for the suspect and contempt for the victim. When two suspects are in custody, one can be played against the other.

Statements made by persons who have been falsely arrested are subject to exclusion by the courts. The fact that a false arrest is followed by valid *Miranda* warnings and that the interview was free from physical duress is not enough to remove the taint of illegality. In *Brown* v. *Illinois*, 95 S. Ct. 2254 (1975), the Supreme Court ruled that the mere recitation of *Miranda* warnings does not sufficiently interrupt the process to render a confession legal. As in a prior Supreme Court case, the officers had made an arrest without probable cause and had forcibly entered the defendants' homes. Such actions, said the justices, affect the voluntariness of confessions, which cannot, therefore, be the products of a "free will."

Not every statement taken following a false arrest should be excluded, however. As the court said:

> It is entirely possible, of course, . . . that persons arrested illegally . . . may decide to confess, as an act of free will unaffected by the initial illegality. But the *Miranda* warnings, *alone* and *per se* cannot always make the act sufficiently a product of free will to break, for Fourth Amendment purposes, the causal connection between the illegality and the confession . . . . While we therefore reject the *per se* rule which the Illinois courts appear to have accepted, we also decline to adopt any alternative *per se* or "but for" rule . . . . The question whether a confession is the product of a free will . . . must be answered on the facts of each case. No single fact is determinative . . . .
>
> The *Miranda* warnings are an important factor . . . but they are not the only factor to be considered. The temporal proximity of the arrest and the confession, the presence of intervening factors . . . and, particularly, the purpose and flagrancy of the official misconduct are all relevant.

The court went on to say that the burden of proving that an illegal arrest did not taint a subsequent confession falls on the prosecution.

(6.3) The *Miranda* Warnings

In its 1966 decision the Supreme Court spoke of four distinct warnings, but did not specify the exact wording. As a result, several acceptable versions are in use today. A suggested warning that is used by many police departments appears below.

ADVICE OF RIGHTS
It is my duty to inform you that you are under investigation by the
_____Police Department.
1. You have the right to remain silent.
2. Anything you say can and will be used against you in court.
3. You have the right to consult a lawyer before answering any questions, and have him present during any interrogation.

4. If you cannot afford to employ a lawyer, one will be provided for you at no cost to yourself.

Once these admonitions are given, before proceeding further, the officer should state the following:

A. Do you understand your rights, as I have explained them?

B. Are you willing to answer questions at this time, without consulting a lawyer, or having a lawyer present?

C. If at any time during the questioning you want to stop answering questions, you may do so and remain silent.

Some law enforcement agencies state the contents of "C" as a fifth warning. Though it is not legally necessary to warn a suspect that he may discontinue the questioning process, once he has expressed this desire all interrogation must cease. It is obvious that the suspect must answer "yes" to "A" and "B" before the interrogation process can begin.

If all four warnings are properly given, a valid waiver by the suspect can be presumed from facts and circumstances other than specific responses to "A" and "B." Officers are *not required* to ask these questions, but should do so if they begin a formal interrogation. A waiver may legally result, and often does, from the mere fact that the defendant freely answers questions put to him. The burden of showing a valid waiver is, however, more difficult for the prosecution in such cases.

Officers should always *read* the warnings from a printed card that they carry at all times. A jury is more likely to believe that the warnings were complete if they were read, as opposed to their being recited from memory. The *Miranda* card is also admissible into evidence at the trial. The card should be read to the suspect and not simply handed to him to read for himself.

Some courts have split hairs over the second warning. A few departments warn suspects that statements "may" be used against them. Others say they "can" be used. A few state they "will" be used. The theory is that "may" implies that leniency is possible, or even likely, if the suspect confesses.

Miranda applies to both exculpatory and inculpatory statements. Thus, should a suspect admit to being present when a criminal act was committed but not having taken part in the act, officers cannot later testify that the suspect acknowledged his presence at the scene of the crime, if the warnings were absent or defective.

If the warnings are defective, the procedure should be repeated, and anything said after the correct warnings are given will be admissible. When officers begin the interrogation process they should make sure that proper warnings were given recently and that the waivers were obtained. If there is any doubt, the admonitions should be repeated. The officers who first gave the warnings will have to appear in court if the waiver is challenged. It is preferable, therefore, for them to conduct the questioning since it minimizes the number of witnesses needed to prove a confession.

(6.4) What Is Custody?

Not every admission or confession must be preceded by warning of rights. As was mentioned above, the *Escobedo* case used the "focus test," that is, whether the investigation focused on the suspect. *Miranda* reinterpreted a suspect's rights under the Fifth Amendment and applied the rule to "custodial interrogations." The court defined this phrase as meaning those circumstances when an accused "is deprived of his freedom in a significant way."

Usually the arresting officers read a suspect the warnings at the time of his actual arrest. It should be noted that an accused does not have a constitutionally protected right to receive these warnings. Rather, his induced statements will be inadmissible in the absence of the warnings. Most departments require that arrested felons be promptly advised of their rights, at the time of the arrest. This does not mean, however, that a person who forcibly resists arrest should be warned during the time of his resistance.

Arrests are often made because a police officer observes the offense taking place in his presence. In many such cases, statements received from the suspect are of little value, and it is unnecessary to question him at the time of the arrest. For example, if a demonstrator smashes a window in front of an officer, the individual should be arrested and booked without interrogation. After the arrest and booking, he should be read the warnings before he is questioned. Nothing in the Fifth Amendment requires an officer to demean himself in the presence of a group of demonstrators.

Should the officers who are transporting the suspect engage in conversation with him, they ought to warn him of his rights unless they are sure this has already been done and by whom. Prisoners frequently become talkative at this stage of the process. They may, for example, express regret that they struck an officer. If they later plead self-defense, accusing the officers of aggressive acts, such statements are invaluable.

Once a suspect has been placed in a cellblock or is taken to the detective bureau for questioning, he should again be warned of his rights, and a clearly expressed waiver should be taken before questioning begins. It makes no difference that the questioning is not accusatory in nature. It is irrelevant that the suspect is in jail for one offense, but is being questioned for another crime. If, however, the officers who are conducting the questioning are from an agency other than the one that first arrested him and are investigating an unrelated case, subsequent statements may be admissible even though the inmate has previously invoked his right to remain silent (*Jennings v. U.S.*, 391 F. 2d 512 [5th Cir. 1968]).

Miranda causes the most problems when the suspect has not been placed under formal arrest. A police station may create an inherently "coercive atmosphere." Warnings should always precede questioning at the station house, even if the person is not a strong suspect, or if he or she voluntarily came to the station without invitation. This does not mean, of course, that everyone who visits a police station should receive *Miranda* warnings. Persons who are reporting the theft or loss of property, who are completing accident reports, or who are seeking assistance obviously should not. But if the visitor is a potential suspect in an unsolved crime and officers plan to question him about that crime, the warnings should be given. Sometimes the existence of a crime will be unknown when an individual goes to a station house. For example, Smith goes to a police station to report a stolen car. During the time his report is being taken, a desk officer learns that the car, driven by a man matching Smith's description, was involved in a holdup. Smith should be given the *Miranda* warnings at this time, and questioning should cease until a valid waiver is obtained. Anything said up to this point would, however, be admissible later.

Miranda warnings should always be given when a suspect is asked to go to a station house to be fingerprinted, to take a polygraph examination, to appear in a lineup, or to give a physical specimen (such as hair or blood).

Persons are frequently asked to get inside a police car for the purpose of giving preliminary information about an incident. Whether the interrogation is custodial or not does not always depend on whether the person was arrested. A coercive atmosphere can also exist in a squad car. If, however, cold weather, rain, darkness, or convenience dictate the location of the questioning, the interrogation is less likely to be considered "custodial."

Most sidewalk confrontations are not covered by *Miranda* until the suspect has been formally arrested. If an officer intends to arrest a suspect regardless of what he says, or if he is questioning him at gunpoint or while the suspect is spread-eagled against a wall or made to lie facedown, coercive factors will, of course, be present and will probably invalidate statements made without the warnings.

When a crime occurs, the officers on the scene often direct everyone present to remain on the premises or at the location and not leave without permission. The Supreme Court made clear in the *Miranda* decision that they did not intend to "hamper" the "traditional function of police officers in investigating crime." Thus, general "on-the-scene questioning" as to facts surrounding a crime is not covered by the *Miranda* ruling. This is true even though the exits are sealed temporarily. Circumstances will affect this rule. A possible suicide at a crowded party will be handled differently from the case where the victim is shot six times in the back and only one person is present at the scene.

Though it was originally thought that residential questioning was never covered by the *Miranda* decision, a case in 1969 (*Orozco* v. *Texas*, 394 U.S. 324 [1969]) made clear that this was not always true. Four officers entered the suspect's bedroom at 4:00 a.m. and interrogated him there. They asked him about a shooting that had taken place earlier and sought to inspect his gun. The lateness of the hour, an uninvited intrusion, and the number of officers present, each standing alone, will not require the admonition of the *Miranda* rights. In combination, however, these factors can create a coercive atmosphere that would require the warnings.

In many cases, the fact that the arrest occurred sometime later than the questioning will avoid the necessity of *Miranda* warnings. Though no rigid rule exists, the courts look more favorably on admitting statements if the arrest occurs on a subsequent day rather than shortly after the crime is committed. If, however, interrogating officers already have probable cause to make the arrest and delay the actual apprehension for reasons of convenience, the statements will be inadmissible.

Places of employment are sometimes the sites of police questioning. An employee under the scrutiny of superiors, subordinates, and fellow workers is in a compelling—if not a coercive—atmosphere. The situation is less coercive if the crime being investigated took place on the premises, and everyone understands why police officers are present. This is particularly true if the investigation results from the officers' appearance on the scene immediately after the commission of the crime.

Routine business inspections do not come under the protection of the *Miranda* decision. These include such occurrences as visits to pawnshops by the theft and burglary details, ID checks in establishments licensed to dispense intoxicating beverages, and the like.

Persons who are present where a search is being conducted pursuant to a search warrant should be advised of their *Miranda* rights, if they are prevented from leaving, if they are asked to participate in the search, or if they are questioned by officers who are making the search. Once contraband or other evidence is found, there is a more compelling reason to warn persons at the scene of the search.

(6.5) What Is Interrogation?

Not every question asked by a police officer constitutes interrogation. There should be some connection between the question and the offense or suspected offense. General questions asked before an officer discovers that a crime has been committed are less likely to be considered interrogation than similar questions asked after a crime has been discovered. This is often the case when suspicious persons are encountered on the streets and in alleys.

Interrogation has been defined as "any questioning likely or expected to yield incriminating statements." General on-the-scene questioning, as mentioned above, is not likely to be held "interrogation." Thus, officers responding to a silent burglar alarm notice a man sitting in a van near the premises. The hour is late, and the street is dark. They ask the man to explain his presence. Such generalized questioning is only preliminary and does not constitute "interrogation." The man's initial answer would be admissible, even if the officers blocked his van and detained him temporarily.

At some point, general questioning may become accusatorial questioning. This comes about in one of two ways. First, the questions become less general and focus on incriminating conduct. Second, the conversation systematically eliminates noncriminal explanations, leaving only a conclusion of criminal conduct. For example, officers respond to a call concerning a shooting. They find a young man, seriously wounded and comatose, and an older man. General questioning reveals the wound was not self-inflicted, that no other persons were present, that the shooting was not accidental, and that self-defense was not involved. As the various noncriminal alternatives are eliminated, suspicion deepens that the older man shot the younger man, without apparent justification. At this stage all questioning should cease until the *Miranda* warnings are given. The conversation is no longer general and therefore constitutes interrogation.

Statements that are volunteered are admissible, even though the person making the statement is in custody. This is because volunteered statements are not the product of interrogation. A "volunteered" statement is different from a "voluntary" statement. The first means the utterance came forth without elicitation. The second refers to a statement that is free of duress and coercion, but is usually elicited by questioning. Volunteered statements are frequently spontaneous and may take officers by surprise. The following are examples of volunteered statements.

1. A man walks into a police station and says, "I just murdered my wife."

2. Police officers knock on a suspect's door, seeking permission to search the premises for narcotics. The suspect says, "That won't be necessary. The dope is under the front seat of my car."

3. A man being driven to the morgue to identify a woman thought to be his wife suddenly says to the officer accompanying him, "Stop. I can't bear to see her. I killed her, and I'm sorry."

"Threshold confessions" are also admissible since they are not the product of an interrogation. They are so called because they are often made as officers cross the threshold of the premises and ask, "What happened?" Once an incriminating statement is volunteered or made in response to a threshold question, further questioning must cease, and the *Miranda* warnings must be given. Anything said up to this point is admissible, without the admonitions. Most courts have held that an officer does not have to interrupt a person who is in the process of volunteering a story or responding to a threshold question. But the longer the story continues, and the more pauses contained in it, the more likely it is that an officer must interject with the *Miranda* warnings.

One of the exceptions to *Miranda* is the situation in which an officer is working undercover at the time a crime is being perpetrated. The person talking or answering questions will not be under arrest, but he will be arrested immediately after the conversation is completed. The officer is not required to interrupt the progress of the crime to warn the person of his *Miranda* rights. There must, however, actually be an offense in progress, or about to take place, for this exception to apply. Thus, it is not permissible to pose as a criminal to interrogate an inmate housed in a jail or prison.

Miranda warnings need not be given to persons responding to questions in an accident report or a similar incident. This is true even if the citizen is suspected of having committed a felony. The purpose of the interview must, of course, be legitimate, such as the completion of a report form. If, during the interview, the citizen makes damaging admissions that are unconnected with the report, the *Miranda* warnings must be given at that point.

(6.6) What Is a State Officer?

The *Miranda* decision only applies to "state action." This means that interrogation by nongovernmental personnel falls outside its mandates. With the exception of Maryland, private security officers in all states are exempt from the *Miranda* decision, even if they possess a commission as a special officer or deputy sheriff. Shopkeepers, under many state shoplifting laws, are granted powers of arrest or detention, but these laws do not transform private action into state action. Citizens' arrests are wholly outside the protection of *Miranda*.

Statements made by an arrested felon, in response to questions asked by civilians, are similarly admissible. Some courts have ruled suspects' statements as inadmissible when an officer requested the civilian to ask certain questions or even when the officer was present at the time the questions were asked. To state the matter simply, the courts will not tolerate subterfuge.

Also outside the scope of *Miranda* are statements made to non-police officials, such as physicians and nurses in city hospitals, school administrators, firemen, and similar personnel. It would be a travesty of justice to exclude such admissions because nonpolice officials and employees would not know the *Miranda* warnings or when to give them. Exclusion of these statements would not punish police misconduct, but would only allow inculpatory remarks to be made outside the "coercive" atmosphere of police interrogation.

(6.7) Applicable Offenses

A survey by the International Association of Chiefs of Police in 1972 indicated wide variance among law enforcement agencies in the interpretation of *Miranda*. Though the decision applies to all felonies, many states have ruled that misdemeanors are excluded from its protections. There is merit to this interpretation if the offense is a petty one, punishable by fine only, or a jail term of short duration (less than six months). Nearly everyone agrees that traffic offenses are outside the scope of *Miranda*, although some courts have extended its protections to serious traffic offenses, such as driving while one is intoxicated.

Officers in states that have not resolved this issue should give the *Miranda* warnings to all persons with an offense punishable by incarceration. This policy will eliminate unnecessary appeals and avoid problems with civil liberties groups.

(6.8) Capacity of Suspects

Statements taken from the insane, persons who are drunk, under the influence of drugs, or who do not speak elementary English may not be admissible. A suspect must make a knowing and intelligent waiver. At what age and level of intelligence a person becomes legally capable of understanding his rights and knowingly waiving them is not subject to definition. The mere fact that a suspect is a juvenile will not invalidate the waiver. In one case a waiver by a thirteen-year-old boy was upheld, as was, in another case, a confession by a fifteen-year-old who was "mildly retarded." In other cases, courts have failed to find a knowing and intelligent waiver when the suspect had an IQ of sixty, an IQ of seventy-two at age fifteen, and when age and retardation or other factors impaired the suspect's judgment.

The testimony of a psychiatrist that the suspect understood the warnings will go a long way in validating the confession.

Insanity may be a complete or partial defense in a crime, but it does not automatically invalidate a confession. One case upheld a waiver by a paranoid schizophrenic. Another admitted statements by a suspect who had the mental state of a six-year-old.

Most courts have refused to exclude statements made under the influence of alcohol or mild tranquilizers. Addiction to heroin is more likely to invalidate a confession, depending on the amount used, the degree of withdrawal, and other factors.

Whether a suspect was suffering from impaired capacity at the time he made incriminating statements is based on the "totality of the circumstances test." There is no "per se" rule unless it it enacted in the penal or evidentiary code. For example, a law in Colorado forbids the police to question juveniles in the absence of their parents.

Police officers who have custody of a suspect who is willing to talk but whose capacity is dubious, should use the following procedure. First, the statement should be taken, accompanied by other questions that tend to indicate the suspect's mental capacity. If the statement is later excluded from evidence, no harm has been done since the alternative is not to interrogate at all. If the impairment is temporary, officers should attempt to take a second statement at a later time. If this can be done, the second statement should not be induced by reference to the prior statement. This is because the first statement might be excluded. The court might conclude that the second statement was obtained by referring to the first statement, and thus the second statement could be excluded.

Even if the statement is of dubious validity, it might encourage a suspect to plead guilty in the hope of being given a lesser punishment, which is certainly better than a straight acquittal.

(6.9) Impeachment and Other Derivative Uses of Inadmissible Confessions

The Supreme Court decided in *Wong Sun* v. *U.S.*, 371 U.S. 471 (1963), that police could not use the results of inadmissible statements to garner additional evidence. In that case federal agents forced their way into the residence of a man named Toy, arrested him without probable cause, and obtained a statement that implicated

Wong Sun and Johnny Yee. The statements led to the arrest of Yee and Wong Sun. Wong Sun later confessed his guilt to the agents. The court concluded that the case against Yee was the result of illegal police conduct, the "fruit of the poisoned tree." Wong Sun was convicted because his subsequent confession was so "attenuated" from the original illegality that all "taint" was "dissipated."

Thus, evidence that is seized or statements that are subsequently obtained as a result of an inadmissible confession are themselves subject to exclusion, as the "poisoned fruit" of the initial illegality. In order for evidence to be admissible, the prosecution must show one of two things: that the police would have obtained the evidence anyway and without the use of the tainted statements, or that the connection between the original misconduct and the subsequent evidence was too remote to require its exclusion.

Another example of the use of evidence derived from statements made in violation of *Miranda* came to light in *Michigan* v. *Tucker*, 94 S. Ct. 2357 (1974). In its decision the Supreme Court upheld the following evidentiary scenario: Tucker, the accused, was given defective *Miranda* warnings. His alibi involved Henderson. When Henderson was questioned, he did not support Tucker's alibi; rather, Henderson's testimony further incriminated Tucker. The court ruled that although Tucker's statements were inadmissible, the police could properly use this information to gain additional evidence against the accused.

In its majority opinion, the Supreme Court said that the law does not require that policemen "make no errors whatsoever. The pressures of law enforcement and the vagaries of human nature would make such an expectation unrealistic." Most lawyers interpret the result in *Tucker* as a loosening of the harsh results of the exclusionary rule rather than as a relaxing of the Poisoned Tree doctrine.

Statements taken in violation of *Miranda* may be introduced at the criminal trial for the purpose of impeaching the credibility of the defendant as a witness if he takes the stand. Suppose, for example, a suspect admits selling heroin, but later denies it at the time of his trial. If the statement is tainted because of a *Miranda* violation, it nevertheless may be read to the jury. The purpose of the prior statement is to impair the believability of the accused, not to prove his guilt. It is admitted to contravene his testimony because, said the Supreme Court (*Harris* v. *New York*, 401 U.S. 222 [1971]), "The shield provided by *Miranda* cannot be perverted into a license to use perjury by way of a defense, free from the risk of confrontation with prior inconsistent utterances."

(6.10) Effect of Immunity or Conviction

The basis for all restrictions on confessions and admissions is the Fifth Amendment, which prevents a person in a criminal case from being a witness against himself. Once an individual is given immunity from prosecution, he can be compelled, under penalty of contempt, to answer questions put to him. The immunity usually takes effect at the time the person is called before a grand jury. The process is later repeated in the criminal trial.

The Supreme Court has ruled that a person is not entitled to "transactional" immunity; he is limited to "use" immunity. This means that the individual still may be prosecuted for the offense, if the police gain their evidence from sources independent of the self-incriminating statements. This has happened occasionally. Thus, under use immunity, the statement itself and the fruits of the statement cannot be used against the accused in a criminal trial. An example follows.

Bruno is granted use immunity before a grand jury and admits that he participated in a counterfeiting scheme. He reveals the location of the printing press (in New Jersey) and the plates (in New York). An accomplice later surrenders himself and brings in the plates from New York. The surrender is not connected with Bruno's statement. Federal agents could not introduce Bruno's statement against him in a criminal trial, but they could introduce it in prosecuting the accomplice. And the accomplice can testify against Bruno. The printing press, if seized on the basis of information in Bruno's statement, cannot be used in Bruno's trial, but could be used in the prosecution of the accomplice. The plates could be used in Bruno's trial since they were turned over to the agents independent of the immunized statement. Had the accomplice been located by using information in Bruno's statement, nothing could be used against Bruno. Had the agents been able to find the accomplice and the plates anyway, Bruno's use immunity would not have prevented the admission into evidence of the plates and the testimony of the accomplice.

Although prosecutors rarely use this technique, a convicted

defendant can be called to the witness stand and be required to give testimony that incriminates himself and others. This tactic has been employed occasionally when one party to the offense has received a light sentence and the others are yet to be prosecuted. The reason it is seldom used is because, in most cases involving multiple defendants, one of them offers to plead guilty and testify against the others in the hope of receiving a reduced sentence.

B. EYEWITNESS IDENTIFICATION

(6.11) Lineups and the Sixth Amendment

In 1967 the Supreme Court under Chief Justice Warren ruled in three cases (*Wade, Gilbert,* and *Stovall,* at 388 U.S. 218, 263, 293 [1967]) that an indicted defendant is entitled to the presence of counsel at a lineup. The rationale behind this rule was that the lineup process is subject to abuse; the abuse might be irremediable; and the presence of a lawyer would help ensure the basic fairness of the procedures utilized. In 1972 the Supreme Court under Chief Justice Burger clarified its original position in *Kirby* v. *Illinois,* 406 U.S. 682 (1972), saying that the right to counsel attaches "only at or after the time that adversary criminal proceedings have been initiated." This means after indictment, arrest by warrant, or arraignment.

In the intervening five years between these decisions, many state courts ruled that the right to counsel is operative at all lineups. While most state courts have reversed themselves in light of the 1972 decision, others have declined to do so. *Kirby* was a plurality decision (that is, two concurring opinions resulting in a holding); because of this, it has not been totally followed by those courts that fail to make a distinction between pre- and postindicted felons.

The rationale for the limitation in the *Kirby* decision is that the government has not committed itself to the prosecution of a suspect until he has been "formally charged." Thus, the right to counsel does not apply before this event since it is not a critical stage of the prosecutory procedures. The rule in *Kirby* will not serve to admit lineup evidence without benefit of counsel if the arraignment is negligently or purposefully delayed.

There is no reason why a defendant cannot waive his right to counsel. (The appendix contains a suggested warning and waiver, in

English and in Spanish.) Waivers are routinely given in police departments of large cities, often on the advice and with the consent of
the public defender. It must be assumed, however, that certain rudi-
mentary records are kept of the proceedings. They include the
following:

1. a frontal and profile color photograph of each participant
   and the entire group assembled;
2. the name, address, race, age, height, weight, and clothing
   worn by each participant;
3. the names of all witnesses and police officers present;
4. the time and place of the lineup;
5. information on whether the participants were required to
   wear specified clothing or masks, assume certain postures or
   walk, repeat directed words or phrases, and so forth;
6. a tape recording, should the lineup contain verbal identification procedures.

In addition, a very thorough written report should be made
immediately following the lineup. Questions asked of each witness
and their response should be transcribed or recorded. Officers must
use great care not to suggest the identification of any particular
participant. Each witness should be interviewed separately and told
not to discuss possible identifications with each other.

Rare is the lineup that includes five whites and one black suspect.
Serious problems have resulted, however, when the police attempt
to find five or six people with peculiar characteristics. It would be
difficult indeed to find six Oriental males in their thirties, who are
six feet tall, have brown hair, walk with a limp, speak with a lisp,
and have a French accent. Obviously, some matches cannot be done,
and professional reasonableness must be the ultimate test. If, for
example, the suspect is very fat, everyone should wear a coat. If the
suspect has a large mole on his nose or a tattoo on his cheek, special
effects, makeup, or bandages can be used. Several courts have held
that officers do not have to go to such lengths when truly unique
features are involved. Cases upholding the admissibility of lineup
identification, notwithstanding certain physical disparities, are: *State*
v. *Tidwell*, 500 S.W. 2d 329 [only one with chin whiskers]; *People* v.
Allen, 327 N.E. 2d 387 [only one with a natural hairstyle]; *People* v.
Broadnax, 325 N.E. 2d 23 [only one bald-headed, all participants
wearing hats]; *State* v. *Tomizoli*, 519 S.W. 2d 713 [only one had

"weather-beaten" appearance]; *Conner* v. *Deramus*, 374 F. Supp.
504 [ages of other participants were eighteen, nineteen, twenty-four,
and twenty-eight; the defendant was forty-seven] ; and *Payne* v. *State*,
210 S.E. 2d 775 [defendant was seven feet, two inches tall, and
stuttered].

To avoid problems of suggestive lineups, officers should arrange
to have five or six persons participate. If one individual has to wear
jail clothing, all should do so. It is never permissible for a suspect to
wear garments resembling the clothing worn by the perpetrator, unless all participants do so. Similarly, five detectives in conservative
suits will impair the effectiveness of a lineup if the suspect is wearing
casual attire. Finally, the suspect or suspects should be randomly
placed in the lineup.

In many communities, particularly smaller ones, the jail population will not have a sufficient number of inmates who resemble the
suspect. Citizen participants must be recruited for this purpose. Even
if they are paid, they should be advised that they are under no
compulsion to participate and are not suspects in the proceedings; a
written consent form can be established for this purpose.

To minimize the number of officers who will have to appear in
court, it is advisable that a single officer conduct the lineup, complete
the reports, interview the witnesses, take the photographs, and perform the clerical tasks. Polaroid photographs will minimize the problems concerned with the chain of evidence, and the officer in charge
should initial the print and staple it to the reports.

To avoid unexpected problems connected with the viewing procedures, it is recommended that witnesses be given a printed sheet
explaining the system. A typical information sheet would advise the
witnesses not to speak unless asked a question by an officer and not
to display recognition of anyone until those individuals in the lineup
are interviewed by an officer. It would, in addition, explain that
they are under no obligation to identify anyone and that, if they do,
certainty of identity is not required.

The attorney representing the accused should be permitted to
view the entire proceedings, including the interview of the witnesses.
This will help ensure that the lineup and the subsequent interview
process are free of suggestive influences. Attorneys for suspects ought
to be told that they should communicate any suggestions or objections
to the officer in charge of the lineup, but that they will not be

permitted to obstruct the procedures. They should not be allowed to interview the witnesses before, during, or after the procedures. If they want to take the deposition of a witness, they should follow the state's rules of criminal procedure designed for that purpose.

An attorney will occasionally be late. The lineup should be delayed for a reasonable time, but for no longer than an hour. If the attorney calls the station and gives a valid excuse, the lineup should be postponed. If, however, no valid excuse is provided, the public defender's office should be contacted, and arrangements should be made for a substitute defense lawyer to appear. A court order can be secured for the purpose of appointing an alternate counsel for a lineup.

(6.12) Right to Compel Attendance

A suspect does not have a constitutional right to refuse to appear in a lineup, providing there is sufficient cause to believe he is a suspect. This does not mean that police officers can conduct a dragnet for dozens of persons who fit a description and forcibly detain them for the purpose of putting them in a lineup. Not only would innocent persons have a right to bring a civil suit for damages, but the perpetrator, if identified, would be entitled to have his identification suppressed because of an illegal "dragnet-type" arrest. This does not mean that the police must have the same quantity or quality of proof required to justify an arrest in order to compel attendance of suspects at a lineup. A lesser standard of proof is sufficient and will support the legality of the proceedings.

It is not uncommon to reduce the number of suspects in a case to not less than three or five individuals. In these cases, officers should apply to a court of competent jurisdiction for an order compelling the attendance of these persons if they do not appear voluntarily. An affidavit, in support of the order, must be filed. The affidavit is similar to that required for the issuance of an arrest warrant, though the proof may be substantially diminished. For example, to obtain an arrest warrant, the affidavit must indicate that there is probable cause to believe that X, a named suspect, committed the offense. In a lineup order it is only necessary to allege that there is probable cause to believe that X, Y, or Z committed the offense, coupled with facts supporting that conclusion.

A lineup order may be issued for several suspects, when only one of them could be guilty, or issued for a single suspect based on less proof than is required for an arrest warrant, because the intrusion on the rights of a participant in such a lineup is less than the intrusion on the rights of an arrested suspect. The lineup procedure takes about an hour; it can be arranged to take place at a convenient time. A suspect is not booked, individually photographed, jailed, or required to post bond. The stigma of guilt associated with an arrest is not present.

As an example of the above, a drugstore was robbed by a gunman who was dressed in the uniform used by deliverymen of the Baker Department Store. Three drivers for that company fit the description and were in the area of the drugstore at the time of the holdup. A court order should be obtained requiring each of the three drivers to appear in a lineup in order that employees of the drugstore might determine whether one of them was the robber.

There are at least two other ways to accomplish the same result. The first is to obtain photographs of each of the three drivers, mix them in with several other photographs of individuals who are similar in appearance and who are dressed in uniforms of the department store, and show these to the witnesses. This is a lesser intrusion on the rights of the innocent drivers and is similarly free of any suggestive techniques. On the other hand, photographs may not truly represent the identity of the accused. Body movements and mannerisms, height and weight, voice and expressions, and other factors cannot be portrayed in pictures. A second way to accomplish this purpose is to conceal a witness on the premises of the department store. As each driver reports to work and leaves, the witness can observe him. This will only be free from improper suggestions when more than one driver is observed.

Although a suspect cannot lawfully refuse to appear in a lineup, there is no practical way to force him physically to do so. What if he must be dragged onstage, screaming and cursing? This will clearly focus attention on him and away from the other participants. On the other hand, a resisting suspect misbehaves at his peril, and he should not be allowed to complain later that he was identified solely because of his performance. Thus, each participant is free to appear as nonchalant and obedient as he chooses. If he intentionally misbehaves, he waives any rights he might have to object to an identification tainted by his own behavior.

(6.13) Confrontations with Single Suspects

Although identifications of single suspects tend to be suggestive, there are three situations where they are completely lawful. The first is when the suspect is located near the scene of the crime at about the time the crime was committed. Most police departments define this time as sixty minutes and set the location as the distance that can reasonably be traveled in that period. The greater the distance from the scene and the greater the time elapsed since the crime, the stronger is the case for a full due process lineup. There is also less likelihood of a faulty identification when the suspect is presented shortly after the commission of the offense. That is, the process is more reliable. Sometimes several suspects may be stopped because they fit a general description. It would be unfair to hold a half dozen persons until a lineup could be put together.

If, on the other hand, a single suspect is stopped, and there is other evidence that he committed the crime, it is a better practice to book him and arrange for a formal lineup. Such other evidence would include a large amount of money or a gun found on his person or in his car, or a confession. A lineup of a single suspect should be avoided when the witness is injured or is extremely upset. It would be a bad practice, for example, to take a suspect back to a grocery store for identification by a woman whose husband was fatally shot by the robber. If this is the only choice without risking a false arrest, it must, of course, be done. When suspects are returned to the scene of the crime, they should not be hauled in at gunpoint or wearing handcuffs. Both of these practices are too suggestive of guilt. If there is more than one witness, each should be asked to step outside to make an identification. This avoids the risk of one witness shouting out his or her identification in the presence of others and thus influencing them.

The second situation justifying a confrontation with a single suspect occurs when a witness is in danger of dying. In these cases the suspect should be taken to the hospital or wherever the witness is for immediate identification.

The third situation is the accepted police practice of having a witness get into a patrol car while the officers ride around the neighborhood looking for the suspect.

It is sometimes thought that a single-suspect confrontation is permissible when the witness knows the identity of the suspect. Examples of this would include a former employee, a resident of the building in which both live, or a relative. It is permissible for the witness to point out such a suspect for the purpose of apprehending him. If the suspect is already in custody, however, the prosecutor should be consulted before allowing a confrontation with the single suspect.

(6.14) Use of Photographs

Police have resorted to the rogues' gallery since the invention of the photograph. There are many reasons why books of photographs are used instead of lineups. First, the police may not know the identity of the suspect, and it is thought that he may be a prior offender. Second, the suspect may have fled, or his whereabouts are unknown. Finally, the police may have the person under surveillance and not want him to know he is suspected of the crime.

Photographs only portray how a person looked at a particular time. Aging, facial hair, a different hairstyle, baldness, and a number of other factors tend to make the process less reliable than a lineup. Nevertheless, such viewings of photographs frequently take place in larger police departments. If no particular person is a suspect before the viewing takes place, it is proper to permit the witnesses, on an individual basis, to look through a book consisting of known burglars, robbers, rapists, or other categories of criminals.

If, however, a particular person or persons are under suspicion, the following procedure should be utilized.

1. All photographs of the suspects should be removed from the books or files in which they are kept.

2. The suspects' photographs should be mixed with pictures of persons with similar features. It is not absolutely necessary that these individuals have been arrested for the crime under investigation, but, if at all possible, they should be.

3. "Mug shots" should not be mixed with other photographs unless there is no alternative.

4. The date of arrest and other ID data that might appear in a mug shot should be covered up. This will minimize the chance that the witness will pick out a recent arrestee when the witness knows that a suspect has been picked up.

5. If a particular person is suspected of the offense, and he is in jail or facing charges, the prosecutor should be consulted. He may want to notify the suspect's attorney of the scheduled viewing.

6. After an identification is made, the officer in charge should record the ID numbers of each photograph shown the witness, if the photographs are displayed separately. If the witness picks the suspect from a book, the pages viewed should be noted. This procedure will enable the officer to reconstruct the viewing process in court, if it becomes necessary.

Many police agencies use a photocomposition process to build a likeness of the perpetrator. Several identification kits are on the market and employ drawings of many types of eyes, ears, noses, and mouths that can be placed together. Their usefulness and legality have been upheld in several court decisions. The officer using such devices should be trained or educated in the proper techniques, and he must be prepared to be cross-examined on this process.

C. OTHER NONTESTIMONIAL EVIDENCE

(6.15) Blood and Breath Samples

When the procedure is done by or under the direction of a licensed physician, blood samples may be taken from the body of a suspect, even if he objects. Because it is an extraordinary remedy, probable cause is a necessary condition when the individual makes an objection. Samples are usually taken to determine the influence of alcoholic beverages or of narcotics. In order to avoid civil liability and not violate the prerequisites of the Fourth Amendment, a court order should be sought and obtained before a suspect is forcibly strapped down and blood drawn from him. If the objections are merely verbal and not physical, a court order is not necessary. The motor vehicle code may provide for forcible samplings under certain conditions. A person can, of course, always consent to the taking of a blood sample. Moreover, it is wise to administer such a test if the suspect insists on it.

A person may be required to breathe into a device that measures his intoxication or other conditions. Again, the motor vehicle code may provide that such a test be given, and a court order can be obtained if he forcibly resists.

In justifying such actions, courts have said the following:

1. There is no privilege against self-incrimination since the evidence is obtained by the labors of the prosecution.

2. There is no right to counsel. Since the suspect does not have a right under the Fifth Amendment to refuse a blood or breath test, he cannot have the right to counsel under *Miranda*, which was decided on the basis of the Fifth Amendment.

3. The action is not an unlawful search and seizure. There is reason to believe the evidence will be destroyed by natural bodily processes unless the tests are administered promptly, and the methods used in extracting the evidence are not unreasonable. No body cavities are searched, and the process does not shock the conscience of the courts.

Not all courts agree on the issue of the degree of force that may be used. In a California case decided in 1970 the officers kept a scissors lock on the suspect and held his arm immobile while he was lying on the floor (*People* v. *Kraft*, 3 Cal. App. 3d 890, 894 Cal. Rptr. 280 [1970]). Though the suspect was "defensive," the officers were aggressive beyond all need. Thus, in California, if excessive force is applied, the evidence will be suppressed.

(6.16) Other Physiological Measurements and Evidence

Samples of hair can be taken over the objection of a suspect. The Supreme Court recently upheld the forcible taking of fingernail scrapings from a suspect (*Cupp* v. *Murphy*, 93 S. Ct. 2000 [1973]). The rationale for this case was that the evidence could be quickly destroyed by cleaning. The warrantless scrapings were based on probable cause.

The so-called moral and privacy considerations surrounding the taking of seminal smears will preclude their use unless the individual gives his consent. A suspect's clothing may, however, be forcibly taken and examined for seminal stains.

For several years legal philosophers have debated whether a bullet could be forcibly removed. Suppose that a policeman is found shot to death, with his gun in hand and a single bullet missing. Suppose, further, that a former offender is found a few minutes later in the next block, suffering from a bullet wound. Suppose, finally, that the gun that fired the fatal shot was found next to the officer, wiped clean of prints, and, again, with a single bullet missing.

On the basis of such evidence, could a search warrant or court order be obtained to extract the bullet from the suspect? If the bullet is removed to preserve his life or well-being, it would, of course, be admissible. By the same token, if removal of the bullet would imperil his life, the court cannot order that it be done. If a decision is made by the prosecutor not to seek a court order, if the suspect refuses to consent to an operation, and if medical evidence all concurs that the bullet could be removed safely, would it be lawful for the prosecution to introduce these facts into evidence against the accused?

As mentioned in Chapter 5, police may not forcibly pump the stomach or forcibly examine the rectal cavity of a suspect. Cases have upheld the administration of an emetic by a physician and the use of such evidence derived from the procedure. If, however, a stomach pump or rectal probe is administered by a physician as a necessary procedure to save the life or preserve the well-being of a suspect, anything recovered during these processes would be admissible.

In general, urine samples may be required of a suspect (for alcohol or narcotics tests). They cannot, however, be forced by inducing the suspect to drink liquids. Because of the problems of dilution, a suspect may be required to urinate in the presence of an officer, with his back toward him (*Quesada* v. *Orr*, 14 Cal. App. 3d 866, 92 Cal. Rptr. 640 [1971]).

(6.17) Summary

Prior to 1964 the only test governing the admissibility of a confession or admission was the voluntariness of the statement. The *Escobedo* and *Miranda* decisions put the lawyer in the middle of the interrogation process. They mandated a litany of warnings that must be recited when the suspect is in "custody."

In recent years the lawbooks have been filled with cases that have searched for the "proper" warnings and have speculated at what point in time the warnings were necessary. Recitation of the warnings is not enough; a "knowing and intelligent" waiver must precede an admissible statement. At what age and in what mental condition a suspect must be have never been precisely defined. Jurisdictions have differed on whether misdemeanors and traffic offenses are includable under the *Miranda* decision.

The Warren Court seemed to infer that full compliance with *Miranda* in every respect was a necessary prerequisite to the admissibility of a statement. The Burger Court has been more flexible and has carved out several exceptions to *Miranda*. For example, statements in violation of *Miranda* may be admitted to impeach a suspect's credibility if he testifies at his trial. The Poisoned Tree doctrine will no longer be automatically applied to tainted confessions.

The Warren Court also put lawyers into the lineup procedures in police stations. The Burger Court qualified that holding and limited this requirement to situations following the initiation of adversary criminal proceedings.

Lineups, blood tests, and other physiological measurements are nontestimonial in nature. A person does not have a constitutional right to refuse to participate in these procedures, if there are reasonable grounds to compel his participation.

7

Discovery

(7.1) Discovery in General

For many years the common-law rule was always that the accused could not inspect any prosecution evidence before trial. This inspection is termed "discovery." "At common law, discovery before trial was generally unavailable in both civil and criminal cases" (*State v. Cook*, 43 N.J. 560 [1965]). Even in relatively recent judicial history, the criminal trial was usually run with neither side revealing anything to the other in advance. Secrecy of the prosecution was upheld on the theory that pretrial revelation of police witnesses or prosecution evidence could lead to intimidation or possible physical danger or death of witnesses. There was also a subconscious reason for secrecy. Everyone considered the criminal trial a legal contest with prescribed rules in which each side tried to beat the other—not as a vehicle for seeking the truth.

Even in civil cases, pretrial discovery of evidence was only narrowly allowed. This attitude in civil suits has now been completely reversed. Experience has shown that, if each side understands the strengths and weaknesses of the other, cases are often settled without necessity of a trial.

This experience in civil cases has greatly affected the court's attitude toward pretrial discovery in criminal matters. As a matter of fact, the old idea against pretrial criminal discovery is now rapidly being discarded. The U.S. Supreme Court decision of *Jencks* v. *U.S.*, 353 U.S. 657 (1957), started this trend. In that case the convicted defendant was denied access to statements made previously by a prosecution witness. The court ruled that the defense must be given the witness's statements for purposes of cross-examining him at the trial. Though the *Jencks* decision involved the trial use of prosecution material, it led to a general recognition of the propriety of allowing the accused to see such material before trial. The present attitude on pretrial criminal discovery is best summarized in a statement from *Williams* v. *Florida*, 399 U.S. 78 (1970): "The adversary system of trial is hardly an end to itself, it is not yet a poker game in which players enjoy an absolute right always to conceal their cards until played."

Coupled with this changing attitude toward pretrial criminal discovery has been an increased emphasis in the courts on protecting the criminal defendant's rights. Now by court decision, rules, and statutes, criminal defendants are being allowed much wider pretrial access to the prosecution's evidence (see statutes in Arizona, Idaho, New York, Vermont, and Wyoming; Federal Rules of Criminal Procedure, 6 [e], 16 and 17; *State* v. *Ford*, 108 Ariz. 404, cert. den. 409 U.S. 1128 [1973]).

The more liberal discovery rights in criminal trials should not be confused with depositions (see the section on "Depositions of Third Parties"). "Discovery" and "depositions" are not the same. According to *Kardy* v. *Shook*, 237 Md. 524 (1965), " 'Discovery' has long been one of the working tools of the legal profession . . . . Discovery suggests the disclosure of facts resting in the knowledge of a party to a suit or the production of . . . things in his possession or under his control . . . . 'Depositions,' on the other hand, indicate the *testimony of a witness reduced to writing* [emphasis added]."

Many older court decisions deny criminal pretrial discovery. These cases should be relied on only with caution, in view of the changing attitude allowing broad pretrial criminal discovery. Because of this changing attitude, the only safe conclusion is that a defendant's right to pretrial discovery of the prosecution's evidence will get broader and broader. The prosecution's right to pretrial discovery of defense evidence will lag behind considerably, but it, too, will gradually be enlarged by court decisions and rulings.

(7.2) Power to Compel Disclosure

Because pretrial criminal discovery was not accepted in common law, the older cases held that the courts were without power to order it (*Rex* v. *Holland*, 4 Durn. & E. 691, 100 Eng. Rep. 124 [K.B. 1792]). Even as late as 1958, the U.S. Supreme Court held that denial of pretrial criminal evidence to the defendant did not violate due process (*Cicenia* v. *LaGay*, 357 U.S. 504 [1958]). A general rule now adopted by state courts is that the court can compel pretrial discovery of prosecution evidence (*State* v. *Superior Court of Cochise County*, 90 Ariz. 133 [1961]).

The court can also, within constitutional limits, allow prosecution discovery of defense criminal evidence. Discovery in federal cases is detailed in the Federal Rules of Criminal Procedure.

(7.3) Propriety of Compelled Disclosure

The accused, even in the modern view, is not entitled to discovery as a matter of right or as a constitutional guarantee (*Palermo* v. *U.S.*, 360 U.S. 343 [1959]). In some jurisdictions, however, it is now spelled out by statute (*People* v. *Muñoz*, 11 A.D. 2d 79, affd. 9 N.Y. 2d 638 [1961]; *Goldman* v. *U.S.*, 316 U.S. 129 [1940]; *U.S.* v. *Fioravanti*, 412 F. 2d 407, cert. den. 396 U.S. 837 [1969]).

In general, discovery by the criminal defendant will be allowed if it is a matter of fairness and if it is a factor in the search for truth. Thus the trial court determines whether to allow the defendant to employ discovery, and the judge is not in error if he refuses to do so unless he has clearly abused his discretion.

The defense counsel must show that the evidence sought is actually needed and is not being requested in the hope that he can learn something useful (*People* v. *Miller*, 42 Misc. 2d 794 [N.Y. 1964]). The courts have, in fact, denied a blanket request by the defense that the state supply copies of all statements in its possession (*People* v. *Terry*, 57 Cal. 2d 538, cert. den. 375 U.S. 960 [1963]). A subpoena to the prosecutor requiring him to bring all statements from his files was also disallowed (*State* v. *Colvin*, 81 Ariz. 388 [1957]). A defense request for all police reports resulted in the same decision (*People* v. *Newville,* 220 Cal. App. 2d 267 [1963]).

A number of older cases hold that only evidence that is admissible can be obtained by discovery (*Fryer* v. *U.S.,* 207 F. 2d 134, cert. den. 346 U.S. 885 [1953]; *Griffin* v. *U.S.,* 183 F. 2d 990 [1950]; *People* v. *Schmitt,* 1 Cal. App. 87 [1957]; *People ex rel Lemon* v. *Supreme Court,* 245 N.Y. 24 [1927]; *People* v. *Riley,* 46 Misc. 2d 221 [N.Y. 1965]). Where not superseded by court rule or statute, these older decisions must now be considered as the minority rule only.

Courts still consider carefully, however, valid arguments by the prosecution that pretrial discovery of prosecution witnesses or evidence might be dangerous to a witness, might improperly reveal the name of an informant, or might otherwise be unfair. In these situations prosecution matters will be protected; the general court attitude concerning them is set forth in *People* v. *Lopez,* 60 Cal. 2d 223, cert. den. 375 U.S. 994 (1963). "There must be a balance of the right of a defendant to discover potentially material witnesses with the probability that such discovery might lead to the elimination of an adverse witness or the influencing of his testimony. In balancing these competing factors the trial court must be allowed great discretion."

(7.4) Matters in the Prosecutor's Files

a. Statements by the Accused

Older case law withheld any pretrial discovery of the defendant's own confession. Under present-day practice, he can gain access to it in almost every court. Part of this change came about as a result of *Jackson* v. *Denno,* 378 U.S. 368 (1964). This decision by the Supreme Court required the judge to hold a separate hearing to determine the voluntariness of the confession. Decisions in various states (such as *People* v. *Huntley,* 15 N.Y. 2d 72 [1965]) have followed this decision, and now pretrial hearings on the voluntariness of confessions are common. Because of such hearings before the trial, defense counsel usually has access to the confession itself. Federal Rule 16 now requires that the U.S. attorney give the defendant access to his statements. A number of states have enacted similar statutes (for example, N.Y. Criminal Procedure Law, 240.20). Aside from these statutory requirements, courts now generally recognize that, as a matter of fairness, the defendant should be allowed to have a copy of his own confession before he goes to trial. Even corporations charged with criminal offenses have been allowed access to pretrial testimony of their employees before the grand jury (*U.S.* v. *Hughes*, 413 F. 2d 1244 [5th Cir. 1969]; *People* v. *Leto Bros.*, 70 M. 2d 347 [N.Y. 1972]). Typical of the modern trend is a decision that allowed a defendant to have copies of his codefendant's statement (*People* v. *Garner*, 57 Cal. 2d 135, cert. den. 370 U.S. 929 [1962]). In that case a man and his wife shot and killed a fellow robber, left his body in the California desert, and fled to Mexico. When arrested, the man made a handwritten statement, which was followed by a joint statement that he and his wife made on tape. The court gave the male defendant his own statement and allowed him to hear the recorded one made with his codefendant. It also granted him permission to make copies.

In a federal charge of criminal conspiracy to steal foreign freight and transport it interstate, the defendant sought statements of coconspirators and codefendants whom the government did not intend to use as witnesses. (A coconspirator is jointly involved, but is not indicted; a codefendant is tried with the defendant.) The court decided that he was entitled to the coconspirators' statements because they were admissible in evidence against him as an exception to the hearsay rule. Thus, they would have the same effect as his own statement. Any statements by codefendants could be given him at the trial court's discretion only if he showed a "particularized need" (*U.S.* v. *Agnello*, 367 F. Supp. 444 [1973]).

Unless there is a rule or statute to cover the situation, the courts are split on the question of discovery of statements by a codefendant or an accomplice.

b. Statements of Witnesses

Once a witness testifies at a trial, opposing counsel has the right to a copy of any prior statement the witness has made. He can then use this information on cross-examination for impeachment purposes (18 U.S. Code 3500; *Jencks* v. *U.S.*, supra). This rule is accepted everywhere by all courts.

The more important question is whether the defendant can obtain the statements of a prosecution witness before trial. Some

courts relax pretrial inspection and give the defense access to statements of all witnesses that the state has obtained. An example of
this is illustrated by *People* v. *Garner*, 18 Cal. Rptr. 40 (1961). In
this case the defendant was charged with performing illegal abortions.
Two women and a man testified at the preliminary hearing. Cross-
examination showed that they had given prior statements to the
police. The defendant demanded copies of these statements, which
were either recorded or taken down in longhand from the police
files before the case went to trial. The court granted the defense
request. It declared that such statements are always allowed at the
trial itself for impeachment purposes, and so there was no valid
reason why the defense should not have access to them before the
trial.

Accessibility of information before a trial takes place can indeed
endanger prosecution witnesses. Some courts will, therefore, not
allow *pretrial* defense examination of statements by prosecution
witnesses (*State* v. *St. Peter*, 63 Wash. 2d 495 [1963]), and it is
forbidden by statute in federal courts (18 U.S. Code 3500).

c. Statements of Victims

Neither rule nor statute generally differentiates between the
availability of a victim's statement and that of any other prosecution
witness. Where the court has discretion, it is reluctant to require
the pretrial availability of a victim's statement. Should there be
a preliminary hearing at which the victim testifies, the defense can,
of course, obtain a transcript of the testimony before the trial
begins. If there is not such a hearing, the court will usually protect
the victim by refusing the defense access to his statement. This
is particularly true for victims of sex crimes (*State* v. *Circuit Court*,
16 Wisc. 2d 197 [1962]).

d. Statements of Police

If a police officer was a *witness*, his statement in the departmental files is as that of any other witness. A statement by a police
officer concerning his investigation and a summary of evidence are
different matters. They are not generally given to the defense in
advance of trial. The court may, however, make them available at
the trial itself to be used in cross-examination of an officer. Indeed,
the Federal Rules of Criminal Procedure, 16 (e), expressly mentions

these matters. Thus, except for such things as the defendant's statements, criminal record, and reports of physical and mental examinations, "This rule does not authorize the discovery or inspection of reports, memoranda, or other internal government documents made by the attorney for the government or other government agents in connection with the investigation or prosecution of the case . . . ."

Police statements summarizing evidence are exactly what they say they are—summaries. They are not actual statements of witnesses. They can be used in evidence only as possible tools for cross-examination impeachment of the officer making the report. Police statements often discuss problems of prosecuting the defendant. Such material will not, of course, be allowed defense discovery (*U.S.* v. *Pfingst*, 477 F. 2d 177, cert. den. 412 U.S. 941 [1973]).

e. Transcripts and Recordings

Investigators are making increased use of tape recordings for taking statements. The fact that the statement is done electronically rather than in writing has no legal effect on its availability to the defense. If the defendant is entitled to a copy, he may be furnished his transcript or be allowed to hear the recording and make his own copy from it. This rule goes as far back as 1950 (*Cash* v. *Superior Court*, 346 P. 2d 407 [Cal. Sup. Ct. 1959]). An undercover agent posing as a coburglar took secret recordings of the planning for the burglary. Court decisions made his recordings available to the defense. New York allows the availability of this type of evidence by statute, except in cases where there was a legal wiretap (N.Y. Criminal Procedure Law, 240.20).

In a case in California the defendant was charged with a sex crime involving children. As part of their interrogation of the man, the police had him listen to a taped conversation between them and the victim. The defendant claimed that he could not remember what he had said. The court ordered that the accused be allowed to hear the recording of himself as well as that of the child (*Vance* v. *Superior Court of San Diego County*, 330 P. 2d 773 [1958]). It is safe to say that tape recordings are normally now made available to the defense (*U.S.* v. *Marshak*, 364 F. Supp. 1005 [1973]).

f. Medical Reports

A report by a coroner or medical examiner is admissible evidence in most courts. In jurisdictions where this is true, the court can make such a report available to the defense before trial. In some jurisdictions, however, the coroner's report may not be made available for technical reasons (*Pinana* v. *State*, 352 P. 2d 824 [Nev. Sup. Ct., 1960]). Reports of physical or mental examinations ordered by the prosecution can normally be obtained by the defendant as a necessary tool in preparing his defense (Federal Rules of Criminal Procedure, 6 [e], 16, and 17.1; N.Y. Criminal Procedure Law, 240.20).

g. Laboratory Findings and Reports by Experts

Courts will usually order that the defendant be given copies of police laboratory reports. This is true even when the report itself cannot be used in evidence and the technician must testify in person.

There are innumerable kinds of these reports. The prosecution can normally use photographs as evidence, and pretrial access to such materials will be given the defendant. Reports by experts and technicians on handwriting, ballistics, fingerprints, and blood will also be ordered shown to the accused. Even organs and bodily specimens may be made available to the defense for examination and testing (*People* v. *Sauer*, 163 Cal. App. 2d 740, cert. den. 359 U.S. 973 [1959]; *People* v. *Dinan*, 15 A.D. 2d 786, affd. 11 N.Y. 2d 350, cert. den. 371 U.S. 877 [1962]; *People* v. *Seaman*, 64 Misc. 2d 684 [N.Y. 1970]; *People* v. *Garner*, 57 Cal. 2d 135, cert. den. 370 U.S. 929 [1962]; *State* v. *Thompson*, 338 P. 2d 319 [Wash. Sup. Ct., 1959]).

A defendant accused of manslaughter was charged with running over a two-and-a-half-year-old girl with his car. His defense was that he was completely unaware that he had hit anything. Scrapings were taken from the car and examined by the F.B.I. laboratory. The court gave the defendant pretrial access to the report, stating that he was entitled to know whether it was positive or negative. If it was positive, the circumstantial evidence would, of course, be used against him (*State* v. *Lackey*, 319 P. 2d 610 [Okla. Crim. Ct. of Appeals, 1957]).

Another accused allegedly killed a man by kicking him in the head. When he was arrested, he had on the same pair of shoes he had worn at the time of the fight. The shoes were taken from him and sent to the laboratory. He argued that the condition of the shoes had been altered; his own laboratory tests would, therefore, be useless. He demanded a copy of the state's laboratory report so that it could be determined if any hair or other material had been found on the shoes. Even though the report was not admissible in evidence, the court granted his request in the interest of justice (*Walker* v. *Superior Court*, 317 P. 2d 130 [Cal. Dist. Ct., 1957]).

Today only an unusual set of circumstances would persuade a court to refuse a defendant access to a laboratory report held by the prosecution.

h. Grand Jury Transcripts

Grand jury proceedings are confidential hearings at which only the state's evidence is normally given. The purpose of the hearing is to determine if the prosecution has sufficient evidence to accuse the defendant of a felony. This process is designed to prevent an individual from being unjustly accused by the state.

There are a number of reasons why grand jury hearings are secret. One is for the protection of witnesses. Another is to provide a way of charging the accused and issuing an arrest warrant for him without his knowledge, should he not be in custody. Most jurisdictions consider unauthorized revelation of grand jury testimony contempt of court or even a criminal offense (N.Y. P.L. 215.70; 18 U.S. Code 3333).

Once a witness has testified at the actual trial, a copy of his testimony before the grand jury will be given to the defense counsel. He may use it as possible impeachment material in cross-examination.

Though pretrial access to grand jury transcripts will not usually be allowed by the court, in some cases a witness who has given evidence before a grand jury may be allowed to see his own testimony before trial (*People* v. *Rosario*, 9 N.Y. 2d 286 [1961]; *Jencks* v. *U.S.*, supra; *re Minkoff*, 349 F. Supp. 154).

i. Names of Witnesses

According to the old rule, neither side in a criminal trial was required to reveal the names of its potential witnesses. Modern procedure requires the prosecution to supply the names of its witnesses unless it can show a valid reason for concealing them. The court must balance the arguments and decide whether to keep the names confidential (*People* v. *Lopez*, 60 Cal. 2d 223, cert. den. 375 U.S. 994 [1963]; *U.S.* v. *Jordan*, 466 F. 2d 99, cert. den. 409 U.S. 1129 [1963]).

A case in Illinois, *People* v. *Martin*, 74 Ill. App. 2d 431 (1966), illustrates the kind of problem that still can arise over the names of witnesses. In this case the prosecution supplied the defendant with a list of names of the state's witnesses, but did not include the name of a confidential informant. The defendant was told orally about the informant and was given a chance to interview him. The informant refused, however, to talk to the defense counsel. Though the defense objected, the trial court allowed the informant to testify. The appellate court upheld this ruling. It pointed out that the defense counsel had the name before the trial and that the informer could not be required to talk to him if he chose not to do so.

j. Criminal Records

If the prosecution is allowed to keep secret the records it has of criminal convictions of the defendant or of any potential witness, the defendant is at a disadvantage. Knowing that a criminal record can have an adverse effect on a jury, the accused may have a problem in determining whether he can safely use a potential witness or even take the stand in his own behalf. Because of this, the defense should have pretrial information on such criminal records. Courts ordinarily grant a defense request for such information. As a matter of fact, several states (such as Arizona, Vermont, and New York) now have statutes requiring the prosecution to furnish such information without a request by the defense (*Losavio* v. *Mayber*, 486 P. 2d 1032 [Colo. Sup. Ct., 1972]; *State* v. *Coney*, 272 So. 2d 550 [1973]).

k. Work Product

The "work product" of an attorney consists of such matters as summaries of evidence, trial strategy, and research. It is part of the pretrial investigation and is not subject to pretrial discovery by either side. Sometimes it is debatable whether an item is evidence or a work product. If the court determines it is the latter, it will be protected (N.Y. Criminal Procedure, 240.10 [3], Federal Rules of Criminal Procedure, 6 [e], 16, and 17.1).

(7.5) Police Files and Records

In the past, defendants were denied access to reports and records compiled by police officers, whether the reports were official or investigative. As with other aspects of discovery, the courts have increasingly liberalized the rules concerning these reports. Some reports, such as those sent to the state after an automobile accident, in some jurisdictions, are available to anyone on the payment of a fee. In other jurisdictions, they are restricted to the persons involved, to owners of the vehicles even if they were not involved in the accident, and to attorneys or insurance adjusters who represent one of the parties involved.

The report on a breath test is usually made available to the person tested if he requests it. As a matter of fact, the report is customarily released on subpoena to any party requesting it, along with photographs of the accident and statements by witnesses. An exception is vehicular homicide, in which matters in police files are protected in the same manner as in other felony cases.

In some jurisdictions, routine police reports sent to the prosecutor will also be turned over to the attorney for the accused; in other jurisdictions, the defense attorney must demand that these items be produced and show that they have some relevancy for the defense effort. The incident report (such as for a burglary, robbery, or theft) is the initial document prepared by police officers; it is usually completed in the field on a standardized form by the patrol officer assigned to respond to the call. It contains little more than bare facts concerning the time of the call and the address where it was received, identity of the victim and his address, one or two sentences describing the event, a description of the alleged perpetrator, a list of witnesses, and other neutral but germane facts. It usually includes additional information for police statistical purposes, such as the amount of light, weather conditions, day of the week, type of property involved, and similar factors that, when aggregated, show criminal patterns.

The follow-up report is written by detectives assigned to the case. It is not neutral because it discloses investigative processes, indicates leads, states conclusions, and generally describes the events and personalities involved. Except for information that can be presented in a strictly factual form, such as data on arrest and loss of property, investigative reports are narrative and therefore vary by the unit and the officer reporting.

A third kind of report is prepared by technicians who are specialists in the field of evidence. They verify the existence of contraband, confirm the identity of fingerprints, conduct paraffin tests, and make comparative ballistic examinations and other scientific studies. Their reports are strictly factual. Thus, if a technician is likely to testify, there is no reason to keep the report from the defense attorney.

The report by a specialized unit such as vice, narcotics, or intelligence is a chronological summary of events leading up to an arrest. These units prepare surveillance reports, reports on interviews with informants, corroborative reports, and investigative summaries. The essential portions of these reports are usually included in affidavits seeking arrest or search warrants. The reports are highly confidential, particularly in investigations that are likely to continue for an indefinite period of time. Gambling, extortion, narcotics, and terrorism are often the offenses investigated. Confidentiality is important because other offenders may be at large, police techniques could be compromised in future cases, and informants might be revealed. Courts should be extremely reluctant to order discovery of these files.

A fifth kind of report is made for the police personnel department or for the purpose of an internal investigation. An officer's personnel dossier lists chronologically all complaints made against the officer and gives a summary of the investigations concerned with the complaints, and conclusions drawn from the investigations, including disciplinary action taken against him, if there was any. These reports are highly sensitive because they may impair the effectiveness of an officer who has been the subject of past investigations, invade his privacy if they are disclosed, and adversely affect police morale.

As was indicated previously, the initial case report is routinely turned over to defense counsel in many jurisdictions and, therefore, does not pose a discovery problem for either side. The follow-up report is sometimes made available if the detective who completed it is to testify on matters contained in it. The theory behind such discovery is that the defense should be allowed access to matters that might impeach the credibility of the officer and prevent a surprise at the trial. Many courts will not require that these reports be produced even if they contain notes of conversations with the accused (see *Annotation*, 7 ALR 3d 8, at 132 ff., Sec. 17, "Police or Investigation Report").

Because they constitute the work product of the state, they are privileged. If, however, defense counsel is able to show inconsistencies in the testimony of one or more officers, there is a stronger likelihood that a court will order them produced. Such inconsistencies may arise at a preliminary hearing or at a suppression hearing.

Surveillance reports are privileged, and a court ordinarily will not compel disclosure. If, however, law enforcement officers used illegal electronic surveillances in conducting their investigation, the accused is entitled to inspect the evidence that was gathered illegally. The purpose of the inspection is to determine whether evidence gathered against him is the fruit of the poisoned tree. The U.S. Supreme Court has ruled that an accused is entitled to obtain records of illegal electronic surveillance without a prior in camera (secret) screening by the court (*Alderman* v. *U.S.*, 394 U.S. 165 [1969]). But he must have standing to object to the act; that is, he must be the party who was overheard illegally or who owned the property on which the surveillance occurred. The court may enter semiprotective orders against disclosure by the accused or his attorney to third parties, such as coconspirators.

Personnel files and reports of internal investigations are ordinarily not discoverable by an accused. A decision in California, which is not law elsewhere, compels production of these records in certain instances (*Pitchess* v. *Superior Court* [*Escheverria*], 1 Cal. 3d 531, 522 P. 2d 305 [1974]). According to that decision, in cases where an officer is the complaining witness (such as a charge of assaulting an officer), the accused can obtain a copy of the officer's personnel dossier. The purpose of such discovery is to locate incidents that might bear on the officer's credibility as a witness. The court held that no prior showing of relevance is necessary and that production is not limited to those matters in the officer's file that report on sustained instances of misconduct. Although there is no common-law privilege concerning officers' personnel files, courts in other jurisdictions do not compel production of police dossiers. It is generally felt that such a file is not relevant to the case being prosecuted, even if the officer will be called to testify.

A privilege against disclosure can ordinarily be waived. This is not necessarily true in the case of certain police records, such as arrest sheets. By federal regulation, law enforcement officers may not disclose an individual's arrest record or juvenile record unless it is allowed by statute, executive order, court order, or court rule. Violation of the regulation subjects police officers to a maximum fine of $10,000. A court can order a police agency to turn over criminal history information to the attorney for the accused, but a particularized need must be shown. For example, if a prosecution witness had ever been arrested for perjury or committed to an institution for the criminally insane, the attorney for the accused needs this information in order to conduct an effective defense. (See the section on "Criminal Records," above.)

(7.6) Matters in Defense Files in General

The idea of letting the state discover matters from the defense has been slow to develop. Some of the older cases, which are probably now obsolete, refused discovery on grounds it would violate the defendant's right against self-incrimination as set forth in the Fifth Amendment (*State* v. *Tune*, 13 N.J. 203 [1953]). In addition to this reason, there was the argument that the prosecution has sufficient pretrial weapons, such as police investigations, grand jury proceedings, and preliminary hearings.

The growing area of pretrial criminal discovery is now allowing both sides more latitude, and it is becoming necessary for the defense to give up information. Statutes in some states require defendants to appear in lineups, give physical samples such as blood and submit to physical examinations, and provide samples of handwriting. Federal rules can require both sides to give the names of their witnesses.

a. Alibis

Most states have statutes requiring prior notice by the accused of a proposed defense based on an alibi. The defense can be required to give the names of proposed alibi witnesses as long as the state, in return, must furnish the names of any witnesses it proposes to use to rebut the claimed alibi (*Warduis* v. *Oregon*, 412 U.S. 470 [1973]).

b. Defense Witnesses

There is, as noted, a growing tendency of each side to furnish the names of its witnesses. Unless there is some compelling reason against it, such as possible danger for a prosecution witness, the courts will generally require that the names be revealed to the other side (*People* v. *Lopez*, 60 Cal. 2d 223, cert. den. 375 U.S. 994 [1963]). The courts have moved so far in the direction of allowing the prosecution discovery that in one case the state was furnished copies of a statement by a defense witness for cross-examination, even though the defense counsel had written out the statement and his witness had not signed it (*State* v. *Montague*, 262 A. 2d 398 [N.J., 1970]).

c. Fingerprints, Handwriting, and Photographs

Fingerprinting and photographing the defendant can be constitutionally required in all felony cases. If these things are not done initially, the courts will order them on application from the state. The accused can also be ordered to give examples of his handwriting, blood samples, and the like. In one case the state was working on a possible criminal charge involving $25,000 in faked automobile insurance claims. The prosecution moved to require a suspect to appear in his office and give handwriting samples. The court ordered that this be done. It pointed out that, while no criminal action was pending, the state's moving papers showed probable cause to identify the suspect as the defendant. He could, therefore, be required to furnish the handwriting samples (*U.S.* v. *Harris*, 453 F. 2d 1317, cert. den. 412 U.S. 927 [1973]).

As early as 1962, the courts in California allowed wide discovery to the prosecution (*Jones* v. *Superior Court of Nevada County*, 58 Cal. 2d 56 [1962]). A rape charge was involved. The defendant claimed that he was impotent and asked for time to get medical evidence and reports on an old injury that had caused his condition. A discovery order was granted the prosecution. It made the defendant surrender the names of the doctors he planned to call and any doctors' reports or X rays he intended to use in evidence. The court excluded only medical reports that had been made for the defense counsel. In its decision, the court gave the pioneering statement on prosecution criminal discovery. It is now generally regarded as the proper rule.

Absent some governmental requirement that information be kept confidential for purposes of effective law enforcement, the state has no interest in
denying the accused access to all evidence that can throw light on issues in the
case. To deny flatly any right of production on ground that imbalance would be
created between the advantages of prosecution and defense would be to lose
sight of the purpose of a criminal trial, the ascertainment of facts.

Similarly, absent the privilege against self-incrimination or other privileges
provided by law, the defendant in a criminal case has no valid interest in denying
the prosecution access to evidence that can throw light on issues in the case.

(7.7) Depositions of Third Parties

In criminal actions the courts are reluctant to grant the right to
take pretrial depositions of third parties (that is, anyone other than
the victim or the defendant). Some states grant it by statute or rule
(Florida Rules of Criminal Procedure, 3.220 [d] ; New York Criminal
Procedure Law, 660.10-680.80). Various decisions, however, refuse
to allow the taking of such depositions, as is routinely done in civil
cases (*Kardy* v. *Shook*, 273 Md. 524 [1965] ; *Reed* v. *Allen*, 121 Vt.
202 [1959]).

The reluctance to order free use of pretrial depositions in
criminal cases is partially grounded on the argument that fear moti-
vates many witnesses where a crime is concerned. Also, witnesses can
develop adverse feelings toward the prosecution if they are subjected
to giving additional pretrial depositions. Thus, while pretrial depositions are acceptable in some cases, there are limits to what the
courts will allow.

(7.8) Effect of Noncompliance

If either side refuses a court-ordered pretrial discovery, contempt
of court is always an available remedy. Though contempt of court
can result in fine or imprisonment, this alone might not deter some
individuals. The court, therefore, has additional remedies. It can
adjourn proceedings until the court order has been followed. If the
state has failed to grant discovery, the charges may be dismissed. This
has been done, for example, in espionage cases, where the government has felt it could not reveal its informant. What is most common
is for the trial judge to refuse to receive the evidence where a discovery order has not been complied with. The court may, in addition,

use any other legal remedy it deems appropriate (*U.S.* v. *Kelly*, 420 F. 2d 26 [2d Civ. 1969]).

(7.9) Summary

The original common-law rule forbade any pretrial discovery in criminal cases. It is now generally agreed that courts do have the power to allow such discovery, and so the modern trend in all courts is to be increasingly liberal in this area.

The accused does not have an absolute right to discovery, and it is still within the court's discretion. Informants for the prosecution, victims of criminal acts, and witnesses who are subject to possible criminal pressures are still protected from defense discovery.

Most evidence in the prosecution's files will be made available to the defense if it can show good cause. Thus, the accused will be given pretrial access to confessions, statements by witnesses, criminal records, laboratory and experts' reports, and similar material.

The defense usually asks for much of the material in police files. Police reports, interviews, and records of internal affairs may be requested. Though courts allow some of this type of material to be used at the trial for cross-examination of an individual police witness, they are generally reluctant to allow pretrial access to it.

The prosecution is gradually being allowed some discovery from defense files. Alibi claims with the names of supportive witnesses, handwriting samples, medical reports, and physical specimens are examples of material that the court will generally order the defense to reveal to the prosecution before trial.

Refusal to grant discovery can result in contempt, dismissal of charges, and other court sanctions.

8

Privileged Communications

(8.1) Common Law and Statutory

A variety of privileged communications cannot be revealed in court. They range from military secrets to communications between husband and wife. The rule of evidence that communications between certain parties should be confidential and immune from testimonial compulsion is based on public policy. Some, such as confidential communications between attorney and client, are historical and part of the common law. Others, such as the confidentiality between doctor and patient, are of modern origin and are usually found in statutes.

"Communication" in these situations is not confined to what one person has told another, but may include such things as written material or observations that could be seen and heard by the person involved in the confidential relationship.

From time to time interested groups seek to enlarge the field of privileged communications by having new laws passed that grant them testimonial immunity. Newspaper reporters, for example, are promoting legislation in some jurisdictions that grants them limited immunity for refusing to reveal their news sources.

For any communication to be excluded from court, the general rule is that it must have some aura of confidentiality about it, and there has to be the required relationship between the parties. If, however, only part of the testimony is privileged, this does not bar the witness from testifying, but only excludes the part that is privileged.

The rule of confidentiality applies to all proceedings, pretrial hearings, grand jury sessions, and the actual trial. There are various exceptions and legal refinements in all areas of privileged communications. Though no constitutional problems are involved, local statutes and court decisions must be consulted in every case to be sure of the particular rule.

(8.2) Marital Privilege

An old English rule disqualified one spouse from testifying *for* the other. This has been completely changed through the years so that now in some cases a spouse cannot testify *against* the other. Only a few remnants of this outmoded English rule remain in a small number of states. The general rule of evidence that forbids one spouse from testifying against the other in criminal proceedings known as "confidential communication" grew up by court decision and became part of our common law. Though the reasons for the rule are obscure, the usual rationale is that "it prevents disruption of the home." In this day of women's liberation, equality of the sexes, and divorce by consent, there is no longer any real basis for retaining the husband-wife immunity rule.

It is interesting that a brother was always allowed to testify against a brother and a father against a child without the court feeling that this was socially disruptive, and yet this could be equally disruptive of family harmony as a situation involving a husband and wife.

The husband-wife testimonial privilege does, however, cause problems for law enforcement personnel, and it promotes more injustice than almost any other rule of evidence. Law books are full of frustrating examples where the rule suppressed the truth and freed guilty defendants. Following are two such examples.

In a case in Ithaca, New York (*People* v. *Daghita*, 299 N.Y. 194 [1949]), a policeman was charged with stealing from the Montgomery

Ward retail store. The store's janitor testified that Officer Daghita often drove him to work in the early morning hours and would go in the store and take merchandise. Many times he carried it away in cardboard boxes. At his larceny trial the state called Daghita's wife and, over objection by the defense, had her testify against her husband. She said that he often brought home articles in his own car or in the police car at 4:00 or 5:00 a.m. She further told how he carried in rugs, clothing, jackets, pillows, and bath towels, often in cardboard boxes. He hid them in the cellar and brought them upstairs later in the day. The husband was convicted and appealed. In New York a statute barred a husband or wife from testifying as to a "confidential communication between them." The appellate court held that even if no word is spoken, the husband's acts done in the presence of the wife were covered and that her testimony in this case was barred. Thus, the conviction was reversed.

A federal case (*Hawkins* v. *U.S.*, 358 U.S. 74 [1958]) involved a defendant who was convicted of taking girls across state lines for immoral purposes, in violation of the Mann Act. The defendant's wife, a prostitute, was called by the government as a witness. In her testimony she described her husband's illegal activities. He was convicted. The United States Supreme Court reversed his conviction, however, stating that her evidence against him was immune under the husband-wife privilege.

Most states do have laws providing for the marital privilege in criminal cases. Following are factors that these statutes generally have in common.

a. Valid Marriage

The parties must actually be married. A mistress or paramour will not qualify, neither will the partner to a bigamous or incestuous marriage or one where there was no marriage license (*People* v. *Glab*, 13 C.A. 2d 528 [1936]). A common-law marriage, where recognized, does, however, qualify for the exclusionary rule.

The general rule is that no privilege attaches to communications before the marriage takes place or after it has been terminated. There are, nevertheless, exceptions. In many jurisdictions a marriage ceremony after the crime will make the earlier communications privileged. Some states even preserve the confidentiality of marital communications after a divorce. The law of the locality must, of course, be consulted in case of a premarital or postdivorce situation.

b. Necessity of Confidentiality

Court decisions are split as to just what husband-wife communications are protected. Most state statutes have attempted to narrow the privilege to cover "confidential communications" only. The prosecutor's problem is that various courts have given a wide interpretation as to the meaning of both "confidential" and "communication." A police investigator may think he has an airtight case because the wife saw some of her husband's criminal activity and no confidential words came from him. When the case comes to trial, the officer may be shocked to find that her testimony is not allowed because it is considered to be privileged.

Many court rulings have regarded conduct observed by a spouse as a "communication." Further, since the acts were done in the presence of the spouse, they are "confidential" because the other spouse committed them in the confidence that he was in the privacy of the marriage situation.

Thus, in barring the testimony of Officer Daghita's wife when she testified about her husband's bringing home the stolen goods, the court stated (*People* v. *Daghita*): "Confidential communication . . . means more than oral communications or conversations between husband and wife. It includes . . . disclosive acts done in the presence [of] the other which would not have been performed except for the confidence so existing."

A criminal indictment was dismissed by a court because a wife testified that she found a pistol in her husband's pocket (*People* v. *Sullivan*, 42 Misc. 2d 1014 [N.Y. 1964]). In another, the wife called police to her home and gave them a loaded pistol her husband had hidden in their liquor cabinet. She was not allowed to so testify (*People* v. *Helmus*, 50 Misc. 2d 47 [N.Y. 1966]). One wife was forbidden to testify that she had found a bag of checks that her husband had hidden in the house. The court held that he must have hidden them there because of his reliance on his marital status (*People* v. *Monahan*, 21 A.D. 2d 76 [N.Y. 1964]). In a murder case an important clue was a piece of cloth found near the victim's body. The defendant's wife testified that her husband left home in the morning of the murder wearing an overcoat of similar cloth and that he had come home that night wearing a different coat. The state's highest court considered this privileged communication, and the testimony was stricken (*People* v. *Woltering*, 275 N.Y. 51 [1937]).

Courts have argued over whether a wife's diary is privileged and even over whether she should be allowed to identify her spouse's handwriting. There is further division concerning the legality of a spouse's testimony in regard to the other spouse's intoxication or mental condition. Merely calling the spouse to the witness stand and making her claim the privilege may be ruled as prejudicial, unless it is done in good faith (*People* v. *Wade*, 53 C. 2d 322 [1959]).

Courts agree that the marital privilege disappears when a third person capable of understanding what is going on is present. In such a situation, confidentiality is lost (*People* v. *Ressler*, 17 N.Y. 2d 174 [N.Y. 1966]). Courts quibble, however, when, for example, the husband was talking to a third party and the wife overheard it. A court in Texas even barred a wife from testifying that she had heard her husband threaten to kill a third person (*Gant* v. *State*, 55 Tex. Cr. 284 [1909]).

c. Exceptions

There are some court-approved exceptions where the marital privilege does not apply. If, for example, a husband commits a crime against his wife, she may testify freely against him. In most jurisdictions this exception has been extended to cover any offense against a family member, such as incest, child abuse, or assault. The exception is based on the theory that such a family offense is in reality an offense against the other spouse (*Commonwealth* v. *Maroney*, 414 Pa. 161 [1964]). According to the same theory, one spouse has been allowed to testify against the other regarding sexual misconduct with any third party.

d. Waiver

The protected person can always waive his privilege and allow the testimony to be used, but the waiver has to be made by both parties (*Wolfe* v. *U.S.*, 291 U.S. 7 [1934]). In a few jurisdictions, however, the protection belongs to the defendant alone. Should the spouse be called as a witness and should the defense make no objection, the privilege is waived automatically.

(8.3) Medical Privilege

Privileged communication between doctor and patient was unknown in common law. The idea began with a nineteenth-century statute in New York. Most states have passed similar laws, so that, in general, communications between doctor and patient are privileged. The term "doctor" includes psychiatrists and other medical specialists. As is to be expected, the privilege has produced many unjust results. An example of this is shown in *People* v. *Decina*, 2 N.Y. 2d 133 (1956).

At 3:30 p.m. on a bright, sunny day Decina was driving alone in his car on a city street. Suddenly he swerved to the wrong side of the road and then to the right and mounted the sidewalk at fifty to sixty miles per hour. On doing so, he plowed through a group of young schoolgirls, killing four of them. The car finally crashed through a brick wall. When he was pulled out of the car, he appeared "dazed" and said "I blacked out from the bridge." The police took him to the hospital under guard. An intern examined him and took his history, all of which was overheard by a police officer stationed at the door of the hospital room. The accused told the doctor, who later testified, that he had suffered from convulsions since childhood when he had sustained a brain injury. Further, for nine years he had been subject to seizures in which his right hand "jumped." Just prior to the accident his right hand acted in that way. Decina was convicted of criminal negligence. The appellate court ruled, however, that, even though the intern was not hired by the defendant, the doctor-patient relationship existed and the information the doctor received was privileged. The conviction was reversed.

Thus, four people were killed by a driver with a long history of epilepsy, and this information was kept out of court. Such a result vividly illustrates the need to reexamine this rule for criminal cases. There is now less reason than in times past to bar evidence of a person's physical condition during a criminal proceeding. Little harm, if any, can come to the individual and much public good can result from revealing the truth where a crime has been charged.

In criminal cases the statutory rule against revealing information that passes between a doctor and his patient is, nevertheless, widespread. Only a few states do not let the medical privilege apply to criminal cases (California Evidence Code, Sec. 998; *Oregon* v. *Belts*, 225 Or. 127 [1963]).

Where the doctor-patient privilege is upheld in criminal trials, there are certain general requirements.

a. Relationship with Patient

There must first be a genuine doctor-patient relationship. The doctor must either be a duly licensed physician or the patient must have, in good faith, believed him to be such. In respect to the privilege, a consulting physician stands in the same position as the regular doctor. The doctor's nurse or the paramedical assistant is generally included.

b. Privileged Subject Matter

Medical privilege is based on the idea that the patient is confiding in the doctor in order that he might be treated. Where the patient is seen for observation only, not to be cured, the information is normally not privileged. A court-ordered physical or medical examination falls into this category. Blood alcohol tests, for example, are not given for treatment. The results are, therefore, admissible (*People* v. *Cook*, 205 N.Y. Supp. 2d 489 [1960]). The same is true of autopsies, since the doctor obviously is not going to treat the corpse.

The doctor-patient privilege covers much more than any confidential matter the patient discusses with him. It includes all information the doctor obtains from the patient that enables him to act (*Renihan* v. *Dennin*, 103 N.Y. 573 [1886]).

c. Exceptions

Some results from applying the doctor-patient privilege have been so extreme that the courts have made exceptions. One of these exceptions is given below.

A physician operated on and removed the bullet from a woman who had been shot. The state had a statute concerning the doctor-patient privilege. It also required doctors to report all gunshot wounds to the police, which the physician did. At the criminal trial the prosecution called the doctor to testify. The defense objected on the basis of privilege, pointing out that the doctor was testifying about treatment. The court overruled the objection and allowed the testimony to stand, stating that the privilege statute was not intended to protect the criminal and that the matter was public information anyway since the physician had to report the wound to the police (*People* v. *Lay*, 254 A.D. 372, affd. 279 N.Y. 737 [1938]).

Another doctor treated an individual who was poisoned. The

patient died, and the doctor was allowed to testify rather than protect the murderer (*Pierson* v. *People*, 79 N.Y. 424 [1880]).

d. Waiver

Only the patient can waive the doctor-patient privilege, since he is the one protected. A stranger to the privilege will, therefore, not be allowed to claim it. In a criminal prosecution for driving while intoxicated, the defendant moved to inspect the hospital records of the deceased accident victim. The prosecution claimed that the victim's death resulted from an embolism that developed from a leg fracture. The defendant wanted his medical expert to examine the hospital records in order to determine whether the blood clot was the result of a nonaccidental factor. The district attorney objected on the grounds of doctor-patient relationship. The court allowed the inspection, holding that the People were strangers to any claim of medical privilege and had no standing to object (*People* v. *Christiano*, 53 Misc. 2d 433 [N.Y. 1967]).

The patient can either expressly waive the privilege or he can fail to object at the trial. He may also lose his privilege by voluntarily disclosing the information to a third party. The courts do not unanimously hold that the privilege is lost if a third party is present during the examination by the doctor. They do agree, however, that the presence of the doctor's nurse or other employee does not waive the privilege.

The patient can lose his privilege if he "opens the door" at his trial by introducing evidence concerning his physical or mental condition, where this is an issue. If his defense is insanity, and he introduces medical evidence to demonstrate his condition, the state will even be allowed to bring in a psychiatrist who previously treated him for insanity. The rationale is that the introduction of defense evidence on mental condition opens the entire field for full exploration (*People* v. *Al Kanani*, 33 N.Y. 2d 260 [1973]).

e. Miscellaneous

Medical privilege generally applies to all matters within the hospital, such as hospital records, X rays, and nurses' notes. Interns and hospital residents are within the area of privilege if they treat the patient, even though they are employed by the hospital. Police may, for instance, overlook the fact that a resident in an emergency room who treats a drunken driver and takes a blood sample in the process may be prevented from testifying.

(8.4) Legal Privilege

The rule of confidentiality of communications between lawyer and client is of ancient origin and does not depend on statute. It is found in civil law in the codes of continental Europe. In English law its history can be traced to the time of Queen Elizabeth.

The rule originated to maintain the honor of the attorney, not to protect the client. At first the counselor was the only one who could waive it, because his honor was involved. As time went on the idea of protecting the lawyer was rejected, and the theory evolved that the privilege belongs to the client. Indeed, the lawyer is now duty bound not to reveal privileged information given by his client and can do so only if the latter consents (*People ex rel Vogelstein* v. *Warden*, 150 Misc. 714, affd. 242 A.D. 611 [N.Y. 1934]).

The privilege applies whenever legal advice is sought from a lawyer and the client makes a confidential communication to him for that purpose. Such information is permanently protected from disclosure, unless the client consents to its revelation.

a. Attorneys within the Rule

"Lawyer" here includes any attorney who is admitted to practice in any state, not necessarily the state where the crime was committed or where the communication was made. The modern trend is to allow the privilege if the client believes that the individual he consults is a licensed attorney (*Wigmore on Evidence*, Vol. 8, Sec. 2302). If the communication was made to the attorney's agent, such as his legal secretary, investigator, or clerk, it is also protected. A law student is not, however, within the protection of the rule, nor is the judge who is consulted as a judge.

b. Relationships within the Rule

The lawyer must be consulted as a lawyer, though it is not necessary that he actually be retained or later hired. "Curbstone advice" is thus not protected.

c. Confidential Communication

Any information the client gives the lawyer for consultation purposes is protected. It need not be labeled "confidential." "Communication" includes words, conversations, or letters from the client.

"Acts" or observations the attorney makes of his clients are somewhat more difficult to classify. An accused thief may pay his lawyer from a large roll of bills. Can the attorney refuse to reveal this? If insanity is an issue, can the lawyer refuse to testify concerning his observation of his client's mental condition? Usually these two questions must be answered in the negative. Facts that anyone could observe are not immune simply because the lawyer saw them (*Oliver* v. *Warren*, 16 C.A. 164 [1911]). If, for the purpose of consultation, the client gives his attorney a voice sample or exhibits a scar, this would be protected.

At times the client may ask a lawyer to do things a layman could do just as well, such as having him witness a bank deposit or listen to a conversation. In this situation there is no privilege.

Attorneys have even claimed that the name of their client was protected. This situation is demonstrated in *People ex rel Vogelstein*, mentioned above. Vogelstein, a New York attorney, appeared in magistrate's court on behalf of fifteen clients who had been arrested for running an illegal lottery. Twelve of these defendants pleaded guilty, and the trial of the other three was pending. Meanwhile, on the theory that organized crime was involved, a grand jury began an investigation. Vogelstein was subpoenaed to appear before the grand jury and was asked who retained him to defend the gamblers. Claiming the attorney-client privilege, he refused to testify. He argued that the information sought by the grand jury might incriminate his client. The judge found him in contempt and had him jailed. Vogelstein appealed. The appellate court affirmed the contempt conviction and held that he must name his client. The names of the fifteen defendants was a matter of public record, the court noted, and so it strongly suggested that there was a wholesale scheme to avoid the law. The decision added that there was no way for the court to know a privileged relationship existed if the attorney would not name his client. It was pointed out, in addition, that the privilege against self-incrimination is personal and does not extend to the attorney. Thus, even that claim did not prevent revelation of the client's name.

A more difficult area is one in which a lawyer receives information regarding physical evidence of a crime. *People* v. *Belge*, 83 N.Y. Misc. 2d 186 (1975), is an example of this situation. Robert Garrow was charged with the knife slaying of an eighteen-year-old boy. His defense was insanity. During preparation for trial, Garrow told his lawyers that he had killed two other people about a year before, and he described the location of their bodies. Though the lawyers located the bodies, they did not notify the authorities. The police did not find either body until three months later. At that time Garrow publicly confessed to the two slayings when he testified in his own behalf at his murder trial. Criminal charges were brought against the lawyers, but were later dismissed at the trial court level.

It is still the law, however, that a lawyer cannot conceal actual physical evidence of a crime that his client has given him. A lawyer was suspended from practice because he saw a sawed-off shotgun and money that came from an armed robbery and intended to conceal this information until after the trial, under a claim of attorney-client privilege. (The general rule is set forth in *People* v. *Lee*, 3 C.A. 3d 514 [1970]; the shotgun case is *In re Ryder*, 263 F. Supp. 360, affd. 38 1F. 2d 713 [1967].)

d. Exceptions

Lawyer-client communication ceases to be protected and loses its confidentiality if there is a third party present who is not in the attorney's employ, who is not a codefendant, or who is not closely associated with the defendant (*People* v. *Kor*, 129 C.A. 2d 436 [1954]). A letter from a third person delivered to the attorney is not confidential, nor is a message from the client to the attorney directing him to deliver it to someone else.

If a lawyer is a party to a crime, or if he is a participant in a conspiracy, there is no privilege. The same is true if the client communicates with the attorney about a proposed crime (*Abbott* v. *Superior Court*, 78 C.A. 2d 19 [1947]).

If the communication itself is criminal, it is, of course, not protected, as illustrated by the case of *People* v. *Farmer*, 194 N.Y. 251 (1909). Mrs. Farmer was indicted for murdering Sarah Brennan. Evidence was presented that she passed herself as Sarah Brennan and signed that name to a deed of Sarah's property. At Mrs. Farmer's murder trial the attorney who prepared the deed was called by the prosecution. He testified that Mrs. Farmer pretended to be the deceased and signed the name Sarah Brennan before him in his capacity as a notary public. The court approved of the testimony, stating that the communication itself was a criminal act on the part of Mrs. Farmer and that "the seal of personal confidence can never be used to cover a transaction which is in itself a crime."

e. Waiver

Since immunity belongs to the client, he must be the one to waive it. In a case in Minnesota (*State* v. *Madden*, 161 Minn. 132 [1924]), a prosecution witness was being cross-examined by defense counsel regarding inconsistent statements the witness had made to an attorney. Because the witness made no objection to the questions, the prosecutor did, saying that whatever the witness had told the lawyer was privileged. The court overruled the objection, stating the privilege belonged only to the witness and not to the prosecutor.

If a defendant chooses to take the stand, his act of testifying does not waive any attorney-client communication that he may have had. Should part of his testimony concern a communication with his lawyer, he has then "opened the door" on the whole subject and has, in effect, waived his privilege.

The privilege survives the death or the discharge of the attorney. Once a communication is protected, it is protected forever, unless it is waived.

(8.5) Paraprofessional Privilege

Some professional fringe areas claim the right of privileged communications. These are occasionally the subject of court decision. Newspaper reporters, as mentioned earlier, are trying to claim the privilege. A privilege of this type ordinarily exists only because a statute grants it.

a. Nurses and Other Medical Personnel

No common-law privilege exists for either of these groups. In some jurisdictions the doctor's nurse is covered under the physician's protective privilege, but the outside registered or practical nurse has no communication privilege unless it is granted by statute. A nurse is allowed to keep a patient's information confidential only when that information is necessary for her to act in her professional capacity (*In re Avery's Estate*, 76 N.Y. Supp. 2d 790 [1948]).

Medical technicians have been excluded from coverage (*Block* v. *People*, 125 Colo. 36 [1951]). Psychologists, psychotherapists, or dentists are not included unless they are specified by statute.

b. Hospital Records

Records of hospitals, both regular and mental, are generally included by statute in the area of medical privilege. The rationale is, of course, that these records contain in written form most of the communications between doctor and patient.

c. Miscellaneous

As was said previously, psychologists and psychotherapists are, from time to time, included in statutes concerning privileged communications. This may affect prosecution of juveniles in cases where the school psychologist is barred from testifying.

Accountants have tried without success to be included (*Himmelfarb* v. *U.S.*, 175 F. 2d 924, cert. den. 338 U.S. 860 [1949]).

With the increase of prosecutions concerning drugs and drug-related matters, the question of confidentiality of pharmacists' prescription records occasionally surfaces. Unless he is included by statute, the druggist cannot claim exemption from revealing his records (*Matter of Probate of Will of Annie Miner*, 206 Misc. 234 [N.Y. 1954]; *Green* v. *Superior Court*, 220 C.A. 2d 121 [1963]).

Telephone and telegraph employees, who are generally forbidden by statue from revealing customers' messages, have occasionally been required to disclose such information as trial witnesses (*Morris* v. *State*, 25 Ala. App. 156 [1932]).

Private detectives have at times been compelled by the court to reveal information regarding their clients even when a statute requires them to respect their clients' confidentiality (*People* v. *Roach*, 215 N.Y. 592 [1915]).

(8.6) Divinity Privilege

Privileged communication between priest and penitent was unknown in common law, but it is now granted by law in most states. The privilege seems, in fact, to be interpreted in the courts more strictly than any of the others.

a. Relationship of the Parties

The usual statute provides confidential protection if the clergy-man involved is a minister of any religion and if the rules of his order forbid him to disclose a confession made to him in his professional capacity.

b. Material Protected

Not every communication with a recognized clergyman is barred. An individual must be consulting him professionally, as he would a physician, and the information must have been given with the understanding that it was to be confidential (*People* v. *Johnson*, 270 C.A. 2d 204 [1969]; see also 22 A.L.R. 2d 1152 [1950]). No promise of confidentiality need be given by the minister, however, as that is understood.

Not every message from penitent to priest is covered. Statements regarding a confederate, codefendant, or other third party are not confessions of the speaker and therefore have no protection. In the same class would be a message that the priest was to give to someone else. By the same interpretation, the privilege does not protect observations the clergyman made.

c. Who Is a Clergyman?

Statutes name "clergymen or priests" and a "clergyman, minister or other person or practitioner authorized to perform similar functions." Problems arise with people who are not officially ministers, but are closely related to religious matters. In a homicide trial in New Jersey (*In re Murtha*, 115 N.J. Superior Court 380 [1971]), a nun refused to testify about a conversation she had carried on with a youth. She was convicted of contempt, and the appellate court agreed with the conviction. It was ruled that she did not perform the functions of a priest and that nothing in Catholic doctrine gave her the right to claim the privilege. Presbyterian elders have been included in the area of religious privilege because in that denomination they are "ministers." Elders of other Christian churches, however, are not included (*Reutkemeier* v. *Nolte*, 179 Iowa 342 [1917]; *Knight* v. *Lee*, 80 Ind. 201 [1881]).

d. Waiver

The divinity privilege is generally conceded to be two sided. The person who confesses has the privilege to protect his confession, and the clergyman has a separate privilege because the rules of his church forbid him to speak. Even if the person who confesses waives his right, the law will not force the clergyman to reveal the confession if it violates the rules of his order. Thus, even if the penitent is dead, absent, or does not claim his privilege, the clergyman may still refuse to testify.

(8.7) Privilege of the Police Informant

There are three kinds of police informants: the good citizen informant, the nonparticipating underworld informant, and the participating informant. Although the identity of the good citizen informant is kept confidential, his reliability must be affirmatively demonstrated in an affidavit establishing probable cause (see Chapter 5 for a more extensive discussion of this type of informant).

a. Nonparticipating Informants

Nonparticipating informants are those who learn of criminal activity and report it to the police, but also desire confidentiality. Their motives for anonymity may be based on a number of factors, such as fear of retaliation or cultural and social ostracism. Many of these informants are paid for their services, and others hope to receive "favors" from officers. The value of such information is significant. Many cases, in fact, could not be solved without it.

In criminal trials, disclosures by informants are not admissible because the accused cannot confront his accuser—a right guaranteed by the Sixth Amendment. Such disclosures are, moreover, hearsay and do not fall within one of the recognized exceptions. Such information may, however, be used to support an arrest or search warrant or in a suppression hearing that attacks the legality of an arrest or search.

In *McCray* v. *U.S.*, 386 U.S. 300 (1967), the Supreme Court held that the confidentiality of unnamed, nonparticipating informants should be preserved. To guard against perjury by the police, however, the judge at the suppression hearing retains the right to examine the informant, in chambers and outside the presence of the accused and his attorney.

b. Participating Informants

Participating informants are those who actually take part in the offense. They may, for example, have bought the capsule or bag of heroin upon which an arrest warrant is based. Because their testimony bears on the ultimate outcome of the trial, an accused may be entitled to learn the identity of these informants (*Roviaro* v. *U.S.*, 353 U.S. 53 [1957]). This exception poses a real dilemma for an investigating officer. If he intends to arrest and prosecute the accused for the crime in which the informant participated, he must be prepared to produce him at a later time. To avoid that situation, another alternative is available. The offense under investigation may be changed to one of a possessory nature. Thus, the informant might purchase narcotics from the suspect, and his information can be used to support a search warrant to look for contraband, which is a continuing and possessory offense. The eventual prosecution of the suspect could take place on the charge of possession of narcotics, which were found pursuant to a search by warrant. If, however, the officer prefers to pursue the more serious offense of sale, the informant would have to be produced in most jurisdictions. In this situation the informant is in a strategic position to exonerate or incriminate the accused, even though substantive circumstantial evidence might also exist.

When offenses are possessory, the officer can testify and respond to cross-examination respecting the existence of contraband on the premises. In determining whether the informant should be identified or produced, courts generally apply a balancing test. Where the informant was the sole participant in the transaction for which the accused is being prosecuted, his confidentiality ordinarily will not be preserved. If, however, there was sufficient evidence in addition to his confidential disclosures, his identity will not be revealed.

For example, an informant is searched and given ten dollars in marked money. The suspect's home has been under surveillance all day, and it is believed that he is alone. Several people have visited under suspicious circumstances; all of them stayed only a few moments. Many are known addicts. The informant is observed as he goes to the suspect's door and is then seen to leave. When he is searched again, the police find that the money is missing and that he has a glassine bag containing a substance that tests reveal to be heroin. To make sure that the informant's identity remains confidential, the surveillance continues until a few more visitors come and go.

In the above example, the officers would have probable cause to arrest the suspect and search his person for the marked money; or they could obtain arrest and search warrants for the suspect and his residence. If heroin was found on the premises, the informant's confidentiality could be preserved. There may even be sufficient corroborating evidence to support a conviction for sale, which evidence would also help contravene any claims that the informant was mistaken in his identity or the events that took place. Should the court rule, however, that the suspect could not get a fair trial without disclosure of the informant's identity or his production as a witness, the charge of sale would have to be dismissed, and the officers would have to be content with the remaining charge of possession.

(8.8) Official Privilege

Matters of state, which, by their very nature, are confidential, are subject to a claim of privilege. When a general is asked questions about a missile, or when a Secret Service agent is asked about precautions taken to protect the President, both may claim executive privilege. If, however, the agent is asked what steps the Secret Service is taking to locate another fugitive or a missing witness, the answer is protected by investigatory privilege. Often the same information will be sought, not in a courtroom, but through interrogatories, by depositions, or by subpoenas duces tecum. The same principles of privilege will often prevent discovery (see Chapter 9).

Several of the Watergate defendants attempted to call former President Richard Nixon as a defense witness. He resisted their subpoenas to testify on the grounds of executive privilege. The Supreme Court stressed, with respect to the presidential tapes, that a court must accord a high degree of deference to such evidence. A judge must balance this solemn responsibility, however, against the needs of criminal defendants (*U.S.* v. *Nixon*, 418 U.S. 683 [1974]; *U.S.* v. *Mitchell*, 397 F. Supp. 186 [D.D.C. 1975]).

It appears, therefore, that there are varying degrees of official privilege, as is the need to know. At the highest level are military secrets, disclosure of which could seriously compromise national security. Of lesser importance is information, which, if disclosed, would reveal negligence of particular officials. Executive privilege is less clearly defined and is not as absolute as military and state secrets. A court might properly refuse to call the President or even the secretary of defense or state, but demand answers from lesser officials. The privilege is not absolute and is based on such factors as the status of the witness, the subject matter of the inquiry, the potential harm to be suffered by the government and the People, and the necessity of the information sought.

It is clear that the courts will not permit the calling of high officials simply to dramatize a cause or to add sensationalism to a trial. Even when considerations of due process mandate the questioning of a high official, it is appropriate to order the taking of a deposition—at the White House, State Department, or Pentagon—to avoid inconvenience to the official and overdramatization of the event.

(8.9) Privilege of the News Media

In the absence of a statute or court rule, a news reporter cannot refuse to disclose the sources of his information. The preservation of confidential sources is, however, in many cases, beneficial to the public, as in the case of police informants. There are also a number of reasons why news sources should remain confidential. First, the information learned serves the public interest. Second, informants would be reluctant to disclose information to reporters if their identities were later made public. Third, informants would be subject to harassment, embarrassment, or, in some cases, physical harm.

California has, therefore, passed a law that protects a journalist from a citation for contempt if he refuses to identify his sources in open court or before a grand jury (California Evidence Code, Sec. 1070). The privilege is limited in that it does not assist a reporter in a civil suit for libel. In a recent case in that state a newsman was put in the county jail for contempt of court because he had refused to obey an order of a state court trial judge to divulge the source of certain information. He sought a writ of habeas corpus from the federal courts; it was denied, and he appealed. A U.S. court of appeals found that the state's interest in protecting the right of due process of the accused outweighed the interest of the newsman in protecting his sources of information. A balancing test was applied. The results showed that the needs of the accused were "more important and compelling," and, in any event, the incarceration did not violate any federally protected constitutional right. Thus, the writ was properly denied (*Farr* v. *Pitchess*, 522 F. 2d 464 [9th Cir., 1975]).

(8.10) Summary

Communications between certain people are legally privileged and cannot be used in court without consent.

Communications between husband and wife are protected by many state statutes. Oral and written communications, as well as one spouse's observations of the other, may be covered. Offenses by one spouse against the other spouse or against a family member are not protected.

Doctor-patient communications, when concerned with treatment, are privileged by statute in various states. Hospital and medical records usually are included.

Confidential communications between a client and his attorney are protected from forced revelation in court. The privilege applies whenever the client seeks his lawyer's legal advice, but ordinary observations by the lawyer, or actual evidence connected with a crime, are not protected.

A communication by an individual to a clergyman is generally protected by statute if the rules of the minister's church forbid its disclosure.

Some miscellaneous privileges are granted by statute to reporters, nurses, and other paraprofessionals. Any of these privileges can be waived, however, and the testimony can be allowed by consent.

Police informants are entitled to maintain their anonymity, and officers can resist demands to identify them on the grounds of privilege. If the informant has contributed information bearing on the identity of the accused or on his guilt or innocence, it may be in the interests of justice to refuse the claim of privilege. Where, however, the informant has merely furnished information constituting probable cause to conduct a search, and the guilt of the accused can be shown by direct testimony, the privilege is respected by the courts.

The government has a privilege not to disclose confidential matters of state, particularly military secrets. This privilege also applies to continuing investigations of a criminal nature.

Statutes written for the express purpose of protecting news sources may grant a journalist limited privilege.

9

Questions, Answers, Impeachment, and Cross-Examination of Witnesses

A. EXAMINATION OF WITNESSES

(9.1) In General

Witnesses testify first by being questioned by the attorney who called them and then by being cross-examined by opposing counsel. This is often followed by a further brief redirect examination by the first attorney and then a recross-examination by the second.

This order is sometimes varied by allowing opposing counsel a preliminary cross-examination on some evidentiary point before the direct questioning is completed. There are rare occasions when a witness, hostile to both parties, is needed. Under these peculiar and infrequent circumstances, the court may call such a witness, who is subject to cross-examination by both lawyers.

Testimony is thus produced by questions asked by attorneys and answers produced by witnesses. Sometimes, in the interest of justice or for the sake of clarity, the court may intervene and question the witness. This is quite proper as long as the judge does not indicate his own opinion, does not take the examination out of counsel's hands, and does not himself ask improper questions over the objections of counsel. A juror may wish to question a witness, but the courts are divided on its propriety. The danger is that an improper question may be asked. Trial courts that permit the practice are most cautious in its use.

All testimony is ordinarily given under oath. Rules on the method of administering the oath are not uniform, but, where a witness has scruples against taking the oath because of its religious connotations, he will normally be allowed to "affirm" to tell the truth without using a Bible. Some courts allow children or incompetents to testify without taking an oath because they do not understand its meaning.

In an administrative disciplinary hearing, the witnesses involved were two inmates of a mental hospital who had IQ's of 43 and 50. A psychologist testified that both knew the difference between the truth and lying. The hearing examiner determined that an oath would be meaningless to them and let them testify unsworn. The appellate court approved of their testifying without an oath, saying that a proper foundation had been laid for it (*Brown* v. *Ristich*, 36 N.Y. 2d 183 [1974]).

A subpoenaed witness receives a small fee allowed by law. Expert witnesses, such as engineers, doctors, and the like are normally paid for their services by the party calling them. It is against public policy for any other witness to be reimbursed in any way.

(9.2) Attendance

Some witnesses appear voluntarily. This would be the usual case with police officers. Others are summoned by subpoena, which is, in effect, a court order issued by the judge, court clerk, or attorney, directing the witness to appear in court at a specified time and place. A subpoena in a state court has no legal effect outside the court's jurisdiction, which usually means within the state. There is a uniform act that provides a way of subpoenaing in criminal cases material witnesses from another state. Federal court subpoenas are not barred by state boundaries. Material witnesses in criminal matters can, in some circumstances, be confined by court order pending trial, thus assuring their appearance when needed.

One can attempt to obtain relief against an improper subpoena by a motion to quash, and this motion will sometimes be granted. Anyone who has material evidence can, however, be compelled to testify, regardless of the inconvenience to the person subpoenaed.

a. Subpoena Duces Tecum

A subpoena duces tecum requires that an individual produce such evidence as documents, books, and so forth. The person who is so subpoenaed must comply by presenting the material in court or sending an employee or other representative who can identify the material. Privileged matter such as doctor-patient records or attorney-client communications cannot, however, be obtained in this way. The protection of privileged material is thus maintained.

A public official cannot be forced to bring a document into court when counsel or the court can easily obtain an official copy.

A problem often arises when incriminating documents are subpoenaed. A defendant cannot be forced to produce incriminating evidence in his possession since this would clearly violate his protection against self-incrimination.

But how about a *witness* who is subpoenaed to bring in incriminating material? A case in point is the following. A grand jury was investigating a criminal charge, and a witness, Ballmann, was subpoenaed to bring in his cashbook, wherein his name apparently was listed with some money transactions. He refused to honor the subpoena, claiming that he could be incriminated in a "bucket shop" gambling charge. The lower court held him in contempt. The U.S. Supreme Court reversed the decision, stating that Ballmann was constitutionally protected and could not be made to produce incriminating evidence by means of a subpoena duces tecum even though it was necessary for the grand jury's investigation (*Ballmann* v. *Fagin*, 200 U.S. 186 [1905]).

The situation differs if the incriminating material is in the hands of a third party who is not involved in any possible criminal activity. In the case of *Couch* v. *U.S.*, 409 U.S. 322 (1973), the Internal Revenue Service subpoenaed the taxpayer's income tax records that he had given to an accountant. When the accountant was subpoenaed, he gave the records to the taxpayer's attorney. A possible crime in relation to income tax was involved. Thus, the claim of possible self-incrimination was made. A federal court found that the accountant was not the taxpayer's employee, refused to honor the last-minute transfer of the records to the attorney, and ruled that the claim of self-incrimination was personal to the accused and held that the accountant could not, therefore, raise it.

Once a subpoena duces tecum is issued, the witness may resort to one of two tactics. He can ask for a protection order, or he can move in court to have the subpoena quashed. The court must then decide if there is any valid reason why the evidence should not be produced. This was the point in question concerning the Nixon tapes, and the courts decided against the President. He made no move to claim the constitutional protection against self-incrimination, and thus his resignation followed.

b. Duty to Testify

It is every person's duty to respond to either kind of subpoena, no matter how inconvenient that might be. Once the subpoena is served, and the witness receives the fee prescribed by law, it is his legal duty to testify. One can only escape by getting court relief in the manner described above. Failure to testify is contempt of court and can result in a fine or imprisonment in some cases. Even the advice of counsel is no excuse for failing to answer the subpoena.

(9.3) Competency of Witnesses

Not every person is legally competent to testify. Age, mental capacity, or other factors may be reasons for disqualification.

a. Children

The trial judge usually makes the decision as to whether children can testify. Some states have statutes that stipulate at what age a child must testify under oath, with younger ones being allowed to testify unsworn if they do not understand the meaning of the oath. If a possible child witness does not understand an oath, it is legal to instruct him about this before he enters the courtroom or in the court itself.

No general rule defines a particular age at which a child is legally capable of testifying. A four-year-old child has, for example, been allowed to testify in a murder case (*Jackson* v. *State*, 239 Ala. 38 [1940]).

In addition to the usual problems that may be involved in using a child as a witness, there is a particular one when a child is connected with a sex crime. Appellate courts are, for some reason, skeptical of the testimony of children concerning sex offenses and will often require corroborating testimony before sustaining a charge of rape or perversion. Because such offenses invariably occur in private, the criminal investigator has real difficulty in obtaining corroboration of the child victim's story. For this reason, many child molesters go unpunished. It is ironic, however, that practicing attorneys, police, and experienced court personnel will believe a child witness rather than an adult avoiding the truth. This practical evidentiary problem in child sex cases is found in all areas where appellate courts take this negative attitude toward the testimony of children involved in sex crimes.

b. Mental Incapacity

Often the only witness may be ignorant, illiterate, mentally retarded, or insane. Such a witness is not barred absolutely from testifying. If he understands an oath and can present a reasonable account, the court will normally allow him to testify. As has been discussed, this has even occurred when the mental ability of the witness was so low that he could not understand the oath. Unless there is a statutory bar against it, even a lunatic may be allowed to testify if he can give an account of events.

A seventeen-year-old boy was found shot to death in the basement of an ice cream parlor. The store manager confessed that he and Krombholz killed the boy because he had been stealing from the till, and the owner of the store told them to do so. Krombholz was a witness for the prosecution. Both defendants were convicted of murder, and the store manager was sentenced to death. After the trial, a mental examination revealed that Krombholz had a long history of mental illness, and he was committed to a hospital for the insane. The court pointed out that even though the witness was mentally ill, that condition did not "per se disqualify him from testifying. He may give evidence provided only that he has sufficient intelligence to understand . . . an oath and give a reasonable accurate account of the subject." A new trial was ordered, however, because his mental condition was not revealed to the judge and jury at the first trial (*People* v. *Rensing*, 14 N.Y. 2d 210 [1964]).

A trial in 1845 illustrates the lengths to which courts can go to allow the handicapped to testify. The defendant was convicted of a rape committed upon the person of Mary Marshall. She was then an inmate of the county poorhouse, "about thirty years of age and of imbecile understanding. One witness considered her an idiot." The act occurred in a woods near the highway. Triskett, the poorhouse keeper, found her shortly after the crime. He testified that, although Mary could not talk, "she communicates her ideas by signs" and that he had no difficulty communicating with her. Triskett stated that "her face was bloody and her clothes soiled." When he asked her what had happened, she told him by signs "that she had been violated." The court, in reviewing the trial, found that it was improper for Triskett to have testified for her and said that there was no reason why Mary herself should not have testified "to give evidence through the medium of this witness as an interpreter by signs" (*People* v. *McGee*, 1 Denio 19 [N.Y. 1845]).

The trend today is to let incapacitated witnesses testify for whatever their testimony may be worth. Even a witness who is under the influence of drugs or alcohol is not incompetent to testify. Whether he testifies is determined by the court. The jury's function is to weigh such testimony.

c. Convicts

In early English common law a person convicted of a serious crime was thereafter completely barred from being a witness. The theory was that such a person was so depraved as to be unworthy of belief. The modern rule is different. Under it, a criminal conviction does not make a witness incompetent to testify. It is up to the jury to judge his truthfulness and accuracy, taking this factor into consideration along with all others. A few areas, however, retain the rule barring testimony by convicts, and some jurisdictions forbid testimony by individuals convicted of specific crimes, such as perjury.

d. Relationships

The relationship of the witness to the individual involved in a crime does not bar his testimony. An exception to this rule is the marital privilege, by which one spouse can prevent the other from testifying in court against him. A blood relative, close associate, or friend may be a witness. The owner of the stolen goods that are involved in the case may testify in a larceny prosecution. A witness who will receive a reward should a defendant be convicted is even allowed to testify. None of these relationships to the crime or the suspect disqualify the witness. It is his believability, not the legality of what he says, that is important.

e. Unsworn Testimony

As has been mentioned, children or witnesses unable to understand an oath may be allowed in some cases to testify without being
sworn. The proposed witness may occasionally be an atheist and
therefore object to taking an oath. In addition, some religious sects
reject the idea of oaths. The court allows these individuals to "affirm
to tell the truth" without using a Bible.

f. Miscellaneous

A particular set of circumstances can disqualify a witness or nullify his testimony. An example follows.

Chicago police entered Albea's apartment and found a girl, Lee
Vaughn, buying heroin from him. The subsequent search, and seizure
of the drugs, was declared illegal by the court. At Albea's trial, the
prosecution had the girl testify only in regard to the events in the
apartment before the entry of the police. She stated that she was an
addict and had gone to Albea's apartment because she wanted "ten
things" (heroin capsules). She paid Albea $12.50, and as he handed
her three capsules there was a knock on the door accompanied by a
voice that said "Western Union." At that point, Albea swallowed the
other seven capsules. Though he was convicted of selling drugs, his
conviction was overturned. The court ruled that the discovery of the
girl witness was the product of an illegal search and that she was incompetent to testify to anything, even events preceding the entry
(*People* v. *Albea*, 2 Ill. 2d 317 [1954]).

A second unusual situation excluding a witness, which is popularly known as the "dead man's statute," exists in many states. These
statutes bar a witness who is interested in the outcome from testifying against the estate of a deceased person concerning a personal
transaction the witness had with the deceased. The reasoning behind
these statutes is simple. Because the dead man cannot deny the
transaction, an interested party should not be allowed to give testimony in regard to it. This situation frequently disqualifies a witness
in civil suits, though it is highly unlikely that the rule could ever be
involved in a criminal trial.

(9.4) Adversary System versus Inquisitorial System

In this country the adversary criminal trial system is used. This system calls for evidence to be produced by two opposing sides, with all witnesses subject to cross-questioning by opposing counsel. The inquisitorial system, which is used in other parts of the world, is quite different. There, the prosecution proves its case by asking questions of the accused, as well as by producing any other witnesses it can find. The defendant is thus forced to defend himself in court by answering the state's questions. The adversary system completely rejects this idea. Here, we have gone so far in the other direction that we protect the accused from having to testify at all.

(9.5) Form of Questions and Duty to Object

All testimony is given in the form of questions and answers. The witness is not allowed to testify in a block by giving a general narrative of events. He presents his story piecemeal in answer to questions. In terms of brevity and clarity this is a handicap, but it is necessary so that no evidence will come out unless it is valid.

Questions should seek testimony based on the facts known by the witness. The answers sought should be factual, not based on the witness' "understanding" of what happened. Questions should be clear. A compound question containing more than one part is improper. A question may not be so general as to include illegal evidence, and it must not be misleading, ambiguous, or indefinite. Any question that does not fit this description is legally objectionable.

In the adversary system, opposing counsel has the opportunity to make legal objection to the question being asked or to the answer being sought. This method thus prevents the introduction of improper evidence. If, however, opposing counsel does not object, any evidence may be used, even though it may be completely irrelevant or invalid.

(9.6) Leading Questions

This type of question suggests the answer, often leaving the witness simply to reply "Yes" or "No." In theory at least, lawyers are not supposed to put answers in the mouths of their own witnesses. Though leading questions will be allowed in preliminary testimony, opposing counsel may properly object to them when the material part of the testimony is reached.

Counsel may ask such preliminary leading questions as "You are Mary Jones?" "You live at 51 Main Street?" "You were home at 10:00 p.m.?" The objection to counsel's asking a leading question would arise if he then queried: "Did the defendant break down your kitchen door and attack you?" Proper questioning would proceed along the following lines. Counsel would call the witness' attention to the critical time and place. He might then ask: "What happened first?" "Then what happened?" "What finally happened?"

Cross-examination introduces an entirely different situation. Counsel is here seeking to test an adversary witness for truth and accuracy. Leading questions are quite proper, and the witness may be led in any direction and to any degree. As a matter of fact, should counsel's own witness prove hostile, he is allowed to ask him leading questions. Counsel can also ask his own witness leading questions when he is in the realm of delicate matters in sex cases, when he is dealing with an immature or incapacitated witness, or when he is attempting to refresh the witness' memory. Leading questions are also generally permissible when counsel is asking about matters that have already been testified to.

(9.7) Assumption of Facts

A question may not assume facts that have not been introduced in evidence. The reason for this is readily apparent. If unproven assumptions are used in questions, both the witness and the jury may be misled. This tactic may, however, be allowed at the court's discretion. Thus, neither on direct examination nor on cross-examination may the questioner misstate the facts or assume something in his question that is not a part of the evidence. Opposing counsel can object to any such question.

(9.8) Argumentative Questions

Lawyers are supposed to question witnesses, not argue with them, although that frequently happens. More leeway is allowed in this area in cross-examination than in direct examination, but it is technically incorrect in both types of examination. Where the question really amounts to arguing with the witness, it is properly objectionable.

(9.9) Asking for Conclusions or Opinions

With a few exceptions, the witness is supposed to confine his testimony to facts, to things that he has personally observed. He is not supposed to give his opinion or conclusion about the case. If this were not so, a trial could be decided by a parade of witnesses on both sides saying what they thought about the defendant's guilt or innocence.

There are, however, several areas involving matters of common observation where lay witnesses are allowed to make estimates or to state an opinion.

In a robbery trial, the defendant claimed that there was no forceful taking of money, but that he had swindled the complainant. His counsel called a defense witness who testified that the complainant told her: "Your friend [the defendant] beat me." The witness then offered to explain that in street talk the term "beat" meant to steal or to defraud rather than physical assault. The trial court refused to accept the explanation, saying it was opinion. The reviewing court disagreed, reversed the conviction, and held that a lay witness can give his opinion as to the meaning of a statement when the words have a doubtful or ambiguous meaning (*People* v. *Irvine*, 40 A.D. 2d 560 [N. Y. 1972]).

Often it is not readily apparent that a question is really calling for a conclusion. For example, an assault victim may be asked: "Did the defendant threaten you?" The question can be properly objected to as calling for a conclusion. To avoid the objection the examiner should draw the witness' attention to the relevant time and place and then ask a series of questions. "What did the defendant do?" "Then what did he do next?" "What did he finally do?" In this way he gets a detailed description of all the actions.

The jury—not the witness—draws a conclusion as to what actually happened. They must decide if the actions of the accused amounted to a threat. When opinion evidence is allowed in any case, either from laymen or experts, the jury is not bound by it. They may reject it or accept it as they wish.

Experts are, of course, allowed to state their opinions. As a matter of fact, the purpose of calling an expert is to get his professional or scientific judgment on a matter outside the realm of common experience. Physicians, engineers, and laboratory technicians are common examples of expert witnesses.

(9.10) Improper Foundation

In a courtroom one may hear an objection to a question on the basis of "improper foundation," and the objection is often sustained, much to the surprise of the uninformed. What usually happens is that a question is asked prematurely or facts are included that have not yet been proven. For example, a question may be asked regarding an exhibit, such as a confession or a photograph, before the exhibit has been admitted in evidence; thus the question lacks a proper foundation. In order to make the question proper, counsel must have the exhibit introduced in evidence or bring out the needed basic facts before he asks it again.

In fact, the physical exhibit itself cannot be introduced without "laying a proper foundation," that is, without proving its relevance, authenticity, and sameness of condition.

(9.11) Parol Evidence Rule

"Parol" is a short way of saying "word of mouth." The parol evidence rule is one saying that, with few exceptions, a written document is what it says it is. For example, ambiguities in documents, such as technical or trade terms, may be explained by verbal evidence. The law will not normally allow oral proof to take precedence over written proof, however, for the spoken word vanishes with the wind, while the written word remains.

Because this rule has little application in criminal trials, it need not be discussed in detail here. It is mentioned only because of its general application in all court proceedings.

(9.12) Self-Serving Declarations

The counsel for the defense is not allowed to introduce in evidence his client's statements demonstrating his innocence. The defendant could write letters in which he declares his innocence to his congressman, the governor, the President, and the newspapers and publicly proclaim his innocence on television. But none of these things has evidentiary value.

Only if a person admits something against his interest can any validity be attached to it. People usually do not make derogatory statements about themselves unless they are true. For this reason, a voluntary confession of a crime is considered the strongest type of evidence against an accused. On the other hand, personal protestations of innocence are regarded simply as manifestations of self-preservation, and so are not admissible as evidence in one's own defense.

Some textbook writers and judges have criticized this blanket ban against the use of self-serving statements as being too broad. It is possible, therefore, to find court rulings in which a defendant has been allowed to show that he made statements indicating lack of motive or interest, demonstrating goodwill toward the victim, or proving that there was a plan not to perform an act (*Wigmore on Evidence*, Sec. 1732; *U.S.* v. *Dellinger*, C.A. [1972], 12 Cr L 2196).

(9.13) Facts Not in Issue

Except for introductory questions to show the background of a witness, all questioning should be material to the issue at hand. If it does not relate to a fact at issue, it is subject to the objection of being immaterial. The trial judge usually determines whether the facts are indeed material.

A line of questioning that seems irrelevant will sometimes be allowed "subject to being connected up." Should the later testimony actually tie the earlier testimony to the case, the latter will be allowed to stand. If not, the court will order the prior testimony stricken from the record and will instruct the jury to disregard it.

As has been said, there is no set of rules to define what is material for the facts at issue. It is actually a matter of common sense, and so the same standards do apply in judging whether a question involves a fact at issue in any particular case.

B. ANSWERS OF WITNESSES

(9.14) In General

A witness' answers should be exactly that—answers. If he digresses, he runs the risk of introducing illegal evidence that could result in a mistrial. He may, however, feel that he should say something that is not a direct answer to the query. In this case, the proper procedure is for the witness to ask the court if he may say something or to ask to step down and confer briefly with counsel before answering.

(9.15) Unresponsive or Improper Answers

The question may be perfectly legal, but the answer may not be. An objection can, therefore, be made to the latter. The witness may, for example, argue, give an unsolicited opinion, or volunteer added information. Opposing counsel can object even after such an answer is given and ask that it be stricken from the record. The court will then order the answer to be expunged and instruct the jury to ignore it.

An example of an improper answer occurred in a larceny trial where the witness committing the legal sin was, of all things, an attorney-accountant appearing on the stand for the prosecution. It was claimed that the accused had defrauded Mrs. Bates of her stock and its proceeds. The above-mentioned witness was asked: "Did you examine the books . . . with reference to Wanita B. Bates' account?" To this the witness replied: "That was one of the various larcenies discovered." The defense attorney promptly called for a mistrial, but the trial judge denied the motion. The appellate court, however, held that the answer was unresponsive and highly prejudicial and therefore ordered a new trial (*People* v. *Robinson*, 273 N.Y. 438 [1937]).

Answers of this kind are as improper as questions of the same type and are always subject to being stricken from the record.

(9.16) Revival of Memory

Witnesses forget, just as the rest of us do. This is especially true in criminal matters where the normal procedure delays considerably the time of the trial from the original date of the crime. The most effective way of solving this problem is for the attorneys to ask leading questions. For example, a witness who cannot recall a date might be asked: "Wasn't it in the winter?" "Do you remember telling me that it was shortly before the end of the school vacation?" Though these questions are leading, they are an acceptable way of refreshing a witness' memory. Another way of jogging a person's memory is to refer to prior statements, testimony, or written memorandums.

(9.17) Past Recollections Recorded

There are times when leading questions, statements, or memorandums do not revive a lost memory. In that case there may still be a valid evidentiary method to produce the needed evidence. If the witness has a written record of the facts that he made shortly after the event, that record may be introduced in evidence as a "past recollection recorded." The witness is shown his own written memorandum, and if, after reading it, he still has no independent recollection of the event, the memorandum may be used as evidence. Though this may sound implausible, it does sometimes happen.

(9.18) Witness' Use of Memorandum or Record

Doctors, businessmen, police officers, and many others in this xerographic age keep a wide variety of written records and memorandums. We are not concerned at this point with how such records can be used against a witness, but with the way the individual who is testifying can use his written records to strengthen his testimony.

He cannot, of course, offer his prior written record to support what he is now saying. As we have seen, this would be self-serving testimony. Neither can he present a diary entry or police reports that say: "Here is what happened. It's all in my record." It is not possible for opposing counsel to cross-examine a piece of paper.

A witness can legitimately use his memorandums to refresh

his memory. Doctors, laboratory technicians, and other expert witnesses could not be expected to recall independently detailed information in individual cases. Such witnesses repeatedly jog their memories by looking at their notes. They are not ordinarily allowed to read directly from these memorandums, but use them only as an aid to memory. It is even more common for the witness to review his memorandums, statements, and records outside the courtroom just before testifying. This is, as a matter of fact, a legitimate and proper way to prepare for giving testimony.

(9.19) Inspection

When a witness uses a written record to aid his testimony, opposing counsel is entitled to inspect that record. The modern trend is to carry this rule further. Even when the witness testifies without using his earlier written records, his counsel is expected to make them available to opposing counsel. The following is typical of this rule.

Rosario and two others were involved in a robbery-murder of a restaurant proprietor. At Rosario's murder trial, one witness testified that Rosario, with his gun in hand, ordered him "into the lavatory." Another witness stated that she was later given the gun. A third witness told how Rosario admitted "shooting" and said, "We all had guns and shot together." As each witness finished his direct testimony, the defense counsel demanded copies of the statements each had given to the prosecutors prior to the trial so that he could use them in cross-examination. The trial judge allowed defense counsel to use only that part of the witnesses' statements that varied from their direct testimony. The appellate court reversed the judge's decision, asserting that defense counsel should be given copies of the complete pretrial statements of any witness even though they were not used as such in the trial (*People* v. *Rosario*, 9 N.Y. 2d 286 [1961]).

Police officers or private investigators should be particularly careful about written reports. A faulty one can lose a case. The example of Officer Dwyer is a case in point. This officer monitored telephone taps during an investigation of ticket scalping. He made shorthand notes of the messages, transcribed them into longhand, and then dictated the material to a court clerk who put it all into a criminal complaint.

Officer Dwyer had previously appeared in court and had been subjected to a long, detailed cross-examination concerning his notes. Because of that, he deliberately destroyed all of his original records in the case of ticket scalping. At the trial, Dwyer stated that he had no memory of these calls and admitted destroying his original notes, but said he could testify by using the complaint he had dictated to the clerk. The appellate courts ruled against this, holding that, where the destruction of records was deliberate, the witness could not use any other record as an aid to his memory. Thus, the case was lost (*People* v. *Betts*, 272 A.D. 737, affd. 297 N.Y. 1000 [1947]).

And so, any witness in modern criminal trials can expect that opposing counsel will see any personal records he uses in testifying. Further, it is likely that the court will allow inspection of any memorandum or records a witness has made prior to his actual testimony.

C. IMPEACHMENT OF WITNESSES

(9.20) Purpose

The purpose of impeaching (discrediting) an adverse witness is to weaken the case of the opposing side, and it is always proper for opposing counsel to use this tactic. He may do so by showing that the witness was inaccurate, untruthful, or unworthy of belief. The most common method of demonstrating the weakness of the witness is to cross-examine him. In some situations, counsel may even be allowed to present affirmative proof that tends to throw doubt on the witness' credibility.

(9.21) Complainants and Defendants

It is obvious that both the complainant and the accused are interested in the outcome of the trial. A complainant in a rape case or the victim of a mugging naturally wants to see the defendant convicted, and every defendant is interested in acquittal.

Because both parties are concerned with the outcome, the jury may consider this as one of the factors affecting their credibility as witnesses. It is legal for the attorneys to bring out such self-interest. This may be done by questioning the witness and by presenting legal arguments to the jury. Both methods are intended to impeach the witness. Such witnesses are also subject to the methods of impeachment discussed below.

(9.22) Competency

Evidence of the witness' lack of normal mental capacity may always be shown by way of impeachment. If a child testifies, for example, his age, his progress in school, and his intelligence as demonstrated by test scores can be scrutinized. Proof of mental retardation, senility, or insanity may also be presented in order to discredit a witness.

(9.23) Bias and Prejudice

Evidence tending to show bias or prejudice on the part of a witness is always relevant and can be introduced, even where the witness has denied it. A number of factors may indicate bias. The opposing attorney may show, for example, that the witness was an accomplice, a friend, or an enemy of either the defendant or complainant. He could also be related by blood or marriage. Any financial or business relationship is relevant. Immoral relations between the witness and one of the parties have a bearing on impeachment. The fact that a witness is a private detective hired by one party could easily bring about a charge of bias.

(9.24) Accuracy of Direct Testimony

The most common method of impeachment is to demonstrate any inaccuracies in a witness' direct testimony. A cross-examiner invariably questions the witness on the minute details of his story. He might ask what time the witness heard a shot. If his answer varies from what he stated in direct testimony, the attorney will forcefully point this out, thus discrediting the witness. It is safe to say, however, that no witness remembers the past exactly, and all observers see things in different ways. But, regardless of the problems involved, bringing out inaccuracies and misstatements is a fair way to attempt to discredit a witness. Juries are affected by the tactic, which is, after all, the reason why trial lawyers use it.

(9.25) Conviction of a Crime

It has been the general rule that a witness could be impeached by asking him about any criminal act of his past life. He could be cross-examined concerning the details of such criminal activity as rape, robbery, or burglary as well as the fact of his conviction for that offense. The universal limit on such questioning for purposes of impeachment is that counsel must have a fair basis for doing so. Every witness automatically presents himself as being worthy of belief. This is the justification for the general rule that any immoral or vicious act in his past life should be allowed to be shown as affecting his credibility.

In some states the field of impeachment is narrowed considerably. California law, for example, restricts cross-examination to the details of offenses that were mentioned on direct testimony (*People* v. *Morgan,* 87 C.A. 2d 674 [1948]). A few states limit impeachment questioning to felony convictions and will not allow inquiries into juvenile adjudications or misdemeanors. All courts bar questions regarding arrests or indictments since they do not involve convictions.

If a defendant takes the stand in his own behalf, he is subject to cross-examination just as any other witness. He can usually be asked about prior criminal convictions within the limitations established by the state in which he is being tried. Should he deny the past conviction, the prosecutor may offer a certificate of that conviction as impeachment evidence.

The attitude of the court toward the use of criminal records as impeachment testimony is currently undergoing change. The new Federal Rules of Evidence (Rule 609, effective July 1, 1975) restrict the use of criminal records to impeach any witness, including a defendant. Barred are the use of convictions over ten years old, juvenile adjudications, misdemeanors, and felony convictions that have been pardoned or granted certificates of rehabilitation. Even felony convictions that are not barred can be excluded as impeachment evidence against the defendant under the federal code. This occurs if the court feels that damage to the accused is greater than the value it might have for the case.

Various court decisions have approved of a procedure whereby defense counsel asks for a ruling in advance of the trial as to which prior criminal conviction can be introduced in evidence. The judge weighs the theoretical prejudice against the defendant the and "probative value" of such evidence and decides which record of convictions, if any, can be used. On the basis of this decision, the defendant with a criminal record can determine in advance of the trial whether or not he wants to take the stand (*Luck* v. *U.S.*, 348 F. 2d 763 [1965]; *People* v. *Beagle*, 6 Cal. 3d 441 [1972]; *People* v. *Sandoval*, 34 N.Y. 2d 371 [1974]).

In all likelihood this trend toward eliminating criminal records for the purpose of impeachment will continue. It is imperative, therefore, that anyone involved in law enforcement keep informed of statutes and current judicial decisions in this field.

(9.26) Drug Use

With the widespread use of drugs, all the way from tranquilizers to heroin, there is an increasing problem with witnesses. Evidence of drug addiction usually impeaches a witness. Some older decisions refuse to allow this evidence to discredit a witness, but the current majority rule is that it may do so. There is, in fact, general agreement that the effect of drugs on a participant at the time of trial can and should be shown, even though it may not be done for the purpose of impeachment.

Gary Pray was tried in Vermont for the murder of his brother-in-law. His defense was insanity. At a pretrial hearing, the defendant turned over a table and tried to attack a psychiatrist who was testifying. The state therefore put him on medication, which made him appear quiet, well oriented, and cooperative throughout the trial. Because the jury was never told that Pray was sedated, they found him guilty. The decision was appealed, and the appellate court held that the state had a duty to reveal the defendant's true condition. It stated: "The jury never looked upon an unaltered, undrugged Gary Pray . . . yet . . . his deportment . . . was a part of the basis of their judgment . . . of his defense of insanity . . . . In fact, it may have been necessary to expose the jury to the undrugged, unsedated Gary Pray in so far . . . as safety might permit." Pray's conviction and life sentence were, therefore, overturned (*State* v. *Pray*, 342 A. 2d 227 [Vt. Sup. Ct., 1975]).

While drug addiction itself may be used to impeach a witness, there are limits to which one can use this type of evidence. A defendant was convicted of selling heroin, largely on the basis of testimony by Giles, who witnessed the sale. Giles was a mainliner with a five-year habit, but he was not under the influence of drugs at the time he testified. In order to impeach the witness, the defense called a doctor to testify on the veracity of addicts. The doctor was asked whether, in his opinion, "a person addicted to [drugs] . . . as a mainliner . . . can testify in a normal manner." The counsel for the prosecution objected to the question. The defense then asked the doctor if, in his opinion, Giles was telling the truth. There was a further objection. The court sustained the exclusion of this evidence. It felt that, while the fact of addiction itself was pertinent, Giles's credibility was entirely up to the jury and that the court would not accept expert testimony that addicts are unworthy of belief (*People v. Williams*, 6 N.Y. 2d 18, cert. den. 361 U.S. 920 [1959]).

(9.27) Immoral Acts

A witness may be cross-examined about any immoral acts in his past, as long as the examiner has a fair basis for asking about them. This is based on the assumption that honesty is associated with morality and good character. Thus, inquiry concerning behavior that demonstrates lack of morality and good character is allowed by way of impeachment.

This presents a real problem in the prosecution of a rape case. The victim must, of course, testify regarding the circumstances of the rape. Defense counsel, in the guise of impeaching her credibility, may cross-examine her regarding her complete moral history, in both major and minor aspects. Even though the victim's answers give no indication of immorality, counsel suggests past indiscretions simply by asking the questions. He is not actually trying to impeach her credibility, but is suggesting that she consented to intercourse. In response to public pressure, some states are enacting laws that limit such cross-examination of complainants in rape cases. Many people have come to feel that this type of question has produced unfair results. These new statutes, therefore, forbid cross-examining the rape victim about her past moral history.

(9.28) Character and Reputation

There is a major exception to the rule barring self-serving evidence. In criminal cases the defendant may offer evidence demonstrating good character. This is usually in the form of testimony by third parties concerning the defendant's reputation in the community. If the defense offers evidence of good character, then the prosecution, in rebuttal, can show impeaching evidence by giving similar proof of poor character.

Also, when any witness, including the defendant, has taken the stand, the adversary party may offer evidence of poor reputation for truth and veracity by way of impeachment. This is done by asking the witness who knows of the reputation if he would believe the prior witness when he is under oath. The other side may then introduce rebuttal evidence to the contrary.

(9.29) Prior Inconsistent Statements

A prior inconsistent statement can always be used to discredit a witness. The examiner must always lay a foundation for using this tactic. First he calls the witness' attention to his prior testimony or statement. Once the witness admits that he made it, or outside proof is submitted showing that he did so, the witness may be queried about the discrepancies. Any variations may then be introduced in evidence.

A witness in a criminal trial can expect that his prior testimony before a grand jury or at a preliminary hearing, as well as any of his earlier written statements, will be used against him in this fashion.

(9.30) Use of Collateral Matters in Impeachment

Questions used in cross-examination by way of impeachment inquiring into past improper acts of a witness are, of course, concerned with side issues that are not involved in the trial before the court. The scope of these impeachment factors must be limited. If it were not, a trial could degenerate into a series of trials within a trial in which opposing counsel would attempt to prove or disprove the alleged indiscretions of the witness. For this reason, a universal rule has been adopted. Except for past criminal convictions, if the witness on cross-examination denies the existence of any alleged disgraceful or vicious act on his part, that ends the matter, and the questioner is bound by the answers.

A case involving stolen property is illustrative of this rule. The defendant testified in his own defense. The prosecutor, on cross-examination, asked the defendant if he had bought and passed counterfeit money at one time. The defendant denied that he had. He was then asked if he had not confessed to doing so at one time. Again he denied the accusation. Though the defendant was shown his signed confession, he continued to deny it was true. At this point the prosecutor read the entire confession to the jury. The defendant was found guilty of the present crime. A higher court set aside the conviction. It was pointed out that, though inquiry into the forgery was a collateral matter allowed by way of impeachment, "the cross-examiner . . . is bound by the answers to his questions on collateral matters" and that "inquiry as to immoral or criminal acts . . . for the purpose of impeaching his credibility is purely collateral" (*People* v. *McCormick*, 278 A.D. 410, affd. 303 N.Y. 403 [1951]).

D. CROSS-EXAMINATION OF WITNESSES

(9.31) Purpose and Character

In contrast to what is portrayed on television, in real courtrooms during cross-examination, witnesses do not break down on the stand and tearfully confess that they committed the crime. One of the general purposes of cross-examination, as has been discussed, is to point out inaccuracies, falsehoods, or collateral matters tending to weaken the believability of the witness. Another general aim of the cross-examiner is to pry out all the favorable information possible from the opposing witness. Police and prosecutors often neglect this area in preparing for trial, forgetting that the defense will attempt to elicit helpful information by cross-examining the People's witnesses.

These two aims, impeachment and the obtaining of favorable information, are the general purposes of most cross-examination.

(9.32) Right to Confront and Examine Witnesses

Cross-examination of witnesses is basic to our adversary trial system. The defendant has a constitutional right to confront the witnesses against him and to cross-examine them (*Boykin* v. *Alabama*, 395 U.S. 238 [1969]).

This presents a problem when there are two or more defendants and the prosecution has confessions he can use in evidence. The following hypothetical situation demonstrates this. In a joint trial the prosecutor uses defendant A's confession, but A does not take the stand. If the confession also implicates defendant B, he loses his chance to cross-question A concerning the incriminating material. The lawyer for B cannot, of course, cross-examine a piece of paper. Under these circumstances, B has a constitutional right to a separate trial from A, where only B's own confession can be used against him. If the prosecution wants to use A's information, it will have to get A to testify in person against B. He will then be subject to cross-examination by B's defense attorney (*Bruton* v. *U.S.*, 391 U.S. 123 [1968]).

(9.33) Scope of Cross-Examination

Every witness who testifies, including the defendant, is subject to cross-examination. Though there are limits as to what may be asked, in general the examiner may question any matter testified to on direct examination. Included within these limits are the usual questions testing credibility. Thus, a cross-examiner is not allowed to question the witness on any unrelated matter. Neither can he badger the witness nor otherwise treat him unfairly. It is up to the trial court to limit such questioning, which means that the judge largely determines the area that is to be allowed.

(9.34) Relevancy to Issues

While there is much latitude in cross-examination, it still must be relevant to the issue. The opponent must object, however, if he wants to keep the examination within bounds.

Anything concerning the accuracy or credibility of the witness is relevant. Questioning based on his direct testimony must relate to material matters recited by the witness. If the direct testimony included immaterial elements, the cross-examiner is not allowed to pursue these further. It stands to reason that facts that were irrelevant in direct testimony are just as irrelevant in cross-examination.

(9.35) Particular Subjects

Illegal evidence, such as privileged communications, cannot be inquired about in cross-examination any more than it can be done in direct questioning. Neither may counsel cross-examine the witness on matters about which he can have no knowledge. In addition, the Fifth Amendment forbids questions by which the witness could incriminate himself.

Should the defendant testify, he does so at some risk since the prosecutor may cross-examine him regarding any fact that may convict him of the crime of which he was accused. The defendant can, however, still claim his privilege against self-incrimination with respect to any other crime, and the cross-examiner will be prevented from inquiring further into such areas (see 35 L.R.A. 518; 21 Am. Jur. 2d Crim. Law, Sec. 358).

Another general area of testimony may be forbidden to the cross-examiner. It arises if he brings out new relevant facts on cross-examination that the witness had not mentioned in his direct testimony. When this occurs, the generally accepted rule is that the examiner has "made the witness his own." In effect, he has adopted this witness as if the examiner had called him. In this event, he can no longer contradict or impeach the witness. Most courts are reluctant to apply this rule rigidly, however, and so some leeway may be allowed in impeachment or contradiction of a witness that one has made his own.

(9.36) Refusal to Answer

On occasion the witness refuses to answer. Though this would normally occur during cross-examination, from time to time a hostile witness might refuse to respond on direct questioning. Before the witness can be held in contempt of court, there must be a genuine refusal to answer. Evasion is not contempt unless the court directs the witness to be more specific and he does not comply. Refusal to answer an incriminating question is not contempt. Failure to reply to a degrading question does not constitute contempt unless the answer is material. Another exception involves a prosecution witness. He can refuse to name an informant unless the court directs him to do so.

Any contempt of court that comes about because of refusal to answer can result in fine or imprisonment. As a matter of fact, in many jurisdictions the recalcitrant witness can be jailed until he does answer.

(9.37) Summary

Our adversary trial system depends on the questioning and cross-questioning of witnesses. Anyone having material information can be subpoenaed to testify and can be made to produce evidence in his possession. The criminal defendant cannot be forced to give testimony.

In direct examination, questions must be relevant, avoid general conclusions, seek facts; they must not be leading or argumentative. In cross-examination much more leeway is allowed in all these areas. Answers must be responsive and produce valid evidence. Opposing counsel must object to any improper question or answer. If he does not do so, even illegal evidence may be used.

Witnesses are not disqualified solely because of age, incompetency, past criminal history, or even insanity. If the court is satisfied that such a witness is able to give a reasonable account of events, his testimony can be taken. These conditions actually affect credibility, not admissibility, of such testimony. Even unsworn testimony is allowed under certain conditions.

A witness may, if necessary, use a personal memorandum or record to aid his memory, but ordinarily he will not be allowed to read this directly to the jury. Opposing counsel may see the record and use it in cross-examination.

Every witness is subject to possible impeachment by any legitimate means. His competency, accuracy, and truthfulness are all subject to question. The witness' interest in the outcome, his relationship to the parties involved, and his bias or prejudice may be shown as bearing on credibility. Cross-examiners commonly inquire into past criminal history, drug addiction, and immoral acts. A witness may decline to answer incriminating questions, as may a testifying defendant, except in relation to the crime for which he is presently being charged.

Any prior inconsistent statement made by the witness may be used for impeachment. The same is true if he has a poor reputation for honesty. A defendant may use evidence of good character as a defense. If, however, he introduces such evidence, the prosecution may show the opposite.

Every defendant has the constitutional right to confront the witnesses against him and to cross-examine them. Though cross-examiners generally must stay within the limits of the direct examination, they may seek out information favorable to their side and can inquire into any legitimate matter of impeachment.

10

Opinion Evidence

(10.1) In General

Witnesses on the stand frequently find their testimony blocked because they have stated an opinion rather than an actual observation. All witnesses have opinions as to what happened, but are generally not allowed to state them. They must confine themselves to facts. This brings to mind Sergeant Friday of the television program "Dragnet." When he was interviewing a witness he frequently cut off her story by saying, "Just give me the facts, Ma'am." This is still a good expression of the rule regarding opinion evidence in court.

This is not to say that a person's opinion is not relevant evidence. There are many situtations where an opinion may be received in court. On the question of one's bias or prejudice, for example, the individual's opinion could be most material, no matter how it is shown. In some cases, a type of opinion evidence is allowed where the witness cannot remember clearly or is not quite sure of a fact. When opinions are accepted, however, they are not allowed to be so broad as to invade the jury's prerogative of deciding guilt or innocence. Nevertheless, opinions from both laymen and experts are received in many situations where the courts have found this to be practical.

Because the rules concerning opinion are not ironclad, the exceptions barring this type of evidence must be learned.

(10.2) Lay Witnesses

A lay witness is any witness who has not been qualified as an "expert witness" or as a "skilled witness."

a. Common Experiences

There are actually large areas where a witness is allowed to state his opinion, mainly in matters of common experience. A layman can say whether it was light or dark and give his estimate of the size, shape, or color of an object. How far away was the defendant? How old was he? How tall? All of these are proper questions, and the opinion answers are allowed as being common observations. In addition, the witness may estimate speed or measurements without being an engineer.

One reason for allowing opinion evidence in matters of common observation such as size, distance, and time is that it is most difficult to get exact data on such matters. Illustrative of this was the evidence in a civil suit over an insurance claim (*Stout* v. *Pacific Mutual*, 130 Cal. 471 [1900]). A man fell from a boat, struck his head, and died. The insurance company questioned the accidental death claim. A witness was the man's young son, who was asked if the blows his father received to the head were light, heavy, or medium. The court allowed his opinion because it felt the testimony was a matter of common observation.

Often the answer by a witness will be part fact and part conclusion. Many times this will pass undetected, but, where an objection is raised, the court must decide on its admissibility. In this situation the court customarily rules that the answer given is the only adequate way the witness can describe an incident and will admit it as a type of "shorthand rendering of the facts."

In a case involving a charge of assault to commit rape (*State* v. *Collins*, 88 Mont. 514 [1930]), the complainant testified she was at a party when the defendant suggested they go into the bedroom. When she refused, he grabbed her by the wrist, pulled her down the hall into a darkened bedroom, and pushed her onto the bed. When she continued to protest and tried to get up, he threw his left leg across hers and "would pull my dress up." The prosecutor then asked if she knew what the defendant was trying to do, and she answered, "Yes." The defense immediately objected, saying she was being asked to give a conclusion. The objection was over-ruled, and she was allowed to answer further. She said: "He was trying to have sexual intercourse with me." The evidence was sustained on appeal. It was held that, however justified the opinion rule was, the answer was based on facts previously testified to and "was a compound of fact and conclusion—a 'shorthand rendering of the facts'—and was properly received."

b. Intoxication

Any witness may testify on the question of intoxication. An individual who has observed drunken people—a common sight in everyday life—can testify directly concerning his opinion on the person's drunkenness or sobriety. A better practice, however, is to have the witness in a case of drunken driving describe the erratic behavior of the car and then give details regarding the defendant's personal appearance, such as slurred speech, staggered walk, and odor of alcohol. Then he should be asked directly: "In your opinion, was the defendant drunk or sober?" This is allowable, even though there is no precise measurement of intoxication and other conditions, such as diabetes or medication, that can produce symptoms similar to drunkenness (*Daniels* v. *State*, 155 Tenn. 549 [1927]). In the opinion of *People* v. *Eastwood*, 14 N.Y. 563 (1856), "A child . . . may answer whether a man (whom it has seen) was drunk or sober: it does not require science or opinion to answer the question, but observation, merely."

c. Identity

Witnesses commonly are allowed to testify as to identity, naming the accused as being the one involved in the crime. Identity is a conclusion about which people often differ, but, regardless of how unreliable it is, such evidence is accepted by the court.

Many years ago in the *Tichborne* case, an English judge, Lord Cockburn, charged the jury in this way:

Frequently a man is sworn to, who has been seen only for a moment. A man stops you on the road, puts a pistol to your head and robs you of your watch and purse; a man seizes you by the throat and while you are half strangled his confederate rifles your pockets; a burglar invades your house by night and you have only a rapid glance to enable you to know his features. In all these cases, the opportunity for observing is so brief that a mistake is possible and yet the lives and safety of people would not be secure unless you acted on the recollection of features so acquired and so retained and it is done every day.

d. Mental Capacity

Because everyone observes "normal" behavior in others every day, any lay witness is allowed to describe "abnormal" behavior in an individual and to give his opinion as to that person's mental condition. He can state whether he thinks the person is sane or insane or had the mental capacity to understand what he was doing.

The layman's opinion must be based on his personal observations and not on an abstract situation. In two cases (*McKenzie* v. *U.S.*, 266 F. 2d 524 [1959] ; *Hixon* v. *State* [Fla. App.], 165 So.2d 436 [1964]) laymen testified on the question of sanity, and the appellate court explained the rules saying that a nonexpert in a criminal case "may be permitted to give an opinion regarding sanity, but it cannot be a general opinion independent of circumstances within his own knowledge." The witness must lay a foundation for his opinion by first testifying as to the "appearances, actions, and conduct . . . of personal knowledge and observation."

It is necessary at this point to introduce a word of caution. While the above is the generally accepted rule of opinion evidence concerning mental condition, some states have statutes limiting this type of evidence in criminal cases. These laws must, therefore, always be consulted.

e. Voices

Testimony on voices is similar to that on identity: a layman may express his view in regard to a person's voice. As long as he has some basis for recognizing the voice, he may give his opinion, even though he never heard the voice before the time of the crime (*Froding* v. *State*, 125 Neb. 322 [1933] ; *People* v. *Harris*, 17 Ill. 2d 446 [1959]).

f. Handwriting

Anyone who knows another person's handwriting may give his opinion as to whether the writing in question was made by that person. Because this is also an area of common observation, all courts agree that a layman who is familiar with a particular handwriting may state his opinion concerning its identity even though he is not a handwriting expert.

In the case of *Criner* v. *State*, 236 Ark. 220 (1963), the manager of a soybean company was convicted of forgery. He would "buy" grain from a fictitious seller, make out a company check to him, forge the seller's name on the back of the check, and pocket the money. The company's secretary, testifying for the prosecution, said that the defendant had a distinctive handwriting and that he was familiar with it. When he was shown a number of questionable checks, he said that, in his opinion, the person who wrote the face of the checks also endorsed them. This testimony by a nonexpert witness was allowed because he stated the facts on which his opinion was based.

Some court decisions hold that a layman can testify on handwriting as long as he has become familiar with the handwriting, even though he has never actually seen the person write (*Phoenix State Bank* v. *Whitcomb*, 121 Conn. 32 [1936]).

g. Demeanor or Appearance

Although some courts take a narrower view, many hold that a witness may describe another's demeanor or appearance by conclusory words, such as "agitated," "nervous," "angry," or "disturbed." Clothing can be described as "messed up" or "disheveled." This testimony showing a person's emotions or appearance may be very important as proof of motive or intent. The reason for allowing this type of conclusion is that it is difficult for the average witness to put such descriptions into words, and this is the most helpful way for him to describe such conditions to the jury (*State* v. *Vanella*, 40 Mont. 326 [1910]; *People* v. *Deacon*, 117 Cal. App. 2d 206 [1953]; *Taggart* v. *State*, 143 Ala. 88 [1905]).

h. Miscellaneous

In some areas commonly thought of as requiring expert, scientific evidence laymen have been allowed to give their opinions, and these opinions have been considered facts of common observation. Courts have, for example, let nonexperts present their opinions on blood, powder burns, the similarity of footprints, tire marks, and the like (*Greenfield* v. *People*, 85 N.Y. 75 [1881]; *Commonwealth* v. *Dorsey*, 103 Mass. 412 [1869]).

i. Qualified Answers

A witness often qualifies his answer by saying "To the best of my knowledge," "I believe," or even "I think." Does this make it simply his opinion, rather than a fact, and thus disqualify the answer? Such language will not ordinarily result in eliminating his testimony as long as he was only explaining a faulty memory or admitting his uncertainty. The court generally allows this type of answer to stand on the ground that it is fully admissible. Its weight, however, is then up to the jury (*Losey* v. *Atcheson, Topeka & Santa Fe Railroad*, 84 Kan. 224 [1911]; *State* v. *Wilson*, 9 Wash. 16 [1894]; *Bachelder* v. *Morgan*, 179 Ala. 339 [1913]).

(10.3) Skilled Witnesses

There is a class of witness between laymen and technical experts, often referred to as a skilled witness, who may be allowed to give his opinion in court in his particular field. A cutlery worker, for example, might testify that the stone and mineral oil found in an accused convict's cell could have been used to grind down a mess hall table knife into the murder weapon used in assaulting another convict.

In a trial in Georgia Clif Byrd was convicted of the shotgun slaying of John Mandeville (*Byrd* v. *State*, 142 Ga. 633 [1914]). A lay witness testified that he examined the gunshot wound inflicted on Mandeville and that, in his opinion, it was done with a "cut shell." The latter, he said, was a shotgun shell with the paper almost completely cut off between the powder and the shot (now often referred to by police as a "wad cutter" shell); thus, when the shot was fired, it stayed together in a lump instead of scattering. He explained that he had fired such shells at objects other than humans and had observed the effects. The court approved the use of his testimony. While not an expert, he was, said the court, a witness experienced in such matters with knowledge on the subject, and he could, therefore, state his opinion.

(10.4) The Scope of Expert Witnesses

The area where opinion evidence is accepted most widely is that of the expert witness. An individual who has special knowledge, education, skill, or experience is qualified to be such a witness. Doctors, engineers, and chemists are among those routinely used as expert witnesses. Under proper limitations, the expert is allowed to state his opinion, which is intended to aid the jury in making its decision.

a. General Limitations

The expert may, of course, give opinion evidence only within the area of his special knowledge. If, however, the matter involved is one on which jurors of ordinary experience can make a decision, an expert will not be allowed to give his opinion. There is no reason, for example, to call a minister or professor to testify that something is obscene. The jury can decide that as a matter of common experience. Neither can a psychologist give his expert opinion that a witness is lying, because this is also a matter of common knowledge for the jury's determination.

In a prosecution for receiving stolen property (*Girson* v. *U.S.*, 88 F. 2d 358, cert. den. 300 U.S. 697 [1937]), the assistant post quartermaster was a government witness. On cross-examination he was handed two pairs of socks, admittedly not stolen, and asked if they did not have the same appearance as the stolen articles. The court properly disallowed the question since this was a matter of common experience that the jury was well qualified to decide.

Many years ago in *Ferguson* v. *Hubbell,* 97 N.Y. 507 (1884), an appellate court stated what is still a correct rule:

It is not sufficient to warrant the introduction of expert evidence that the witness may know more of the subject than the juries; . . . the jurors may have less skill and experience than the witness and yet have enough to draw their own conclusions . . . where the facts . . . are of such nature that jurors generally are just as competent to form opinions . . . there is no occasion to resort to expert or opinion evidence.

Even where expert opinion is properly used, it is still just that, an opinion. The jurors may accept or reject it. They still are the sole judges of the facts, not the experts.

b. Province of the Jury

An expert cannot give his opinion on the ultimate question to be decided by the jury. Even the most experienced criminologist or investigator is not allowed to testify that the defendant is, in his opinion, innocent or guilty.

In an interstate case involving a stolen automobile (*Gibson* v. *U.S.*, 363 F. 2d 146 [1966]), the charge was that a car had been taken in Georgia and sold in Alabama. An F.B.I. witness was asked: "Do you know whether he stole the automobile or how he got it?" He answered: "I believe he did." The appellate court, in reversing the conviction, held that this questioning invaded the jury's province, since the witness was being asked to give his opinion on the defendant's guilt or innocence.

While questions of this scope still will not be allowed, there is a growing tendency for courts to widen the area of expert testimony. In many cases the testimony is allowed in evidence for what it may be worth, even though technically the expert's opinion invades an area in which the jury must make a decision (*People* v. *Ciucci*, 8 Ill. 2d 619 [1956]; *Rabata* v. *Dohner*, 45 Wis. 2d 111 [1969]).

(10.5) Qualifications of Experts

Before an expert witness can give his opinion, the foundation for it must be laid by showing his qualifications, education, experience, and training. This is ordinarily accomplished by having the witness recite the facts of his experience and his background. At this point, opposing counsel is often allowed a preliminary cross-examination to question the expert's qualifications. It can happen, however, that counsel will state that the witness is an expert and that his qualifications need not be questioned. This commonly occurs when doctors are testifying.

The court must always be satisfied that the witness is a qualified expert before it will allow him to testify.

Expert witnesses are normally paid a fee for testifying, and in some cases the fee is very substantial. This is a proper procedure and provides no grounds for disqualifying them from testifying.

(10.6) Hypothetical Questions

A common method of obtaining the opinion of an expert witness is to ask a hypothetical question. This is done by requesting
that he assume certain facts about which other witnesses have testified
and then ask for his opinion based on the assumed facts. Doctors
testifying in homicide cases are routinely questioned in this way.
Previous testimony may have shown that the deceased had a split
skull and that a bloody ax was found at the scene. Questioning of
the doctor might proceed thus:

Q. Assume Doctor, that the deceased was found with a wound at the top
of the skull approximately four inches long, a half inch wide, and extending
into the brain and that this ax, Exhibit 1, was found near the body. Can you
state with reasonable medical certainty whether or not Exhibit 1 could have
caused such a wound?
A. I can.
Q. You may state your opinion.
A. In my opinion Exhibit 1 could have produced the wound you have
described.

In the past, hypothetical questions were universally used to
solicit the opinions of experts. They do, however, cause problems.
In the first place, the question itself must be precise, and one can
only assume the exact facts already in evidence. If anything beyond
these facts is assumed, both the question and the answer are improper.
In the second place, doctors and other expert witnesses have resisted
the use of the hypothetical question because they consider it unduly
restrictive and a handicap to the presentation of their findings.

Modern decisions and some procedural statutes avoid the
hypothetical question on direct examination and simply let the
doctor or other expert tell what his examination revealed and what
his conclusions are. The hypothetical question is still widely used on
cross-examination, however, to test the expert's findings and to try
to impeach his conclusions. Opposing counsel may assume only part
of the evidence in his question and base his hypothetical questions
on his own view of the facts (71 ALR 2d 16-18).

A hypothetical question may be used only with expert witnesses.
The nonexpert who is allowed to state an opinion must base it on
his own observations and nothing else. Thus, theoretical or hypothetical questioning of a lay witness is improper (*People* v. *Dolbeer*,

149 Cal. 227 [1906]; *People* v. *Vehler*, 114 Ill. App. 2d 171 [1969]).

(10.7) Basis for Opinion

The expert may give his opinion from personal observations. When a psychiatrist has made a mental examination, he may base his opinion regarding sanity entirely on this examination. A pathologist who has performed a postmortem examination may give his opinion on the cause of death on the basis of that examination. The lay witness, as has been said, can base his opinion solely on his personal observations.

The expert may base his opinion on past medical history and hospital records as well as on personal observations. He can also draw his conclusion entirely from the hypothetical question that assumes the facts and then asks for his opinion.

(10.8) Scientific Books

Scientific books cannot be used on direct examination to back up the expert's findings. Otherwise each side would present titles of learned tomes to prove the view of each witness, and the jury would be left to read all of the books cited in order to reach a decision. Even if a single book were introduced to prove a point, it would not be allowed because opposing counsel would be denied the right of cross-examination. Only mathematical or mortality tables can be quoted.

The expert can say that his opinion may have been formed in part by his study of scientific books, even though he cannot read from them in testifying. The expert must give his own opinion, not that of someone else.

Material from scientific works can be effectively used in cross-examination. Counsel can ask his opponent's expert if he recognizes certain authorities and then point out conclusions in these books that differ from his opinion. The court has discretion in this matter and will not let books be used in cross-examination merely as an excuse to put contrary opinions before the jury (*Pahl* v. *Troy City Railroad*, 81 A.D. 308 [N.Y. 1903]; *O'Connell* v. *Williams*, 17 Misc. 2d 296 [N.Y. 1958]; *People* v. *Riccardi*, 285 N.Y. 21 [1941]).

(10.9) Subject Matter of Expert Opinion

A number of considerations govern this area. A discussion of each follows.

a. Legal Opinions

Legal opinions ordinarily are not a proper subject for an expert witness. The expert may give his opinion of facts, not of the law. A lawyer cannot be called in to give his opinion as to the meaning of a local law applying to the case. That would be a conclusion of law for the trial judge, not for the witness. There is, however, at least one exception to this rule. If foreign laws are involved in the case, a legal expert might be allowed to give his opinion concerning these laws.

b. Estimates

Opinion regarding value must frequently be given by an expert. Stolen property or buildings destroyed by arson do not have a definite market value, and therefore, estimates of value by experts must be used. Because there was no actual sale between a willing buyer and seller to fix the market price, estimated value cannot be exact. Estimated value by an expert in the field is the best possible measure.

c. Time, Speed, Weight, Duration, and Number

Time of death, speed of vehicles, direction, and similar measurements can seldom be determined with mathematical certainty. As stated, lay witnesses can estimate such things on the basis of their observations. The fact that laymen may give such opinion evidence does not mean that experts are not allowed to do the same. The expert may give similar estimates on the basis of both the evidence in the case and his technical background. An accurate estimate of speed may be obtained from such information as the weight and size of the vehicle and skid marks. A contractor or engineer might estimate the number of cubic yards of fill placed on a land area. The direction from which a blow is struck and shots were fired would also be proper subjects for expert opinion (*Hopt* v. *Utah*, 120 U.S. 430 [1886]; *Ford* v. *State*, 96 Ark. 582 [1910]).

d. Mechanical and Agricultural Matters

An endless variety of mechanical and agricultural matters can involve expert testimony. Problems involved with the safety of machinery and with construction, such as the strength of structures, all involve expert testimony. Examples of agricultural items calling for expert evidence include value of a crop loss, whether or not milk has been adulterated, and whether stolen timber came from the complainant's woodlot.

(10.10) Physicians and Psychologists

Medical witnesses are the most common of all expert witnesses; their usefulness is discussed here.

a. Injuries

Almost all criminal cases involving injuries call for expert testimony from physicians. Is there tissue injury indicating force in a rape case? Was "serious physical injury" inflicted? A doctor's opinion is obviously necessary in this kind of situation. Physicians can give opinion evidence as to type, extent, and cause of wounds and injuries. Some states even allow them to state whether they feel the wound was self-inflicted.

A defendant, charged with murdering a woman with whom he had been living, argued that her death from gunshot was suicide, not murder. The pathologist who performed the autopsy found that death came from a bullet that entered below the left armpit, traveled across the thorax, penetrated the heart and lungs, and struck the right arm three inches below the shoulder. He was asked if, in his opinion, the wound could have been self-inflicted. Over objection, the court permitted him to reply, and he said it "would be a very unusual pattern for a self-inflicted wound." The court allowed the answer to stand, even though this was the crucial fact in issue. It held that self-inflicted wounds were not such a matter of common experience as to exclude expert testimony (*People* v. *Cole*, 47 Cal. 2d 93 [1965]; see also 56 ALR 2d 1435).

b. Physical Condition

There are times when it is necessary to have expert opinion on an individual's physical condition. If, for example, the defense claims a forced confession was beaten from the accused, and the prosecutor says that the man beat his own head against the cell bars, the jail physician who examined the defendant is the most qualified expert witness to help resolve the question. Another example arises when there is a claim of self-defense. In this case the general physical condition of both the accused and the victim of an assault is pertinent. An extremely important contemporary example concerns the necessity of a physician's opinion when a defendant contends that medication was the cause of his condition, rather than intoxication or unauthorized drugs. There are, of course, countless other factual situations where expert medical testimony is required in criminal cases.

c. Mental Condition

Only in rare cases is an individual so obviously deranged that the testimony of a trained psychiatrist, physician, or psychologist is not needed. Though the court usually accepts the expert testimony of a general practitioner on sanity, a few jurisdictions require the opinion of a specialist.

d. X Rays

Laymen are not capable of interpreting X rays. If X rays are to be used in evidence, they must be introduced through expert testimony and interpreted for the jury by either a qualified physician or a radiologist.

(10.11) Cause of Death

Expert testimony is ordinarily required in statements regarding cause of death. While it is true that laymen often observe death and dead persons, they have no common knowledge as to its various causes.

The pathologist studies tissues and organs to determine the cause, while the medical examiner may discover that the cause was the result of wounds, drowning, burning, and the like.

Where special knowledge is necessary to find death's cause, the prerogative of the jury is not violated.

(10.12) Fingerprints and Documents

In cases where fingerprints have been found, a fingerprint expert must give testimony concerning them; as only he can explain the points on which he has based his opinions.

Determination of the authenticity of documents—faked stock certificates, wills, letters, and others—requires examination by an expert. Typewriters differ by make, model, and even by individual machine. Here, too, an expert, by careful examination and with the aid of enlarged photographs, can identify and authenticate the typewritten material in question. Laymen can give testimony concerning handwriting, but experts in the field are frequently needed for an examination and a professional opinion.

(10.13) Character and Reputation

So-called "character evidence" is often used by the defendant in criminal trials. This is done by having witnesses testify as to the defendant's good reputation in the community. The theory, which is not terribly sound, is that an individual's misdeeds are generally known by friends and acquaintances. Thus, a good reputation is evidence of one's innocence of the crime charged. Such evidence is generally accepted as sufficient to raise a reasonable doubt among members of the jury.

If the defendant offers character evidence, the prosecutor may introduce evidence of poor character in rebuttal. In addition, character witnesses can be cross-examined as to whether they have heard of specific improper acts on the part of the defendant.

In a related area, evidence of a poor reputation for truthfulness and accuracy can be presented as impeachment material against a witness.

No one can testify as an expert on an individual's character and reputation, since the basis for such testimony is public discussion by people in the community. Therefore, those who are qualified to give testimony are laymen, people familiar with the individual's reputation.

(10.14) Modern Developments in Opinion Evidence

The field of expert testimony that is accepted by the court expands as scientific knowledge increases. Those who examine questioned documents can now testify freely on typewriter comparisons. Evidence based on breathalizer tests is now allowed to prove intoxication when the test was administered by trained personnel, and the results are, in effect, conclusory. Expert testimony on voiceprints is now being offered and accepted in some courts. Poly-graph investigations are routinely used and relied upon by police forces everywhere. Properly administered by trained and experienced experts, the polygraph has proved itself a reliable guide in the search for truth. And yet, with few exceptions, courts have refused to accept the results of polygraph tests. Only gradually are they being allowed as evidence.

In the area of narcotics, expert opinions on the effects of drugs and the way they are used and administered are increasingly being accepted. Even nonscientific personnel with experience in the drug field have been allowed to qualify as skilled witnesses and to give opinion testimony (*People* v. *Smith*, 253 Cal. App. 2d 711 [1967]; *People* v. *Moore*, 70 Cal. App. 2d 158 [1945]; *People* v. *Chrisman*, 256 C.A. 2d 425 [1967]).

There is now wider acceptance of expert testimony on modus operandi, where actions that seem normal on the surface are actually methods of committing a crime. Gambling, bookmaking, lottery, and even burglaries are examples. For instance, in a trial in California the defendant was charged with a form of burglary known as "till tapping" (*People* v. *Clay*, 227 Cal. App. 2d 87 [1964]). Testimony indicated that the defendant stood by the store's checkout counter and asked for a number of grocery items that caused the clerk to turn his back. A customer saw the defendant's accomplice withdraw his closed hand from the cash drawer. Testifying as an expert in the area of "till tapping," a police officer stated that this was the usual method of committing such a crime. The court allowed this testimony because the defendant's conduct at the checkout counter appeared normal, and, for this reason, the jury might have found him to have been an innocent bystander.

The theory behind this loosening of the strict ban on opinion evidence was set forth in a federal case involving five thousand dollars in counterfeit money found in the defendant's dresser drawer (*U.S.* v. *Petrone*, 185 F. 2d 355, cert. den. 340 U.S. 931 [1950]). He told the F.B.I. agent that counterfeiting was not in his "line" and that a "rat" had left the bills there the night before. During the agent's testimony he was asked if the defendant had not given him the "impression" that he did not know the bills were in his room. The trial judge would not allow the question since it called for a con-clusion. The appeals court, however, said that the question and an-swer should have been allowed. It stated that a blind following of the rule against conclusions "may . . . become a substantial obstacle to developing the truth . . . for our perceptions are always 'conclusions.' The rule should be held lightly and in many cases let the witness state his opinion and leave to cross-examination a searching inquisition to uncover its foundations."

(10.15) Summary

Though witnesses are supposed to recite facts, not opinions, there are wide areas in which opinion evidence is accepted.

Lay witnesses may estimate speed of vehicles, distances, time, and other measurements. They are also allowed, solely on the basis of their own observations, to state their opinions on another person's identity, handwriting, voice, sanity, and even his state of intoxication.

An expert witness is in a different class. He is called for the sole purpose of stating his expert opinion about some facet of the case. He cannot, of course, go so far as to decide the case for the jury. They are free to accept or reject his conclusion as they see fit.

Once having established his credentials in court, the expert can give his opinion, not only from his own observations, but from an assumed state of facts based on the evidence in the case. The expert may sometimes give opinions in the same areas as laymen, such as measurements, handwriting, and the authenticity of documents.

Many areas of opinion evidence, such as fingerprints and scientific, engineering, and mechanical matters, come only from experts.

Physicians are commonly needed for opinion evidence regarding physical condition, types and extent of injuries, and the cause of death.

Character evidence is a common defense in criminal trials. This is nonexpert testimony concerning the reputation one has in his community and is based on discussions of local people. If the defendant produces evidence of good character, the prosecution may offer proof of poor character. A witness may be attacked by evidence of poor reputation for truth. Though character evidence is pure opinion, it is, nonetheless, legal.

11

Hearsay Evidence

(11.1) What Is Hearsay?

The subject of hearsay is widely misunderstood. This need not be. All that is needed is some initial analysis, followed by a two-step process, which is given below.

The ban against hearsay is of ancient origin. The general concept of hearsay is the idea that a witness is forbidden to mention what someone else has told him. This is not so. Many out-of-court statements must be allowed in evidence. The first thing to do is to understand exactly what hearsay is.

"Hearsay" is an out-of-court statement offered to prove the truth of the matter contained in the statement. It is only hearsay *if it is offered to prove that the statement itself is true.* If it is introduced for some other purpose, it is not hearsay. It may be objected to on other grounds, but not on the basis of hearsay.

This is the most important step in recognizing hearsay, and one that even many attorneys miss. The first question to be asked is "What purpose is the conversation being offered for?" If the offeror does not care whether the statement is true or false, then it is *not* hearsay.

For example, Davis is being tried for murder, and his defense is insanity. His lawyer offers to prove that shortly before the shooting Davis was seen standing on the corner of Main and Delaware, wearing a cocked hat, with his hand in his shirt front, shouting "I'm Napoleon." An objection is raised on the grounds that the statement is hearsay. No one was claiming that he was Napoleon. The statement was offered to prove Davis was insane. Therefore, it was *not* hearsay.

So whenever a question of hearsay arises, remember this Napoleon example. If the conversation is not offered to prove its truth, it is not hearsay.

Make your own analysis. Do any of the following situations involve hearsay?

1. A spectator offers to testify that just before the complainant was struck with a beer bottle, he shouted at the defendant, "Hit me and I'll kill you."

2. A bank customer, now a witness in an armed robbery trial, offers to testify that he heard the teller say to the defendant, "Don't shoot me. Don't shoot me. I'll give you the money."

3. The charge is blackmail. The prosecution offers a legally recorded telephone conversation in which the defendant said to the victim, "Pay me five bills or I'll tell your wife what went on in room 209 of the Paradise Motel last night."

4. The bank officer is accused of embezzling $100,000 from dormant bank accounts. The state produces a fellow employee who offers to testify that on several occasions during the period in question, he heard the defendant say, "A man can't live on the stingy salaries this outfit pays."

5. The charge is burglary of the Empire Warehouse. The first officer who arrived at the scene in his patrol car testified that just before this, he had received a radio message saying, "Go to the Empire Warehouse at the corner of Main and Elm."

None of these can be classed as hearsay. The offeror does not care whether or not any of the statements is true. The answers to the illustrations are as follows.

1. This was offered to show provocation or self-defense, and it matters not whether the victim would have killed his assailant or not.

2. The teller's "Don't shoot" statement is evidence that she was giving up the funds under fear of physical harm, which is an element in robbery. Even if the bank robber only had a water pistol and

could never have shot her, the statement is proper to show her state of mind.

3. The blackmailer's threat may well have been pure bluff and entirely untrue. True, or false, it is only offered to show the threat as part of the crime, and the truth of the threat is immaterial, and so it is not hearsay.

4. Whether or not he could live on his salary is immaterial. The statement was not offered to prove that the bank was penurious. Its purpose was to show the defendant's motive for stealing. Hearsay was not, therefore, involved in his testimony.

5. The radio call was not offered as proof that there was a burglary, but simply to show why the officer went there. It would not have mattered if the dispatcher had been giving him a false instruction. Since the truth of the message was not involved, it was not hearsay.

Statements that show motive, intent, or bias are not always hearsay but can easily be confused with it. Usually, such statements are offered, not to prove the content as being true, but to show a state of mind like the earlier example of Napoleon. For instance, a husband is accused of murdering his wife. The People offer evidence by a neighbor who overheard him calling her a whore, just before the fatal shot. The evidence is accepted, not to prove that she was immoral, but that he hated her enough to kill her. In addition, the prosecution might reveal that, before the murder, the defendant told a third person that he was going to marry a long-time woman friend. Whether or not he was going to marry her is beside the point; a statement is properly received in evidence to prove that he intended to and hence had a motive for murder. Courts normally accept this type of statement for the purpose of showing mental operations.

It is not just an oral statement that can be classified as hearsay. A "statement" can be oral, written, or even nonverbal conduct that conveys a message. The basic objection to hearsay is that, if it is used, the opponent is denied his right to confront and cross-examine the person who made the statement. It is not possible, of course, to cross-examine an out-of-court statement. This is the reason why an expert is not allowed to bolster his testimony by reading from a scientific book. The testimony would be offered to prove the *truth of the matter in the book*, and there is no way counsel can cross-examine a volume. Thus, such testimony is objectionable as hearsay.

For the same reason, a case cannot be proven by submitting a sworn affidavit, instead of having the live witness. Cross-examination and confrontation would be lost. If the affidavit would be offered to prove its truth, it would be objectionable as hearsay.

Gestures often are questioned as possibly being hearsay. In *People* v. *Plummer*, 36 N.Y. 2d 161 (1975), a defendant was convicted of armed robbery of a store clerk. The defendant and two others went into a store, held a knife to the clerk's throat, and the defendant said that if she did not cooperate, he "would slit [her] throat." They took her wallet and over two hundred dollars from the cash drawer. Three days later, she saw the defendant in front of the same store looking at her and crossing his throat with his finger. He did this several times later and also pointed to his head, imitating a pistol. The defendant's sister also made threatening gestures. Though objection was made to the evidence of these threats, the appeals court ruled that this evidence was all admissible.

The question of hearsay was not actually raised, but what if such an objection had been made? The gestures were a message. The defendant was telling her what was going to happen if she did not cooperate. This evidence would be acceptable, not as proof that they actually were going to kill her, but as evidence of the defendant's state of mind, his animosity, all of which was relevant to the charge of armed robbery.

(11.2) Exceptions to the Hearsay Rule

Whether the problem involves an out-of-court conversation, document, or message type of action, your analysis must always begin with the first step. Stop. Ask yourself, what purpose is it being offered for? If offered to prove the truth, then it is hearsay.

This does not end your hearsay inquiry. It only begins it. Practicality dictates that a great number of out-of-court statements must be allowed in evidence. Contracts are made by word of mouth. Threats and promises may be made the same way. There are, then, a number of exceptions to the hearsay rule that are allowed in both civil and criminal litigation.

Having first determined if the evidence offered is basically hearsay, the next step to determine is: does it fall within any of the many exceptions to the hearsay rule?

(11.3) Confessions

The confession of an accused is probably the most commonly understood exception to the hearsay rule. Such an out-of-court statement is offered to prove the truth of its content, and as such it is hearsay. It is, however, allowed as an exception to the hearsay rule.

The reasoning behind this is that people do not ordinarily admit to a criminal act. If they do, it is likely that their statements are true. Thus, if the confession is voluntary and meets the necessary constitutional requirements (detailed in Chapter 6), it will be allowed as an exception to the hearsay rule as evidence against the person who confesses.

a. Admissions

An admission is a kind of miniconfession. Though the accused might never have actually confessed, he might have made a partial admission regarding the crime. Perhaps he told a girl friend that he was at the scene of the crime or showed her a gun that he claimed was used in an armed robbery. If voluntarily made, such an admission can be used as evidence against an accused, as an exception to the hearsay rule.

b. Admission by Silence

On rare occasions there may be an admission or a complete confession simply by silence. There is a widely held misconception about this. Many practitioners think that if a defendant is present during a conversation then the words can be used as evidence against him. This is not true.

The mere presence of a defendant does not in itself make the conversation admissible. If a statement (not written) is made in the presence of the accused incriminating him *under circumstances calling for his denial*, only then is his silence deemed an admission. For example, if he is arrested, and the lieutenant says, "You stole this gun," the defendant's silence means nothing, for he has a constitutional right to remain silent. So, if the accusation is made in open court, or while the man is in custody, his silence is not an admission. If, on the other hand, there is a street fight, and the victim confronts a man saying "You cut me," the man's silence can be taken as an admission of guilt. The statement "You cut me" could be introduced in evidence by any witness who heard it.

In a case of murder on an Indian reservation (*Arpan* v. *U.S.*, 260 F. 2d 649 [1958]), an Indian was convicted of killing his wife. The evidence showed that the husband had been on a drunken spree, came home, and shot his wife. His defense was that he was so drunk he did not know what happened.

After the shooting, the defendant ran to his parents' home. Another Indian testified as a prosecution witness that he went to the parents' house and questioned the people who were there. "In the defendant's presence" he asked the father what happened, and the father answered that the defendant had said, "I killed Jeanette." Because this was a third party, not the father testifying, it was not in the nature of a confession the witness had heard from the defendant. The trial court admitted the statement by a third party because it was "made in the defendant's presence."

The appellate court properly reversed the conviction. It noted that, according to the record, the investigating Indian first sat by the defendant, but when he spoke to the father, he moved to another part of the room. The defendant may never have heard the conversation, or, if he did, he was admittedly in shock and recovering from intoxication. There can be no admission by silence unless all the circumstances call naturally for a denial from the accused. Only if the circumstances are so strong that the defendant's silence amounts to an acquiescence, may the accusatory conversation of a third party be admitted as an exception to the hearsay rule.

c. Confessions of a Codefendant

As discussed earlier, a defendant's confession is admissible only against the defendant. It cannot be used against a codefendant because it is pure hearsay in regard to the other party. It is admitted only against the person who confesses, as an exception to the hearsay rule, on the common-sense premise that people do not ordinarily admit a crime of their own unless it is true. But there is no reason to be afraid to say that someone else committed a crime. It is only when an individual implicates himself that the statement has the ring of truth.

(11.4) Statements of Coconspirators

A conspiracy is an agreement between two or more people to commit a criminal act. The conspirators are then partners in crime. In civil law, one partner is bound by the actions of the other if they are performed in the course of their business partnership. Each is, therefore, the agent of the other. It is the same with a criminal conspiracy. The federal rule is generally applicable. It holds that the statement of a coconspirator is admissible in evidence against all conspirators under three conditions. First, the conspiracy must be established by independent evidence. Second, the statement must be made in furtherance of the conspiracy. Third, it must be made during the conspiracy. The following cases illustrate this: *Mares* v. *U.S.*, 383 F. 2d 805, cert. den. 394 U.S. 963 (1967); *U.S.* v. *Coppola*, 479 F. 2d 1153 (1973); *Grunewald* v. *U.S.*, 353 U.S. 391 (1957).

In a federal vice case (*Krulewitch* v. *U.S.*, 336 U.S. 440 [1948]) the defendant was accused of conspiring with his wife to transport another woman from New York to Miami for prostitution. After the prostitute had been taken to Miami and the defendant arrested, she came back to New York. This ended the conspiracy. Then the prostitute and the defendant's wife had a conversation in New York. At his trial the prostitute was allowed to relate the conversation she had with the wife in New York as follows: "The wife said 'You didn't talk yet?' and I says 'No' and she says 'Well don't . . . until we get you a lawyer . . . . Be very careful what you say . . . . It would be better for us two girls to take the blame than Ray [defendant] . . . . He couldn't stand to take it.'" Partially on the basis of this testimony, the man was convicted. His conviction was eventually reversed by the Supreme Court because the conversation took place after the prostitution conspiracy ended. Thus, what the two women said was not binding on the husband and was inadmissible hearsay.

For the same reason a *confession* of one conspirator is not admissible against the others. Because the conspiracy was over by the time the man confessed, his confession, like that of any codefendant, was binding only against himself (*U.S.* v. *Register*, 496 F. 2d 1072 [1974]).

(11.5) Declaration against Interest

Declarations against interest are out-of-court statements by one who is not a party to the crime and can be used as evidence when a witness is not available.

Ordinarily, a person does not publicly admit things that are harmful to (that is, against) his own interest. If he does, it is a good indication that what he says is true. One example is a declaration against pecuniary interest, such as admitting a debt. More commonly involved in criminal trials is the declaration against penal interest, where an individual other than the defendant admits to a criminal act. As a matter of fact, these declarations, which are exceptions to the hearsay rule, always apply to people other than the defendant. If we were talking about a defendant's statement, this would be a confession admissible against him under that exception.

The declaration against penal interest ordinarily constitutes evidence that the defendant tries to use in his own behalf. He offers it to prove that *someone else has admitted committing* the crime he is accused of. In the past the declaration against penal interest was not usually considered an exception to the hearsay rule (*Donnelly* v. *U.S.*, 228 U.S. 243 [1912]). The modern trend of court decisions, however, is to recognize this type of declaration as an exception to the hearsay rule and to admit it under certain circumstances.

The pioneer federal decision in this area is *Chambers* v. *Mississippi*, 410 U.S. 284 (1973). Chambers had been convicted of murdering a policeman during a demonstration in Mississippi. As the policeman fell, he turned and fired his gun, wounding Chambers. A man named McDonald left town shortly after the shooting, but later returned and confessed to Chambers' lawyer that he, not Chambers, had actually shot the policeman. When McDonald was called as a defense witness, however, he repudiated his confession. Chambers offered the testimony of three of McDonald's friends that McDonald had admitted to the shooting. The court refused to allow this. Chambers was convicted.

The Supreme Court, in reversing the conviction, recognized the reliability of a declaration against penal interest where the circumstances such as these indicated the truthfulness of the statement. The court avoided the usual requirement that a declaration against penal interest cannot be offered unless the declarant is unavailable, by pointing out that McDonald was there, and he could have been cross-examined. Various states are following this example and are now admitting the declaration against penal interest in evidence.

Another case involving the declaration against penal interest is *People* v. *Brown*, 26 N.Y. 2d 88 (1970). Brown was convicted in New York of murder. He claimed self-defense, saying that the deceased had a pistol in his hand when Brown shot him. The fact that the police found no other pistol near the body seemed to negate his claim. At the time of Brown's trial, Seals was in jail for robbery. Seals told Brown's lawyer that he "picked up a gun" immediately after the shooting. When he was called as a witness at Brown's trial, Seals refused to testify on the basis of his rights under the Fifth Amendment. The trial court refused to allow testimony concerning Seal's conversation with Brown's lawyer. The appellate court, however, reversed the conviction. It recognized the validity of Seal's declaration as being against penal interest because his statement would constitute the admission of a crime on his own part. In the court's opinion, when the declarant is dead, when he is beyond the court's jurisdiction, or when he refuses to testify, his admission against penal interest should be received in evidence.

In two modern decisions (*Commonwealth* v. *Hackett*, 307 A. 2d 334 [Pa. App. 1973] ; *Commonwealth* v. *Colon*, 337 A. 2d 554 [Pa., 1975]) the state of Pennsylvania has accepted the declaration against penal interest as a recognized exception to the hearsay rule. The federal courts also recognize this exception, making it part of the Federal Rules of Evidence (Section 804). Some court decisions now approve the use of a declaration against penal interest whether or not the speaker is available to testify.

It is undoubtedly true that, with the limitations traditionally applied to the declaration against penal interest, third-party confessions to a crime will increasingly be allowed in evidence as part of the defendant's case.

A word of caution about relying on the use of a declaration against penal interest should be mentioned. It may not be used unless the speaker is actually faced with the possibility that he will be punished. If he cannot be punished for what he says, it is not an acceptable declaration against penal interest. This is graphically demonstrated by *U.S.* v. *Dovico*, 380 F. 2d 325, cert. den. 389 U.S. 944 (1967) (see also *U.S.* v. *Seyfried*, 435 F. 2d 696 [7th Cir. 1970] ; *Commonwealth* v. *Colon*, supra).

A man named Dovico and a codefendant were convicted on a drug charge. While the codefendant was in a federal penitentiary, he told a cellmate that he, not Dovico, was the one who had put the cocaine in the trash. The codefendant never testified at Dovico's original trial and died before the case was appealed. Because of the codefendant's death, Dovico sought to use the statement to the cellmate. The reviewing court determined, however, that the statement was not a declaration against penal interest. By assuming all the blame when he made the statement, the codefendant was not subjecting himself to any possible additional punishment. He had already been convicted of the crime, and, because he had never testified in court on the matter, he was not even opening himself to a possible charge of perjury. Since no additional criminal punishment was possible, this was not a genuine declaration against penal interest.

a. Homicide or Suicide?

Declarations of suicide are admitted as an exception to the hearsay rule. They are similar to other declarations against interest on the logical basis that threatening suicide is generally regarded as a disgraceful act that an individual ordinarily would not falsify. It is true that the declaration of suicide is offered to show a state of mind, but normally its purpose is also to prove the truth of the matter contained in the statement. It is unimportant whether the statement is made orally or is in the form of a suicide note. The result is the same. All such statements are hearsay, but are received as exceptions to the rule (*People* v. *Tugwell*, 28 C.A. 348, 359 [1915]; *People* v. *Selby*, 198 C. 426).

A defendant named Salcido was convicted of murder. He had been riding in the backseat of a car with his girl friend (*People* v. *Salcido*, 246 C.A. 2d 450 [1966]). They began to argue, and it appeared that he threatened her with his gun. A witness in the front seat heard a shot and saw that the girl was wounded and that the defendant was wiping his gun. The defense attempted to prove that, on the way to the hospital, the victim told the ambulance driver and the defendant that she had shot herself. The trial judge would not allow this testimony, and Salcido was convicted. The appellate court reversed the conviction. It stated that, though the suicide statement was offered to prove the truth of the matter in the statement, it was receivable as an exception to the hearsay rule.

(11.6) Dying Declarations

The dying declaration of a homicide victim has long been accepted as an exception to the hearsay rule. In order for the declaration to be considered an exception, however, certain conditions must be met. First, the victim must be "in extremis." Second, he must know that he is dying and that he has no hope of recovery. Third, if he were living he would be competent as a witness. Fourth, his statement must relate to the cause of his death. Courts have based this exception on the theory that if a person knows he is about to die, he is unlikely to lie about who injured him. What he says is thus guaranteed to be true as much as if it had been under oath in court.

People v. *Coniglio*, 79 Misc. 2d 808 (N.Y. 1974), demonstrates a dying declaration. A police officer called to the scene of a shooting found a woman lying on the floor bleeding from bullet wounds. As he bent over her, she said: "Benny shot me. Benny shot my husband and he's dead and I'm going to die too." The officer asked: "Benny who?" She answered: "Benny Coniglio." "Where is Benny?" he asked. She replied: "Around the corner on 11th Avenue." She was taken to surgery and died a few hours later.

The trial court found that her statement met all the conditions for a dying declaration in a homicide case. It ruled, however, that only those portions of the statements bearing on her own death, not on that of her husband, were admissible.

In the absence of authority granted by statute, courts have refused to accept the following types of statements: the dying statement of a burglar that his codefendant was innocent; the dying victim's statement where the crime charged was assault with intent to kill rather than homicide; and the statement of a convicted murderer about to be executed that his codefendant was innocent. None of these statements are true dying declarations in homicide. Neither would they be received as declarations against penal interest, as the dying speaker could in no way be subjecting himself to any further punishment, knowing that his life was about to end.

In the past the classic restriction on the use of a dying declaration has been to apply it only to homicide cases. Some jurisdictions have now widened the rule to apply to matters other than homicide, but limit it to the declarant's description of the circumstances of his own death.

(11.7) Res Gestae

The term "res gestae" (literally meaning "things done") is a general catchall used by courts for admitting various conversations that are connected in some way with a transaction.

One judge complained about the use of the term (J. Hauser dissent, in *Coryell* v. *Reid*, 117 Cal. App. 534 [1931]), saying, "Definitions of the term 'res gestae' are as numerous as the various cures for rheumatism and about as useful."

Courts continue to misuse the term, mistakenly admitting conversations as res gestae exceptions to the hearsay rule, when they really are not hearsay at all. The illustration used earlier—of a witness testifying that the bank teller said to the robber, "Don't shoot me. Don't shoot me. I'll give you the money."—would in most courts be admitted as part of the res gestae if there were a hearsay objection. As was previously pointed out, it is not hearsay in the first place and stands in its own right as a relevant proof that the teller was parting with money in fear, which is an essential element in robbery. It was not proof of a shooting.

The best way to handle the problem of res gestae is to realize that judges generally admit conversations, words, or acts that are incidental to and explanatory of the fact in controversy. This is, of course, an ill-defined and inexact way to rule on the admissibility of hearsay evidence. A much better way is to understand that there are three classes of genuine hearsay exceptions under the classification of res gestae: excited utterances; explanatory statements; and verbal acts. It is always preferable to use their correct names even if the judge terms them res gestae.

a. Excited Utterances

A speaker's spontaneous words made while he was under the stress of excitement caused by the event will be admitted *even as proof of the matter contained in the statement*. This type of statement, which is made under stress, is reliable because the speaker did not have time to fabricate. Thus, his words are spontaneous, generated by the circumstances themselves. The key to the admittance of an excited utterance is its spontaneity. In this way it differs from the dying declaration in a homicide case. The validity of the latter is based on the solemnity of the occasion and must meet all the requirements given previously. A murder victim's excited utterance made at the time of the crime is admitted because of the spontaneous nature, even though the victim is unaware of his imminent death.

A good example of this is *State* v. *McClain*, 25 N.W. 2d 764 (1964). The defendant, McClain, returned home at about 3:00 a.m. after a heavy drinking spree. He argued with his wife, hit her, and she fell across the bed. McClain then went into the kitchen and ate two sandwiches. He claimed that he came back to the bedroom, found the mattress on fire, threw it out the window, and went out looking for his wife.

The state's story was quite different. The prosecutor produced a neighbor who testified that he heard the McClain family argument and that the wife came to the neighbor's front porch afterward and asked him to "Call the law." The neighbor refused. The burned wife came out and sat on the steps, rocking back and forth and screaming. She accused her husband, saying: "Don't touch me under here, I'm burned up . . . Mac poured gas on me and burned me up." She died thirteen days later in the hospital. The court ruled that her statement was a spontaneous declaration made under stress, even though it was subsequent to the event, and was properly admitted in evidence as an exception to the hearsay rule. McClain was thus convicted.

The excited utterance is allowed in evidence even if made by a third party because the basis for its truth—spontaneity—is the same whether said by a participant or a spectator (*Swensson* v. *Albany Dispatch Co.*, 309 N.Y. 497 [1956]; *Ollala* v. *State*, 157 Tex. Cr. 458 [1952]; Federal Rules of Evidence, Sec. 803 [2]).

The admission of the excited utterance is gaining wider acceptance in court decisions. It is generally admitted as part of the evidence, whether or not the speaker is available as a witness. Many decisions, like the McClain case, also admit excited statements that are not strictly "contemporaneous" as long as they were made spontaneously under the stress of the event (*State* v. *Ehlers*, 119 Atl. 15 [N.J. 1922]; *People* v. *Costa*, 40 Cal. 2d 160 [1953]).

In a case in Colorado the victim, who was found in the street immediately after the defendant ran her down with his car, said that the driver was her husband. She stated: "That is my husband. He is drunk. He is trying to kill me." The court admitted her statement in evidence (*Dolan* v. *People*, 449 P. 2d 828 [Colo. 1969]).

b. Explanatory Statements

Conversations accompanying the fact in issue will be admitted to explain ambiguous actions, even if they are offered to prove the truth of the statement itself. The conversation must actually "explain" the conduct. It must outline and give meaning to the act.

Much evidence of the explanatory type is not hearsay. Like the statement "I'm Napoleon," it is not offered for the truth, but to explain conduct or to show a mental condition.

Explanatory conversations occasionally are presented to explain, and the statement is also offered for its truth. This makes it a true hearsay exception. One such situation involved the defendant, Alexander, who was accused of murdering his partner, Stedman (*Alexander* v. *U.S.*, 138 U.S. 353 [1890]). Stedman had disappeared and was found ten days later shot through the head. Alexander maintained his innocence and argued that someone else had shot his partner. The defendant introduced evidence that, after Stedman had disappeared from town, a story circulated that he had run off with House's wife and that House and his friends armed themselves and went to look for the missing man. Alexander also offered proof that House, during this time, threatened to kill Stedman, and the trial judge excluded this evidence. Alexander was subsequently convicted. The Supreme Court reversed the decision. It stated that, since evidence was allowed showing that House was looking for Stedman, his threats accompanying this search explained his actions and were admissible.

c. Verbal Acts

"Verbal act" is a term that is frequently used loosely. A contemporaneous type of statement is often admitted into evidence under the label "verbal act" because the statement accompanied the act. This use of the term is too broad. It is more accurate to confine the definition to a statement that is itself a fact and is an integral part of the action under investigation. A verbal act is actually what it says it is—an action by words.

If a pickpocket steals a man's wallet, he has committed a larceny with his hands. If he swindles him out of the same money by a dishonest investment scheme, he has committed larceny by word of mouth. Thus, his conversations on the latter subject would be admissible as a spoken form of larceny, that is, as a verbal criminal act. A criminal conspiracy is a similar example of a verbal act. In this case, every word of the criminal participants is admissible. The words of the conspirators thus amount to an act of crime—a verbal act.

In *Ward* v. *U.S.*, 296 F. 2d 898 (1962), the defendant, convicted of offering a bribe to a juror, appealed, claiming the trial court allowed some hearsay evidence. A witness, Staley, had testified that the defendant hired him to offer two hundred dollars to a prospective juror in order to obtain a hung jury. Staley offered the money to the juror, but the latter declined. Staley reported this to the defendant. The court allowed all of Staley's testimony. When the defendant appealed the decision, the appellate court affirmed the conviction, saying that Staley was the defendant's agent and that the conversation with the jury was a verbal act—the very crime of offering a bribe to a juror.

(11.8) Complaint of a Sex Victim

A complaint made by a victim of a sex crime will be admitted under certain conditions as an exception to the hearsay rule *as proof that the crime itself took place*. If the statement is made at the time of the attack, it is admissible as an excited utterance, but the type of exception being discussed here is a complaint made after the attack, when the stress of events may have passed.

If there has been a rape or an act of nonconsensual perversion, the victim usually complains about it at the first possible opportunity. Should the woman not complain, one might assume that she was not violated, but had consented to the act.

The person who heard the complaint can testify concerning it since the complaint is a natural, instinctive type of utterance and so bears a presumption of truthfulness. It is also allowed to overcome the negative reaction to silence on the part of the victim and to corroborate the victim's testimony if she is impeached as a witness. The victim's statement must not be too remote and must actually be a complaint.

In *Callahan* v. *U.S.*, 240 F. 683 (1917), there was a prosecution for statutory rape. An adult male was accused of having intercourse with a girl under the age of fourteen. Shortly after the intercourse took place she met her girl friend outside the house. The friend, called as a prosecution witness, testified that the girl had told her that she had gone to the house willingly, had intercourse with the defendant, and then showed the three dollars that he had paid her. The defendant was convicted and appealed. The reviewing court reversed the conviction, saying that the girl's statement was not a complaint or expression of outraged feeling nor even an excited utterance. It was merely interesting information passed on in a conversation with an intimate friend and was therefore hearsay.

Thus, in order for the sex victim's complaint to qualify for this hearsay exception, it must be recent, it must be given voluntarily at the first natural opportunity, and it must be an actual complaint.

(11.9) Business Records

Over the years the courts have developed a set of rules for admitting business records in evidence. Sometimes known as the "Shop Book Rule," it is now usually referred to by a term such as "business records as evidence act."

This hearsay exception has evolved as a matter of practicality. For example, if a merchant suing a customer in regard to his charge account had to produce each clerk who made every sale, the employee who made the delivery, and the bookkeeper who made the account entry, it would clutter the courtroom endlessly and make proof extremely difficult. Thus, the rule has developed over the years allowing records regularly made in the course of business to be admitted in evidence as an exception to the rule against hearsay.

The rule has recently been expanded. It now includes records that are not strictly "business records" if they are made in the regular course of the "business," near the time of the event, and if, in the opinion of the court, the sources of information and the purpose of keeping the record were such as to justify its admission. Under this expanded interpretation, accident reports, police reports, and other regularly kept records not involved in any commercial business are often allowed in evidence in criminal cases. A police report can, however, normally be used only if the writer of the report was a witness to the facts or if the person giving the information to the writer was under any obligation to relate the facts (*Hole v. N.Y.*, 32 A.D. 2d 47 [N.Y. 1969]).

In criminal trials the defense ordinarily asks for the production of police witnesses' notes, police records, and the like. As previously noted, the defense uses these in cross-examination. Occasionally, however, the defense may offer such a record in evidence under the business records exception as proof of the actual matter contained in the report.

(11.10) Prior Statements of a Witness

Many types of earlier statements made by a witness may be allowed as evidence. If a witness has testified previously in the same case at an earlier trial, at a pretrial hearing, or in an examination before trial, when he could have been cross-examined, the record of his testimony can ordinarily be used in the later trial, should the witness be unavailable. His earlier testimony is then used as direct proof of its contents, just as though he were on the stand testifying in person.

In *California* v. *Green*, 399 U.S. 149 (1970), the Supreme Court announced an extension of the rule by allowing the use of earlier testimony in the situation even where the witness was available. In that case a sixteen-year-old boy was arrested on a drug charge, and he named Green as his supplier. He testified to this at Green's preliminary hearing. At the trial, however, the boy took the stand and said he had been taking LSD and could not remember. The prosecution then read from his testimony at the preliminary hearing and had an officer testify that the boy had orally named Green as his supplier. This was the state's only proof that directly linked Green to the drug sale. The Supreme Court approved this evidence, saying that the boy had testified at the trial and could have been cross-examined thoroughly in regard to his prior statements and his present testimony. The court further pointed out that it was not an unconstitutional deprivation of the right of cross-examination to use the prior statements as direct proof of the crime.

The use of a prior statement of a witness often becomes involved in cases of identity, where the witness identifies the defendant from the stand during the trial and has, of course, identified him earlier at the station house or in a police lineup. The general rule has been that prior identification is equivalent to a prior statement. If the witness had failed to identify the defendant earlier, that fact would be allowed as impeaching evidence to weaken the present testimony. If, on the other hand, it was a consistent identification whereby the witness had identified the same man twice, the prior identification would not be allowed in evidence unless the identity had been attacked and it was necessary in order to rehabilitate the witness.

A rule that is now evolving in court decisions is to admit the evidence of the earlier identification, even if it is consistent, on the theory that it was fresher and more reliable in the first instance than it is during the trial. Judges maintain that this situation is similar to that of *California* v. *Green*. Thus, when the identifying witness is on the stand, he can be thoroughly cross-examined, and, for this reason, the testimony of both identifications should be allowed. States still vary in this interpretation. Some, for example, will not allow testimony regarding prior identification simply to bolster the witness then on the stand. Some states also have statutes governing identity testimony (*People* v. *Rosati*, 39 A.D. 2d 592 [N.Y. 1972] ; *People* v. *Caserta*, 19 N.Y. 2d 18 [1966] ; N.Y., CPL 60.25).

(11.11) Miscellaneous Exceptions

A number of minor hearsay exceptions—official records, such as certificates of conviction, records of vital statistics, family records, and ancient documents—occur infrequently in criminal cases.

Some states now admit hearsay in general at administrative proceedings or preliminary hearings before indictment. Hearsay is also widely allowed as a basis for arrests and warrants. Some types of hearsay, such as official laboratory reports, may be introduced before a grand jury. A few jurisdictions have laws that permit the use of various declarations of persons since deceased. As previously mentioned, a written record of a "past recollection recorded" may sometimes be used where the witness has no present memory of the event.

(11.12) The Two-Step Rule for Determining Hearsay

There is a simple two-step rule that anyone can use to determine if evidence offered is hearsay. All you need to do is ask yourself two questions.

First, is the statement offered to prove the truth of its contents? If it is offered for some purpose other than to prove its truth, it is not hearsay. Remember the Napoleon illustration of the man on the street corner with his hand in his shirt, saying "I'm Napoleon." That statement was receivable, not to prove he was the Emperor, but to show that the speaker was insane.

Always do this *first*, and you will find that most conversations or writings offered are not hearsay, and the problem is eliminated.

Many attorneys, and even some judges, miss this first step. In all fairness, it must be said that this is easy to do, unless in the first instance you stop and say to yourself, "Is this offered to prove it is true, or is it offered for another purpose?"

So—should hearsay arise, Napoleonize.

Next, if it is offered to prove its truth, the statement is hearsay, but it still may be usable.

A hearsay objection?
Try all the exceptions.

So, secondly, you must ask yourself, "Does the statement fall within any of the exceptions to the hearsay rule?" Number the exceptions off mentally. Is it a confession, an admission, an excited utterance, a dying declaration, an explanatory statement, or some other exception? Now, you have the final answer.

Follow the two-step rule and you will always find the answer to the hearsay question.

(11.13) Summary

Hearsay is an out-of-court statement offered to prove the truth of the matter contained in the statement. An oral or written statement offered for purposes other than its truth is not hearsay. Many written and oral statements are admitted as evidence, however, not to prove their truth, but to demonstrate motive, intent, bias, or other state of mind. They are not hearsay.

There is a two-step exercise in deciding hearsay. First, is the statement offered to prove its truth? If so, it is classed as hearsay. Second, if it is hearsay, does it fall within any of the exceptions?

Several recognized exceptions to the rule exist, even though they may actually be classified as hearsay. The best-known exception is a confession, which is an out-of-court statement received for its own truth. Admissions, even admissions by silence, fall in the same class. Statements of coconspirators made during and in furtherance of a conspiracy are usable against all conspirators as an exception to the hearsay ban.

Declarations made by a witness against his own pecuniary or penal interests are received in evidence as proof of the content of the statement itself. A dying declaration of a homicide victim is allowed, provided he knew that death was near and then subsequently died. By their very nature they are considered reliable and hence received in evidence, though they are plainly hearsay.

Many utterances accompanying or near in time to when the crime was committed are accepted, even though they are offered to prove their truth. Among these are excited or spontaneous utterances, explanatory statements delineating ambiguous conduct, and verbal acts that, in themselves, constitute a crime. Contemporaneous complaints by the victim of a sex crime are recognized as valid proof of the matter contained in the complaint even though they are properly classed as hearsay.

Records that are regularly kept in the course of any business are generally accepted. These include, among others, business and police records. Prior testimony and prior statements of a witness can be used in some circumstances as direct proof of the matter in the statement. Minor varieties of other hearsay exceptions include records of family lineage, official records, vital statistics, and records of criminal convictions.

12

Documentary Evidence, Photographs, Demonstrations, and the Best Evidence Rule

(12.1) Documentary Evidence in General

Legal evidence is not, of course, limited to the oral testimony of witnesses. Tangible objects that can express a fact or that tend to clarify the truth or untruth of the issues in question are admissible and fall under the classification of documentary evidence. This broad category includes private writings, documents, official records, newspapers, maps, or any other object on which symbols have been placed with the intention of preserving a record of events or impressions.

Documentary evidence is subject to the same rules that govern oral testimony. It must, therefore, satisfy the threefold test of materiality, relevance, and competence. The issues of the case determine the materiality and relevance of the document; such determinations are within the bounds of discretion granted to trial judges. The competence or reliability of documentary evidence presents problems that do not exist in the context of oral testimony. Thus, the basic question is whether or not the document offered as evidence has a sufficient guarantee of reliability. As a result, the judge is often called upon to make a judgment on the inherent reliability of the type of document offered. One important, if somewhat overly flexible, standard states that documentary evidence satisfies the test of competence if the document was made and preserved in such a way as to appear to state directly, accurately, and truthfully a fact relevant and material to the legal issue in question (*Curtis* v. *Bradley*, 65 Conn. 99, 31 Atl. 591 [1894]).

Once the tests of materiality, relevance, and competence are met, the category of admissible documents becomes very broad. The document may be in the form of letters, numbers, marks, or symbols upon any type of surface or substance. When one is determining the admissibility of writings, the significant question to ask does not necessarily involve the specific type of writing offered, but rather the contents of the document or the purpose for which it is offered as evidence. Under such a subjective test of admissibility, many types of documentary evidence become admissible; they include private writings, memorandums, and letters; church and family records; books, newspapers, and scholarly works; tables, charts, and graphs; commercial paper of all types; business or corporate records; and the reports and records of public officials and agencies.

(12.2) Authentication of Documents

Before a writing can be admitted as documentary evidence it must be authenticated. Authentication is a legal process of proof that is designed to establish the genuineness of the writing and may be accomplished in a number of ways. The document may, for example, be supported by an authenticating witness, whose function is to establish that the writing is what it purports to be and that it was made by the party to whom it has been attributed. In some cases the authenticating witness is not necessary. The opposing party may concede the genuineness of the document, or it may fall within one of the limited exceptions to the authentication requirement. The party offering the document as evidence should, nevertheless, always be prepared to establish its authenticity. In all cases the genuineness of the writing must be demonstrated to the satisfaction of the trial judge before it will be formally admitted into evidence. If he is not persuaded that the writing is authentic, the writing will not be allowed to be read or shown to the jury or to be considered by the judge in a nonjury trial.

It is important to remember that the authentication process should never be confused with the necessity to establish proof of the writing's contents after the documentary evidence has been received at trial. After the judge is convinced that the writing is what it purports to be, the party introducing the evidence must still convince the jury that the content of the document is truthful.

Though there are many ways to authenticate a document, the final determination of its authenticity and reliability remains a matter firmly within the discretion of the trial judge. The easiest way to authenticate a document is, of course, to obtain the stipulation of the opposing party that the document is genuine. It is more common, however, to do so by locating the author of the document or one who observed the making of the document and placing him on the stand as an authenticating witness. Such persons are regarded as persuasive guarantors of the document's source and genuineness.

In some cases such formal authentication is not required because the nature of the writing is such that its authenticity can be presumed as a matter of law. The most prominent example of self-authentication are ancient documents and official records.

A former ironclad rule of authentication required that, whenever a writing offered as evidence carried the signature or mark of an attesting witness, the witness should be called to prove the fact of execution, unless, of course, he was incompetent or incapable of testifying. Failure to produce such a witness had to be explained to the judge's satisfaction. If it was not, the evidence would become inadmissible. The apparent reasoning behind this rule was that the subscribing witness was considered by the writer of the document to be an appropriate person to establish the fact of execution; thus, he probably had a greater knowledge of the document's authenticity than any party other than the writer.

Many states have modified this rule by statute. Such statutes generally make attested writings provable without the testimony of the attesting witnesses. This does not affect the duty of the party offering the document to establish its authenticity; it merely relieves him of the obligation to account for the whereabouts of the attesting witnesses.

When the attesting witness is used to authenticate a document, whether or not he is required by law to do so, he need not be able to recall the transaction or to have an independent recollection of the contents of the document. It is sufficient for the attesting witness to be able to identify his signature or mark on the document; he can thereby establish that the document was executed in his presence. This satisfies the requirement of authentication since the objective is only to establish the genuineness of the writing, not the truth of its contents.

If the attesting witness or author of the writing is unavailable or unable to authenticate the writing, it is possible to prove the document's authenticity through the use of circumstantial proof. In the case of a handwritten document, there are three ways to establish authenticity. First, a person who is familiar with the alleged writer's handwriting can identify the document. Second, courts have allowed the testimony of handwriting experts to establish authenticity. The expert compares the questionable document to an authentic example of the writer's handwriting and is thus able to express an expert opinion on whether or not the two documents were written by the same person. Though the expert is not required to explain the reason for his judgment, the value of his opinion will be greatly enhanced if the judge or jury is made to understand the basis for his decision. As in all cases of expert testimony, the court is free to give little weight to the opinion or even to reach an opposite conclusion. Most courts, however, consider handwriting expertise a valuable tool in the authentication process (see, however, *Keeney* v. *Arp de la Gardee*, 212 Iowa 45, 235 N.W. 745 [1931]). Third, one may present the sample and the questioned handwriting to the jury itself. This can only be done after the comparisons have been entered in evidence and will usually serve to evaluate the judgment of a handwriting expert.

Another means of authenticating a questioned document through the use of circumstantial evidence arises when a reply is requested to a letter. By referring to the content of the return letter, the courts have held that it is possible to authenticate the identity of the writer of the reply. This ruling is based on the theory that only the party who had received the original letter would be familiar with the subject matter contained in the reply (*Anstine* v. *McWilliams*, 24 Wash. 2d 230, 163 P. 2d 816 [1945]).

The ancient document rule is an exception to both the rule excluding hearsay evidence and that requiring authentication of documents. The traditional rule was that a writing that was thirty or more years old, if relevant to the inquiry and free from suspicion, was admissible in evidence without the ordinary requirements of proof of execution. The Federal Rules of Evidence (Secs. 803 [16] and 901 [b] [8]) reduced the definition of "ancient" to twenty years and also indicated that if a document is ancient, the proof of its age suffices as authentication.

(12.3) Specific Kinds of Records

If the litigants are the two parties to a transaction, a receipt, or notation of payment, will generally be admissible in evidence. A receipt of full payment is proof of a settlement and is not merely evidence of the sums specified in the note. On the other hand, a receipt for the payment of an account is not evidence that the account was due if the existence of an account is the question in issue. A receipt will not be competent evidence against a person who was not a party to that transaction, for such evidence is hearsay, as concerns the parties to the case. Many states have adopted provisions concerning business records that exclude from the hearsay rule written records made in the regular course of business. The rule under the Federal Rules of Evidence (Sec. 803 [6]) is slightly broader as it refers to "regularly conducted activity." If the receipt can be fitted into one of these exceptions, it will be admissible in evidence against third parties as well.

a. Church Records

Church records and baptismal, marriage, and other certificates are admissible as evidence if made by the clergyman, official, or other person authorized to make such records. Because these records are private, they do not fit within the range of public reports for which authentication is unnecessary. If the clergyman who made the record is still living at the time of the lawsuit, he will be required by some courts to authenticate the reliability of his records. Such records can only serve the limited purpose for which they were intended; they cannot be used for extraneous purposes. For example, in *State* v. *Larocca*, 157 La. 50, 101 So. 868 (1924), a priest was not allowed to testify concerning the age of a party when his information was based on the age he had been told to place on the party's baptismal certificate.

It is well established that entries in a family Bible or similar record can be entered in evidence when offered to prove the birth,

death, marriage, or other fact of history there recorded. The entry
must be duly authenticated and is subject to the best evidence rule
that would prefer public or official documents if they are available.
It is not necessary to prove the identity of the individual who made
the entry, but it should be shown that the Bible had been taken from
the custody of the family in question, that there was some guarantee
that the date was recorded at the approximate date of the occurrence, and that the family generally accepted the record as accurate.
The timing and purpose of the entries may have considerable significance in the effort to establish the competence of the entry as it
relates to the issue on trial.

b. Letters

Letters are a frequent form of documentary evidence and are
admissible if they are communications between the parties and are
properly authenticated. To be documentary evidence, letters must
be relevant and material to an issue of the lawsuit, but they need
not have been written after legal action was commenced. Previous
letters written between the defendant and victim may be relevant to
the case if they are informative concerning the writer's state of mind,
motives, or plans. A letter written by a defendant after his arrest
usually meets the requirements of relevance and materiality, but is
inherently suspect as self-serving. It will, therefore, probably be
given little weight by a jury.

Authentication is a vital element of a letter offered as documentary evidence. The fact that the letter purports by its signature to
have been written by a particular party on a particular date is inconclusive in a determination of authenticity. When it is impossible
to obtain authenticating evidence from the alleged author or from a
witness, and handwriting comparisons fail to settle the issue, courts
have allowed circumstantial or secondary evidence to complete the
authentication. This type of evidence may include the style or tone
of the letter if it is in any way distinctive or proof that only the
alleged author could have had the knowledge required to write the
particular letter.

Letters written between third persons are generally excluded
from evidence on the basis of their being outside the scope of the
trial (irrelevant) or violative of the hearsay evidence rule (incompetent). They may be admitted, however, if it can be shown that the

person against whom the evidence is presented was in some way aware of the communications or if they are used to prove a collateral issue such as the person's state of mind or location at a particular time.

c. Telegraph Messages

These messages are subject to the same rules of evidence as all other types of documentary evidence but with an additional twist. A telegram may be accidentally or intentionally altered by telegraph operators at either end of the line. This means that telegrams are subject to the rule that prefers the original written message as evidence if it is still available. Should it not be available, the sender is faced with a major problem of authentication; he must prove that a telegram was sent in his name and that he authorized or caused the telegram to be sent in his name on a particular date.

d. Books

Books or other publications will not usually be received as documentary evidence, despite their usefulness as sources of information. This is in keeping with the general rule barring hearsay evidence, which specifies that such publications are thought to be written records of information on which persons could be called to provide oral testimony. There are several recognized exceptions to this general rule. If, for example, a particular book is the work of a deceased author who is unquestionably reliable, and if the book concerns general facts of history, the work will be admitted. In cases where the author of the work is still living or where the facts are of such recent interest that many persons would be able to give oral testimony concerning these facts, however, these persons should be called as witnesses, and the book will be inadmissible.

e. Newspaper and Magazine Articles

Newspaper articles or magazine accounts usually will not be admissible. The statements made in these publications were not made by a party under oath, and there is no opportunity to cross-examine the author. A newspaper account may be admissible if it concerns historical events of obscure or ancient origins that cannot appropriately be the subject of oral testimony. A newspaper account can also be accepted as evidence if it qualifies as an ancient document.

In all cases, printed material, whether a newspaper, a magazine, or a book, must be adequately authenticated to the satisfaction of the trial judge. *Dallas County* v. *Commercial Union Assurance Co.*, 286 F. 2d 388 (5th Cir., 1961), involved a newspaper account of a fire in a clock tower, an issue relevant to the trial. The court admitted the account as evidence, not because it was fifty-eight years old and was an ancient document, but because it felt that the requirements of materiality, relevance, and reliability were all satisfied, and there was no other means of obtaining the information contained in the article.

f. Learned Treatise

The use of a learned treatise as documentary evidence has recently been redefined by the Federal Rules of Evidence. Most jurisdictions had refused to admit medical and scientific treatises as evidence of the theories and opinions they stated. Rule 803 (18) allows such evidence once its authoritativeness has been established before the trial judge. For the first time it may be used as substantive evidence in federal courts rather than merely as a means of impeaching the expert testimony offered by the opposing side. If, in the past, an expert accepted a treatise as authoritative, and the treatise contained information that contradicted his testimony, the opposing attorney could use these contradictions to impeach the witness. He could not, however, enter the treatise as substantive evidence.

In those states that still exclude treatises from being offered as substantive evidence, the hearsay rule is the basis for the exclusion. That is, there is no way to evaluate the validity of the opinions contained in the book since there is no opportunity to challenge or cross-examine the author, and the opinions were not made while under oath. This rule may be relaxed when the treatise is used to impeach the oral testimony of an expert witness. In that case the evidence is not being offered as the truth, but is introduced to challenge the oral testimony given under oath.

g. Commercial and Scientific Publications

The rule against hearsay evidence is further relaxed regarding the use of commercial or scientific publications, which include market quotations, scientific treatises, histories, atlases, and similar reference publications. In the case of the exception for commercial publications, the rationale parallels that for business records, which constitutes a major exception to the hearsay rule. It is expected that the information in commercial publications, such as catalogues, price lists, and indexes, will be relied upon. If it is established that the commercial world does indeed rely on these figures, the document will be admitted as evidence. The rationale for allowing scientific publications and histories is not as strong since it is more difficult to establish their authoritativeness or reliability. There is, however, a basis for their exception in that such works are the products of expert authority and can usually be checked against corroborative evidence and research data.

h. Official Records

Official records and other official writings are significant exceptions to the hearsay rule. When a document sets forth the record, report, statement, or data compilation of a public agency or official, and when it is the duty of that agency or official to make such a report, the records are public in nature and will usually be admissible in evidence without requiring proof by the person who actually made the entries. There must, however, be some indication that the official making the report had firsthand knowledge of its contents; otherwise the evidence would be no more than hearsay on the part of the reporting officer. Many states have statutes dealing with official reports or certified copies of those reports. They provide that reports concerned with a matter within the officer's statutorily defined duty should be admitted as evidence of the facts contained in those reports. The Federal Rules of Evidence (Sec. 803 [8]) go beyond the state rules and allow the receipt in civil cases and against the government in criminal cases of findings from investigations made pursuant to a legally granted authority.

i. Records Concerning Death

Death certificates and autopsy reports are special types of documentary evidence, combining an investigating and a recording function. Either the original certificate or certified copies are admissible evidence of the facts contained in those reports. In addition, the records of the coroner and his staff or copies of those records are accepted as evidence. These reports are not conclusive evidence, however, and are subject to impeachment and contradiction.

(12.4) Tables

Most charts, graphs, and tables constitute another form of documentary evidence that is subject to the same requirements of relevance, materiality, and competence as are all forms of written evidence. They must also be authenticated before they are received as competent evidence. Some tables, however, are used so frequently and unquestioningly that they have generally become admissible without further proof of authenticity. As an example, life insurance companies prepare mortality or life expectancy tables to establish the probable remaining life expectancy for a person at any given age. Since these tables are compiled by disinterested parties and come as close as is humanly possible to statistical exactitude, courts will usually admit them without question when a determination of life expectancy is relevant to the issue on trial. In all cases involving tables, of course, the trial judge must be satisfied that the tables are authentic and accurate. If the court is not satisfied, it will be necessary to establish the authenticity of the table through the presentation of competent evidence.

(12.5) Vital Statistics

Data relating to birth, marriage, death, or other vital statistics that are collected by a public official pursuant to a requirement of the law are admissible as evidence on judicial notice, and there is no requirement of authenticating such documents. A distinction should be made here between a public official responsible for compiling such statistics and the clergyman or family member who may keep a parallel record. Because the official is under a duty to maintain accurate records, certified copies of these records are admissible without further authentication. On the other hand, persons who are not public officials are under no obligation to record such matters, and the accuracy of their reports cannot be presumed. Thus, these records must be authenticated.

(12.6) Business Records

The business records exception to the hearsay rule grants an important concession to the modern business world. If the hearsay rule were strictly applied, evidence arising in the course of business operations would only be admissible when the individual who made the specific business entry or wrote the particular check could be placed on the stand. With the advancing complexity of most business operations, it became necessary to find a compromise between the rigid requirement of the hearsay rule and the desirability of receiving evidence where there is a sufficient guarantee of reliability.

The result is, of course, the business records exception. Thus, courts usually admit business records without the authenticating proof of the person who made the entry. There are two reasons for this exception. First, business records could only rarely be accepted since it is virtually impossible to trace the activities and duties of each employee in a modern business operation. Second, courts accord business records a high presumption of reliability because they are the main source of information on which business decisions are made, and, thus, they can be expected to be carefully prepared and preserved.

Five basic requirements must be met if a writing is to be brought within the business records exception to the hearsay rule:

1. The record must be a writing of some type, which has been interpreted to include all kinds of commercial paper, journal entries, and even computer printouts. Oral business records have not, however, been incorporated into this exception.

2. The entry must be made in the regular course of business. This is a most flexible standard, but it excludes writings incidental to the business made by individuals who could, under the general rule, be able to claim the protection of the exception. The theory is that only matters arising in the regular course of business have the inherent qualities of reliability that underlie the exception.

3. The party offering the evidence must be able to show that the custom of the business was to record the particular type of transaction at the same time the record was made or within a reasonable period of time thereafter. For two reasons this is a further guarantee of reliability. First, it establishes that the entry was probably recorded soon after the transaction. Second, there is little danger that the person who made the entry has a faulty memory of the event.

4. If the party offering the information was not connected with the business, the entry will not be admissible. This is because

information supplied by an outsider lacks assurance of reliability.

5. The record must be authenticated as being what is purports to be. This does not mean that every business entry must be authenticated, for this is what the exception was designed to eliminate. Instead, the offering party is merely required to prove that the entry was made in the usual place for such entries and that the book in which it was recorded be the actual record kept by the business.

The usual procedure is for the custodian of the records to bring the account book, checkbook, or whatever document is sought as evidence. He must then prove to the court's satisfaction that what he brought is the authentic record of business activities. If the court is so convinced, the business record is entered into evidence although no one has authenticated the making of the actual entry sought as evidence.

(12.7) Demonstrations in General

Demonstrative evidence can be classified as two basic types. The first, selected demonstrative evidence, also known as preexisting evidence, is used to give a jury a better concept of an item of evidence. In a murder trial, for example, a woman raises as a defense that she was incapable of wielding the alleged murder weapon, a baseball bat. The prosecution may introduce a baseball bat as evidence to impeach that claim, even though the bat is not the actual murder weapon, but is only a preexisting sample of a typical bat.

The second type of demonstrative evidence, prepared or reproduced, includes, among other things, photographs, scale models, drawings, and casts. Such evidence is prepared and offered in court to aid the jury in understanding the issues and testimony of the trial. If these representations can be shown to be accurate and correct, courts will usually admit them as evidence on the theory that they constitute a tangible form of testimony from a qualified witness that he may use instead of more detailed and possibly less graphic oral testimony.

It is necessary to establish the authenticity of all demonstrative evidence offered for admission. If, for example, the diagram or exhibit is not made in the presence of the court, evidence must be offered to establish the accuracy of the representation. In this respect, the requirements of authentication do not differ from those required of all evidence offered by an out-of-court party. In order to satisfy the tests of the hearsay rule, it is necessary to establish the reliability of the evidence to the satisfaction of the trial judge. If the evidence consists of a drawing or diagram made in court by a witness, its admission is not likely to be challenged since the evidence was produced in court while the witness was under oath. It is thus sufficient to satisfy the requirements of the hearsay rule.

a. Photographs and Recordings in General

If counsel lays a proper foundation of accuracy and reliability, photographs and sound recordings may be accepted as evidence if they are relevant and material to the issues and if they are not unduly prejudicial. Photographs are probably the most commonly used form of demonstrative evidence. The reliability of their reproduction is generally accepted, they are a relatively inexpensive means of representing the actual physical evidence, and they are very convenient.

As with all other evidence, a photograph must be shown to have some relevance to the matter in controversy at the trial in order to be admitted. The trial judge determines the relevance, which is based on the relevance of the photograph itself, not that of the fact the offering party is attempting to establish. If it is determined that the photograph is not relevant to the purposes of the trial, the fact may be established through the use of some other evidence.

b. Accuracy of Representation and Authentication

A photograph cannot be submitted anonymously and be accepted as evidence. Without a sponsoring or authenticating witness, a photograph has no value as evidence because it is impossible to establish what the photograph shows. Thus, a competent witness must provide the court with evidence that the photograph is a fair and accurate depiction of persons, objects, or scenes. It is not necessary for the photographer to establish the accuracy of his work, although in some cases that may be the best way to establish authentication. Any witness who is competent to speak from personal experience on the accuracy of the scene depicted is suitable as an authenticating witness. If the witness is someone other than the photographer, he need not have been present when the photograph was taken. His presence would, however, add weight to his testimony.

The trial judge has considerable discretion in ruling whether the photograph was substantially accurate. He may even allow its admission when there are contentions that the photograph is inaccurate. In those cases, however, the jury must weigh the evidence in order to determine the accuracy of the photograph.

c. Time and Changes of Conditions

One of the basic questions that must be clarified before the court will allow a photograph in evidence is that of change or the possibility of change in the contents of the photograph. There is, in addition, basically a question of relevance. For example, even if the depiction is an absolutely accurate portrayal of the present condition of a railroad crossing, it may have no relevance to a trial concerning the way the crossing appeared twenty years ago. Thus it is necessary to establish two separate and distinct proofs. First, the photograph must be an accurate depiction of the subject that it appears or purports to represent. Second, the scene must be shown to have some relevance to the issue at trial. This can only be established by showing through competent proof that the photograph aids in understanding the conditions of the subject as it appeared at the time with which the trial is concerned.

The fact that there was a lapse of time between the incident in question and the making of the photograph need not result in a ruling of inadmissibility. If the party offering the photograph as evidence can produce witnesses to testify that the photograph fairly depicts the subject as it appeared at the time in question, the photograph should be admitted. If, on the other hand, a photograph was made immediately after the incident, but conditions had materially changed before the picture was taken, the photograph has little relevance and will probably be excluded. Every effort should be made, of course, to see that conditions in the photograph closely approximate those existing at the time of the incident. Thus, if the issue is visibility along a train track, the photograph should be taken with the approximate amount of daylight as was present at the time of the incident. A photograph that does not coincide in every detail with conditions at the time of the incident may be admitted. The jury must, however, be instructed to consider it only for a certain limited purpose. For example, in a case of battery the victim was pushed over a bannister. A photograph taken after the bannister was removed might be admissible for the limited purpose of showing where the battery took place. That is, as long as the changed conditions in the photograph do not unduly influence the jury, a trial judge may be persuaded to admit the photograph as evidence.

d. Prejudicial Use of Gruesome or Nude Photographs

Since the judge must approve all photographs before he admits them into evidence, there is a natural obstacle to the submission of photographs that are unduly prejudicial. If a photograph is inflammatory, horrifying, or gruesome, it will be admissible only if the judge feels it would be helpful to the jury in understanding a case. If, on the other hand, the value of these photographs is outweighed by the danger they pose in prejudicing the interests of either party, they are properly excluded. Thus, judges usually apply a balancing test between the probative value of the evidence and its prejudicial effect.

e. Colored Photographs and Motion Pictures

Colored photographs and slides are admissible as demonstrative evidence and are subject to the same limitations placed on black-and-white photographs. Though color photographs provide a more accurate depiction of appearances and conditions than do those in black and white, there is a greater danger that they might be unduly prejudicial and inflammatory. Colored photographs may, in fact, be excluded in their entirety when an inaccurate portrayal of colors raises the possibility of misleading a jury.

Motion pictures are also admissible as evidence when properly authenticated. The authentication procedure may be more complex than that for a still photograph because of the possibilities of inaccuracy. A motion picture consists of a series of still photographs exhibited in sequence. It is, therefore, possible for a motion picture of an actual event to be tampered with in such a way as to be imperceptible to the untrained viewer. Lens settings, interruptions of the photographic process, elimination of unfavorable frames, and tampering with the sound track are only the most obvious examples of abuse.

Because of these factors, courts have placed a heavier burden on counsel seeking the admission of moving pictures in evidence than they have for the admission of a still photograph. Evidence must be provided of the circumstances in which the pictures were taken, with particular attention paid to technical aspects. The manner and circumstances in which the film was processed and developed must be established, and the court may require evidence of the accuracy of the speed at which the movie is shown and the size of the depiction on the screen. It is also necessary to have available a person who was present at the making of the film in order that he might testify that the movie is an accurate portrayal of the events filmed.

The fact that a motion picture film has been edited will not render it inadmissible if the court is satisfied that the accuracy of the representation is established. In some cases, a court may even direct the party offering the film in evidence to edit it in order to remove irrelevant materials. There is, of course, always an inherent danger of deception whenever motion pictures are offered in evidence. If, however, they are properly authenticated and clearly relevant to an issue at trial, they are acceptable forms of demonstrative evidence.

f. Videotapes and Sound Recordings

The increased use of videotapes in recording events has led to suggestions that they be introduced as evidence in legal proceedings. At this point it appears that they will be subject to the same rules that apply to the admission of motion pictures. Once again there is a danger of tampering, but, if the foundation of accuracy and relevancy is adequately established, there is no reason why these tapes should not be an acceptable form of demonstrative evidence.

It is generally accepted that sound recordings are admissible if they are appropriately authenticated. The process of authentication includes a demonstration that the recording device was capable of making an accurate recording, that the operator of the device was authentic and accurate, that there were no additions to or deletions from the recording, that the recording was properly preserved, and that voices or other sounds on the recording were properly identified by the offering party. At the preliminary hearing concerning admissibility, the judge may instruct the offering party to erase irrelevant or incompetent materials, which do not, of course, affect an otherwise admissible sound recording.

In spite of the general acceptance of sound recordings as demonstrative evidence, they may be held inadmissible if they violate a rule of competency. If the recording was made through the use of an illegal wiretap, it is incompetent and hence inadmissible in a federal court. Recorded admissions and confessions are inadmissible if they were obtained by unconstitutional means. Tape recordings do, however, present a potentially valuable tool to police in establishing that a confession was voluntarily given with full knowledge of the party's *Miranda* rights. If used properly and authenticated to the judge's satisfaction, such recordings should be admissible as evidence.

g. Models and Casts

A trial judge has the discretionary power to admit any model into evidence if he is satisfied that it is relevant to the issues in a trial and is an accurate replica or representation of the object in issue. If it is likely that a model will mislead or confuse a jury, it may be excluded from evidence. If, however, the discrepancy between the model and the actual object can be explained to the jury, the model should be admitted.

Models often help the jury to understand complex physical conditions or such things as the layout of a building or any other structure with which they could not be familiar but which they must understand in order to render a verdict in the case. Perhaps the most common type of model are reproductions of the human body, its skeleton, and organs, which are used to illustrate the expert testimony of a medical authority.

Another common type of demonstrative evidence is the plaster cast, which reproduces an impression made in mud, sand, or a similar substance. As an effective substitute for photography, the cast is often used by police to present a three-dimensional reproduction for the purpose of recreating a mark left at the scene of the crime. If a proper foundation of relevancy and accuracy is laid, judges generally admit casts in evidence.

h. Experiments

To the extent that experiments conducted by police are relevant to the issues of a trial, they should be admissible as evidence. When these experiments are performed outside the courtroom, the party offering the evidence should show that the tests were made under circumstances similar to those existing at the time of the incident or crime. Among the experiments that are treated with great respect by the courts are ballistics tests, tests of various parts of motor vehicles such as brakes and headlights, tests of the sensory powers of a witness, and chemical tests for intoxication. This type of evidence can be very persuasive as well as being an important source of factual information. Since accuracy is the single most important test of admissibility, these experiments should be conducted by qualified experts whenever possible. Courts do not generally favor proposals for the jury's participation in experiments that take place in the courtroom. And, where test results are inconclusive or might be confusing to the jury, the trial judge should properly exclude them from evidence.

i. Diagrams, Drawings, and Graphs

While photographs are often an important aid in recreating the scene of the incident at issue, they do not always tell the whole story. It may be necessary to provide additional drawings and diagrams in order to describe a particular locale thoroughly. For example, photographs of a murder scene may inadequately portray the overall appearance of a room, and a photograph taken at a distance necessarily sacrifices specific details. The solution to this problem is often a diagram, either drawn by a third party and corroborated by the witness or drawn by the witness himself.

The fact that these diagrams or drawings are not made strictly to scale does not automatically render them inadmissible. It may, however, have a considerable impact on the judge who must determine whether they will aid or hinder the jury in its consideration of the case. A certain amount of latitude for minor inaccuracies is allowed where the exhibit is intended only to act as a guide to the testimony of the witness. If, on the other hand, the diagram is to be used as substantive evidence, such as to prove the location of boundary lines or a topographical feature of a landscape, great care should be taken to establish the accuracy of the exhibit.

The use of maps and graphs as an aid to comprehending testimony is also common. In many cases, under the rules of documentary evidence, it is unnecessary to establish the factual basis for the exhibits such as the process of gathering data on which the graph is based or, in the case of a map, the accuracy of the surveyor. Even if these documents fit within the applicable hearsay exception, it is still necessary to establish that the particular graph or table offered is the one it purports to be. Should it be necessary to enlarge the original graph, the enlarging process must be authenticated.

(12.8) Best and Secondary Evidence Rule

The *best evidence rule* is actually an expression of the legal system's preference for the strongest or most authentic evidence available. Although the rule generally applies only to documents in writing, the Federal Rules of Evidence (Sec. 1001) also make the rule applicable to recordings, photographs, X rays, and films.

The rule requires that the contents of any writing be proven by the contents of the writing itself or that failure to do so be adequately explained. If the trial court finds the explanation satisfactory, the judge has the discretionary power to admit secondary evidence of the writing, usually in the form of a carbon copy or other copy. When there are no secondary sources, oral testimony concerning the contents of the writing is admitted so long as the court is satisfied that no superior (that is, written) evidence is available.

The best evidence rule does not involve a judgment on the persuasiveness or conclusiveness of evidence. Indeed, that entails a strategic decision that must be made by the attorneys for each side. The primary purpose of the best evidence rule is to prevent fraud. The most effective way to prove the contents of a written document is, of course, to introduce the document itself. When an unexecuted copy of a document is offered to prove the contents of the original, the possibility always exists that the copy is not an accurate representation of the parties' intentions at the time the document was signed.

In order to have secondary evidence of a writing admitted, the offering party must go through a three-part proof. Thus, he must prove:

1. that the original existed at one time;
2. that the original was genuine and represented the intent of the parties;
3. that there was an adequate explanation for the failure to produce the original.

There are many acceptable reasons for not producing the original document. The purpose of the best evidence rule is not to ban the use of nonoriginal writings, but to be certain that the original is no longer available. Two of the most common reasons are that the original was destroyed by the offering party without fraudulent intent or that the original was lost and a diligent search has failed to produce it.

a. Legal Documents and Public Records

If the evidence sought concerns a legal proceeding, the best available evidence is always the official record of the proceeding. It thus becomes necessary to produce the official transcript or record to establish any evidence made public at a trial. A witness is not allowed to give oral testimony concerning the outcome of a trial or testimony given at trial if an objection is made under the best evidence rule. Secondary evidence of legal proceedings is admissible only where the judicial records are no longer available or where the trial record is incomplete with respect to the issue at trial.

The best evidence rule also applies to records kept by public officials or agencies and to the proceedings of public bodies. Secondary evidence is only admissible when there is no available official record.

b. Photographic Copies, Duplicates, and Carbon Copies

The traditional application of the best evidence rule barred photographic duplicates of an original where the failure to produce the original was not adequately explained. These copies are not regarded as duplicate originals of the documents since they were not executed at a point simultaneous to the execution of the original; thus, the possibility of fraudulent alterations still exists. Increased sophistication of and reliance on photoduplication equipment have, however, seriously undercut the application of the best evidence rule in this area. A number of states have passed statutes that allow qualified photographic reproductions to be admissible as evidence and with the same status as the original writing. This parallels developments concerning documentary evidence that admit a certified copy of a public record with the same authentication process required of an original.

The courts have generally held that photostatic copies of public records are admissible. Because the courts seem to have taken judicial notice of the accuracy of photographic reproduction, it is not necessary to include a scientific explanation of the camera's accuracy as a part of the authentication process. Issues in which the courts assume accuracy of reproduction are sometimes termed "self-authenticating."

If the original document cannot be located, but the offering party is able to offer a duplicate original, the best evidence rule will not exclude the duplicate original. The clearest example of a duplicate original is a legal document, which is normally executed in tripli-cate. Because of the nature of the execution and the identity of the documents themselves, there is no basis for distinguishing the original from the duplicates.

There is a division of opinion concerning the application of the best evidence rule to carbon copies of the original document. Some jurisdictions treat carbon copies as the equivalent of duplicate origi-nals even when there has been no formal execution of the copies. In such cases, the carbon copy must still be authenticated in some way as having been made at the same time as the original.

Where either the original document or the copy of the original has not been accounted for, the rule operates to exclude a copy made from a copy, unless it is the best evidence available.

(12.9) Form of Proof, Adverse Production, and Complex Documents

The objective of the party seeking to have secondary evidence introduced is to convince the trial judge that he has exhausted all reasonable avenues of discovery and has been unable to locate the original writing. Any competent proof may be used to establish that the original has been lost, destroyed, or otherwise made unavailable. It is not necessary to offer positive proof of a writing's destruction. If the trial judge has any suspicion that the document is being improp-erly withheld, however, he may deny the admission of secondary evidence by invoking the best evidence rule.

It is not sufficient for the party seeking to produce secondary evidence of a document to indicate that the adverse party is in possession of the original. In order to fulfill the requirements of the best evidence rule, he must be able to show that he has given the opponent a request for production (notice), and there has been a failure to comply. The requirements of notice vary among juris-dictions, but generally include a written request for production of the document and allowance of a reasonable period in which to produce it. If the document is clearly unavailable by reason of its remoteness, it is within the court's discretion to order admission of the secondary evidence. In addition, most jurisdictions do not require a defendant to produce a document that incriminates him.

When the best evidence rule is made inapplicable by the vast number of documents or when the complexity outweighs their value as evidence, the court has discretion to authorize or to order an approximate summary. This occurs most frequently in complex commercial cases where it is impractical to require the production of thousands of canceled checks or a complete accounting of a firm's financial status. In such cases, the original documents must be submitted to the adverse party so that the accuracy of the summary can be tested on cross-examination.

(12.10) Summary

Most of the underlying rules governing admissibility of documentary evidence do not differ in principle from those regulating testimonial evidence. Like hearsay, there are well-recognized rules governing particular types of documents, such as church records, letters, books, and other publications.

Official records are usually admissible if made by a public servant who had firsthand knowledge of the information recorded. Photographs, motion pictures, and videotapes are also admissible if there are sufficient indicia of reliability. Like models, casts, and diagrams, they assist in the fact-finding process.

The best evidence rule serves to ensure that the most original record or copy will be the one received in evidence. Duplicates and copies of copies will not be excluded if originals are not available, but the rule requires parties to make an effort to locate documents that are more likely to be trustworthy.

13

Physical and Scientific Evidence: Preservation and Custody

A. ROUTINE PHYSICAL EVIDENCE

(13.1) In General

Any physical evidence that tends to prove or disprove the crime charged may be offered. If it is relevant, and the proper foundation laid, it will be admitted as part of the proof. The range of objects and materials that may be offered in evidence is limitless. Relevancy is the key word.

(13.2) Admissible Objects

No rule excludes any particular object as evidence. As long as the evidence tends to prove the issue, it should be usable.

If, however, the exhibit is too gruesome or inflammatory, the court will exclude it on these grounds. In a homicide case arising out of an illegal abortion, for example, the dead fetus may have been preserved and offered in evidence. It would be excluded on that ground, no matter how relevant it might be to the proof. If the exhibit can be misleading, such as an unfair or slanted photograph, it will be rejected if there is an objection.

(13.3) Fruits of the Crime

"Fruits of the crime," such as loot from a robbery or a burglary, are relevant and admissible in evidence. If it is impracticable to bring the actual objects into court, photographs of them can be used in evidence. A stolen car or truck, for example, would be returned to the owner and would be described by witnesses with the aid of photographs.

(13.4) Instrumentalities

Anything used to commit crime is relevant evidence. A murder weapon, a gun employed in a robbery, a burglar's tools, an acetylene torch used to open a safe, a gasoline can from an arson scene—all such objects may properly be offered in evidence in each particular case.

(13.5) Masks and Clothing

Any type of mask used during the commission of a crime would be admitted in evidence. Police sometimes overlook clothing as evidence of a crime. If, however, the clothing is some type of disguise, it would be strong evidence. More frequently the suspect's or victim's clothing may yield stains, foreign substances, powder burns, or wound marks that make the clothing very useful as evidence.

At one time a medical examiner in Maryland issued a death certificate stating that a man had died from natural causes. The deceased, a middle-aged man with a history of heart trouble, was found dead, lying across the bed in his motel room, clad in his underwear. The cause of death was determined to be heart disease. Because of an anonymous telephone tip suggesting murder, the medical examiner reopened the case. The examiner found a tiny hole in the front of the man's undershirt with a bloodstain on it. The autopsy revealed that he had been stabbed to death with one blow of an ice pick, which was apparently delivered by the other occupant of the room, his paramour. Thus, the overlooked undershirt was a prime bit of evidence in the prosecution's murder case.

(13.6) Changes in Objects

If an exhibit is to be admitted in evidence, it must reasonably be in the same condition at the time of the trial as it was at the time of the crime. In the event it has been altered because of laboratory or scientific testing, expert witnesses can describe the changes, and the evidence will still be admitted, even though it is in a different condition. Though some types of evidence deteriorate naturally, they still may be allowed in evidence if they remain usable and if the change in condition is not prejudicial in some way.

If, however, the evidence has been carelessly handled or damaged so that it has been changed materially, the defense has valid grounds to object to its use, and court may exclude it.

(13.7) Exhibition of Persons

As has been mentioned in Chapter 6, the defendant can be ordered to present himself in a lineup. He can also be made to rise in court or otherwise exhibit himself or any part of his body, if this is relevant to the proof. He may have, for example, been described as strong and husky. The court may thus allow him to remove his shirt and show that he really is of slight physique or that he has a physical impairment, such as a crippled arm.

Exhibiting the body or any part thereof is also left to the discretion of the judge. He will allow nothing of this nature if it is indecent or inflammatory in the court's judgment.

B. SCIENTIFIC EVIDENCE

(13.8) In General

With the advance of science, scientific evidence allowed in court has changed. Pictures of bank robbers taken by hidden cameras or closed-circuit television, for example, are now used in evidence. Such proof was unknown years ago. Acceptance by the courts of new types of scientific evidence is slow, however, and does not keep pace with the latest advances in science. Whenever a new type of scientific evidence is offered, considerable expert testimony must support it.

In addition, a time of successful use must first be shown before the courts will allow the new method in evidence.

(13.9) Firearms and Ballistics

Much valuable evidence can be obtained by firearms and ballistics tests, but they are not completely perfect as popularly imagined.

In case of close-range firing, reliable tests exist to measure burning, powder marks, and other residues. Tissue may be burned or fabrics scorched. Carbon or powder particles may penetrate or adhere to the surface of the wound. Such proof is often crucial in determining whether a shooting was suicide, accidental, or homicide.

Firearms themselves may be identified through restoring obliterated serial numbers. Gun barrels leave distinguishing marks on bullets. Shell casings also receive individual markings that can often identify the weapon from which the shell was fired. Bullet or shell comparisons, however, are not always completely conclusive, depending on the fragment recovered at the time of the crime. Experts can often state only that the bullet could have come from the weapon in question. The evidence is still acceptable, although it is not conclusive proof of the connection between the projectile and the weapon.

Gunshot residue tests from a suspect's hands—the so-called paraffin tests—have been known for many years. Many experts now doubt their value, largely because similar residues may be found on an innocent person's skin (see Inbau, Moenssens, and Moses, *Scientific Evidence in Criminal Cases*, Sec. 4.12).

(13.10) Tool Marks and Micrography

Photographs taken through a microscope and then enlarged often provide strong circumstantial evidence for use in court. Pry marks from a forced entry may show identical markings with a tool when they are compared microscopically. Other examples include broken tools compared with a piece recovered at the scene of the crime, knife marks on bone, cut marks on wires, and crimp marks on detonators.

Microscopic examination of such evidence is often successful. The term "comparative micrography" is used to describe such examinations where a hard object is applied against a softer one. Tool marks, as has been said, can be examined in this way. The mark itself, or a cast impression, is microscopically compared with the mark made by the suspected tool on a soft substance such as lead. A photograph of the mark is termed "photomicrography." Matching striations, a piece of the blade from a suspect's knife, or a portion from a broken tool can often be successfully demonstrated by photomicrography. Because the photographs often contain areas of apparent differences that the expert must interpret and explain, however, it is not unusual for him to testify without using photomicrography.

(13.11) Forensic Pathology

The trained medical examiner can often supply the best evidence of the details of a suspected crime. In all suspicious or violent deaths an autopsy is required. The pathologist determines the cause and the approximate time of death. Was it a drowning, or did death occur outside the water? The postmortem tells.

Bruises and wounds can be measured and photographed. Hairs, blood, bodily fluids, stomach and blood contents, and condition of the body and wounds—all reveal a story to the trained examiner. In the case of sexual offenses, seminal and other stains may be analyzed. Blood alcohol is commonly tested where intoxication is involved. Evidence concerning poisons, drugs, and many other physical conditions is often given by pathologists.

(13.12) Toxicology and Chemistry

When poisoning is suspected, the pathologist performing the autopsy removes the bodily material such as blood, urine, stomach contents, or tissue from vital organs. He then turns the material over to a toxicologist (a specialist on poisons and their effect) for his examination. The toxicologist presents his findings in a report.

A chemical expert may be called in for laboratory tests in cases concerned with drug abuse or situations involving intoxication. These tests include the use of chemical reagents, crystalline comparisons, chromatography, and other methods of chemical testing. All methods have strengths and weaknesses, and an investigator or attorney should be aware of them as they relate to evidence involved in a criminal prosecution.

Alcohol tests are the most frequently encountered by the officer in the field. Blood, breath, urine, or saliva can all be checked for the presence of alcohol. A police investigator must, however, take certain precautions. The breath test may be defective if the machine has not been aerated to remove moisture. Sterilizing the skin with any kind of alcohol may contaminate a blood sample that is taken for alcohol testing. A blood sample taken at a postmortem to determine the amount of alcohol is useless if the body has been embalmed.

Various factors weaken the effectiveness in court of a blood test for alcohol where intoxication is involved in the criminal charge. After the blood sample is taken, the chemist will actually be unable to state exactly what the alcoholic content of the blood was at the time of the event. It is obvious that the sample had to be taken at some point after the alleged crime. Heavy drinking just before the crime would produce a high percentage of alcohol in the blood at the time of the test. Because of the time necessary for alcohol to be absorbed in the bloodstream, a laboratory expert would have to admit that the blood-alcohol level at the time of the crime would have to have been lower. Experienced defense attorneys are aware of such test deficiencies where alcohol is involved, and they can often convince juries of the weaknesses in such proof.

(13.13) Serology

A serologist is used to analyze bodily fluids such as blood, semen, saliva, and the like. Analysis of blood is the most common.

Several tests are conducted first to classify the specimen as blood. Lipstick, catsup, even iodine are some of the substances that resemble blood. Further tests indicate whether it is animal or human blood. Once it is found to be human, blood is divided into types, either A, B, AB, or O. The types can be readily determined. Approximately 40 percent of Americans are type A, 43 percent are type O, 14 percent are type B, and 3 percent are type AB. There are other systems as well for classifying human blood. Unlike fingerprints, blood samples cannot specifically identify any one individual. An expert can only testify that the blood samples are of the same group, not that they are from the same person. He can, however, eliminate a possible source if the two samples are of different classes.

Those people who have type A, type B, or type AB secrete the antigens characteristic of these blood groups in such bodily fluids as saliva, tears, semen, and perspiration. Blood grouping tests from these bodily secretions can, therefore, be made for about 80 percent of the population.

In cases involving rape or perversion, serology tests are often made to determine the presence of semen and sperm cells. Seminal fluid is secreted by the glands along the seminal tract to which sperm is supplied from the testes. Sperm will not be present if the suspect has had a vasectomy or if too much time has elapsed between the crime and the taking of the sample. The specimen may be tested for acid phosphatase to reveal if it is human seminal fluid. Swabs may be taken from the vaginal or cervical area of the female. In cases of perversion anal or oral swabs are used. Stains may be found on the clothing of the victim or suspect or at the scene of the crime.

Saliva stains are not often thought of, and yet they may be found on cigarette butts, cigars, pipes, or other objects. As has been said, they can often be used to classify blood types. Similar results can also be obtained from perspiration stains, which normally remain on coats, hats, shirts, and dresses. Even fecal matter and vomitus yield test results to the serologist.

(13.14) Narcotics and Drugs

Because the use of narcotics and various drugs has become so widespread, law enforcement personnel continuously find themselves deeply involved in drug control.

It has even been a legal problem to devise a definition of "narcotic" that is scientifically correct. Those who draft statutes have avoided the problem by simply listing a series of drugs that must be labeled "controlled substances." Some jurisdictions have statutes that attempt not only to regulate narcotics traffic but to make it a crime to be a user. California attempted this with a possession statute making it a crime to "use or be under the influence, or be addicted to the use of narcotics."

In *Robinson* v. *California*, 370 U.S. 660 (1962), a suspect arrested under this law had needle marks and scabs on his inner arms. He confessed to the use of narcotics. A police narcotics officer testified that, in his opinion, the marks on the defendant, Robinson, resulted from the use of a nonsterile hypodermic needle. When Robinson took the stand, he repudiated his confession and said that the marks came from an allergy contracted in the military service. Robinson was, nevertheless, convicted. The U.S. Supreme Court finally overturned his conviction. It pointed out that, while the state can legally regulate narcotics traffic, here they were making a crime of addiction, even if the drugs were used outside the state of California. The court reasoned that this would be similar to considering mental illness or venereal disease a crime. In the opinion of the court, this amounted to cruel and unusual punishment and violated the Eighth and Fourteenth Amendments.

a. Types of Drugs

Opiates are one of the general classes of drugs. Derived from the opium poppy, they include opium, codeine, morphine, heroin, and synthetics such as methadone and meperidine. All opiates are addictive and are labeled narcotics.

Marijuana, often listed as a narcotic, is correctly classified as a hallucinogen, as are mescaline and LSD. As the term indicates, users of hallucinogens perceive sights, sounds, and colors that are not real. Though none of these drugs are considered addictive, many are dangerous.

Cocaine is an alkaloid derived from cocoa leaves. A stimulant, it reduces inhibitions. Extended use may produce hallucinations. It is normally taken by sniffing or by injection.

Barbiturates are used as sedatives, hypnotics, and antispasmodics. Overuse produces symptoms similar to intoxication and can result in physical dependence.

Amphetamines are stimulants. Their use does not cause physical dependence.

b. Tests for Drugs

The police chemist is frequently called on to identify unknown materials in order to determine if they are drugs or narcotics. In cases of deaths and of traffic violations, tests of blood or urine are used to provide information concerning the use of drugs. These range from relatively simple physical and chemical tests to nuclear activation analysis.

Tests to determine addiction to narcotics are among those

generally employed by police laboratories. Urinary analysis is the best-known method. Laboratory findings based on urinalysis are accepted as legal evidence. One problem with urinalysis is that police are often careless in obtaining and preserving the sample.

In the 1950's, the nalline test was developed to discover narcotic addiction or recent use by individuals. The test involves injecting a drug, nalorphine, into a subject and measuring the reaction of the pupil of his eye.

An early California case ruled on the admissibility of nalline test results for narcotics use (*People* v. *Williams*, 164 Cal. App. 2d 858 [1959]). Two suspects had been arrested as being drug users. Each admitted to having used drugs previous to that time, but denied recent use. Both of them had old and new needle marks on their arms. The doctor who administered the test testified in court that the subjects were injected with nalline after having their pupils measured with a test card that contained a series of dots. Thirty minutes later their pupils were measured again. A comparison of the measurements showed that each one had dilated pupils. The appellate court approved the use of the test results in conjunction with the expert's opinion that both defendants were then under the influence of narcotics. While the nalline test itself has limitations, such as the possibility of inaccurate readings of the pupillometer, it is now generally received in court.

Courts now routinely allow witnesses to testify concerning needle marks ("tracks") on a suspect's arm and to give an opinion as to whether they are recent or old. Such evidence has been received as proof in possession of heroin.

A wide variety of scientific tests for narcotics and drugs are accepted by modern courts, providing there is proper identification of the sample, its custody, and the qualification of the expert witness.

(13.15) Fingerprints

The skin of a person's fingers, palms, toes, and feet contains a series of friction ridges, which is nature's method of giving man traction. These ridges form patterns that remain the same from birth to death. All friction skin has perspiration pores, and body oils leave a pattern wherever the skin ridges touch a smooth surface. Impressions accidentally left on such a surface are called latent prints.

Though they are normally invisible, they can be made visible by means of powders, vapors, or chemicals. They can be lifted by the use of a transparent adhesive tape or other means and kept as a permanent record. The latent prints once brought to life can be photographed and then compared with known fingerprints.

All fingerprints can be classified under an accepted formula, which makes it possible for them to be filed and retrieved. Identifying the unknown latent print with the known one is entirely different from classifying it. There can be an untold number of prints in the same general class, but only one print of a particular individual.

To identify the particular print, the expert looks for four elements. The standard rule is that there must be at least eight identical ridge comparisons; generally, more concordances are desired. The latent print at the scene of the crime is usually used to identify the defendant and to place him at the scene.

Thus, fingerprint evidence has two uses: to prove the identity of the accused or of the victim or to provide evidence that the defendant committed the crime.

Testimony regarding fingerprints must come from an expert trained and experienced in the science of classifying and identifying them. This type of evidence is so widely accepted that the defense now has little room for attacking the technician's testimony. There are, in fact, a number of cases in which a conviction has been won and sustained even though it is based mainly on fingerprints.

People v. *Rodis*, 145 Cal. App. 2d 44 (1956), concerned the burglary of a drugstore in California. The burglar entered the store through a rear window that was nine feet from the ground. A screen was removed, and the defendant's fingerprint was found on the outside of the window. At the trial the only evidence against the defendant was this fingerprint. Contrary evidence was provided by his family who testified that he was at home the night of the burglary. The defendant himself took the stand and denied ever having been in the store. In spite of the evidence provided by the defense, the defendant was convicted on the strength of the fingerprint evidence. The appellate court affirmed the conviction, pointing out that the fingerprint was found on the outside of the window, nine feet from the ground. Thus, it would have been necessary for a person to use a ladder or a platform to remove the screen. All of these facts militated against any innocent placement of the fingerprint. There is, however, a more generally accepted rule regarding fingerprint evidence. It holds that, in cases where the only evidence of guilt consists of fingerprints found at the scene, the evidence, to be legally sufficient, must be coupled with proof of other circumstances tending reasonably to exclude the idea that the fingerprint was left at a different time. Unless these circumstances are present, the courts will not sustain a conviction based only on fingerprint evidence. This was demonstrated in *Barum* v. *U.S.*, 380 F. 2d 590 (1967), and 380 U.S. 2d 595 (1967), plus *Fladung* v. *State*, 4 Md. App. 664 (1968).

Often it is important to know when a latent print was made, but it is doubtful if such proof can be obtained from fingerprint evidence. The courts sometimes make unusual decisions on this point, as illustrated by the two *Barum* cases cited above. In one of these, Barum was convicted of stealing from a private home a valuable coin collection contained in two empty jars. His fingerprints were found on the jars, but the government's witness admitted that the prints could have been on the jars "for a period of . . . years." The appellate court reversed the conviction. It held that there was insufficient evidence to convict and said that the prosecution should have produced evidence to show that the prints "were placed on the jars at the time of the crime." Barum's other burglary conviction resulted from fingerprints found on three objects in a house, a tea canister, a metal cash box, and a glass table top. The appellate court upheld this conviction on the theory that Barum could have had no previous access to these articles.

In presenting fingerprint evidence, the prosecution must demonstrate the qualifications of its expert and his method of gathering the evidence and its custody, the means of expert examination, and his opinion. The defense may counterattack by attempting to show errors made by the technician and irregularities owing to dirt, variations in finger pressure, scars, and excess use of ink. If the fingerprints were incident to an unlawful arrest, the defense can have them exluded from evidence (*Davis* v. *Mississippi*, 394 U.S. 721 [1969]).

As has been illustrated previously, if the defendant can show that he had innocent access to the scene of the crime, the fingerprint evidence will lack value. The defense may also be allowed to offer evidence that there were no fingerprints at the scene (*State* v. *Cooper*, 2 N.J. 540 [1949]). In this situation the state may rebut the defense by offering proof to show why no fingerprints were found (*Draper* v. *State*, 192 Ark. 675 [1936]). The fact that other fingerprints may have been present at the scene of the crime may not be relevant evidence and will thus be excluded by the trial court. In a bank robbery case, *U.S.* v. *Farley*, 292 F. 2d 789 (1961), the defense was an alibi. The prosecution introduced evidence that the defendant's fingerprint was on the bank window. Farley offered to introduce evidence that other fingerprints were on the window besides his. The court properly denied his offer of proof. It stated that the presence of his prints were shown to disprove his alibi defense. If fingerprints belonging to someone else were there also, it was immaterial.

(13.16) Questioned Documents

The modern specialist who examines documents has come a long way from the so-called "handwriting expert" of previous years. Aided by present-day scientific developments, he is able to do many more things than analyze handwriting. It is true that a questioned document often involves handwriting comparisons, and the expert is called in solely to perform this function. He might, for example, identify the author of a written extortion or ransom note, a forgery, or a letter. He is often asked to do more than this. Has the original document been changed? Were words inserted? Have pages been added? Is the entire paper a fake? These and many similar questions are often submitted to the examiner of questioned documents for his analysis and for his subsequent court testimony.

During the last hundred years, the science of document examination has grown and become more sophisticated. There were initially many so-called experts whose court testimony was based more on self-confidence than on expertise. While there is no recognized professional course of study for a document examiner, the individual must have a technical background and much experience in his field. Those prerequisites will qualify him as an "expert." Though document examiners sometimes vary in their opinions, this does not occur often. When they do disagree, it is usually because they did not have the same materials or they worked under different conditions.

What is a questioned document? It may be a letter, a check, a contract, or a will. It may, in fact, be any material that contains a mark or signature. Criminal cases often involve a variety of things, from the psychopath's scrawled message in lipstick on a mirror to hotel registers, drivers' licenses, and passports. Whenever a document or any part of it is questioned or its authorship is in doubt, the examiner is called in to analyze it and to give his opinion.

The document itself must be treated with great care by the field investigator. Handling is avoided whenever possible so that fingerprints will not be added or minute changes made. The document will usually be picked up with tweezers, placed in a plastic envelope, and sealed. The investigator's mark will then be put on the outside of the container, not on the item itself.

If handwriting is involved, the examiner must have as many genuine exemplars as possible. The defendant can be ordered to furnish these specimens. The expert prefers examples of the suspect's handwriting that use the same words as those appearing in the questioned document. Similarities as well as differences are important in arriving at an opinion on handwriting.

A typewritten document can often be traced to a particular machine. The document examiner keeps a file of samples of the type from various kinds of typewriters. This often allows him to determine immediately the make or model of the typewriter involved. Because each machine develops its own particular characteristics, such as type wear and varying impressions, the expert can go on to make a precise identification of the typewriter used. It is even possible to identify typewriters with revolving elements, although this type of machine does cause added problems for the expert examiner. The trial of Alger Hiss was one of the most widely publicized cases in which the conviction was largely based on typewriter evidence.

In the field of altered documents the skilled examiner can often show the most dramatic results. By using infrared or ultraviolet light and other methods, he may be able photographically to reproduce charred documents, disclose words previously removed by chemicals, or even reproduce the original writing from indentations transferred to paper that lay underneath.

The document examiner may use demonstrative evidence for the jury to illustrate his testimony. Some courts criticize him when he uses this device, and others criticize him when he does not. In *People* v. *White*, 365 Ill. 499 (1937), the defendant was accused of forging a signature on a promissory note. The state claimed that a genuine signature was first traced on the note with carbon paper and then written over in ink. The expert for the prosecution claimed that this left flecks of carbon on the paper. A microscope was set up in the courtroom, and each juror was allowed to look through it. The expert asked each in turn if he saw the flecks, and every answer was "Yes." The appellate court very properly criticized these actions and said that such a demonstration and interrogation of the jurors was improper.

It is interesting to contrast this with a federal case involving income tax fraud (*U.S.* v. *Bruno*, 333 F. Supp. 570 [1971]). The IRS received a forged letter that was allegedly signed before May 1967. The government expert testified that the signature was made with an ink that was not manufactured until after that time. To prove his contention concerning the ink, he performed a demonstration in the courtroom. He punched holes about the size of a hypodermic needle from the questioned signature and dissolved these small pieces of paper containing the ink in a solution that was then placed on a coded plate. The ink separated into its component dyes, and the expert compared this unknown ink with chromatograms. He testified that the original comparison chromatograms were made on glass plates that fade quickly. The court criticized the expert for not taking colored photographs of the plates and offering photographs in evidence. The court pointed out that the actual demonstration provided no way for the jury to see what the basis for his comparison was. Had they been shown colored photographs or slides, they could have assigned proper weight to his testimony.

Thus, when materials are properly handled in the field and when the modern qualified document examiner is provided adequate handwriting exemplars, he can often be the strongest witness the state can produce.

(13.17) Microanalysis

The term microanalysis refers generally to analysis of minute particles of evidence and not just to evidentiary testing by microscope. Microscopes of various kinds are used by technicians in this process.

Examination of small particles of hair, paint, fibers, soil, and glass frequently yields significant results. Paint smears from burglaries or chips from an automobile accident, for example, can often be analyzed and classified by such testing. Paint may be many layers, and the number and kinds of layers can reveal matching characteristics.

Glass fragments from car headlights, broken windows, eyeglasses, and the like may be important evidence. Particles may be found in a suspect's clothing or matched with those in a suspected vehicle. Various techniques of microanalysis can also reveal the chemical or physical characteristics of glass for scientific comparison.

One can test hair to discover whether it is human or animal. It is possible to identify hair from different areas of the body. Racial differences and sometimes sex can be determined by the examination of human hair.

Fibers are of varied types, from synthetic to animal, and the examiner can usually classify them and make accurate comparisons. Even in very small quantities, fibers yield information that can be useful. Those obtained from clothing, for example, may match those from insulation where burglars forced an entry through a wall or ceiling. Tools, clothing, and fired bullets may have fibers connected to them. Threads found on a murder or rape victim may help identify the suspect.

Soil may either be left or removed from the location where the crime occurred. Proper preservation by the investigator enables laboratory technicians to obtain useful evidence from soil, but comparisons are very difficult.

(13.18) Neutron Activation Analysis

One by-product of atomic science, which has been employed since 1964, is neutron activation analysis of evidence in criminal cases. This process involves bombarding the evidence with a stream of nuclear particles from a nuclear reactor that is used for research. This produces radioactivity in the bombarded material. The radioactive material "decays," and in so doing it gives off gamma rays. The rays are counted and their intensity measured. This information is then compared with known data to give an analysis of the quantity of the elements present in the evidentiary sample. Gunshot residue, soils, paint, grease, drugs, and a variety of other substances can be tested by this method. It is obvious, of course, that the facilities for this type of testing are limited.

U.S. v. *Stifel*, 433 F. 2d 431, cert. den. 401 U.S. 994 (1970), is the leading case supporting evidence obtained by neutron activation analysis. Orville Stifel was convicted of murdering Dan Ronec, in his parents' home, by sending a bomb through the mail. The package was in the form of a mailing tube that exploded when Ronec unscrewed the top. The evidence against Stifel was circumstantial, the alleged motive being jealousy over a woman. Stifel had worked for a large soap company and had access to its mailing tubes and labels. The government used neutron activation analysis on these, and its expert testified that the mailing label and tube fragments were the same "elemental composition" as those of the company. The metal cap and the tape "were the same manufacture" and were produced on the same day as the ones made for the company. The court admitted the evidence resulting from the neutron activation analysis, pointing out that no appeals court had refused it and that its scientific basis had been widely accepted by a variety of state decisions.

More recently, in 1974, the Minnesota Supreme Court approved the use of this type of scientific evidence, with a slight warning. In the case involved in this decision, *State* v. *Spencer*, 216 N.W. 2d 131 (Minn., 1974), the defendant had been convicted of aggravated assault and of shooting an off-duty policeman. When the suspect was arrested, his hands were swabbed with nitric acid solution, and the swabs were sent to the Treasury Department laboratory in Washington for neutron analysis. At the trial, the expert testified that the test results showed the presence of barium and antimony on the defendant's right hand and that this meant that the defendant had fired a gun. On cross-examination the expert admitted that there were about a hundred other ways that these chemicals could have contacted the defendant's hands. The court approved the use of the the neutron activation analysis evidence. It pointed out, however, that the expert should only have been allowed to state his opinion that the chemicals came from firing a gun. He should not have been allowed to state this as a positive conclusion.

There appears to be no serious court opposition to the use of this new method. While its access to the police is necessarily somewhat limited, the results can be spectacular.

(13.19) Polygraph

This is a widely used device for testing a person's truthfulness. Developed a number of years ago, it operates on the theory that lying produces tension even in the hardened criminal. This in turn affects bodily reactions such as blood pressure and respiration. These are measured by the machine as the subject is being questioned, and they are recorded on a continuous graph. By reading the graph, a well-trained operator can determine the speaker's truthfulness with great accuracy.

Police forces everywhere have used the polygraph for a number of years in criminal investigations. Was the woman raped, or did she consent? Did the witness see the shooting, or is he purposely accusing an innocent man? Prosecutors and police need to know the truthfulness of witnesses and complainants, and the polygraph has been a useful aid in determining this.

An accused sometimes submits to a test voluntarily. If the machine indicates his protestations of innocence are true, the prosecution is ordinarily dropped. If it shows that he is lying, a confession may follow. Even where there is no confession, and the machine points to guilt, the police at least know that they are on firm ground in making the charge against him.

If a suspect refuses to be tested, the prosecution usually feels that he is guilty. An innocent person has nothing to fear, and the device should show his innocence.

It occasionally happens that both the defense and the prosecution stipulate that a polygraph test be given and the test results used in evidence. Without such a stipulation, most courts will refuse to admit polygraph evidence. They feel that the machine is being used as a substitute for the court's and the jury's determination of truthfulness.

New York's highest court excluded polygraph evidence in *People* v. *Leone*, 25 N.Y. 2d 511 (1969). Oklahoma also refused to admit it in *Fulton* v. *State*, 541 P. 2d 871 (Okla. Cr App. 1975), even though both sides had agreed by stipulation that the results could be used.

Ballard v. *Supreme Court*, 64 Cal. 2d 159 (1966), illustrates the narrow view that courts can take regarding polygraph tests. Walter Ballard, a physician, was charged with raping a woman patient. He was alleged to have given her a drug to prevent her resistance

and then to have had sexual intercourse with her. The police physician
examined her and found semen on her clothing. Later the police put
a microphone in her purse and had her see the doctor in his office
while they recorded their conversation outside. They also did the
same thing by having her call the doctor on the telephone. The police
subsequently gave her a polygraph test. When the doctor was arrested,
he demanded the results of the test in order to prepare for trial. The
court refused his request, saying that polygraph test results could
not be used in court, and, therefore, the evidence was inadmissible.
It did, however, allow him to be given the questions asked and her
replies to them.

As has been said, most courts have consistently refused to allow
such test results to be used. At present, however, there are a few
indications that polygraph test results will be allowed under prescribed restrictions. One such indication came in *State* v. *Dorsey*,
532 P. 2d 912 (N.M. App. 1975), aff'd 539 P. 2d 204 (N.M., 1975).
In that case the defendant was accused of attacking another person
with a knife. He claimed self-defense, saying that he did not pull his
knife before leaving his car and that the alleged victim struck the first
blow. A polygraph test indicated that the defendant was telling the
truth. He offered the test result to support his statement. The prosecution objected, and the trial court excluded the evidence. The appeals
court held that this was in error. It ruled that, even though there had
been an objection, the use of the polygraph was now a scientifically
approved test, and, within the reasoning of *Chambers* v. *Mississippi*,
supra, it should have been admitted.

It is inevitable that the use of the polygraph will be approved
more extensively in court decisions, but its acceptance is extremely
slow.

(13.20) Voiceprints

Another scientific device now coming into wider use is the
voiceprint, which reproduces a person's voice spectrographically. The
test is based on the fact that no two people have the same voice
characteristics. This is because the vocal cavities and organs of
articulation—lips, tongue, teeth, and the like—all vary from individual
to individual.

The voice spectrograph electronically analyzes the complex

speech sounds, disburses them into their various parts, and reproduces them on current-sensitive paper. This visual result is the voiceprint. When certain cue words are compared with previously recorded voice-prints of the same words, identification of the voice becomes possible. The prints lend themselves to computerized classification so that a central file can be compiled. This file makes it possible, for example, to compare a kidnapper's or a blackmailer's telephone call with voiceprints of known criminals with similar backgrounds.

Scientific opinion regarding voiceprints is presently divided, despite their very high degree of accuracy. Both federal and state courts are also divided. At this point, however, courts in Massachusetts, California, and Minnesota have accepted voice spectrograms as evidence of identification in criminal cases, as have a few federal courts. *Commonwealth* v. *Lykus,* 327 N.E. 2d 671 (Mass., 1975), involved the kidnapping and murder of a young boy. The police taped the kidnapper's ransom calls. A specified amount of money was dropped, and, after three attempts, the suspect collected it. When it was traced to him, he admitted that he had picked up the money. He stated, however, that he had been hired to do it for $500 by a man who was involved in drug traffic, and he claimed that he had left the money where this person had instructed him to do so. The boy was found shot to death in a wooded area. At the trial, six witnesses identified the defendant's voice, but one could not. A voiceprint expert testified that the defendant was the one who made the calls. He based his statement on the tapes and voice exemplars. The defendant was found guilty and appealed. The appellate court approved the use of the voiceprint evidence and upheld the conviction.

The Minnesota courts have similarly approved voiceprint evidence; the leading case there is *State ex rel. Trimble* v. *Hedman,* 291 Minn. 442 (1971). A decision in Ohio, *State* v. *Olderman,* 336 N.E. 2d 442 (Ohio App. 1975), and one in Maryland, *State* v. *Reed,* 18 Crim. L. Rptr. 2011 (Cir. Ct. Md. 1975), have followed these cases and admitted voiceprint evidence.

The latest device designed to evaluate the voice electronically is the psychological stress evaluator. The theory behind this machine is similar to that of the polygraph in that it measures certain stress-related parts of speech. Involuntary indications of stress made by the voice are traced on a graph, and the results are interpreted. Unlike a polygraph, the machine does not have to be attached to the subject.

It is necessary only to make a recording of the questions and answers. The recording of the interview is later fed through the evaluator, and the voice reactions are charted. The psychological stress evaluator is presently being used as an investigative tool in law enforcement agencies and in the business world, but it has not yet received court approval.

(13.21) Narcoanalysis and Hypnosis

Scopolamine, sodium pentothal, and the like, often labeled truth serums, are, at times, used as an interrogation or diagnostic tool. The technique is known as narcoanalysis and is based on the theory that this type of drug will break down the subject's mental resistance so that he will respond truthfully to questioning. Suspects may consent to such a test in order to clear themselves, or both counsel may stipulate that the test be given.

Courts consistently reject the introduction of any statement, by either a defendant or a witness, made under the influence of these drugs. They hold that the validity of the test has not been scientifically proven. Cases illustrative of this rejection by the courts are *People* v. *McCracken*, 39 Cal. 2d 336 (1952); *People* v. *Harper*, 111 Ill. App. 2d 204 (1969).

Statements made while the subject is under hypnosis are viewed by the courts in the same way as those made while an individual is undergoing narcoanalysis. A hypnotized person is, of course, powerfully subject to suggestion. Stage performers for many years have used posthypnotic suggestions to induce subjects to perform actions after the hypnotic trance is over. And yet, in spite of the court's rejection of these tests and of the widespread nonprofessional use of hypnosis, both hypnosis and narcoanalysis have legitimate investigative and diagnostic applications.

The human mind is a strange and largely unknown mechanism. Even the process of memory is not fully understood. People remember by different means. Some remember consciously less than others. Also, many tend to erase unpleasant or horrible experiences from their minds. What of the rape victim who cannot recall the events of the assault? Narcoanalysis or hypnotism may actually allow her to remember. This very situation occurred in *People* v. *Harper*, supra. However, the court rejected the victim's statement made to her psychiatrist while she was under the influence of a drug.

Narcoanalysis is, however, a recognized method used by psychiatrists to diagnose mental illness. But the information the patient gives the psychiatrist when drugs are administered for the purpose of diagnosis cannot be admitted as proof of the truth of what was said. An example of this occurred in a murder case in New York (*People* v. *Esposito*, 287 N.Y. 389 [1942]). In response to the defendant's request for a sanity test, one examining psychiatrist used a drug injection as a method of diagnosis to determine whether the defendant was insane or malingering. The trial judge allowed the doctor to describe this method of testing and to give his resulting opinion on the sanity of the subject. The physician was not, however, allowed to relate any admissions or drug-induced statement that the defendant may have made. The appellate court approved this decision and affirmed the conviction.

A more difficult problem exists when a statement is given after the truth serum treatment is completed. A similar situation can occur where the defendant is an addict and he has been given medication to ease his withdrawal symptoms, and then confesses. At the time of trial, he may claim that his confession was drug induced and thus involuntary.

In *People* v. *Townsend*, 11 Ill. 2d 30 (1957), the defendant, Townsend, was convicted of a mugging murder in which $4.80 was involved. While he was being interrogated, at the time of his arrest, he complained of stomach pains. A doctor was called in and found that the suspect was an addict suffering withdrawal symptoms. He administered phenobarbital and other drugs to relieve him. The defendant later gave a detailed statement confessing to the murder. He was subsequently sentenced to death. On appeal, Townsend claimed that his confession was drug induced and thus involuntary. The Illinois court affirmed his conviction, saying that the fact that he was given beneficial drugs to ease his pain was not proof that he was drugged for the purpose of securing a confession.

Six years later Townsend took his case to the U.S. Supreme Court via habeas corpus (*Townsend* v. *Sain*, 372 U.S. 293 [1963]). It found that one of the drugs given Townsend for treatment of his pains was hyocine, which is the same as scopolamine—a truth serum. For this reason, the court found that there was a real possibility that Townsend's later confession was drug induced, not voluntary. Thus, they remanded the case to the district court for a complete hearing on the subject.

Posthypnotic statements have, on occasion, received less harsh treatment from reviewing courts. In cases of amnesia, for example, posthypnotic suggestion is a legitimate means and a recognized method of restoring memory. If hypnosis is carefully used, with no suggestion made to the subject other than that he will be able to remember when his trance is ended, his later statement might possibly be allowed in evidence. The court would have to be assured that the test was so administered, however, because any posthypnotic statement is highly suspicious.

People v. *Leyra*, 302 N.Y. 353 (1951), was a case in which a son was convicted of the hammer slaying of his aged parents. When he was interrogated, he gave partial and conflicting statements. The police called in a doctor who questioned Leyra at length, using suggestion and other psychological tools. The defendant subsequently confessed orally to a police captain, to his business partner, and to the district attorney. During Leyra's first trial, at which he was found guilty, the taped interview with the doctor was heard by the jury. When the decision was appealed, the defendant claimed that he had been hypnotized and that none of his statements had been voluntary. The appellate court reversed the conviction and ordered a new trial. It stated that the recorded interview should not have been heard on the question of his guilt and that its only relevance could have been on the question of voluntariness.

Leyra was retried, and this time the doctor's interview was not used, only the subsequent confession. He was convicted again. His case was finally taken to the U.S. Supreme Court via habeas corpus (*Leyra* v. *Denno*, 347 U.S. 556 [1954]). There his conviction was reversed a second time, the court holding that his statements to the doctor were coerced psychologically and that the other confessions followed so closely that they were one continuous process and were all involuntary.

In at least one reported incident—in a murder trial in Ohio— hypnosis was allowed in the courtroom (*State* v. *Nebb*, no. 39, 450 [Ohio Cm. Pl. 5/28/62]). The jury was excused, and, by agreement of attorneys, the defendant was hypnotized in the presence of the judge. The prosecution then questioned him. As a result of the questioning, the prosecutor reduced the charge to manslaughter.

Witnesses have been allowed to testify concerning their recollections, even though their present memory was acquired through hypnotism. This was the case in *Harding* v. *State*, 5 Md. App. 230, cert. den. 395 U.S. 949 (1969), and *Cornell* v. *Superior Court*, 52 Cal. 2d 99 (1959).

Thus, while both narcoanalysis and hypnosis are recognized scientific tools for investigation and treatment, their results are narrowly circumscribed in the courts.

(13.22) Miscellaneous

Fluorescein powders have long been in use. Though invisible to the naked eye, they produce a fluorescent glow when excited by an ultraviolet lamp. They are frequently used to catch sneak thieves, such as dishonest employees.

In a highly publicized case in suburban Chicago, police suspected a dentist of performing indecent acts upon his female patients after administering gas. One woman volunteered for "dental treatment" and was gassed. Her private parts had been lightly covered with gynecological jelly mixed with fluorescein paste. When the dentist was later confronted, his face and sexual organs fluoresced.

At least one case (*Brock* v. *U.S.*, 223 F. 2d 681, 685 [5th Cir. 1955]) has held that the use of ultraviolet lamps on a suspect's outer clothing or hands is not a search within the meaning of the Fourth Amendment. Thus, a search warrant is unnecessary.

A variety of other things provide scientific proof in criminal cases. Dentistry, for example, is increasingly used as a method of identifying unknown bodies. This method is highly reliable because it is unlikely that any two people exist with the same dental history. Dentists' records are carefully kept and so provide good scientific evidence. Anthropologists and others may, in much the same way, be able to supply information on sex, race, and other characteristics from human remains found many years after death.

As science progresses, new fields of scientific evidence in criminal cases will continue to develop.

It is necessary to insert a word of caution concerning scientific proof that depends on scientific measuring instruments. There are no American court decisions holding that evidence of measurements by mechanical means or scientific instruments are presumed to be correct. Seldom does the defense raise the objection that there has been no proof of the accuracy of the scientific measuring device used by the expert witness. The legal question is open, however, and anyone offering scientific proof should be aware that the problem exists (21 ALR 2d 1200).

C. PRESERVATION AND CUSTODY OF EVIDENCE

(13.23) In General

Evidence is of no value to the prosecutor unless it can be used in court. The police must, therefore, exercise care in collecting, identifying, and preserving any physical evidence connected with the crime. Unless properly connected with the crime and sufficiently authenticated at the trial, the evidence cannot be used.

(13.24) Collection

Evidence at the scene of the crime cannot be collected too carefully. Photographing the weapon at the scene of a murder or the tool marks of forced entry where a burglary occurred should, for example, be routinely done. The evidence itself must be kept free of contamination, fingerprints, or damage so that its original condition remains unchanged. If the item is numbered, the numbers should be written down for the police records. Exhibits should be carefully placed in separate evidence envelopes, preferably of clear plastic, and should be tagged immediately.

(13.25) Marking

Where possible, evidence should be marked by the officer who first recovers it. His initials may be put on the exhibit. The butt plate from a rifle, for example, can be removed and the initials scratched on the stock before replacing the plate. If the object itself cannot be marked, the envelope or other containers should be labeled with the investigator's initials. Where glass or tube containers are used, it is a sound practice to seal them with tape and then sealing wax, with the officer's fingerprint placed on the warm wax.

(13.26) Preservation

All evidence should be placed in a locked cabinet. Valuable and dangerous items should be kept in a fireproof, locked vault or safe.

Laboratory technicians ought to preserve by chemical or other methods anything that might decompose, such as bodily tissue. Any article taken into custody or removed should be logged in and out in in an evidence register. The 3M Company markets a specially developed tape that is transparent except for the word "Evidence," which is in red letters. The tape is designed to be affixed over initials or a signature. It destroys itself in a noticeable manner whenever it is tampered with.

(13.27) Testing

Testing, whether done by the laboratory or by a firearms expert, may consume part or all of an exhibit. This is acceptable, and the expert witness can easily explain it in court. Any material remaining after the tests are made must be returned to police custody for later use at the trial.

(13.28) Chain of Custody

The general rule of "chain of custody" (which is more accurately termed "chain of identification") applies to evidence that has undergone expert analysis, such as a blood sample or material from bodily specimens. The side offering the evidence must show that the technician received the same sample that was originally taken from the person involved or from the place in question. It must also lay a foundation by testimony from every person who had the object in his custody, beginning with the officer who originally took it through the technician who examined it. If one person who had it in his custody cannot be found to testify to this, the court will usually rule that the chain has been broken and that the object will not be admitted into evidence. It is obviously impossible to follow the chain of custody rule exactly. If, for example, a specimen is mailed to a laboratory, every postman and clerk who handled it cannot be produced in court. Proof of mailing and the laboratory receipt of the package will suffice. What is required is proof that the exhibit now in court is the same one that was tested. It is extremely important for police authorities to keep the chain of custody unbroken and to maintain an exact record of everyone who had any object in his possession.

This rule usually applies only to exhibits that are part of an expert's testimony. If the knife found at the scene of a murder is proved by a witness to be in the same condition as when found, it generally is admissible in evidence without the various police evidence custodians having to testify that it was in their possession.

(13.29) Courtroom Authentication

There is a standard way of introducing an exhibit. First, it is marked for identification. Next counsel says: "I show you Exhibit 2 for identification. What is it?" The witness identifies the object and describes finding it. He is then asked: "Is it in the same condition now as when you originally found it?" If he answers in the affirmative, the exhibit is sufficiently authenticated to be offered in evidence.

(13.30) Destruction of Evidence

Evidence must be preserved during the time of trial and any appeals, including postconviction attacks through habeas corpus. Once the process has ended, the evidence can be safely returned to its rightful owner. In some cases, the defendant, through his attorney, will acknowledge the existence of an item, its value, and the description of it. This enables the owner to obtain his property much sooner, and thus prevent a hardship. Police often receive a court order allowing the destruction of evidence from closed cases some time before they actually dispose of it. Because of growing police corruption arising from narcotics, some jurisdictions provide for analysis of the evidence and a court-ordered destruction of the drugs even before the trial (see N.Y. CPL, Article 715 [1973]).

Destruction of evidence can create problems. In *Brady* v. *Maryland*, 373 U.S. 83 (1963), the police secretly videotaped a jailhouse visit two people made to an accused murderer. The district attorney viewed the tape to see if it contained anything that would be helpful to the defense. Finding nothing, he erased the tape. One of the visitors was later a prosecution witness at the trial. Brady was found guilty and appealed. During the second trial the defendant argued that the destruction of the tape violated his right to impeach the witness. Though the court affirmed the conviction, it warned that if the police destroy evidence as being nonmaterial without first notifying the defendant, the burden will be on the prosecution to show that this destruction did not prejudice the defense.

In the past, police in California encountered a problem concerning destruction of evidence because they routinely destroyed breathalizer ampules that had been used to detect the presence of alcohol in those accused of driving while intoxicated. Thus, a defendant contesting the result could not retest the ampule. The court ruled, therefore, that they should not be destroyed (*People* v. *Hitch*, 527 P. 2d 361 [Cal. 1974]).

A safe rule to follow before destroying evidence is this, notify the defendant and seek court approval where it is appropriate.

(13.31) Summary

Physical evidence relevant to the crime can be used if properly taken and preserved. Fruits of the crime, burglar's tools, clothing, even the defendant's person, may be relevant evidence.

Much scientific proof, such as fingerprints, ballistics tests, and chemical analysis, is available. Tests for narcotics are now commonplace. Document examiners using modern methods can give detached proof of forgeries, handwriting comparisons, and even individual typewriter identification.

Microanalysis of soil samples, paint chips, or fibers often can supply dramatic evidence against a defendant. Neutron activation analysis is a more recent method of identifying the elements present in evidentiary samples. It has been used to identify the place and even the date of manufacture of items. Courts are now recognizing the validity of neutron activation analysis.

Polygraph and voiceprint analysis are both widely used investigative tools. Courts still reject polygraph results, but are beginning to allow voiceprint evidence in court.

Narcoanalysis and hypnosis are medically approved diagnostic tools, but any courtroom use is narrowly circumscribed.

Proper care must always be taken in the collection and custody of both physical and scientific evidence. Evidence collected at the scene must be properly labeled and preserved. The chain of custody of any bodily sample used in a laboratory test must be carefully recorded and then testified to in court.

Any after trial destruction of evidence should normally be done under court order.

14

Special Problems of Proof

A. MOTIVE, KNOWLEDGE, AND INTENT

(14.1) Essential Elements

Criminal statutes speak at various times of knowingly, willfully, maliciously, or intentionally committing a crime. The fact that these words are similar in connotation does not mean that they may be used interchangeably. These terms do, however, describe the essential elements of a crime. The state's proof must, therefore, fulfill the statutory definitions of these terms, or the evidence will not satisfy the requirements of the particular charge. It is thus easy to see why an adequate understanding of the terms used in each particular jurisdiction is absolutely necessary if criminals are to be prosecuted successfully.

Motive, intent, or knowledge in the commission of a crime is seldom proved by developing direct evidence. Certain crimes incorporate, nevertheless, criminal intent as an element of the offense. In the prosecution of these offenses, such as assault with intent to kill, proof of the defendant's state of mind is a critical element of the state's case. If this essential element is not proved beyond a reasonable doubt, an acquittal will result. The defendant might, of course, still be convicted of a lesser offense where criminal intent is not a necessary element, such as the discharge of a firearm within corporate limits.

It is probable that the accused never directly revealed his motive, intent, or knowledge of the crime with which he is charged. The law must infer these elements from his words or actions. The inference must, however, relate to a state of mind that existed at the time of the criminal act. It cannot be inferred from subsequent events or statements.

(14.2) Knowledge

One is not usually guilty of a crime unless he is aware of all existing facts that make his conduct criminal. Where knowledge of certain facts by the accused is a material element of the crime with which he has been charged, knowledge must be proved beyond a reasonable doubt. Since proof of knowledge is necessarily an elusive task, courts are willing to admit a broad spectrum of evidence as an aid to the jury in determining the defendant's level of awareness. Knowledge can be proved by affirmative statements or admissions by the accused or by the development of collateral evidence. The jury is often allowed to infer the defendant's knowledge from his specific acts or from other circumstances.

The element of knowledge required in a criminal prosecution should not be confused with intent to commit a crime. A defendant will not be acquitted merely because he was unaware that his conduct violated the criminal code. One of the basic principles of criminal law is that ignorance of the law does not excuse the illegal conduct of any person. The requirement of knowledge is satisfied, however, when it is proved that the accused had knowledge of the facts that make his conduct criminal under the laws of the particular jurisdiction.

Two simple examples demonstrate this distinction. A merchant is being prosecuted for having received stolen goods. The criminal code declares that a person who obtains control over stolen property, knowing the property to have been stolen, and who conceals the property to deprive the rightful owner of its use commits theft. The merchant's defense is that he did not know that keeping stolen goods was a crime. In this case the decision would be based on the fact that the merchant knew the goods to be stolen. The requirement regarding knowledge was satisfied by the fact that he was aware of all the factual circumstances that made his conduct illegal. In contrast, suppose a hunter shoots at a pheasant. The bullet passes through a bush and kills a child who was hiding behind it. While the hunter had the intent of firing his gun, he did not have knowledge of the child's presence. He could not, therefore, be charged with knowledge amounting to a murderous intent.

The defendant's knowledge need not be actual or direct. It is sufficient if the circumstances of the transaction make him aware of the likelihood of certain facts. This is known as "constructive knowledge." In the example of the stolen goods, the prosecution would not have to prove that the merchant personally observed the goods being stolen from the true owner. The requirement concerning knowledge is satisfied when the defendant would reasonably have believed, on the basis of facts and circumstances, that the goods had been stolen.

(14.3) Willfulness

This concept is often incorporated into criminal statutes, and, when present, it is an essential element of the crime that must be proved beyond a reasonable doubt. Mere carelessness is not willfulness. It is not enough that the criminal act was the result of negligence on the part of the accused. A design or purpose to inflict injury or to do wrong must also have been present. A wide scope of evidence will be admitted where it is relevant to the determination of the defendant's design or purpose.

An inference of willfulness can be drawn when a person acts with intentional disregard for the safety of another person or for property. One can, therefore, infer that his intent was willfully to inflict injury.

The crucial element creating an inference of willfulness is an intent to do wrong without a justifiable excuse. When, for example, a defendant is accused of failing to file federal income tax returns without a justifiable excuse, one could infer that his intent was to conceal his tax liability from the government. Thus, the element of willfulness is established. Willfulness can also be established when the accused has exhibited a willingness to inflict injury, even though he bore no specific ill will toward the particular party who was injured. In this respect, willfulness can be distinguished from other statutory elements, such as malice or intent.

(14.4) Malice

Malice can be viewed as an extension of willfulness. It has been defined as a wicked or coldhearted purpose, but it is often difficult to distinguish the elements of malice from those establishing willfulness.

Crimes concerned with an intent to injure the interests of a particular individual most frequently involve the element of malice. Some courts, however, have considered malice a general disregard of duties owed to society and to all individuals. These courts do not require that the defendant acted out of ill will for a particular victim. For instance, when a person fires a gun into a crowded room, there may be no intended victim, but the general malice of the offender's conduct is interpreted to include an element of malice toward the victim who is actually injured.

Another facet of malice is the doctrine of transferred malice. When an injury intended for one victim is accidentally suffered by another, the law finds malice in the actions of the accused even though the ultimate result was not that which he had intended. For example, a chemist prepares a poisoned apple with the intent of murdering his wife, but the wife gives the apple to a neighbor boy who eats it and dies. The chemist would be found to have acted with malice toward the boy even though his actual malice was directed toward his wife. It should be noted, however, that the doctrine of transferred malice only applies if the unexpected injury has the same legal consequence as that which was originally intended. In the example of the apple, it would be the death of the boy.

The unifying aspect of crimes requiring proof of malice is that the act itself cannot be excused on legal grounds. Courts are generally liberal in permitting the admission of evidence that either tends to show or to rebut an inference of malice. Signs of previous ill will or hostility exhibited by the defendant are useful to prove the existence of actual malice at the time the crime was committed.

(14.5) Intent

Proof of intent to commit a crime is an essential element of many criminal statutes. It is usually described as the purpose, aim, or design that leads to the criminal act. It is unfortunate for the prosecution that intent is usually not revealed directly, but must be inferred from the conduct of the defendant. A wider range of evidence, both direct and circumstantial, is allowed than would normally be permissible when it is material to proving the elements of the criminal conduct. If this latitude concerning the admission of evidence were not permitted, it would be virtually impossible to prove intent, which often lies at the heart of the offense or which itself constitutes a criminal act. Further, an important doctrine of criminal law is that of *presumed intent,* which holds the accused accountable for all natural and probable consequences of his acts.

In most jurisdictions, an accused is allowed to testify concerning his intent, if that is an essential element of the crime and if his conduct leaves the issue of intent open to interpretation. There are, of course, obvious problems connected with his testimony. First, the defendant's recollection of his intent will be colored by his self-interest. Second, it is difficult to supply evidence that contradicts such testimony. The rationale for allowing his testimony is that the judge and/or the jury should be allowed to hear all relevant testimony and determine the degree of credibility to which it is entitled.

When an individual has the intent to do something that the law recognizes to be a crime, it does not matter that his plan may not have included a desire to break the law. The intent required to comply with a criminal statute is not an intent to break the law, but an intent to do an act that society has determined to be wrong.

If the intended injury occurs in an unexpected way, the element of intent is still present. For instance, an assassin shoots at a government official. The shot misses him, but strikes the automobile's gasoline tank, which ignites and causes the official's death by burning. Because the intent to commit murder was originally present, the assassin would be charged with that crime even though the murder did not occur in the manner he had intended.

The fact that the offender's intended act could not possibly have succeeded will not excuse his conduct, and the element of intent to commit the particular crime will be found to exist. Suppose, for example, a burglar intends to break in and steal a painting he knows to be in a particular house. By mistake, he breaks into the wrong house and is apprehended. The fact that he intended to commit a burglary overrides the fact that his mistake made it impossible for him to achieve his objective.

(14.6) Motive

It is often difficult to distinguish motive from intent. While intent is often the most important element of the crime that the prosecution must prove, motive is usually not an essential element. For example, a husband who murders his wife in order to collect her life insurance has an intent to kill and a motive of getting the money. In prosecuting the man, the state would have to prove his murderous intent but not his reason for killing his wife. The fact that the defendant had a motive for committing the crime is almost always material and relevant; it provides persuasive circumstantial evidence that the defendant committed the crime. Proof of that fact is, however, usually not an essential element of the crime. It is not necessary for the prosecution to dismiss a charge solely because the defendant's motive cannot be established.

This is not to say that motive is completely immaterial to proving whether or not the specified crime was committed. For instance, when an intruder is caught breaking into a house, his motive is crucial because the crime becomes only burglary if the motive for the break-in was to steal property. Proof of a good motive may establish the absence of the requisite intent, or it may establish mitigating or extenuating circumstances, which, in turn, affect the type of sentence that will be imposed.

Evidence of other crimes committed by the accused is admissible to establish his present motive if the test of relevancy is met. Although such evidence is almost certainly prejudicial, the judge usually instructs the jury that such evidence should be considered only on the question of motive, not as evidence to prove guilt.

A moral reason for committing a crime will not serve as a legal defense. The assassination of a political tyrant may, for example, be undertaken with the noblest of motives, but the act remains murder in the eyes of the law. To hold otherwise would permit each man to substitute his concept of right and wrong for the law.

B. COMMON SCHEME OR DESIGN

(14.7) General Rules Relating to Other Crimes

A well-established rule of criminal procedure is that proof of the previous commission of crimes and offenses will not be competent or admissible to prove the commission of the crime with which the defendant is presently charged. This rule is, of course, designed to prevent the conviction of an accused solely on an inference that, because he had committed crimes in the past, he was likely to have committed the present crime. The rule also applies to accusations of having committed other crimes and to proof of threats, willingness, or intent to commit other crimes.

The rule recognizes that past offenses have no necessary relevance to finding a defendant guilty beyond a reasonable doubt. Otherwise, it would be extremely unlikely that a habitual criminal would ever be cleared of charges, even when he was innocent of the crime for which he was being tried. The rule also avoids the problem of requiring the defendant to respond to unrelated issues and of diverting the jury's attention from the facts of the particular case on trial.

As with most procedural rules that are not stipulated in the Constitution, but are merely designed to guide judicial discretion, there are several recognized exceptions. Thus, while past criminal conduct may not be used to infer guilt, it may be admitted to establish other essential elements of the crime, such as identity of the accused, knowledge, intent, and motive. This evidence can also be offered to prove the existence of a criminal plan or to establish the fact that the present crime was not the result of an accident or mistake. And so, in summary, evidence of a past crime should only be admissible if a legal connection exists between previous incidents and some essential element of the crime with which the defendant is presently charged. Because it is likely that such evidence will be highly prejudicial to the defendant, courts insist on clear proof of this connection.

In one area—that of sex crimes—the rule against the use of prior offenses as evidence of present guilt has been relaxed. Some courts have stated that evidence of prior sex offenses has peculiar relevance for proving the propensity of the accused to commit such crimes. The real problem is to balance the importance of the testimony against its potential for prejudice. Some courts have, therefore, been willing to admit evidence of previous sex offenses for the purpose of establishing the defendant's state of mind as long as the prior conduct is not too remote in time.

(14.8) Consecutive Crimes Showing a Common Scheme or Design

A major exception to the rule barring evidence of prior offenses to prove the present crime applies to evidence of a common scheme, plan, or series of crimes. The law permits proof of a scheme to commit a series of crimes including the specific crime charged. In order to prove the existence of that scheme, the prosecution may offer evidence of the commission of other crimes if the interrelationship of time, place, and circumstances supports the inference that the specific crime in question was a part of that overall scheme.

The basic test for admissibility in this area thus depends on the interdependence of the consecutive crimes. It is within the discretion of the trial court to determine that the crimes are sufficiently related, and its decision will only be reversed if that discretion has clearly been abused. If the first crime prepared the way for the second, and the second depended on the first to assure its commission, the two crimes become consecutive and interdependent.

Proof of the prior offense is relevant for establishing motive and intent for the present crime if the events are sufficiently close in time. For instance, evidence in a homicide prosecution that the accused had stolen a pistol on the day before the crime, and had used the weapon when committing the crime, would be admissible as interrelated crimes relevant to establishing the criminal intent of the accused at the time of the shooting. In such cases, the length of time that elapsed between the consecutive crimes does not determine the admissibility of the evidence, but merely the weight it should be accorded.

Opinion is divided on whether proof of the prior offense may be placed in evidence when it does not tend to establish directly a common scheme or design. In light of the policy underlying the exception, it would seem that admissibility should hinge on proving the existence of a common scheme. The more relaxed approach adopted by a minority of jurisdictions is, in reality, little more than an attempt to establish guilt by reference to similar past conduct, which may be of questionable relevance to the present charge.

(14.9) Continuing Acts Distinguished

What excludes continuous crimes from the rule barring evidence of prior offenses is that the essence of a continuous crime is the total pattern of conduct, which is itself illegal. Evidence of a habit or common practice is not used, therefore, to suggest that the accused committed a separate crime, but, rather, serves to establish the crime itself. If, for example, a person is on trial for illegally manufacturing liquor, it would be appropriate to admit evidence that, at a point prior to his arrest but within the period specified by the indictment, the defendant was operating a still. Such evidence serves to establish the practice, habit, or course of conduct that constitutes the alleged offense. It would, on the other hand, be improper in a prosecution for auto theft to offer proof of prior or subsequent convictions for the same offense. This evidence would have no relevance in proving the guilt on the particular charge since each auto theft represents a separate offense rather than one continuing act. To admit such evidence would raise all the problems of prejudice to the defendant that the rule against evidence of prior offenses was designed to eliminate.

(14.10) Particular Offenses

a. Gaming Offenses

In a prosecution for violating the statutes that prohibit gambling and related activities, evidence of offenses similar to the one charged is admissible if it satisfies the requirement of relevance and if it is sufficiently proximate in time. Evidence of similar activities can be introduced to prove the use and character of the business of the accused; to establish the role of the accused in illegal activities; to prove intent, motive, knowledge, and identity of the accused; to establish the ownership, possession, or control by the accused of the premises in question; and to establish a common criminal scheme or conspiracy. Individual offenses that constitute a single part of a continuing act are also admissible. Evidence of unrelated criminal activities will, however, be excluded under the general rule prohibiting the evidentiary use of irrelevant evidence.

b. Liquor Offenses

When the defendant is accused of one of the variety of liquor offenses, evidence of distinct and unrelated offenses is inadmissible in accordance with the general rule. Evidence of independent sales may, however, be admitted if they are not too remote to establish a connection between the accused and the present offense.

Many crimes involving liquor fit within the concept of continuing offenses. The state can, therefore, use evidence of prior offenses of a similar nature—illegally engaging in the business of selling liquor, maintaining a liquor nuisance, illegally keeping a place where liquor is sold—to prove the elements of the charge. In these cases, evidence is admissible if it tends to establish the crime charged even when the evidence discloses the existence of other crimes.

In other cases involving liquor, the crime for which the defendant is charged is more closely related to a specific incident. Evidence of independent offenses unrelated to the principal crime is, therefore, inadmissible except as used to establish intent, knowledge, identity, or other similar points. Examples of noncontinuing criminal acts include illegal sales, transportation, importation, manufacturing, possession of equipment and ingredients, and possession of liquors.

It is possible in these cases to exaggerate the distinction between the two classes of crimes. When a person is arrested for illegally selling bootleg liquor, and there is evidence that he has been previously convicted of similar offenses, the state should charge the defendant with illegally engaging in the business of selling liquor rather than with the isolated crime of an illegal sale. The reason, of course, is that the elements of a continuing offense are present; evidence of the prior offenses could not otherwise be used to establish guilt.

c. Prior Attempts to Kill, Rape, or Rob

The general rule that excludes evidence of prior independent crimes also excludes prior attempts to commit crimes. Exceptions to this rule do, however, permit the introduction of this evidence for certain limited purposes (see 14.7). A significant exception concerns a defendant who has previously been convicted or accused of attempted homicide, rape, or robbery.

In the case of a homicide prosecution, evidence of certain facts that aid in understanding the present crime but disclose a separate and distinct crime can be admitted into evidence. Thus, evidence of a prior attempt on the life of the deceased might tend to show the defendant's state of mind, malice, premeditation, knowledge, intent, or the existence of a plan or scheme. None of the factors would constitute evidence of guilt, but the prior offenses could be used to reinforce the essential elements of the present charge.

When an accused is charged with rape, evidence of related crimes will be admissible if it is relevant to an issue at trial. Courts will not exclude such testimony solely because it tends to show the accused was guilty of other sex crimes, but the relationship to the charged offense must be clear. The mere fact that the accused was guilty of previous similar crimes or other sexual offenses against a third party will not be allowed as evidence to prove the guilt of the accused. If, however, evidence of the prior sexual crimes established the existence of a plan or design or proves the mental state of the defendant, the prior offenses will be allowed in evidence. Some jurisdictions even permit the introduction of prior offenses against third persons to establish the defendant's general lustful intent and to infer a common design of sexual deviance.

The same general rules apply to evidence of prior robbery attempts. There must, however, be a clearly visible connection between the crime charged and the prior offense, particularly when the prior crime was committed in another locality or in a different manner. The degree of proof required to establish a common scheme between present and previous crimes is left to the discretion of the trial judge. In general, the prosecution is allowed to show that there are sufficient similarities between the robberies to eliminate the possibility of coincidence, thereby raising the inference of a common scheme or design.

d. Arson

In a prosecution for arson in which the state attempts to prove a common scheme, it must be established that prior fires were the result of arson, that they were set by the accused, and that there was a clear connection between the crimes. To prove this connection, the state has been allowed to introduce evidence of intent to burn another building, of previous plans to burn the same building, and of similar methods used in a prior attempt. Unless this connection can be made, the general rule against the introduction of evidence will apply, and the evidence will only be admissible to infer intent, knowledge, and similar issues.

e. Possessory Offenses

Possession of certain types of items has been made a criminal offense in some jurisdictions although, strictly speaking, possession would not seem to fit the requirement of a criminal "act." The explanation is that possession (whether it be narcotics, burglary tools, or whatever) is construed to mean conscious possession. If the possessor knowingly received an illegal item and had an opportunity to reject it but did not do so, the requirement of conscious possession has been met. If evidence of other crimes tends to prove the existence of a common scheme or plan, it is admissible. Thus, prior convictions for burglary can be introduced to establish the element of intent to commit burglary—a requirement in many statutes that makes the possession of burglary tools a criminal offense.

f. Fraud

Evidence of false representations made by the accused either before or after the conduct alleged to be fraudulent, and evidence of similar fraudulent practices not too remote in time, will be admitted to prove that the accused knew his statements to be false at the time he made them and that he had an intent to commit fraud. Related conduct can also serve to establish a common scheme or plan. In these instances a standard procedure is usually followed. First, the jury is required to find from other evidence that a misrepresentation was made. After that requirement is met, prior offenses may be used to establish that the defendant made the statement knowing it to be false and that it was part of a scheme. The usual prerequisite for proving a fraudulent scheme is merely that the transactions be similar in outline, even though they may differ in details.

g. Stolen Goods

In accordance with the general rule, evidence of other offenses is admissible only to the extent that it bears on issues in the present case. In the case of receiving stolen goods, evidence of prior crimes will be admitted if it helps to explain motive, intent, knowledge, or a common scheme or design. Evidence that the accused received other stolen property at approximately the same time can, in particular, be used to help prove knowledge or a common scheme. This is especially true where the prior receipt of stolen goods is inseparably related to the current charge. Some judges have even allowed evidence of a postcriminal delivery of stolen goods to the defendant to establish the existence of a common scheme or plan.

(14.11) Proof of Subsequent Offenses

As has been said, evidence that the accused committed a number of crimes subsequent to the one for which he is standing trial has generally been admissible to establish the existence of a common scheme or design. The law allows testimony on the crimes other than the one for which the defendant is being tried, but only to the extent that the crimes are sufficiently related in time, character, and location so as to be relevant to the question of a common design. As in all questions of relevance and admissibility, the ruling is made by the court.

The above position represents the majority view on use of subsequent offenses to prove a common scheme or design. Some courts, however, have taken a broader approach, and others a more restrictive one. Some state courts have ruled that subsequent offenses of a similar nature may not be used as evidence of improper intent in the commission of the first offense. On the other hand, a California court ruled in a rape prosecution (*People* v. *Ing*, 65 Cal. 2d 603, 55 Cal. Rptr. 902, 422 P. 2d 590 [1967]) that evidence of a similar crime committed fifteen years *earlier* (that is, a prior offense) was relevant to the question of common scheme or design, despite the usual requirement that the events be proximate in time. The court allowed the jury to decide the weight to be placed on the evidence.

(14.12) Relation to the Defense of Entrapment

When a defendant is accused of committing a crime, he is allowed to raise the positive defense of entrapment. This defense claims that the accused was improperly induced by police officers to commit a crime he would not otherwise have committed. When a defendant raises this defense, the prosecution is entitled to use evidence of past criminal acts to respond to and rebut his claims. The purpose of the prosecution's evidence is to prove the defendant's criminal disposition. Prior convictions would, of course, cast doubt on the defendant's claim that the crime would never have occurred without the planning and active encouragement of the police department.

C. CONSPIRACY AND ACTING IN CONCERT

(14.13) Conspiracy in General

Conspiracy (an agreement among conspirators) is a common-law crime that has been codified in each jurisdiction. The agreement itself is punished, not the purpose of the conspiracy. To prove the offense, the prosecution must show an agreement by two or more people to perform an unlawful act or to perform a lawful act by unlawful means. An example of the latter would include the operation of a legitimate business using illicit methods. Although it is not a necessary element of the common-law offense, statutory conspiracies also require proof of an overt act in furtherance of the conspiratorial purpose. This act need not be a crime, but must further the unlawful aims of the conspirators.

Conspiracy laws are useful in prosecuting organized crime and corruption cases in which it would be difficult to prove a multitude of well-concealed crimes. It is, further, unnecessary to prove that each conspirator was an equal partner in the arrangement. Because of the terroristic acts often associated with criminal conspiracies, the size of the organization itself, the psychological pressures to remain in the group, and the mutual encouragement of continued illegal behavior, the crime is of a nefarious nature.

Because it is the act of agreement that constitutes the crime, not the overt acts in furtherance of the conspiracy, the conscious and continuous union of minds to engage in unlawful activity forms the bases of prosecution. No particular words or "forms of agreement" are necessary to form a conspiracy. Since it is unlikely, without testimony from a coconspirator, that the agreement can be reconstructed in court, the conspiracy may be proved by the conduct of its participants. It is not sufficient to show that a particular defendant had knowledge of the agreement; he must actually have agreed to be a part of the conspiracy, either by word or deed.

(14.14) Parties to a Conspiracy

Not all conspirators are equal partners. Some might receive large profits while others suffer losses. It is unnecessary to allege or to prove that each coconspirator knew the identities of all other conspirators. Many defendants do not, in fact, know the size of the conspiracy or the number of participants. It is necessary to prove only that the particular defendant knew that he was joining an organization that had an unlawful purpose or used an unlawful means to accomplish a lawful purpose.

There are often multiple conspiracies that include gambling, prostitution, narcotics offenses, and loansharking. One or more individuals may be conspirators in all of these multiple conspiracies, but others may be involved in only one or two. Because it is the agreement, not the acts, that is illegal, it is not necessary that an individual be involved in all the illegal purposes of a conspiracy. If, however, a conspirator knows of all the illicit purposes of the organization, he becomes a conspirator for all those purposes, even though his participatory role is limited.

For this reason, some defendants may have to be severed from the principal trial, although protection of these defendants from prejudicial evidence can be accomplished by numerous indictment counts and careful jury instructions.

Because each agreement constitutes a separate offense, it is proper to try an individual several times for his involvement in a number of coexisting and related conspiracies. A continuous operation over a span of many years may, however, still be a single conspiracy. As unlawful purposes are added to or dropped from the organization's operation, new conspiracies do not necessarily begin and end. Unlike a legitimate partnership, a new organization is not created every time a conspiratorial "partner" is dropped from or added to the conspiracy.

One unusual aspect of conspiracy prosecutions is that a person who joins a conspiracy with full knowledge of its prior acts of misconduct becomes fully liable for such acts. For example, a person joins a narcotics conspiracy knowing that the organization has committed murder. When he is prosecuted for membership in the conspiracy, proof of the murder may be admitted in his trial. It must be remembered, however, that he will be tried for conspiracy, not murder. On the other hand, it is also possible to try a defendant for conspiracy to commit a substantive crime when he has been acquitted of the substantive crime itself. This is because of the conceptual differences between conspirators and accessories. Once a conspirator severs his relationship with a group, he is no longer liable for future conspiratorial acts, even though he might have formed the illegal combine himself.

A party to a conspiracy need not be acquainted with the intimate details of the plan. It is not necessary for him to know the identities of the victims, or even how many victims will be involved. Liability attaches to insignificant participation as well as to leadership roles. Punishment might differ, of course, but, again, it is the act of agreement and not its purposes that the law punishes.

(14.15) Knowledge and Intent

The prosecution must allege and prove that each conspirator knew that he was engaging in criminal activity. Even when it is unnecessary to show criminal knowledge in the prosecution of the substantive offense, knowledge is a necessary element of proof in conspiracy to commit that offense. It is not necessary, for example, to prove that a defendant knowingly violated customs laws, but a prosecution for conspiracy to violate customs laws and regulations requires such proof.

It is also necessary to prove that each defendant had criminal intent. The courts have held that if two persons are tried for conspiracy, and criminal intent can be proved only against one of them, he may use it as a defense, but the one whose intent was evident cannot. It may be necessary in some federal crimes to show an "anti-federal" intent in addition to a "guilty mind," that is, an intent to violate a law that is federal in nature.

A conspiracy may be prosecuted either in a federal court, state courts, or both.

(14.16) Acting in Concert

Two or more persons may act together for a criminal purpose and still not be coconspirators. A burglar may act in concert with a fence, a bet taker with a layoff operator, a policy wheel operator with a numbers printer, or a car thief with the owner of a paint and body shop. Such arrangements take on the character of a conspiracy only when there is a conscious agreement, knowledge, intent, and an overt act.

The distinction has given rise to the so-called Wharton rule, named after the famous author of a treatise on criminal law. It states: "If only a minimum number of parties logically necessary to commit the substantive offense are involved, conspiracy indictments will not lie." This is because no greater danger to the public is posed if the exact number of people necessary to commit the crime are involved. Thus, it would be improper to prosecute a "conspiracy" to commit adultery, incest, bigamy, sodomy, a simple bribery, or other substantive offenses requiring at least, but not more than, two people. When, however, two individuals agree to bribe a third, the minimum number of actors is exceeded, and prosecution would be proper.

It has been held that a person can conspire with a corporation, and each can be prosecuted. If, however, the corporate soul is the same mind as one of the conspirators, the corporate entity cannot be counted as another "person."

(14.17) The Overt Act Requirement

In common law a conspiracy was indictable as soon as the unlawful agreement was formed. The statutory versions require proof of an overt act. Though the act is usually a crime, it may be a misdemeanor, or even noncriminal behavior in furtherance of the conspiracy, such as the purchase of equipment. The act must occur after the agreement was entered into and before it was terminated. The statute of limitations runs from the time the act took place, since it is a necessary element of the offense. In most jurisdictions, however, continued overt acts prolong the statute of limitations.

(14.18) Problems of Proof

Unlike prosecutions for other crimes, at a conspiracy trial circumstantial evidence may be admitted with wide latitude. Inferential evidence may be needed, since the underlying agreement could be impossible to prove otherwise. It is possible for the words, deeds, books, and records of one conspirator to be admitted into evidence against the penal interests of all other conspirators. Some jurisdictions allow hearsay evidence against alleged conspirators. Finally, one conspirator may testify against the interests of all other conspirators, including those he has not met.

D. ACCOMPLICES

(14.19) What Is an Accomplice?

To understand the role the accomplice plays in the law of evidence, it is first necessary to understand how the law defines an accomplice. It must be said at the outset that the courts have been unable to arrive at a universally accepted definition. The term could be broadly defined as any persons who participate in a crime, whether they be principals, aiders and abettors, or accessories before the fact. There is an obvious problem with this approach: the exclusion of all evidence offered by such "accomplices" would often have the effect of providing an insufficient evidentiary basis for convicting the principal. Courts that have followed this broad definition of accomplice have, therefore, also been compelled to establish arbitrary exceptions to the definition in order to obtain the desired testimony.

The more established rule is to treat as accomplices all persons who could be indicted, either as a principal or as an accessory, for the same offense as that with which the defendant is charged. He must have knowingly, voluntarily, and with common intent united with the principal offender in the commission of a crime. Thus an accomplice may be either an active participant in the crime or one who advised or encouraged another to commit a crime (aider or abettor). While an individual need not have been present at the time the crime was committed, knowledge and voluntary action are necessary in order for him to be viewed as an accomplice.

The mere fact that a person was present or acquiesced in the commission of a crime is not sufficient to make him an accomplice. Knowledge that a crime is about to be committed or the failure to report a crime is also insufficient to make the person an accomplice.

Either the judge or the jury determines whether or not an individual is an accomplice. It need not be established beyond a reasonable doubt that a witness is an accomplice, but, if the testimony of the individual raises a strong presumption to that effect, it has been considered sufficient to justify the application of the special rules of accomplice testimony.

Whether a person is an accomplice also depends on his legal capacity to commit a crime. A child or adult who is not of sound mind (non compos mentis) cannot be either a principal or accessory to a crime.

(14.20) Credibility

It should be obvious that the testimony of an accomplice is properly viewed as having questionable reliability. The testimony of an accomplice is likely to be colored by his perception of hostility, threats, hopes of leniency, and a number of other factors. He is unlike most witnesses in that his testimony can and will have at least an indirect effect on the subsequent treatment he will receive from the legal system. The testimony of an accomplice has, therefore, historically been received with caution.

As the trier of fact does with all witnesses, he must weigh the credibility of the accomplice's testimony. Judges often caution a jury, however, concerning the problem of credibility posed by uncorroborated testimony offered by an accomplice (see 14.25-14.28). Such an instruction still permits the jury to believe the accomplice's testimony.

In common law it was well established that the uncorroborated testimony of an accomplice could form the sole basis for a guilty verdict. Many jurisdictions have stopped that practice by declaring, either in statutes or judicial decisions, that such testimony must be corroborated to support a conviction. Other jurisdictions require corroboration where the defendant is accused of certain types of offenses. Where an accomplice is testifying against the defendant and the charges against him are dropped or he is acquitted of the charge, the witness remains an accomplice for purposes of his testimony. Thus, corroboration is still necessary for an acquitted accomplice in jurisdictions that require corroboration to convict.

(14.21) Feigned Complicity

To be an accomplice as defined by law, the individual must share the defendant's criminal intent. When, therefore, an individual participates in a crime in order to obtain evidence to convict the other participants, he is not an accomplice, and his testimony is not subject to any requirement of corroboration that would otherwise be imposed by law.

If the witness claims his complicity in the crime was feigned, but there is evidence to the contrary, the jury must decide whether the witness is a real or only a feigned accomplice. It should be noted that the facts considered in such cases are similar to those raised when the defense claims solicitation or entrapment by police officers. The primary difference is that the question of whether an accomplice is real or feigned is not an element of the accused's defense, but merely gives weight and sufficiency to the evidence offered.

(14.22) Admissions and Confessions by Accomplices

When an accomplice is willing to admit his guilt and is prepared to testify against the accused (in other words, is willing to "turn state's evidence"), there is no principle in the law of evidence that will prevent the prosecution from using the testimony. Since the accomplice is present in the courtroom and is subject to cross-examination by the defendant's attorney, there can be no objections based on either the clause concerning confrontation of witnesses in the Constitution or the hearsay evidence rule. The attorney for the accused will, of course, question the accomplice to determine if he anticipated receiving a benefit in return for his cooperation, and he will remind the jury of the low regard accorded the testimony of accomplices.

A completely different situation arises when an accomplice has confessed his personal guilt and the prosecution attempts to introduce his confession as evidence of the defendant's guilt. While the confession will undoubtedly be used against the person who made it, it cannot be used against other participants in the crime who are mentioned in it. With respect to these associates, the statement would be hearsay evidence and, hence, inadmissible.

The practice of courts conducting a joint trial in which one of the defendants made a confession has recently changed. In the past, the confession was allowed in evidence against the confessor, but the jury was instructed not to consider the statement as evidence against any other persons. The Supreme Court recognized that the practice almost certainly results in prejudice to the codefendants who did not make the confession. It therefore forbade its use in the important case of *Bruton* v. *United States*, 391 U.S. 123, 10 L. Ed. 2d 476, 88 S. Ct. 1620 (1967). As a consequence of this decision, the prosecution must now either try the person who confesses and the other defendants in separate trials or seek the convictions of all parties in a joint trial without making use of the confession. If the confessor repeats on the witness stand the assertions contained in his confession, the application of the hearsay evidence rule is avoided because the confession is then subject to cross-examination by the defense attorneys.

When an accomplice makes a confession in the presence of the defendant and the latter assents to that confession, it becomes admissible against him. The defendant's assent may be a positive acceptance, or it may be implied from his silence or failure to deny the statements of the accomplice.

(14.23) Compelling the Testimony of an Accomplice

a. Immunity

When a person is asked a question that may implicate him in a crime, he is not obligated to answer it. His constitutional right to remain silent—known as the privilege against self-incrimination—is protected by the Fifth Amendment. Despite some criticism by legal commentators, the privilege has prevented prosecutors from commenting on the refusal by a witness to answer questions and the jury from drawing conclusions from his exercise of this right.

The state often finds it necessary and desirable to use the knowledgeable testimony of an accomplice to convict a defendant. This usually involves a decision by the prosecutor to allow one party to a crime to go free in order to catch "the big fish."

It frequently happens that the only evidence sufficient to convict the defendant is the knowledge possessed by a conspirator or an accomplice. In such cases, the accomplice is often offered immunity in exchange for his testimony. Anything less than an offer of immunity (such as a lesser charge or a reduced sentence) is unpersuasive to the accomplice because he knows that the likely alternative is a dismissal of all the charges against the defendant for lack of evidence sufficient to convict.

The privilege against self-incrimination can be claimed only by a person facing the risk of prosecution and conviction. The purpose of immunity is to eliminate that risk and to compel the accomplice to respond freely to what would otherwise be incriminating questions.

Three basic forms of immunity may be granted a witness. He may be given immunity to prevent the use of his compelled testimony at a subsequent trial in which he is a defendant (use immunity) or from the use of any evidence derived from that compelled testimony (derivative use immunity). A much broader grant of immunity protects the witness from prosecution for any offenses to which the compelled testimony relates (transactional immunity). The Supreme Court has ruled that a grant of use and derivative use immunity serves to supplant the privilege against incrimination (*Zicarelli* v. *New Jersey State Commission of Investigation*, 406 U.S. 472 [1972]). A witness who refuses to answer questions after receiving use and derivative use immunity is not protected by the Fifth Amendment and can be found in contempt of court. It is not necessary for the state to extend the broader protection of transactional immunity in order to compel the testimony of an accomplice.

b. After Conviction

If the accomplice has been convicted of the crime, he can still be compelled to testify against the defendant. He can no longer claim the privilege against self-incrimination since he has already been prosecuted and convicted of the acts at issue in the criminal proceeding. Unless the accomplice is entitled to certain testimonial privileges, established either by common law or statute, he can be made to testify; a refusal to do so is punishable as contempt of court. The accomplice cannot refuse to testify simply because a question is embarrassing.

In addition to the state's power to compel the presence and testimony of any witness, including convicted accomplices, the Supreme Court has ruled that a defendant has an absolute right to obtain and present witnesses in his defense. This constitutional right, as set forth in the Sixth Amendment, states that every individual is entitled to the best possible defense.

(14.24) Distinguishing Accomplices from Accessories

An accessory before the fact is one who does not take part in the actual commission of the crime, but whose prior acts of advising or counseling are sufficient to make him a participant in the crime. Accessories before the fact fit within the definition of an accomplice. Some state statutes have abolished the distinction between principals and accessories before the fact, allowing the latter to be indicted, tried, and convicted as a principal.

Accessories after the fact do not begin their participation until after the crime has been committed. At that point, they receive, relieve, or assist a felon with the knowledge that a felony has been committed. To be an accessory after the fact, the individual must have had knowledge that a felony had been committed, must have known that the person he was aiding was the felon, and must have intended to be aiding the felon in some way. If any one of these elements is missing, he is not chargeable as an accessory.

An accessory after the fact is seen as committing a separate offense from that committed by the principal. The prescribed penalties are, therefore, usually less severe than those imposed against principal offenders or accessories before the fact.

E. CORROBORATION

(14.25) Corroborating Evidence

Corroborating evidence supplements and supports previously offered evidence. While corroborating evidence is directed at the same issue as the initial evidence, it comes from a separate source and is designed to enhance the credibility of the prior testimony. Thus, the use of corroborating evidence serves the same purpose as proof of the good character of a witness, proof of his reputation for telling the truth, proof of prior consistent statements, and disproof of contradictory evidence.

Direct evidence by any one witness is sufficient to prove any fact. When, however, a witness has been impeached or contradicted by other testimony, the side that introduced him is allowed to produce evidence that tends to support his testimony and credibility. This supporting evidence is termed corroboration. Some courts have observed that once a witness has been impeached, he cannot be corroborated unless his impeachment has not been conclusive. It has generally been held that when the first witness has been discredited, the supporting evidence must be credible and unimpeached to effect corroboration.

Specific rules of evidence govern the use of corroborative evidence. Proof, by other evidence, of a fact stated by a witness will properly be rejected when there has been no contradiction of his testimony. This is merely an application of the rule that prevents either side from offering evidence that only repeats uncontradicted testimony and is therefore cumulative in nature.

Considerable latitude is usually allowed in the admission of corroborative evidence, with the trial judge exercising a large degree of discretion concerning its inclusion. The weight attributed to corroborative evidence depends on its nature and credibility. Though corroboration need not be direct or conclusive, it must meet the usual test of relevance, materiality, and competence. It is not permissible to corroborate a witness by referring to collateral or irrelevant matters, and testimony regarding his general reputation for truthfulness will not serve as corroboration. The corroborating witness must testify in detail and to all particulars that are to be corroborated. He may not merely testify that the testimony of a prior witness was accurate.

As a general rule, the prior similar statements of a witness cannot be used to corroborate his present testimony. In addition, one cannot infer the truth of his present testimony from his acts. There are, however, exceptions to the general rule concerning the use of prior testimony to corroborate. For example, the testimony of a witness is attacked on the grounds that it was recently fabricated or was produced by self-interested motives. Under these circumstances the side that offered the testimony is allowed to refute the charges by establishing that the witness had previously made statements of a similar nature. This exception to the hearsay evidence rule is a narrow one that is applied very cautiously by most judges. Another exception concerns identification testimony. When such testimony is impeached, evidence of prior consistent identifications may be used in corroboration. This exception is especially useful in those cases that raise claims of mistaken identity.

Once a witness' testimony has been sufficiently corroborated, the jury may not reject that testimony even when it would have been contradictory and inconsistent if uncorroborated. When corroboration has been completed, the other party may introduce matters that tend to lessen the impact of the corroborative testimony. A prominent example of this practice occurs when a wife corroborates her husband's alibi testimony. By pointing out the natural tendency of a wife to stand by her spouse, the prosecution lessens the effectiveness of the corroborative evidence.

In some jurisdictions the criminal code has departed from the common-law rule that permitted the direct evidence of any witness to support a conviction. These statutes specify that in the case of a guilty verdict the crucial testimony must be corroborated by another witness. This means, in effect, that the testimony offered by the party against whom the statute operates is not legal evidence and should be given no weight whatsoever.

(14.26) Sex Crimes

At common law, it was generally held that the unsupported testimony of the victim of a sex crime would be sufficient to sustain a conviction, if the testimony was not contradictory or inherently improbable. In the case of a rape charge, this was true even when the victim was under the age of consent, when the underaged female admitted that she had consented to the intercourse, and when she had a reputation for a lack of chastity. Thus, regardless of facts tending to diminish the credibility of the complaining witness' testimony, juries could still accept that uncorroborated testimony and use it as the sole basis for a conviction.

Some jurisdictions have amended this principle by judicial decision. Recognizing that a charge of rape or seduction is one that is easily brought but difficult to disprove, these courts have required that convictions on such charges be based on both the testimony of the complaining witness and independent corroborating evidence tending to strengthen or confirm the original testimony. Other jurisdictions have gone beyond this and require corroboration as a statutory element of the crime. Thus, the courts have no discretion by which they can base a conviction on the uncorroborated testimony of the complaining witness. The degree of specificity needed to corroborate the victim's testimony is, however, a fairly light burden for the prosecution to satisfy. The complaining witness need not be corroborated on each of the essential elements of the crime, but only on the act of intercourse. The statutory requirement of corroboration is met by any testimony tending to show the defendant's guilt or establishing the credibility of the complaining witness.

(14.27) Confessions

A defendant frequently makes a confession outside the court-room and then refuses to repeat it on the witness stand. Such an extrajudicial confession is not generally admitted into evidence unless it is corroborated by other evidence. The corroborative evidence must prove or tend to prove a material element of the crime charged. In its most basic form, the rule requires that, before an uncorroborated confession is accepted as evidence of guilt, there must be proof that the alleged crime actually occurred. This requirement may be expressed in another way: there must be independent evidence that sufficiently supports the admitted facts in order that the jury may infer the truth of the confession.

The evidence offered as corroboration must be substantive and cannot merely be an allegation that the confession was true. It is not necessary, however, that the corroborative evidence be sufficient by itself to establish a preponderance of guilt. For example, a statement by the accused that he murdered his wife is not enough to support a murder conviction. The discovery of her body is, however, corroborative evidence of the truth of that confession. Once the commission of the crime by someone is established, the corroborative connection has been made between the confession and the crime.

(14.28) Corroboration of Accomplices

The role of the accomplice's testimony was analyzed above (see 14.22). It can take one of two forms. First, the prosecution can develop evidence following the accomplice's testimony that tends to support its truth. Second, it can develop facts that serve to establish a connection between the accused and the crime that indirectly corroborates the testimony. The testimony of an accomplice must generally be corroborated by an independent source and not by another accomplice. Once an accomplice's testimony has been corroborated, it is usually entitled to great persuasive weight.

At common law, the testimony of an accomplice could support a conviction whether or not it was corroborated. With the passage of statutes that require corroboration for an accomplice's testimony to serve as the basis for a conviction, however, most courts make every effort to impair its use. Especially in those cases where the accomplice's testimony is suspicious, contradictory, inconsistent, or unreasonable, corroboration will be required as a matter of law. It is not necessary that every fact or any particular fact be confirmed. If the probative force of the accomplice's testimony is strengthened and confirmed, it will be corroborated as a matter of law and can, therefore, stand as the sole basis of convictions in jurisdictions that have altered the common-law rule.

(14.29) Summary

Often difficult to prove directly, several crimes incorporate intent or knowledge as an element of the offense. Intention is provable by the conduct and statements of an accused. Knowledge, on the other hand, does not refer to the recognition that an act is criminal; proof that the accused was aware of the facts that made his conduct criminal is sufficient. Ignorance of the law is no excuse. Motive is a different concept; it is never an element of an offense. It is admissible where intent is an element of the offense, and provides persuasive circumstantial proof that the defendant committed the crime.

Ordinarily, evidence that an accused has committed other crimes is not admissible. Where, however, one offense is related to another, such evidence is admissible and relevant. Similarly, where otherwise unconnected offenses can be shown to be a part of a common scheme or design, such proof will be allowed where the interdependence is shown.

A conspiracy is a separate offense, which is the conscious agreement of two or more persons to commit one or more offenses, coupled with an overt act in furtherance of the aims of the conspiracy. Equal participation in the scheme or the equal sharing of benefits is not necessary. A coconspirator may not even know the identity of all other participants. Often there are several conspiracies in simultaneous existence, and only a few of the participants may be active in multiple conspiracies.

Accomplices may be either active or passive participants in a crime. An accomplice does not need to be present during the commission of the offense; knowledge and assent are sufficient. Prosecutors frequently offer accomplices immunity from prosecution, in return for their testimony against the principal offender.

Corroborating evidence supplements and supports previously

offered evidence. Proof of uncontradicted testimony may be rejected as cumulative. On the other hand, certain kinds of testimony require corroboration. A confession is not admissible against an accused unless the crime itself is proved. Sexual offenses, by judicial decision and often by statute, require corroboration.

15

Grand Juries, Suppression Hearings, Appeals, and Forfeiture Proceedings

A. GRAND JURIES

(15.1) Grand Juries in General

The grand jury is part of our legal inheritance from England. Its origin goes back many hundreds of years. Originally the grand jury accused and tried persons for crimes. Later, it became, as it is today, an accusatory body, charging suspects with serious crimes. It functioned both as an arm of government, processing felony complaints against individuals and as a shield, protecting individuals against unjust prosecution by the king. Its use is essentially the same today.

The term "grand jury" comes about because it is composed of a larger number of people than the traditional trial jury of twelve persons. The function of the grand jury is to inquire into felonies committed within its particular district. Its purpose is to determine whether the prosecutor has sufficient evidence to justify accusing a person of a felony. If so, it indicts the suspect by presenting the trial court with a written paper—an indictment—charging him with a specified crime. If it finds insufficient evidence against him, it returns a "no bill." The charge is then dismissed, and, if the defendant is in custody, he must be released.

The grand jury ordinarily hears only the evidence presented by the prosecutor, who is required to present a prima facie case. Most charges are brought by the prosecuting attorney, but a citizen may bring a criminal complaint to the grand jury's attention, or the jury itself may request an investigation.

In some jurisdictions a grand jury may investigate a matter that does not result in an indictment, but makes a "presentment," calling attention to wrongdoing, usually affecting public officials. Many courts restrict the use of such presentments by keeping them sealed and allowing publication only by court order. Grand juries can also issue their own subpoenas. They hold their hearings under the direction of the prosecutor without the presence of a judge. The court is, however, always available to them for advice or assistance if it should be needed. Their procedure is private and somewhat informal.

Since the grand jury is an accusatory body, not a trial court, the accused has no right to give evidence himself or to produce witnesses in his own behalf (*Charlton* v. *Kelly*, 229 U.S. 447 [1912]). He may, however, request the right to testify. If he is allowed to do so, he will first be required to sign a waiver of immunity. Otherwise, his protection under the Fifth Amendment would bar any subsequent indictment of him. If he does give evidence before the grand jury, he must do so without the assistance of counsel, unless a statute allows representation in his particular jurisdiction.

Sometimes the prosecution is willing to have a criminal suspect testify in order to indict a third party. All jurisdictions have procedures whereby such a witness may be granted immunity. When the witness has been granted immunity, he can be compelled to testify before the grand jury on pain of being held in contempt. A grant of immunity will not, of course, protect him against the subsequent charge of perjury should his grand jury testimony prove to be deliberately false.

The grand jury has now been abolished in England. In some jurisdictions in the United States the grand jury has been largely superseded by the use of a prosecutor's information instead of an indictment. The grand jury is still in wide use, however, and it is a constitutional requirement in many jurisdictions.

(15.2) Use of Tainted Evidence

The grand jury, like a trial court, must base its findings on legal proof. With minor exceptions, it must follow the same rules of evidence as every other court. In some states, however, there are statutory exceptions that allow the use of hearsay in the form of official laboratory and medical reports.

Since there is usually no defense attorney present to raise an objection, it is easier for improper evidence to creep in before a grand jury than would be allowed in an actual trial. The grand jury occasionally hears tainted evidence, such as a confession that is subsequently ruled to be involuntary or evidence from a search and seizure that is suppressed. The fact that a grand jury has heard illegal evidence will not in itself invalidate the indictment. If, after excluding the illegal evidence, the court finds that the grand jury heard sufficient legal proof to sustain the charge, the indictment will stand (*U.S.* v. *Calandra*, 94 S. Ct. 613 [1974]).

(15.3) Secrecy of Records and Transcripts

Grand jury proceedings are held in secret. All jurors take an oath of secrecy, and some jurisdictions even require such oaths from witnesses who testify before it (*Goodman* v. *U.S.*, 108 F. 2d 516 [1939]). This secrecy is so protected that in many jurisdictions revelation of grand jury proceedings is a crime. At the very least, it may be a contempt of court. Newspaper reports as to the scope of grand jury investigations or the names of witnesses appearing before it do not violate grand jury secrecy. The court, however, is the only one that can order grand jury proceedings made public, and it may do this at any time in the interest of justice.

There are valid reasons for grand jury secrecy. First, it greatly encourages reluctant or fearful witnesses to reveal information. They can thus testify in confidence, knowing that their testimony will not become public until the time of an actual trial. Second, grand jury members are protected from pressure or actual harm, since their testimony and even their individual votes are kept confidential. Third, an accused who is not in custody can be indicted secretly and can be successfully arrested without being alerted to the fact that he is wanted.

After an indictment is made public, defense counsel routinely requests the court's permission to inspect the grand jury minutes. If an accused testified before it, he may be given a copy of his own testimony, but, at this point, all else remains secret. Only the prosecutor and the court have access to the minutes and the transcript of the proceedings. In response to a motion to inspect the minutes, the judge ordinarily reads the minutes in camera and either sustains or dismisses the indictment, depending on the validity of the proof. His decision is made without allowing the defense to inspect the transcript. As a matter of fact, this inspection is rarely allowed by the court and only then on good cause and in the interest of justice.

When an indictment finally results in a trial, defense counsel is allowed to have a copy of any testimony by a prosecution witness before the grand jury. This is used in cross-examination of that witness.

(15.4) Composition of Grand Jury

Grand juries have consisted traditionally of more than twelve but not more than twenty-three members. Their number and composition are controlled by statute and by the constitution of the particular jurisdiction. During the grand jury proceedings, the number of jurors present and voting can vary from case to case, as long as the statutory quorum is present. A unanimous vote is not required. Agreement by twelve is normally sufficient for a decision, either to indict or to hand down a no bill.

The general makeup of any grand jury is subject to constitutional tests for fairness. There must, for example, be no exclusion from membership because of race or ethnic background. Some jurisdictions do, however, have special constitutional membership rules. In New York City, for instance, convicted felons are barred from membership (New York Judiciary Law, Sec. 609), but, in general, grand jury lists are made up from a cross section of the population.

B. SUPPRESSION HEARINGS

(15.5) In General

The exclusionary rule comes into focus in a proceeding called a suppression or exclusionary hearing. Lawyers for defendants make formal motions to "suppress and reject" either tangible or intangible evidence that has allegedly been illegally obtained. Such motions are in the nature of affirmative defenses; that is, counsel for an accused must move for suppression, or any objection to evidentiary use is waived.

The rule is usually thought of in terms of tangible evidence that has been seized as the result of one of the following:

1. *defective search warrant*: missing dates, bad or insufficient address, missing signature, or staleness;
2. *extension of warrant beyond scope*: small containers such as envelopes opened on authority of a warrant for large objects, or additional unnamed premises searched;
3. *improper execution of a search warrant*: outside jurisdiction, wrong class of officer, or defective announcement;
4. *warrantless entry of premises*: no exigent circumstances in justification;
5. *extension of protective search*: drawers, boxes, or suitcases searched in adjacent rooms incident to a custodial arrest;
6. *no probable cause*: arrest, arrest warrant, or search warrant made on insufficient grounds;
7. *defective consent*: consensual search predicated on coerced consent, consent by a party not in lawful possession, or consent by a person not of sound mind or age.

Intangible evidence will also be suppressed if it has been illegally seized. Illegal electronic surveillance, unauthorized wiretaps, or conversations overheard through a trespass are prime examples.

Physical identification evidence, if improperly obtained, is subject to suppression. This includes fingerprints, blood or urine samples, fingernail scrapings, removal of hair, body impressions, and clothing worn.

Eyewitness identification, when obtained through nonconstitutional methods, will be suppressed. A suggestive lineup, coaching of a witness, or disregard of lineup procedures are frequent bases for such motions.

Violation of the rule against self-incrimination, in any of its facets, warrants suppression of the statements or admissions. In addition to *Miranda* violations, testimonial evidence is also inadmissible if it is the product of coercion.

Noncompliance with statutes or court rules can result in the exclusion of evidence. A willfully delayed arraignment might, for example, vitiate an otherwise voluntary confession.

Evidence that is discovered or obtained as a result of a prior improper act is tainted and is, therefore, usually inadmissible. This is the so-called Poisoned Tree doctrine.

Finally, evidence that is obtained by "shocking" police conduct is subject to suppression. The Supreme Court, for example, reversed a conviction based on evidence seized after the defendant's stomach was forcibly pumped *(Rochin v. California*, 342 U.S. 165 [1951]).

Suppression hearings are scheduled after the arraignment, but usually before the trial. Many state codes parallel Federal Rule of Criminal Procedure 41(e) in this respect. It is possible in federal court to institute a suppression hearing in anticipation of an indictment. This procedure may be ineffectual, however, since a grand jury can consider illegally seized evidence.

The law presumes proper police practices until they are challenged. At the opening of the suppression hearing, the defense has the burden of going forward. As the moving party, the defense attorney normally asserts the nature of his defense and then presents evidence in support of his motion.

The quantum of evidence necessary to shift the burden of proof to the prosecution depends on the nature of the claim. If the defense utterly fails to show any illegality, the motion will be denied at that stage of the hearing. When, however, the defense succeeds in raising an inference of illegality, the burden of persuasion shifts to the prosecution. In cases where a warrantless arrest or search has uncovered tangible evidence, the prosecution must then assume the burden of persuasion. The opposite is true when the challenged evidence was obtained with a search warrant or incidental to an arrest by warrant. This is because a neutral and detached magistrate, in an ex parte proceeding, has already made preliminary findings of probable cause.

The defendant may or may not be called to present testimony. Such testimony is useful in cases where a frisk or warrantless arrest is contested. Since a defendant can still refuse to testify at his trial, and since a suppression hearing is held outside the presence of a jury, the defense counsel is less reluctant to call his client as a witness.

The defendant's testimony at the suppression hearing is usually inadmissible at the trial stage. Prior to the Supreme Court's opinion in *Simmons* v. *U.S.*, 390 U.S. 377 (1968), this testimony was admissible when it concerned his guilt or innocence. This created a true dilemma. In order to prove police misconduct, the defendant often had to testify regarding acts of an inculpatory nature. Should the motion to suppress be denied, these admissions would gravely prejudice the outcome of the trial. Although the decision in *Simmons* only applies to Fourth Amendment challenges, its logic has been cited in cases involving suppression of confessions. *Simmons* also restricted for impeachment purposes the use of the defendant's statements "on the issue of guilt." This does not mean, however, that the defendant can perjure himself with impunity at the time of trial.

The question of the legality of a search often necessitates disregarding as untruthful the testimony of the defendant or of the police. A suppression judge seldom accepts the defendant's uncorroborated version of the facts.

Although suppression hearings are less formal and more flexible than trials, cross-examination of witnesses is limited to the scope of their direct evidence. This rule must, however, be invoked by counsel. As is the case with postconviction appeals, the findings of fact will not be disturbed on appeal unless they are clearly erroneous. Inasmuch as the basis for suppression of evidence often rests on the credibility of witnesses, it is important for the defense to elicit inconsistencies or irregularities in the statements of the prosecution's witnesses.

A significant aspect of exclusionary hearings is that hearsay and otherwise inadmissible evidence may be introduced to demonstrate the existence of probable cause. This takes three common forms:

1. *Statements made by confidential informants.* The informants are not present in court, are not cross-examined, and their identities are not revealed. Moreover, the officers who obtained or received disclosures by informants might not be present either, depending on circumstances. In possession cases, for instance, the state's witnesses might be limited to the principal arresting officer and the affiant on the search warrant affidavit. Such hearsay is admissible.

2. *Surveillance reports made by other officers.* Once again, the affiant can rely on statements made to him by fellow investigators. Surveillance officers could be recognized in court, and, in most cases, their appearance is unnecessary. This form of hearsay is deemed reliable per se.

3. *Arrest records of the defendants.* Prior arrests of the defendants and persons with whom they had contact during surveillances are admissible to establish probable cause.

Each state is free to set its own rules on the conduct of suppression hearings. There is no constitutional requirement that such motions be heard before a different judge than the one who will preside at the trial, but this is usually the case in larger communities. It is important that a record be kept for reasons of appellate review and possible postconviction collateral attack through federal habeas corpus proceedings.

Although the state cannot appeal an acquittal, it routinely appeals motions to suppress that have been granted. The latter are proper because a defendant has not been placed in jeopardy until the jury is sworn or waived. Such appeals are handled in the usual fashion of written briefs and, frequently, oral arguments to the appellate court. During the period of appeal, the defendant is continued on bond.

Once a motion to suppress has been granted and sustained on appeal, the property is returned to the defendant. In federal courts and in many states the judge orders such return; in other states the defendant must file a civil action in replevin. In no case, however, will a court order the return of contraband to the person from whom it was taken since no one can lawfully possess or own contraband. Stolen goods will not be returned to a defendant. The court can order them restored to their lawful owners.

C. APPELLATE ADVOCACY

(15.6) In General

Before a criminal trial begins, the advantage is said to be completely with the state, with its police, its prosecutor's staff, and its unlimited financial resources. Once the trial starts, the advantage shifts to the defendant. He can rest on the presumption of his innocence and on the fact that he does not have to prove a thing. When the trial is over, his advantage is even more pronounced for he has all the legal weapons at his disposal. If the defendant is acquitted, that ends the matter completely. The state cannot appeal because that would amount to double jeopardy. If he is convicted, however, the defendant has the right to appeal.

Most jurisdictions provide two higher levels of appellate courts. To one, the defendant can get to as a matter of right. The second, he may reach only by court consent. The right to appeal is not guaranteed by the Constitution and so is regulated by statute. The Constitution does, however, assure all defendants, rich and poor, that they will be treated alike. Thus, indigent defendants are allowed to appeal. The state assigns them counsel and assumes all expenses.

(15.7) Interlocutory Appeals

The general rule is that only the final judgment in a criminal case can be appealed. If the parties to a criminal action could routinely appeal preliminary court rulings, the actual trial could be postponed for months or even years.

Pretrial motions and hearings fall within the category of interim matters and, therefore, do not result in a final determination. If a motion to suppress has been granted, the state may bring an appeal on that point. Should the motion lose, however, the matter will not be a part of any appeal until and unless a conviction results (*DiBella* v. *U.S.*, 369 U.S. 121 [1962]). Once a criminal case is finished and an appeal is made by the defendant, all preliminary matters are reviewed by the appellate court as part of the entire record (*Parr* v. *U.S.*, 351 U.S. 513 [1956]).

(15.8) Appeal of the Law

A criminal appeal is confined, theoretically, to the consideration of questions of law. Did the judge make an error in his charge to the jury? Was there an improper court ruling on evidence? Was the indictment legally defective? Was the statute unconstitutional? These and similar legal questions are all properly reviewable on a criminal appeal.

Is the evidence sufficient as a matter of law to prove guilt beyond a reasonable doubt? Though this question actually involves a matter of fact, it is considered a legal matter and, hence, is proper for an appellate decision. In some jurisdictions an appellate court can overturn a conviction "in the interests of justice." This broadly defined term gives the reviewing court an unlimited right to consider any area involved in a trial, even though it may not strictly concern a question of law.

(15.9) Appeal of the Facts

All appellate courts review the entire factual proof and reverse a conviction if they find that there was insufficient legal evidence before the trial court to prove guilt beyond a reasonable doubt. In addition, the appellate court must always decide the legal question of the validity of any material evidence that was accepted by the trial court over a sound objection. Appellate courts cannot, of course, substitute their judgment for that of the jury, who are the triers of the fact. Such matters as the credibility of witnesses and the resolution of disputed fact questions are for the jury alone to determine (*State* v. *Dantonio*, 18 N.J. 570 [1955]).

(15.10) Disposition of Appeals

a. Affirmance

If there was sufficient legal evidence to support the conviction, and if there was no reviewable error of law or trial procedure, the appellate court will affirm (uphold) the conviction.

b. Remand

An appellate court may, in some cases, avoid making a final decision and remand (return) the case to the lower court for further proceedings. Additional hearings on confessions or the refusal to allow withdrawal of a guilty plea are matters that are typically remanded.

c. Modification

Many appellate courts have the right to modify the criminal judgment. For example, one or more counts of a multicount indictment may be dismissed, a sentence may be reduced, or a fine may be remitted. Appellate courts can, however, only mitigate or reduce the punishment. Under our system, it is unconstitutional for them to increase the sentence in any way (*Commonwealth* v. *Garramone*, 307 Pa. 507 [1932]).

d. Reversals

All appellate courts have the power to reverse a conviction of any criminal case that is properly brought before them. That is, they may send the case back to the original court to be tried again. They may even dismiss the charge entirely if there are proper legal grounds for doing so.

The legal theory is that an appellate court should reverse a conviction only if the error it finds is a substantial one. There is, of course, no such thing as a perfect trial, and any trial record contains matters that are legally arguable. Legal errors of an unsubstantial nature are, therefore, supposedly ignored by an appellate court.

The theory of criminal appeals often varies from the practice. In their desire to protect the rights of individuals, appellate courts are apt to reverse any conviction, sometimes on the basis of even the smallest of technical errors. Thus, in criminal appeals today, the advantage is decidedly with the defendant.

(15.11) Postconviction Remedies

Once convicted, the defendant has his right to an appeal. When this is finished, the general assumption is that the matter is ended. The prosecutor should feel that he can move on to the next case. But this is not so. Though the trial may be over and the appeal finished, often the case is only begun. The convicted defendant has two powerful postconviction remedies—*coram nobis* and habeas corpus— that he often carries on endlessly from behind bars, seeking continuously to overturn his conviction.

a. Coram Nobis

One remedy that is often used to fight a criminal conviction is the writ of error called *coram nobis*. This petition to the original court seeks to set aside a conviction on some alleged error that does not appear on the record. Among typical examples is the claim that the sentencing court was misled or defrauded by such things as a plea bargain broken by the prosecutor, a prosecutor's concealment of evidence favorable to the defendant, or a sentence that is unduly harsh based on an unconstitutional or illegal predicate (prior) conviction. In some jurisdictions the right of *coram nobis* is a matter of common law, and in others it is set out in statutory form. There is generally no time limit on its use, and repeated petitions are often accepted by the court even though they may be somewhat repetitious.

b. Habeas Corpus

English-speaking courts began using this postconviction remedy before Magna Charta (1215). In its simplest form, it is a petition to the court to inquire into the legality of any imprisonment. When the court receives a proper petition in habeas corpus, it must cause the prisoner to be brought before it and must inquire into the legality of his conviction. Failure to do so may result in a penalty against the court itself.

It is unfortunate that this postconviction remedy is often abused. Even before an appeal is completed, an inmate may attempt to get faster relief by filing a habeas corpus petition. When it is refused, he often simply files it again. When it is denied, he appeals the decision. If the inmate finally exhausts all his appeals and his state habeas corpus remedies, he has further recourse. He may start all over again in federal court, claiming lack of due process or other constitutional grounds that allegedly make his conviction improper. First, he has access to the federal district court from which he can attempt to carry his case through the federal appellate level all the way to the Supreme Court. He may, of course, be defeated in this effort. If so, he has the right to try again should he find a new legal argument to present against the validity of his conviction. It is obvious, therefore, that, under our dual court system, postconviction litigation by prisoners can be an extremely lengthy process.

In a case of great significance, the U.S. Supreme Court has ruled that a convicted defendant may not attack his conviction on Fourth Amendment grounds, absent extraordinary circumstances (*Stone* v. *Powell*, 96 S. Ct. 3037 [1976]). Prior to this landmark decision, many inmates and defendants awaiting incarceration would routinely attack their convictions on the grounds that these were procured by evidence that was illegally seized. Previously, a federal district court was not bound by the conclusions of legality made by state trial and appellate courts. Federal judges frequently interpreted the Fourth Amendment more liberally in favor of a defendant than did state courts.

Stone v. *Powell* holds that a defendant may not attack his conviction upon an allegation of illegal search and seizure if he has had an opportunity to challenge the search in the state courts.

D. FORFEITURE PROCEEDINGS

(15.12) Personal Property

In Exod. 21:28 is the first recorded law of forfeitures, which states that if an ox gores a man or a woman to death, it shall be stoned and its flesh shall not be eaten, but the owner of the ox shall be clear. From the time of Moses, there has existed a philosophy that recognizes the personality and responsibility of inanimate objects. Blackstone noted, for example, that a weapon used to slay another must be forfeited to the crown. Thus, although the owner of the ox or the weapon might be excused, punishment would be inflicted on the property.

Since 1789 the federal code and most state statutes have provided for forfeiture of enumerated goods and chattels when employed in a proscribed manner. Included are motor vehicles, aircraft, and ships that are used to transport contraband or violate customs laws and gambling paraphernalia, obscene objects, whiskey stills, counterfeit presses, and listed weapons. In cases involving the syndicate, currency used or gained from enumerated activities is subject to confiscation.

Forfeitures are not automatic. They are civil actions, penal in nature and effect, that are brought against items of personal property. Some statutes protect innocent owners; others do not. If, for example, a person's car is stolen and is subsequently used to transport narcotics, the vehicle will be returned. If, however, the owner lends his car to a drug dealer, forfeiture can be effected, even though the owner did not know or consent to the illegal use of his car.

Statutes that expressly authorize relief for nonculpable owners of personal property are called remission laws. Many of these laws were enacted to protect mortgagees and lessors. In order to obtain the benefits of a remission, the owner or holder of a security interest must show the following:

1. that he had no knowledge of the wrongdoing;
2. that reasonable inquiry would not have revealed an illicit purpose;
3. that dealings with the perpetrator were businesslike;
4. that the facts known to the nonculpable party were consistent with innocent use.

A remission cannot be granted in the case of blood relatives, partners, unindicted coconspirators, and controlled corporations. If this were not the case, criminals could avoid forfeitures through contrived mortgages, leases, and other equitable interest instruments.

(15.13) Nature of Proof Required

Despite their penal attributes, forfeiture proceedings remain civil actions. This means that it is unnecessary to prove culpability beyond a reasonable doubt. And, unlike criminal cases where the burden of proof falls almost entirely on the prosecution, the government need only show a prima facie case in order to recover the item in question; the burden of proof shifts to the owner to establish a defense or mitigation. Thus, the rules of criminal procedure do not apply in pretrial proceedings and evidentiary matters.

Although the exclusionary rule is not usually employed in civil actions, an illegal search or seizure will vitiate a forfeiture action. In order to benefit from the exclusionary rule, however, the victim of the police misconduct must be the claimant of the property. For example, if police officers learn of a boat loaded with heroin through a confession taken in violation of the *Miranda* warnings, the boat would still be subject to forfeiture if it was owned by someone other than the individual who made the confession. Thus, to state the matter in its simplest terms, the claimant must have standing in order to object to the illegal search or interrogation.

The Supreme Court has ruled that a claimant to seized property has a constitutional right to remain silent. In the opinion of the justices, there is no difference between a person who pays a criminal fine and one who forfeits a valuable item of personal property. This means that the traditional tools of discovery, such as interrogatories and depositions, cannot be used to incriminate the claimant or to facilitate forfeiture of his property.

Once valuable items are forfeited, they are usually sold by the sheriff to the highest bidder. Proceeds are turned over to the state treasurer, who deposits them in the general fund. In the case of a vehicle, the court can order a change of title to the law enforcement agency that seized it. This is a prime source of the undercover cars used by narcotics and gambling units.

(15.14) Contraband

Contraband, the possession of which is unlawful, can have no owner. It would, of course, be a travesty if a person could recover contraband because of an illegal search or of defective interrogation. An item of personal property is not, however, automatically "converted" to contraband because of an improper use. For this reason, a statute that labels gambling proceeds as contraband does not exempt currency seizures from a challenge under the Fourth or Fifth Amendments.

Heroin, machine guns, counterfeit money, bombs, and other items that cannot be lawfully possessed by citizens under any circumstances will never be returned to the parties who were in possession of them. It might be argued that this rule of law encourages improper police practices. One must remember, however, that the exclusionary rule would still prevent prosecutions, and the civil courts could grant injunctive relief against a pattern of police misconduct.

(15.15) Summary

The grand jury originated in England. It is a group of from twelve to twenty-three persons who inquire into serious offenses and either accuse suspects of crime by indicting them or release them by finding a "no bill." Their proceedings are secret. At the trial, later, a witness' grand jury testimony can be used by the defense in cross-examination.

Suppression hearings are usually pretrial proceedings seeking to suppress illegal evidence, improper confessions, or invalid identifications. Such matters as defective search warrants, illegal arrests, lack of *Miranda* warnings, and the like can be inquired into.

Criminal appeals normally can only be taken by the defendant after he is convicted. If the prosecution could appeal from an acquittal, it would be double jeopardy. Interlocutory rulings must wait until the conviction is appealed, but the state can appeal from the granting of a suppression motion.

A convicted defendant has two additional postconviction remedies, *coram nobis* and habeas corpus. *Coram nobis* is a petition to the original sentencing court seeking to set aside a conviction on the grounds of error outside the record. Habeas corpus is a court-ordered inquiry into the cause of one's imprisonment and can be brought repeatedly in both state and federal courts.

Forfeiture proceedings are civil actions seeking to confiscate property that has been used in an illegal manner. The government need only show a prima facie case, leaving the owner to prove a defense or mitigation. Innocent owners may get relief.

Contraband, such as heroin, counterfeit money, and the like, will never be returned to the possessor.

Appendixes

Appendix A. Tips on Testifying

The Police Witness

As a law enforcement officer, you may find yourself a witness in court. You could be the one who caught the burglar red-handed, confiscated his burglar's tools, and took his confession. All of this is unimportant, however, unless you know how to tell your story in court, answer the lawyers' questions, and convince the jury that you are honestly and accurately telling them what happened.

There are many things that you as a police witness can do to help the presentation of your own case. Some points on testifying are obvious; some are not. However, they all add up to one thing, winning the lawsuit. You can contribute to this by being a better witness.

1. Witness' Appearance and Dress

First, remember that you, as a witness, may be a complete stranger to judge and jury. They are the ones who will judge you for truthfulness and accuracy. The jury can believe you or not, as they choose. If they believe that a witness has lied to them about any material matter, they can disregard his entire testimony or believe that part that they choose to believe and disregard the rest. They are the sole judges of the facts in our jury trial system.

In everyday experience, how do you judge a person whom you meet for the first time? Your initial decision about him is often based on his appearance. You may change your mind later, but your first and most lasting impression of him is governed by the way he looks. So it is with the witness.

Your very physical appearance will set a picture of yourself as you take your oath and enter the jury box. A person's clothing, a woman's hairdo, neatness, and cleanliness are important. These are not small details.

If you are a uniformed officer, wear your uniform in court. You should be proud of your badge, police insignia, and uniform. The jury will sense this. If you are a plainclothes officer, wear conservative clothes.

Another caveat for the police witness concerns his weapon. The last thing an officer should do before coming into a courtroom to testify is to remove his gun. Never testify while armed, even if the weapon is concealed, unless the prosecutor wants you to. A wise cross-examiner is going to ask you if you are armed, and you will have to reveal it. This can put you at a psychological disadvantage with the jury. Who loves a man armed with a gun?

At a recent murder trial, a psychiatrist was a witness for the defense. He came in to testify wearing sport slacks, a sport shirt open at the neck, no necktie, and a casual jacket. His Vandyke beard was untrimmed. He could not have looked any more unprofessional if he had tried. This was the defense star witness, but he lost the psychiatric ball game before even throwing the first ball. He created such a poor impression that the court gave little weight to his expert opinion regarding the defendant's sanity.

Though these may seem to be small points, cases are won or lost this way. They all add up to the picture of you in the jury's mind.

2. Manner of Speaking

Witnesses do come into court chewing gum, sucking candy drops, and talking with chin in hand. Others talk softly, drop their voices at the end of sentences, or otherwise speak poorly. You are not going to do any of these, of course.

A good police witness sits up, speaks up, and answers questions firmly and directly. When giving an important answer, he will look at the jury directly. He is, after all, trying to convince the jurors, not the lawyers. The prosecutor already believes him, and the defense counsel never will.

3. Pretrial Conference

Never testify if you can help it without first having a pretrial conference with the prosecuting attorney assigned to try the case. If the prosecutor thinks he is too busy to talk to you, then you might send word you are too busy to testify. You need to know the general picture of the case and what testimony he expects from you. The prosecutor needs to know what you can testify to of your own personal knowledge.

There is no such thing as a perfect lawsuit. Each case has its weak points and strong points. If there is some problem, such as one concerning evidence, tell the prosecutor beforehand. He needs to know all of the facts, both good and bad, before the trial begins.

Also, as a witness, remember that you too will be on trial. Any unfavorable item in your own past is fair game for the cross-examiner. So, if you have any skeletons in your personal closet, tell the prosecutor. He can then put the best possible light on the matter.

If you have forgotten a date, misplaced a note, or are unclear on any item, the time to straighten the problem out is before trial, not from the witness box. There are often areas of improper evidence that might cause a mistrial if referred to, and counsel can advise as to this. There is nothing wrong or unethical about going over your testimony in advance with trial counsel. Admit this freely if asked about it on cross-examination.

You will find that a proper pretrial conference is the best preparation you can have to ensure accurate, truthful testimony on your part.

4. Officers' Homework

By the time any police witness comes into court, he will have already told his story several times in written statements, police reports, or at preliminary court hearings. Read these and learn them. Defense counsel will have access to these, and he loves to cross-examine about small differences between earlier statements and your in-court testimony.

Lawyers know that the smallest discrepancy may have an effect on the jury, leaving them with the feeling that you are either careless, mistaken, or untruthful. Lawsuits are often lost in just this way.

Do your homework on pretrial statements, and you will pass your witness examination.

5. Use of Notes

A good officer takes notes. If you are called as a witness, you may bring your notes or other memorandums with you. In fact, if you do not use them on direct examination, defense counsel will invariably ask if you took notes and, if so, where they are. The court generally will allow him to see them. If, by chance, your notes contain any embarrassing information, leave them home and rely on your memory. The judge will ordinarily not let you testify directly from any written memorandum. It should be used to refresh your recollection only. The proper way to do this is to say to the court, "May I look at my records?" When the judge consents, take out the writing, read it to yourself, then look up and give your answer. Theoretically, you have "refreshed your recollection" and are testifying from your own mind, not simply reading from a written record.

You might find that you have no recollection of the evidence even after reading the memorandum. In that case, the writing itself may be admitted in evidence as an exception to the hearsay rule as a "past recollection recorded." Though this is unusual, it can be done.

Knowing the proper use of notes and memorandums can make you a better witness.

6. Anticipating Cross-Examination

A generation reared on "Perry Mason" expects to see the cross-examined witness suddenly (just before the commercial) break down and confess that his entire testimony was a lie. This only happens on television, not in courtrooms.

When defense counsel cross-examines you, he does not expect to prove you a liar, but he may hope to suggest it. Primarily, he has other things in mind. First, he is seeking any item of testimony that will help the defense. Perhaps no fingerprints were found on the murder weapon, or no blood-alcohol test made on the drunken driver. He may be able to get this into evidence through you.

Second, the cross-examiner will often try to get you to answer something that you really do not know. He may, for example, ask you to name a distance or give a definite time.

In these instances, the lawyer will be friendly, helpful, and urgently persuasive, trying to get you even to estimate this. He tends to make you feel that you ought to know the answer even though you do not. The best procedure is to say you are not sure and hold firmly to that position. Once you give in and say, "It was about fifty feet" or "One forty-five in the morning" when you do not know, defense counsel may use that answer very effectively later with some other evidence to discredit the prosecution.

Third, the defense attorney will quiz you thoroughly as to any of your earlier testimony or statements. Be prepared for this through your pretrial homework. A favorite trick of some examiners is to stand some distance away from the witness box, appear to read from a paper, and then ask the witness if he had made such a statement previously. This is improper, but some lawyers get away with it. If this happens to you, make the lawyer show you the prior statement, point out the pertinent part, and allow you to read it to yourself before answering. If you do this, the examiner cannot make up a mythical question and answer, but must make honest use of the material, with the witness being given a fair chance to explain himself.

In connection with cross-examination there is a widely held belief that a questioner can force you to answer "Yes" or "No." There is no such rule. The witness can always explain himself. The only time a judge will confine you to a yes or no answer is if you are avoiding giving an honest answer to a question.

An effective defense against a cross-examiner, and one that is often overlooked, is courtesy. It pays in the courtroom as it does in everyday life. Nothing discourages even the most hard-bitten criminal lawyer so much as the police witness who continually answers, "Yes, sir," "No, sir," or "I'm sorry, counsellor, but I said nine o'clock." Keep this up, and you will be the one to "keep your cool," not he.

Finally, it almost goes without saying that your best weapon as a witness is truth. Truth often is stretched, bent, or broken in the courtroom. Do not do this. A truthful witness need never fear a cross-examination.

Someday, you may be that witness in the box. A good appearance, good speaking habits, a pretrial review, and the use of your own notes will make you a better witness. Truth will make you the best.

Appendix B. Fundamentals of Legal Research*

Federal Law—Congress of the United States

All the laws of a general nature passed by Congress are compiled by the federal government in the *United States Code* (U.S.C.). The West Publishing Company has taken the U.S.C. and annotated it by listing after each section the court decisions and legislative history of the section. This set of the code is called the *United States Code Annotated* (U.S.C.A.) and is the one you will find cited most often. The code is grouped under fifty headings (called "Titles" instead of "Chapters"), and any federal law of a general nature can be found under one of these. For appropriation acts the *Statutes at Large* must be consulted. The *Statutes at Large* are comparable to the session laws published by the states.

State Statutes and Constitutions

One of the primary sources of state law is the state code (also named General Statutes, Revised Statutes, Annotated Statutes, etc.). The state code is a compilation of all the laws of a *general nature* passed by the state legislature. It is arranged under chapters or titles according to the various subjects. The code normally does *not* contain appropriation acts or resolutions of the legislature. It is kept up to date by cumulative pocket parts or supplements which are usually

---

*Reproduced with permission from "Finding the Law," a student study guide prepared by the Legal Division staff of the Traffic Institute, Northwestern University.

issued after each session of the legislature. The code is often published by one or more private publishers.

The state constitution is usually found in the same set of books containing the state code.

Annotated Statutes

It is frequently advisable to obtain the interpretation or construction which the appellate courts have made of the various provisions of the state statutes. As a guide to the court decisions, many states, as a part of their state code, annotate each section of the statutes. By *annotate* is meant that after each section of the statute any appellate court decision which has construed or interpreted that section is listed along with a short statement of the holding of the court. Annotations normally contain the legislative history of the section.

Session Laws

The Session Laws or Acts and Resolves, etc., are published after each session of the legislature. This volume or volumes contain *all* the laws, including appropriation acts and resolutions, enacted at that particular session. They are usually referred to by the year in which the legislative session was held, e.g., the 1971 Session Laws contains *all* the laws enacted at the 1971 session of the legislature.

Bill Index

Many states through the legislative reference bureau, or other legislative service agency, publish listings of bills before the legislature and indicate the status of the bills. These listings show such things as the title of the bill, author, general subject matter, and action taken, if any.

Appellate Court Decisions

The decisions of the highest appellate state court are collected and reported in bound volumes called the *state reports*. (The highest appellate court is, in most states, called the state supreme court.) In those states with intermediate courts of appeal between the trial court and the state supreme court, a separate series of reports is frequently published.

Each volume ordinarily contains a subject index and digest of the cases in that volume. It will also contain a table of cases which lists in alphabetical order the names of the cases in that volume.

Each decision reported will show the date it was handed down by the court and at the beginning of each case the compiler will write head notes or syllabi. Head notes are short statements of the points of law decided in that case. These head notes ordinarily are not a part of the decision and should not be quoted as the holding in that case, except where it is noted they have been written by the court.

State Digests

The opinions of the higher courts of the state (and of the lower courts where their opinions are reported) frequently are compiled by topic and outline arrangement into digests of law. By determining what specific point is in issue and under what topic it would be found, it is possible to ascertain what cases, if any, have been decided pertaining to that point. State digests are kept up to date by the issuance of supplements.

Federal Court Decisions

In general, there are three levels in the federal court system which report their decisions. The U.S. District Courts, courts of general jurisdiction, are the trial courts. Decisions of these courts are published in the *Federal Supplement* (F. Supp.). At the next higher level are the Courts of Appeal, the intermediate appellate courts. The decisions of the Courts of Appeal are published in the *Federal Reporter* (F.) or (F. 2d).

The highest court in the land is the Supreme Court of the United States. The decisions of this court are reported in three main sets of reports. The official reports are entitled *United States Reports* and cited as "U.S." The West Publishing Company publishes the *Supreme Court Reporter* (S. Ct.), and Lawyers Co-operative Publishing Company publishes the *United States Supreme Court Reports* (L. Ed.) or (L. Ed. 2d).

The National Reporter System of the West Publishing Company

This set of reports covers the *Supreme Court Reporter, Federal Reporter, Federal Supplement,* and, in addition, the cases from the fifty states. The latter are grouped as follows:

Atlantic (A.)   Connecticut, Delaware, District of Columbia, Maine, Maryland, New Hampshire, New Jersey, Pennsylvania, Rhode Island, Vermont.

North Eastern (N.E.)	Illinois, Indiana, Massachusetts, New York, Ohio.
North Western (N.W.)	Iowa, Michigan, Minnesota, Nebraska, North Dakota, South Dakota, Wisconsin.
Pacific (P.)	Alaska, Arizona, California, Colorado, Hawaii, Idaho, Kansas, Montana, Nevada, New Mexico, Oklahoma, Oregon, Utah, Washington, Wyoming.
South Eastern (S.E.)	Georgia, North Carolina, South Carolina, Virginia, West Virginia.
South Western (S.W.)	Arkansas, Kentucky, Missouri, Tennessee, Texas.
Southern (So.)	Alabama, Florida, Louisiana, Mississippi.

For two states, California and New York, separate units are published:

New York Supplement (N.Y.S.)	Court of Appeals, Appellate Division of the Supreme Court, Supreme Court and other Courts of Record. (Cases of the Court of Appeals, the highest appellate court, also appear in the North Eastern Reporter.)
California Reporter (Cal. Rptr.)	Supreme Court, District Courts of Appeal, and Appellate Department Superior Courts. (Decisions of Supreme Court of California also appear in Pacific Reporter.)

By reference to these units of the National Reporter System, it is possible to keep up with all of the reported court decisions throughout the United States. Prior to issuance in bound volumes the cases come out in paperbound copies known as Advance Sheets. Reference to the appropriate Advance Sheet will give the most recent reports of any particular jurisdiction. The National Reporter System started in 1879 with one unit and by 1888 embraced the entire country.

Decennial Digest

The Decennial Digests are an integral part of the National Reporter System. These digests are compilations of reported cases for a ten-year period, indexed by subject matter, each of which is identified with a "key number."

The whole area of the law has been grouped under topics. Each topic is then outlined with a key number for each subject under that topic. For example under the topic "Automobiles," Key No. 5 deals with the power to regulate and prohibit. Key No. 5 is then further divided into subheads such as (1) In general, (2) Equipment, lights, and signals, (3) Stopping, parking, or standing, etc. By taking "Automobiles Key No. 5 (3)" it is possible to find every case decided in the United States since 1897 on the power to prohibit or regulate parking of automobiles by consulting the Decennial Digests under that topic and key number.

The proper key number can be found by consulting the index at the beginning of each topic, or the subject index.

Cases reported prior to 1897 are to be found in the Century Digest. This set of books digests all reported American cases dating from 1658. The cases are summarized in a manner similar to the Decennial Digest. The reference numbers are not the same, however, and it is necessary to consult cross-reference tables in going from the Century Digests to the Decennial Digests or vice versa.

On the matter of key numbers, it is worth noting that each syllabus point of every case reported in the National Reporter System is indexed by reference to the corresponding key number in the Decennial Digests. By having a particular case in point, reference can be made to the key notes appearing in the beginning of the case in the reporter system (N.E., S.E., etc.). By then searching that title through the Digests it is possible to find all of the cases from over the United States on that subject. In those states where the state digest is published by the West Publishing Company, publishers of the National Reporter System, it is possible to obtain a key number in the state digests and track it down under the same heading in the general digest.

Law Encyclopedias

The current leading law encyclopedias are *Corpus Juris Secundum* (C.J.S.) and *American Jurisprudence* (Am. Jur.). *Corpus Juris Secundum* is a successor to Corpus Juris (C.J.), which replaced the Encyclopedia of Law and Procedure (Cyc.). *American Jurisprudence* is the successor to Ruling Case Law. *American Jurisprudence* has recently been revised and published as *American Jurisprudence Second*

Edition (Am. Jur. 2d). It is cross-referenced to an annotated case series, American Law Reports (ALR), and its predecessor, Lawyers' Reports Annotated. Both C.J.S. and Am. Jur. 2d are kept up to date by pocket supplements.

American Law Reports

American Law Reports (ALR) is a valuable source for finding selected cases on certain points of law. It is basically a compilation of cases with annotated comment. ALR is composed of three parts: the First Series (ALR) contains 175 volumes; the Second Series (ALR 2d) has 100 volumes; the Third Series (ALR 3d) is the current set. Each series has its own Index and Supplemental Service.

Another part of this set is the American Law Reports Federal (ALR Fed) which started in 1969. This series is devoted to federal legal problems and has a "Quick Index."

Finding a Given Case

A typical "citation" of a case is as follows: *Jones* v. *Smith*, 185 Kan. 230, 358 P. 2d 890 (1959).

The case name is "*Jones* v. *Smith*." All of the state reports (bound volumes containing the decisions of the highest appellate court or intermediate appellate court) are listed by the abbreviation of the state name, e.g., Ill., Mich., N.Y., etc. The number preceding the state name is the number of the volume, and the figure following the name is the page in that volume where the particular decision will be found. The capital "P. 2d" is an abbreviation for Pacific Reporter, Second Series. And again the number in front is the volume number, and the number following is the page of this particular decision. The figure in parenthesis is the year in which the case was decided. Thus for most cases you have two sets of books in which the case can be found—the state reports or the National Reporter System. However, a few states have discontinued their state reports and rely on the National Reporter System for publication of their court decisions.

The "2d" following the abbreviation indicates that that series of reports has gone into a second series. That is, after reaching 200 or 300 volumes in the series, the compiler decided to begin with Volume 1 again, and to distinguish the second series from the first a small "2d" is used. Most of the units in the National Reporter System have gone into the second series in numbering the volumes. Several states have also started into the second series on their official state reports—Wash. 2d, Ill. 2d, N.Y. 2d, Utah 2d, Cal. 2d, for example.

If one has the name of a case and knows the state from which it has been issued, reference is had to a table of cases to be found in the state digest. The general digest system also has comparable tables of cases which, however, embrace the entire United States. Given a definite volume number and the name of a case but not the page number, reference to the particular volume and the table of cases contained therein will supply the appropriate page.

If a state citation is supplied and it is desired to obtain the Reporter System citation, refer to the reporter Blue Book where the appropriate citation will be found, either in the basic Blue Book, the 1936, 1948, 1960, or 1970 supplement, or the current paperback volume. In addition, if a federal case has had a descriptive name attached to it such as the "Sick Chicken" case or the "Slaughter House" case, or whatever the popular name may be, there is a book containing cross-references to popular case names in which the citation can be found. This is in the M-Z volume of the index to the Sixth Decennial Digest.

Law Dictionaries

Black's Law Dictionary or *Bouvier's Law Dictionary* are ready sources for the definition of legal terms. They also contain such things as explanations of written expressions, the meanings of various practices and procedures, and a list of common legal abbreviations to be found in both American and English reports.

A Brief List of Common Legal Abbreviations

A. or Atl.	Atlantic	A. 2d	Second Series
A. D. or App. Div.	Appellate Division Reports, N.Y. Supreme Court	A. D. 2d	Second Series
ALR	American Law Reports	ALR 2d or ALR 3d	Second Series or Third Series
ALR Fed.	American Law Reports Federal		
Am. Jur.	American Jurisprudence	Am. Jur. 2d	Second Edition
C.A. or Cal. App.	California Appellate Reports	C.A. 2d or C.A. 3d	Second or Third Series
Cal. Rptr.	California Reporter		
C.J.	Corpus Juris		
C.J.S.	Corpus Juris Secundum		
Cr.L. or Crim. L. Rptr.	Criminal Law Reporter (weekly loose-leaf)		

Cyc.	Cyclopedia of Law and Procedure		
F. or Fed.	Federal Reporter	F. 2d	Second Series
F.R.D.	Federal Rules Decisions	(opinions, usually interim, interpreting the Federal Rules of Civil and Criminal Procedure)	
F. Supp.	Federal Supplement		
L. Ed.	U.S. Supreme Court Reports (Lawyers Co-op. Publ. Co.)	L. Ed. 2d	Second Series
L.R.A.	Lawyers' Reports Annotated		
Misc.	New York Miscellaneous	Misc. 2d	Second Series
N.Y.S.	New York Supplement	N.Y.S. 2d	Second Series
N.E.	North Eastern	N.E. 2d	Second Series
N.W.	North Western	N.W. 2d	Second Series
P. or Pac.	Pacific	P. 2d	Second Series
R.C.L.	Ruling Case Law		
S.E.	South Eastern	S.E. 2d	Second Series
S.W.	South Western	S.W. 2d	Second Series
So.	Southern	So. 2d	Second Series
S. Ct.	Supreme Court Reporter (West Publ. Co.)		
U.S.	United States Reports	(official government edition)	
U.S.L.W.	U.S. Law Week	(weekly loose-leaf)	

Appendix C. Warnings

The English versions of the following warnings were prepared by the Police Legal Unit of the Metropolitan Dade County Public Safety Department, Miami, Florida. The Spanish translations were provided by Public Safety Advisors of the Agency for International Development. The translations are worded in such a way as to be universally acceptable for use with suspects from Central America, Cuba, Mexico, Puerto Rico, South America, and Spain. Police agencies that deal predominantly with a single Spanish-speaking group may wish to rephrase them, employing local expressions. The warnings may be reproduced without further permission by law enforcement agencies for investigative purposes.

Constitutional Rights Warning: Interrogation

BEFORE YOU ARE ASKED ANY QUESTIONS, YOU MUST UNDERSTAND YOUR RIGHTS.

1. You have the right to remain silent. You need not talk to me or answer any questions if you do not wish to do so.
2. Should you talk to me, anything which you say can and will be introduced into evidence in court against you.
3. If you want an attorney to represent you at this time or at any time during questioning, you are entitled to such counsel.
4. If you cannot afford an attorney and so desire one, one will be provided without charge.

I HAVE READ THE ABOVE STATEMENT OF MY RIGHTS AND AM FULLY AWARE OF THE SAID RIGHTS.

I AM WILLING TO ANSWER ANY QUESTIONS ASKED OF ME.

I DO NOT DESIRE THE PRESENCE OF AN ATTORNEY AT THIS TIME.

THIS STATEMENT IS SIGNED OF MY OWN FREE WILL WITHOUT ANY THREATS OR PROMISES HAVING BEEN MADE TO ME.

_____   _____
Witness   Signature of Subject

_____   _____
Witness   Date-Time

Advertencia de los Derechos constitucionales para un Interrogatorio

ANTES DE QUE SE LE FORMULE NINGUNA PREGUNTA, UD. DEBE SABER SUS DERECHOS.

1. Ud. tiene el derecho de guardar silencio. Ud. no tiene la obligación de hablar conmigo ni de contestar mis preguntas si no lo desea.

2. De hablar Ud. conmigo, cualquier cosa que Ud. diga puede ser presentada y será presentada en la corte como evidencia en contra suya.

3. Si Ud. desea que un abogado lo represente en este momento o en cualquier momento durante el interrogatorio tiene todo el derecho para ello.

4. Si Ud. no puede pagar los servicios de un abogado, y sin embargo lo desea, podemos facilitarle uno sin costo alguno por parte suya.

HE LEIDO LO EXPUESTO ARRIBA ACERCA DE MIS DERECHOS, Y LO COMPRENDO PERFECTAMENTE.

DESEO CONTESTAR CUALQUIER PREGUNTA QUE SE ME HAGA.

NO DESEO LA PRESENCIA DE NINGUN ABOGADO EN ESTE MOMENTO.

PARA CONSTANCIA DE QUE NO SE ME HA AMENAZADO, NI SE ME HA HECHO NINGUN OFRECIMIENTO, VOLUNTARIAMENTE FIRMO LA PRESENTE DECLARACION.

Testigo	Firma del sujeto
Testigo	Fecha y hora

Constitutional Rights Warning: Consent Search

BEFORE ANY SEARCH IS MADE, YOU MUST UNDERSTAND YOUR RIGHTS.

1. You may refuse to consent to a search and may demand that a search warrant be obtained prior to any search of the premises described below.

2. If you consent to a search, anything of evidentiary value seized in the course of the search can and will be introduced into evidence in court against you.

I HAVE READ THE ABOVE STATEMENT OF MY RIGHTS AND AM FULLY AWARE OF MY RIGHTS.

I HEREBY CONSENT TO A SEARCH WITHOUT WARRANT BY OFFICERS OF THE _____ POLICE DEPARTMENT OF THE FOLLOWING: (Describe premises or automobile).

_____

_____

_____

I HEREBY AUTHORIZE THE SAID OFFICERS TO SEIZE ANY ARTICLE WHICH THEY MAY DEEM TO BE OF EVIDENTIARY VALUE.

THIS STATEMENT IS SIGNED OF MY OWN FREE WILL WITHOUT ANY THREATS OR PROMISES HAVING BEEN MADE TO ME.

_____   ·   _____
Witness   Signature of Subject

_____   _____
Witness   Date-Time

Advertencia de los Derechos Constitucionales para el Consentimiento de un Registro

ANTES DE QUE SE PRACTIQUE REGISTRO ALGUNO, UD. DEBE CONOCER SUS DERECHOS.

1. Ud. puede negarse a que el registro tenga lugar, y Ud. puede exigir que le presenten una orden judicial antes de hacer registro alguno en el local o locales que se describen abajo.

2. Si Ud. permite se haga el registro, cualquier cosa de posible evidencia que sea confiscada, puede ser y será presentada en la corte en contra suya.

HE LEIDO LO EXPUESTO ARRIBA ACERCA DE MIS DERECHOS Y LO COMPRENDO PERFECTAMENTE.

POR LA PRESENTE DOY PERMISO A LOS FUNCIONARIOS DEL DEPARTAMENTO DE POLICIA. PARA QUE LLEVEN A CABO EL REGISTRO EN EL AUTOMOVIL Y LUGAR O LUGARES QUE SE SENALAN, SIN LA NECESIDAD DE LA ORDEN JUDICIAL. (Describe el automóvil o lugares aquí.)

_____

_____

_____

POR LA PRESENTE AUTORIZO A LOS FUNCIONARIOS MENCIONADOS A QUE CONFISQUEN CUALQUIER COSA QUE ELLOS CONSIDEREN COMO EVIDENCIA DE VALOR.

PARA CONSTANCIA. DE QUE NO SE ME HA AMENAZADO, NI SE ME HA HECHO NINGUN OFRECIMIENTO, VOLUNTARIAMENTE FIRMO LA PRESENTE DECLARACION.

_____   _____
Testigo   Firma del sujeto

_____   _____
Testigo   Fecha y hora

Constitutional Rights Warning: Lineup

BEFORE YOU APPEAR IN A LINEUP, YOU MUST UNDERSTAND YOUR RIGHTS.

1. You will be placed in a lineup for identification purposes.

2. You may not refuse to participate in the lineup.

3. You have the right to the presence of an attorney during the lineup.

4. If you cannot afford an attorney, one will be provided without charge.

I HAVE READ THE ABOVE STATEMENT OF MY RIGHTS AND AM FULLY AWARE OF THE SAID RIGHTS.

I DO NOT DESIRE THE PRESENCE OF AN ATTORNEY AT THIS TIME.

THIS STATEMENT IS SIGNED OF MY OWN FREE WILL WITHOUT ANY THREATS OR PROMISES HAVING BEEN MADE TO ME.

_____   _____
Witness   Signature of Subject

_____   _____
Witness   Date-Time

Advertencia de los Derechos Constitucionales para Participar en una Rueda de Presos

ANTES DE QUE SE PARTICIPE EN UNA RUEDA DE PRESOS, UD. DEBE CONOCER SUS DERECHOS.

1. Ud. aparecerá en una rueda de presos para fines de identificación.

2. Ud. no debe de oponerse a participar en la rueda de presos.

3. Ud. tiene el derecho de la presencia de un abogado mientras esté en la rueda de presos.

4. Si Ud. no puede pagar los servicios de un abogado, y sin embargo lo desea, se le puede facilitar uno sin costo para Ud.

HE LEIDO LO EXPUESTO ARRIBA ACERCA DE MIS DERECHOS, Y LO COMPRENDO PERFECTAMENTE.

NO DESEO LA PRESENCIA DE NINGUN ABOGADO EN ESTE MOMENTO.

PARA CONSTANCIA DE QUE NO SE ME HA AMENAZADO, NI SE ME HA HECHO NINGUN OFRECIMIENTO, VOLUNTARIAMENTE FIRMO LA PRESENTE DECLARACION.

Testigo	Firma del sujeto
Testigo	Fecha y hora

Appendix D. Criminal Forms

STATE OF NEW MEXICO   (COUNTY OF _____)

                                         (CITY OF _____)

             IN THE _____ COURT

(STATE OF NEW MEXICO)

(CITY OF _____)

            v.   No. _____

John Doe

AFFIDAVIT FOR SEARCH WARRANT

_____ , being duly sworn, on his oath, states that:

(check one)

[ ]   he has reason to believe that   [ ]   he is positive that

(check one or both)

[ ]   on the following described premises   [ ]   on the person of

(here name person and/or describe premises)
in the above described (city) (county) and state there is now being concealed certain property, namely: *(describe property as particularly as possible)* which: *(check appropriate boxes)*

[ ]   has been obtained or is possessed in a manner which constitutes a criminal offense

[ ]   is designed or intended for use, or which has been used, as a means of committing a criminal offense

[ ]   would be material evidence in a criminal prosecution

and that the facts tending to establish the foregoing grounds for issuance of a Search Warrant are as follows: *(include facts in support of the credibility of any hearsay relied upon; if necessary, continue on reverse side of this form)*

Subscribed and sworn to before me in the above named (county) (city) of the State of New Mexico this .... day of ...., 19......

Judge, Notary or Other Officer Authorized to Administer Oaths	Signature of Affiant
Official Title	Official Title (if any)

Search Warrant

STATE OF NEW MEXICO   (COUNTY OF............)
                                        (CITY OF.................)
            IN THE ....COURT
(STATE OF NEW MEXICO)
(CITY OF............................)
            v.   No.....................
John Doe

SEARCH WARRANT

THE (STATE OF NEW MEXICO) (CITY OF............................)
TO ANY OFFICER AUTHORIZED TO EXECUTE THIS WARRANT:

Proof by Affidavit for Search Warrant, which is attached to and hereby made a part of this warrant, having been submitted to me by.., who

(check one)
   [ ] has reason to believe   [ ] is positive
that there is now being concealed

(check one or both)
   [ ] on the premises described in the Affidavit
   [ ] on the person named in the Affidavit
the property described in the Affidavit, which *(check appropriate boxes)*

   [ ] has been obtained or is being possessed in a manner which constitutes a criminal offense

   [ ] is designed or intended for use or which has been used as a means of committing a criminal offense

[ ] would be material evidence in a criminal prosecution and that the facts tending to establish the foregoing grounds for issuance of a Search Warrant are set forth in the Affidavit for Search Warrant, which is attached to and hereby made a part of this Search Warrant.

I am satisfied that there is probable cause to believe that the property described in the Affidavit is being concealed on the *(check one or both)* [ ] person   [ ] premises described in the Affidavit and that grounds for the issuance of the Search Warrant exist.

(If the Warrant may be served at any time, the court must have found the proof to be positive and must also check the following finding)

> [ ] I further find that there is probable cause to believe that the property described in the Affidavit may be moved or destroyed unless seized immediately.

YOU ARE HEREBY COMMANDED to search forthwith
(check one or both)

> [ ] the person   [ ] the place described in the Affidavit

for the property described in the Affidavit, serving this Warrant and a copy of the Affidavit, and making the search

> [ ] between the hours of 6:00 a.m. and 10:00 p.m.,
> [ ] at any time of the day or night

and if the property be found there, to seize it, leaving a copy of this Warrant and a receipt for the property taken, and prepare a written inventory of the property seized and return this Warrant, the return and inventory list to this Court within three days after seizing the property described.

Dated this_____day of _____, 19_____.

_____
                                                           Judge

If the sworn written statement is positive that the property is on the person or in the place to be searched and states probable cause to believe that the property may be moved or destroyed unless seized immediately, the Warrant may direct that it be served at any time.

Return and Inventory

I received the attached Search Warrant on _____ , 19_____, and executed it on _____, 19_____, at _____ o'clock (a.m.) (p.m.). I searched the [ ] person [ ] premises described in the Warrant and I left a copy of the Warrant with

----
(name the person searched or owner at the place of search)
together with a receipt for the items seized.

The following is an inventory of property taken pursuant to the Warrant: *(Attach separate inventory if necessary.)*

This inventory was made in the presence of ------------------------------
Signature

and------------------------------------
Signature

This inventory is a true and detailed account of all the property taken by me on the Warrant.

Officer

Return made this ------day of ------------------, 19------, at------------ (a.m.) (p.m.).

(Judge)   (Clerk)

After careful search, I could not find at the place, or on the person described, the property described in this Warrant.

Officer

Date

Application for Inspectorial Search Order

STATE OF NEW MEXICO   (COUNTY OF------------)
                                     (CITY OF------------------)
          IN THE ------------------------COURT
(STATE OF NEW MEXICO)
(CITY OF----------------------)
          v.   No.------------
John Doe

APPLICATION FOR
INSPECTORIAL SEARCH ORDER

----------------------------------, being duly sworn, on his oath, states that:
1. he is an officer authorized by law to make inspectorial searches;
2. inspection of the following described *(check appropriate box)*
    [ ] premises: *(describe premises to be searched as particularly as possible)*

    [ ] vehicle: *(describe vehicle as particularly as possible)*

is necessary for the purpose of ascertaining the existence or non-existence of the following described conditions *(set forth purpose or reason for search, and facts)*.

in accordance with the requirements prescribed by *(check appropriate box or boxes)* [ ] fire [ ] housing [ ] sanitation [ ] welfare [ ] zoning requirements;

(check if appropriate; complete if checked)
3. [ ] permission to inspect at night is requested for the following reasons: *(set forth reasons search may be reasonably conducted at night)*

(check appropriate box)
4. [ ] he has been refused consent to make an inspectorial search after having given seven days notice of the time and purpose of the proposed inspectorial search;

　[ ] an inspectorial search by consent of the owner of the *(premises) (vehicle)* is not obtainable within a reasonable period of time;

(check if appropriate and complete)
　[ ] it is necessary that the applicant be accompanied at the time of any search by one or more law enforcement officers *(set forth reason)* --

----

Subscribed and sworn to before me in the above named (county) (city) of the State of New Mexico this ------- day of ------------, 19-------.

Signature of Affiant

Title

Judge, Notary or Other Officer
Authorized to Administer Oaths

Inspection Order and Return

STATE OF NEW MEXICO   (COUNTY OF ....)
                                       (CITY OF ....)
          IN THE .... COURT
(STATE OF NEW MEXICO)
(CITY OF ....)
          v.
John Doe

INSPECTION ORDER
THE (STATE OF NEW MEXICO) (CITY OF ....)
TO ANY OFFICER AUTHORIZED TO MAKE AN INSPEC-
TORIAL SEARCH OF PREMISES OR VEHICLES:

An application for an inspectorial search order, which is attached
to and hereby made a part of this order, having been submitted to me
by .... , who has made a sufficient showing that inspection of the *(check appropriate box)* [ ] premises [ ] vehicle described in the application is in accordance with reasonable legislative
or administrative standards.

(check appropriate box)
     [ ] I am satisfied that seven days notice has been given to the
          owner of the (premises) (vehicle) described in the applica-
          tion and consent has not been given to make an inspectorial
          search.

     [ ] I am satisfied that an inspectorial search by consent of the
          owner of the (premises) (vehicle) described in the applica-
          tion is not obtainable within a reasonable period of time.

(check if appropriate)
     [ ] Inspection of the (premises) (vehicle) at night is reasonable
          under the circumstances described in the application.

YOU ARE HEREBY COMMANDED TO SEARCH FORTH-
WITH:

(check one or both)
     [ ] the premises   [ ] the vehicle
described in the application
     [ ] between the hours of 6:00 a.m. and 10 p.m.
     [ ] at any time of the day or night

(check if appropriate)
> [ ] You are hereby authorized to be accompanied by one or more law enforcement officers.

You are to return this order within three days after the search is completed to make a sworn report of the circumstances of the execution or failure to execute this order.

Judge

RETURN

---------------------------- , being duly sworn, on his oath, states that: he received the attached Order on ----------------------------, 19------, and searched the (premises) (vehicle) described at --------------------- o'clock (a.m.) (p.m.) on ---------------------, 19-------.

The following is a report of the circumstances of execution or failure to execute the order of the court: *(set forth record of proceedings taken subsequent to issuance of order)*

Signature of Affiant
Inspection Officer

Title

Subscribed and sworn to before me in the above named (city) (country) of the State of New Mexico this ------- day of -----------, 19 -------.

Judge, Notary or Other Officer
Authorized to Administer Oaths

Official Title

Complaint for Preliminary Examination

FELONY

STATE OF ILLINOIS ⎱ ss.   THE CIRCUIT COURT OF COOK COUNTY
COUNTY OF COOK ⎰

The People of the State of Illinois   COMPLAINT FOR PRELIMINARY
              Plaintiff   EXAMINATION
        v.   No._____

_____
              Defendant

_____complainant, now appears before
        (Complainant's Name Printed or Typed)

The Circuit Court of Cook County and in the name and by the authority of the

People of the State of Illinois states that _____
                                                        (defendant)
has, on or about_____at _____
                        (date)   (Place of offense)
committed the offense of _____ in that he
                                        (offense)

_____

_____

_____

in violation of Chapter _____ Section _____

ILLINOIS REVISED STATUTE AND AGAINST THE PEACE AND DIGNITY
OF THE PEOPLE OF THE STATE OF ILLINOIS.

                                    _____
                                      (Complainant's Signature)
                                    _____
                                    (Complainant's Address)   (Telephone No.)

STATE OF ILLINOIS ⎱ ss.
COUNTY OF COOK ⎰   _____
                                    (Complainant's Name Printed or Typed)
being first duly sworn, on_____oath, deposes and says that he has read the
foregoing complaint by him subscribed and that the same is true.

                                    _____
                                      (Complainant's Signature)
Subscribed and sworn to before me _____ , 19 _____ .

                                    _____
                                      (Judge or Clerk)

I have examined the above complaint and the person presenting the same and
and have heard evidence thereon, and am satisfied that there is probable cause
for filing same. Leave is given to file said complaint. Warrant issued.
                        Bail Fixed at $_____
                        Judge_____

THE CIRCUIT COURT OF COOK COUNTY, ILLINOIS

_____
Plaintiff

v.

_____
Defendant

ARREST WARRANT

THE PEOPLE OF THE STATE OF ILLINOIS TO ALL PEACE OFFICERS IN THE STATE—GREETING:

We command you to arrest _____
(Defendant)
for the offense of _____ stated in a
(offense)
charge now pending before this court and that you bring him instanter before

The Circuit Court of Cook County at _____
(location)
or if I am absent or unable to act before the nearest or most accessible court in

Cook County or if this warrant is executed in a county other than Cook, before

the nearest or most accessible judge in the county where the arrest is made.

Issued in Cook County _____ , 19 ____

Bail fixed at $ _____

_____
Judge

WITNESS: MATTHEW J. DANAHER, CLERK OF THE COURT

and the Seal thereof, at Chicago _____

_____19 _____

_____
Clerk

Appendix E. Selected Cases

The following important decisions demonstrate various points made in the text.

Chapter 1: Introduction to Evidence

George A. Luria v. United States,
Supreme Court of the United States, 231 U.S. 9 (1913)

Mr. Justice VAN DEVANTER delivered the opinion of the court:

This appeal brings under review a decree setting aside and canceling, under § 15 of the act of June 29, 1906, as fraudulently and illegally procured, a certificate of citizenship theretofore issued to George A. Luria by the court of common pleas of the city and county of New York, 184 Fed. 643 ....

Section 15 of the act of 1906, under which this suit was conducted, is as follows:

If any alien who shall have secured a certificate of citizenship under the provisions of this act shall, within five years after the issuance of such certificate, return to the country of his nativity, or go to any other foreign country, and take permanent residence therein, it shall be considered prima facie evidence of a lack of intention on the part of such alien to become a permanent citizen of the United States at the time of filing his application for citizenship, and in the absence of countervailing evidence, it shall be sufficient in the proper proceeding to authorize the cancellation of his certificate of citizenship as fraudulent, and the diplomatic and consular officers of the United States in foreign countries shall from time to time, through the Department of State, furnish the Department of Justice with the names of those within their respective jurisdictions who

have such certificates of citizenship and who have taken permanent residence
in the country of their nativity, or in any other foreign country, and such
statements, duly certified, shall be admissible in evidence in all courts in proceedings to cancel certificates of citizenship . . . .

Objection is specially directed to the provision which declares
that taking up a permanent residence in a foreign country within five
years after the issuance of the certificate shall be considered prima
facie evidence of a lack of intention to become a permanent citizen of
the United States at the time of the application for citizenship, and
that in the absence of countervailing evidence the same shall be
sufficient to warrant the cancellation of the certificate as fraudulent.
It will be observed that this provision prescribes a rule of evidence,
not of substantive right. It goes no farther than to establish a rebuttable presumption which the possessor of the certificate is free to
overcome. If in truth, it was his intention at the time of his application to reside permanently in the United States, and his subsequent
residence in a foreign country was prompted by considerations
which were consistent with that intention, he is at liberty to show it.
Not only so, but these are matters of which he possesses full, if not
special, knowledge. The controlling rule respecting the power of the
legislature in establishing such presumptions is comprehensively stated
in Mobile, J. & K. C. R. Co. v. Turnipseed, 219 U.S. 35, as follows:

> Legislation providing that proof of one fact shall constitute prima facie
> evidence of the main fact in issue is but to enact a rule of evidence, and quite
> within the general power of government. Statutes, national and state, dealing
> with such methods of proof in both civil and criminal cases, abound, and the
> decisions upholding them are numerous . . . .
>
> That a legislative presumption of one fact from evidence of another may
> not constitute a denial of due process of law, or a denial of the equal protection
> of the law, it is only essential that there shall be some rational connection
> between the fact proved and the ultimate fact presumed, and that the inference
> of one fact from proof of another shall not be so unreasonable as to be a
> purely arbitrary mandate. So, also, it must not, under guise of regulating the
> presentation of evidence, operate to preclude the party from the right to present
> his defense to the main fact thus presumed.
>
> If a legislative provision not unreasonable in itself, prescribing a rule of
> evidence, in either criminal or civil cases, does not shut out from the party
> affected a reasonable opportunity to submit to the jury in his defense all of the
> facts bearing upon the issue, there is no ground for holding that due process of
> law has been denied him . . . .

Nor is it a valid objection to such legislation that it is made
applicable to existing causes of action, as is the case here, the true

rule in that regard being well stated in Cooley's Constitutional Limitations, 7th ed. 524, in these words:

> It must also be evident that a right to have one's controversies determined by existing rules of evidence is not a vested right. These rules pertain to the remedies which the state provides for its citizens; and generally in legal contemplation they neither enter into and constitute a part of any contract, nor can be regarded as being of the essence of any right which a party may seek to enforce. Like other rules affecting the remedy, they must therefore at all times be subject to modification and control by the legislature; and the changes which are enacted may lawfully be made applicable to existing causes of action, even in those states in which retrospective laws are forbidden. For the law as changed would only prescribe rules for presenting the evidence in legal controversies in the future; and it could not therefore be called retrospective, even though some of the controversies upon which it may act were in progress before . . . .

Finding no error in the record, the decree is affirmed.

Chapter 2: Admissibility of Evidence

Mary P. Reynolds v. *United States,* U.S. Court of Appeals, Ninth Circuit, 238 F. 2d 460 (1956)

HAMLEY, Circuit Judge.

Mary P. Reynolds was acquitted of the crime of murder in the second degree, but convicted of the lesser and included offense of manslaughter. On this appeal, she questions the sufficiency of the evidence and the giving of certain instructions.

The facts essential to a consideration of the specifications of error may be briefly stated. Duncan Wallace McIntosh was killed by a shot fired from a 9 mm. Luger pistol at 3:04 a.m., April 8, 1954. This occurred in the apartment shared by appellant and McIntosh. No one else was present when the shot was fired.

The two had been drinking excessively at several bars before going to their apartment shortly after 2:30 a.m. Appellant was also subject to diabetic comas. She testified that she did not know whether it was McIntosh or she who fired the shot. She further testified, however, that McIntosh had struck and choked her, water had been thrown on her, and McIntosh had threatened her with the gun. One witness testified that appellant admitted shooting McIntosh. Another witness testified to a telephone conversation shortly after the shooting, in which a woman, who gave her name as "McIntosh," stated that she had shot McIntosh. On the other hand, a man who lived in the apartment below testified that he had heard the pistol shot, and that about five minutes later he heard a woman exclaim, "Why did you do it? Why did you shoot yourself?"

There was a good deal of additional evidence concerning the activities of appellant and McIntosh earlier in the evening; what was found when officers and friends reached the apartment after the shooting; the conclusions to be drawn from the bullet holes and lack of powder burns; and other matters. Appellant was found to be bruised around the throat and drenched with water. McIntosh, in addition to the bullet wound, had deep scratches on his face.

At the trial, appellant defended on two alternative theories: (1) That McIntosh committed suicide; and (2) that if appellant did shoot McIntosh, she did so in self-defense.

Considering the evidence in the light most favorable to the government, as we are required to do, it is our view that there was sufficient competent evidence to sustain every element of the crime of manslaughter.

Appellant contends that the second paragraph of the following instruction on the presumption of innocence is an incorrect statement of law, and that its giving was prejudicial error:

> The law presumes every person charged with crime to be innocent. This presumption of innocence remains with the defendant throughout the trial and should be given effect by you unless and until, by the evidence introduced before you, you are convinced the defendant is guilty beyond a reasonable doubt.
>
> This rule, as to the presumption of innocence, is a humane provision of the law, intended to guard against the conviction of an innocent person, but it is not intended to prevent the conviction of any person who is in fact guilty, or to aid the guilty to escape punishment.

In Gomila v. United States, 5 Cir., 146 F.2d 372, an instruction on the presumption of innocence, containing what was, in effect, a similar qualification, was held to be not a correct statement of the law. Considering the cumulation of this and other errors, the court reversed and remanded for a new trial.

In Moffitt v. United States, 10 Cir., 154 F.2d 402, certiorari denied, 328 U.S. 853, 66 S.Ct. 1343, 90 L.Ed. 1625, it was held that an instruction containing about the same qualification was a correct statement of the law. The court reasoned that, when read with the other instructions, this qualification did not imply that the presumption was to be used only if the jury should feel the defendant was innocent.

In United States v. Farina, 2 Cir., 184 F.2d 18, 23, certiorari denied, 340 U.S. 875, 71 S.Ct. 121, 95 L.Ed. 636, it was held that the statement that the presumption of innocence was not intended as a bulwark behind which the guilty might hide, was, in a general sense, true. It is objectionable, said the court, only if it might lead a jury to suppose that the presumption could not be invoked until a defendant has dispelled proof of his guilt. The court held that, read in context with other instructions, the language in question would not have that effect.

In the Farina case, the court distinguished Gomila v. United States, supra, expressing the view that the instruction given in Gomila might have led a jury to suppose that a defendant could invoke the presumption only after he had established his innocence. It was also pointed out that the reversal in Gomila was for a "cumulation" of errors. Judge Frank filed a vigorous dissent in Farina, stating that were it necessary he would hold that the " 'presumption of innocence' error" alone warranted reversal.

Instructions on the presumption of innocence containing a similar qualification have been approved in Illinois, in a long line of cases extending from Spies v. People, 122 Ill. 1, 12 N.E. 865, 17 N.E. 898, pet. for writ of error dismissed, 123 U.S. 131, 8 S.Ct. 22, 31 L.Ed. 80, to People v. Henderson, 378 Ill. 436, 38 N.E. 2d 727. Such a qualification of this instruction has apparently not been sanctioned in the recent decisions of any other state.

The presumption of innocence is predicated not upon any express provision of the federal constitution, but upon ancient concepts antedating the development of the common law. Wigmore points out that, while this presumption is another form of expression for a part of the accepted rule concerning the burden of proof in criminal cases, it does serve a special and additional purpose. It has been characterized as one of the strongest rebuttable presumptions known to the law. Bradford v. United States, 5 Cir., 129 F.2d 274, certiorari denied, 317 U.S. 683, 63 S.Ct. 205, 87 L.Ed. 547.

The presumption of innocence was developed for the purpose of guarding against the conviction of an innocent person. It was not developed for the purpose of aiding the guilty to escape punishment. It is nevertheless perfectly plain that the presumption, together with the related rule on the burden of proof, in guarding against the conviction of an innocent person, may in some cases prevent the conviction of a person who is actually guilty. Thus, where the prosecution is unable to muster evidence sufficient to overcome the presumption, there will be an acquittal, even though the defendant be actually guilty.

This is a calculated risk which society is willing to take. It does so because it regards the acquittal of guilty persons less objectionable than the conviction of innocent persons.

The inclusion of the qualification in question in an instruction on the presumption of innocence is designed to curb that calculated risk. It accomplishes this by implying that society is just as anxious to convict the guilty as it is to acquit the innocent. The implication is false, else there would be no presumption of innocence. It subverts the presumption, since it distracts attention from its paramount purpose of protecting the innocent. When this qualification is added to an instruction on the presumption of innocence, the result is to leave matters about where they would have been had no instruction on the presumption been given.

Since it is right to instruct on the presumption of innocence, it is wrong to add this self-defeating qualification. We therefore find ourselves in agreement with Gomila v. United States, supra, and with Judge Frank's dissent in United States v. Farina, supra. We conclude that it was prejudicial error to give the instruction in question.

Reversed and remanded for a new trial.

People of the State of Colorado ex rel. Edward N. Juhan v. *District Court for the County of Jefferson,* Supreme Court of Colorado 439 P. 2d 741 (1968)

MOORE, Chief Justice.

The district attorney for the First Judicial District commenced this original proceeding to secure a determination of the constitutionality of an act of the legislature dealing with the defense of insanity in criminal cases . . . . The statute in pertinent part reads as follows:

Plea of insanity—(3) (a). Upon the making by the defendant of the plea of insanity at the time of the alleged commission of the crime, a jury shall be impaneled as in criminal proceedings and the issue of the defendant's sanity or insanity shall be decided by such jury in accordance with section 39—8—3. The burden shall be on the DEFENDANT to prove by a preponderance of the evidence that HE was INSANE at the time of the alleged commission of the crime.

The trial court sustained the motion of counsel for Fulmer, holding that the above quoted statute violated the Constitution of the State of Colorado. Thereupon this original proceeding was commenced and we issued a rule to show cause as prayed for in the petition. The respondents have appeared, briefs have been filed, and oral arguments have been heard . . . .

There are a number of fundamental principles of law applicable to criminal cases which have been so universally accepted and applied in this country as to have become component parts of our understanding of the term "due process of law." Among such basic concepts we find the doctrine that, at the outset of the trial, an accused person is presumed to be innocent of the offense charged against him; that the state must satisfy the jury of the guilt of the defendant beyond a reasonable doubt; and that if upon any material issue of fact essential to guilt the jury has a reasonable doubt, the defendant is entitled to the benefit of that reasonable doubt and a verdict of not guilty. Numerous cases decided by this court have imbedded these basic fundamentals in the main stream of the criminal law . . . .

The language of these cases has taken such form over a period of many years as to become part and parcel of our concept of constitutional "due process of law." As thus interpreted by the judiciary over the years the due process clause of the state constitution includes the doctrine that the state must prove guilt beyond a reasonable doubt, and that the accused cannot be required by legislative enactment to prove insanity or any other defense by a preponderance of the evidence.

Interpretations given constitutional provisions by the judiciary are not subject to change by the legislature. The interpretations given by the courts to the constitution are incorporated in the instrument itself and are beyond the power of the legislative branch of government to change. This of course is not true of legislative acts. If the courts misconstrue or misinterpret the intent of the legislature concerning a statute, there is nothing to prevent it from correcting the error and making clear that which was intended.

There is not the slightest requirement that the meaning of "due process of law" shall be the same in each of the fifty states. The Supreme Court of the United States has never nullified an interpretation of due process by a state supreme court which might be given by a federal court construing the Constitution of the United States. No state has yet been required to accept as all inclusive or all exclusive the federal court determination of what activities of the state fall within or lie without the ambit of due process of law under the United States Constitution. What the United States Constitution does to state authority is this: It says that the state cannot deny a right or impose a liability which is contrary to the federal concept of due process of law. It does *not* say that a state has no right, under its state due process clause, to create protections for its citizens which might not be required under the federal concept. So long as state action does not deny a right protected under the federal concept of due process, or impose a liability prohibited thereby, the federal power will not nullify the rights and protections which, within the state, are recognized as part and parcel of due process under the state constitution; and that is exactly what happened in Leland v. State of Oregon, 343 U.S. 790, 72 S.Ct. 1002, 96 L.Ed 1302. See Snyder v. Commonwealth of Massachusetts, 291 U.S. 97, 54 S.Ct. 330, 78 L.Ed. 674.

Under the old 1864 Oregon statute an accused who defended on the ground of insanity had the burden of establishing insanity beyond a reasonable doubt. This procedure was always followed in that state. In 1948 the Oregon court held that the statute did not violate either federal or state due process. Obviously at the state level there had not developed a body of law creating a "principle of justice so rooted in the traditions and conscience of our people as to be ranked fundamental." Brown v. State of Mississippi, 297 U.S. 278, 56 S.Ct. 461, 80 L.Ed. 682. Exactly the opposite has occurred in the State of Colorado. The effect of the decision of the U.S. Supreme Court was to say: "If that is what the State of Oregon wants under state due process it can have exactly that, because it does not violate the federal concept of due process." Certainly if the Supreme Court of Oregon had developed a deep-rooted concept of criminal justice in this particular, as has been done in Colorado, and if Oregon had said that the statute in question offended a "fundamental" concept of due process, the Supreme Court of the United States would have been obligated to affirm. Again, we say that there is no requirement that due process of law shall operate as a "straight jacket" forcing every sovereign state to give *no more*, as well as no less, protection than that which would be recognized at the federal level . . . .

All Colorado decisions from the beginning of territorial days to the present require application of the rule that total guilt must be established beyond a reasonable doubt. Mental capacity to commit a crime is a material part of total guilt for there can be no crime without the *mens rea* . . . .

No one has yet contended that mental capacity to commit a crime is not a "material element" of the crime of murder, or any other offense . . . . So in the case at bar if the evidence of insanity offered by the defendant created a reasonable doubt *as to that fact*, "it would be sufficient to rebut the presumption" of sanity which attends prior to plea raising the issue . . . .

[This cannot be changed] by act of the legislature for the very simple reason that in this state our concept of due process of law prohibits it. In the instant case the trial court ruled properly.

The rule to show cause is discharged.

Yee Hem v. *United States,* Supreme Court of the United States, 268 U.S. 170 (1925)

Mr. Justice SUTHERLAND delivered the opinion of the court:

Plaintiff in error was convicted in the court below of the offense of concealing a quantity of smoking opium after importation, with knowledge that it had been imported in violation of the Act of February 9, 1909, chap. 100, 35 Stat. at L. 614, as amended by the Act of January 17, 1914, chap. 9, 38 Stat. at L. 275, Comp. Stat. § 8800, 3 Fed. Stat. Anno. 2d ed. p. 723. Sections 2 and 3 of the act as amended are challenged as unconstitutional, on the ground that they contravene the due process of law and the compulsory self-incrimination clauses of the 5th Amendment of the Federal Constitution.

Section 1 of the act prohibits the importation into the United States of opium in any form after April 1, 1909, except that opium and preparations and derivatives thereof, other than smoking opium or opium prepared for smoking, may be imported for medicinal purposes only, under regulations prescribed by the Secretary of the Treasury. Section 2 provides, among other things, that if any person shall conceal or facilitate the concealment of such opium, etc., after importation, knowing the same to have been imported contrary to law, the offender shall be subject to fine or imprisonment or both. It further provides that whenever the defendant on trial is shown to have, or to have had, possession of such opium, etc., "such possession shall be deemed sufficient evidence to authorize conviction unless the defendant shall explain the possession to the satisfaction of the jury." Section 3 provides that on and after July 1, 1913, "all smoking opium or opium prepared for smoking found within the United States shall be presumed to have been imported after the first day of April, nineteen hundred and nine, and the burden of proof shall be on the claimant or the accused to rebut such presumption."

The plaintiff in error, at the time of his arrest in August, 1923, was found in possession of and concealing a quantity of smoking opium. The lower court overruled a motion for an instructed verdict of not guilty, and, after stating the foregoing statutory presumptions, charged the jury in substance that the burden of proof was on the accused to rebut such presumptions; and that it devolved upon him to explain that he was rightfully in possession of the smoking opium, —"at least explain it to the satisfaction of the jury." The court further charged that the defendant was presumed to be innocent until the government had satisfied the minds of the jurors of his guilt

beyond a reasonable doubt; that the burden to adduce such proof
of guilt beyond the existence of a reasonable doubt rested on the
government at all times and throughout the trial; and that a conviction could not be had "while a rational doubt remains in the minds
of the jury."

The authority of Congress to prohibit the importation of opium
in any form, and, as a measure reasonably calculated to aid in the
enforcement of the prohibition, to make its concealment with knowledge of its unlawful importation a criminal offense, is not open to
doubt. Brolan v. United States, 236 U.S. 216, 59 L. ed. 544, 35 Sup.
Ct. Rep. 285; Steinfeldt v. United States, 135 C. C. A. 549, 219 Fed.
879. The question presented is whether Congress has power to enact
the provisions in respect of the presumptions arising from the unexplained possession of such opium and from its presence in this
country after the time fixed by the statute.

In Mobile, J. & K. C. R. Co. v. Turnipseed, 219 U.S. 35, 42, 43,
55 L. ed. 78, 80, 81, 32 L.R.A. (N.S.) 226, 31 Sup. Ct. Rep. 136,
Ann. Cas. 1912A, 463, 2 N. C. C. A. 243, this court, speaking
through Mr. Justice Lurton, said:

> The law of evidence is full of presumptions either of fact or law. The
> former are, of course, disputable, and the strength of any inference of one
> fact from proof of another depends upon the generality of the experience upon
> which it is founded . . . .
>
> Legislation providing that proof of one fact shall constitute prima facie
> evidence of the main fact in issue is but to enact a rule of evidence, and quite
> within the general power of government. Statutes, national and state, dealing
> with such methods of proof in both civil and criminal cases, abound, and the
> decisions upholding them are numerous . . . .
>
> That a legislative presumption of one fact from evidence of another may
> not constitute a denial of due process of law, or a denial of the equal protection
> of the law, it is only essential that there shall be some rational connection
> between the fact proved and the ultimate fact presumed, and that the inference
> of one fact from proof of another shall not be so unreasonable as to be a purely
> arbitrary mandate. So, also, it must not, under guise of regulating the presenta-
> tion of evidence, operate to preclude the party from the right to present his
> defense to the main fact thus presumed.

The legislative provisions here assailed satisfy these requirements
in respect of due process. They have been upheld against similar
attacks, without exception so far as we are advised, by the lower
Federal courts. We think it is not an illogical inference that opium,
found in this country more than four years (in the present case, more
than fourteen years) after its importation had been prohibited, was

unlawfully imported. Nor do we think the further provision, that possession of such opium, in the absence of a satisfactory explanation, shall create a presumption of guilt, is "so unreasonable as to be a purely arbitrary mandate." By universal sentiment and settled policy, as evidenced by state and local legislation for more than half a century, opium is an illegitimate commodity, the use of which, except as a medicinal agent, is rigidly condemned. Legitimate possession, unless for medicinal use, is so highly improbable that to say to any person who obtains the outlawed commodity, "since you are bound to know that it cannot be brought into this country at all, except under regulation for medicinal use, you must at your peril ascertain and be prepared to show the facts and circumstances which rebut, or tend to rebut, the natural inference of unlawful importation, or your knowledge of it," is not such an unreasonable requirement as to cause it to fall outside the constitutional power of Congress.

Every accused person, of course, enters upon his trial clothed with the presumption of innocence. But that presumption may be overcome, not only by direct proof, but, in many cases, when the facts standing alone are not enough, by the additional weight of a countervailing legislative presumption. If the effect of the legislative act is to give to the facts from which the presumption is drawn an artificial value to some extent, it is no more than happens in respect of a great variety of presumptions not resting upon statute. See Dunlop v. United States, 165 U.S. 486, 502, 503, 41 L. ed. 799, 804, 805, 17 Sup. Ct. Rep. 375; Wilson v. United States, 162 U.S. 613, 619, 40 L. ed. 1090, 1094, 16 Sup. Ct. Rep. 895. In the Wilson Case the accused, charged with murder, was found, soon after the homicide, in possession of property that had belonged to the dead man. This court upheld a charge of the trial court to the effect that such possession required the accused to account for it, to show that, as far as he was concerned, the possession was innocent and honest; and that, if not so accounted for, it became "the foundation for a presumption of guilt against the defendant."

The point that the practical effect of the statute creating the presumption is to compel the accused person to be a witness against himself may be put aside with slight discussion. The statute compels nothing. It does no more than to make possession of the prohibited article prima facie evidence of guilt. It leaves the accused entirely free to testify or not, as he chooses. If the accused happens to be the only repository of the facts necessary to negative the presumption arising from his possession, that is a misfortune which the statute under review does not create, but which is inherent in the case. The same situation might present itself if there were no statutory presumption, and a prima facie case of concealment with knowledge of unlawful importation were made by the evidence. The necessity of an explanation by the accused would be quite as compelling in that case as in this; but the constraint upon him to give testimony would arise there, as it arises here, simply from the force of circumstances, and not from any form of compulsion forbidden by the constitution.

Judgment affirmed.

Chapter 3: Detention and Arrest in General

John W. Terry v. *State of Ohio,* Supreme Court of the United States, 392 U.S. 1 (1968)

Mr. Chief Justice WARREN delivered the opinion of the Court.

This case presents serious questions concerning the role of the Fourth Amendment in the confrontation on the street between the citizen and the policeman investigating suspicious circumstances.

Petitioner Terry was convicted of carrying a concealed weapon and sentenced to the statutorily prescribed term of one to three years in the penitentiary. Following the denial of a pretrial motion to suppress, the prosecution introduced in evidence two revolvers and a number of bullets seized from Terry and a codefendant, Richard Chilton, by Cleveland Police Detective Martin McFadden. At the hearing on the motion to suppress this evidence, Officer McFadden testified that while he was patrolling in plain clothes in downtown Cleveland at approximately 2:30 in the afternoon of October 31, 1963, his attention was attracted by two men, Chilton and Terry, standing on the corner of Huron Road and Euclid Avenue. He had never seen the two men before, and he was unable to say precisely what first drew his eye to them. However, he testified that he had been a policeman for 39 years and a detective for 35 and that he had been assigned to patrol this vicinity of downtown Cleveland for shoplifters and pickpockets for 30 years. He explained that he had developed routine habits of observation over the years and that he would "stand and watch people or walk and watch people at many intervals of the day." He added: "Now, in this case when I looked over they didn't look right to me at the time."

His interest aroused, Officer McFadden took up a post of observation in the entrance to a store 300 to 400 feet away from the two men. "I get more purpose to watch them when I seen their movements," he testified. He saw one of the men leave the other one and walk southwest on Huron Road, past some stores. The man paused for a moment and looked in a store window, then walked on a short distance, turned around and walked back toward the corner, pausing once again to look in the same store window. He rejoined his companion at the corner, and the two conferred briefly. Then the second man went through the same series of motions, strolling down Huron Road, looking in the same window, walking on a short distance, turning back, peering in the store window again, and returning to confer with the first man at the corner. The two men repeated this ritual alternately between five and six times apiece—in all, roughly a dozen trips. At one point, while the two were standing together on the corner, a third man approached them and engaged them briefly in conversation. This man then left the two others and walked west on Euclid Avenue. Chilton and Terry resumed their measured pacing, peering and conferring. After this had gone on for 10 to 12 minutes, the two men walked off together, heading west on Euclid Avenue, following the path taken earlier by the third man.

By this time Officer McFadden had become thoroughly suspicious. He testified that after observing their elaborately casual and oft-repeated reconnaissance of the store window on Huron Road, he suspected the two men of "casing a job, a stick-up," and that he considered it his duty as a police officer to investigate further. He added that he feared "they may have a gun." Thus, Officer McFadden followed Chilton and Terry and saw them stop in front of Zucker's store to talk to the same man who had conferred with them earlier on the street corner. Deciding that the situation was ripe for direct action, Officer McFadden approached the three men, identified himself as a police officer and asked for their names. At this point his knowledge was confined to what he had observed. He was not acquainted with any of the three men by name or by sight, and he had received no information concerning them from any other source. When the men "mumbled something" in response to his inquiries, Officer McFadden grabbed petitioner Terry, spun him around so that they were facing the other two, with Terry between McFadden and the others, and patted down the outside of his clothing. In the left breast pocket of Terry's overcoat Officer McFadden felt a pistol. He reached inside the overcoat pocket, but was unable to remove the gun. At this point, keeping Terry between himself and the others, the officer ordered all three men to enter Zucker's store. As they went in, he removed Terry's overcoat completely, removed a .38-caliber revolver from the pocket and ordered all three men to face the wall with their hands raised. Officer McFadden proceeded to pat down the outer clothing of Chilton and the third man, Katz. He discovered another revolver in the outer pocket of Chilton's overcoat, but no weapons were found on Katz. The officer testified that he only patted the men down to see whether they had weapons, and that he did not put his hands beneath the outer garments of either Terry or Chilton until he felt their guns. So far as appears from the record, he never placed his hands beneath Katz' outer garments. Officer McFadden seized Chilton's gun, asked the proprietor of the store to call a police wagon, and took all three men to the station, where Chilton and Terry were formally charged with carrying concealed weapons.

On the motion to suppress the guns the prosecution took the position that they had been seized following a search incident to a lawful arrest. The trial court rejected this theory, stating that it "would be stretching the facts beyond reasonable comprehension" to find that Officer McFadden had had probable cause to arrest the men before he patted them down for weapons. However, the court denied the defendants' motion on the ground that Officer McFadden, on the basis of his experience, "had reasonable cause to believe . . . that the defendants were conducting themselves suspiciously, and some interrogation should be made of their action." Purely for his own protection, the court held, the officer had the right to pat down the outer clothing of these men, who he had reasonable cause to believe might be armed. The court distinguished between an investigatory "stop" and an arrest, and between a "frisk" of the outer clothing for weapons and a full-blown search for evidence of crime. The frisk, it held, was essential to the proper performance of the officer's investigatory duties, for without it "the answer to the police officer may be a bullet, and a loaded pistol discovered during the frisk is admissible."

After the court denied their motion to suppress, Chilton and Terry waived jury trial and pleaded not guilty. The court adjudged them guilty, and the Court of Appeals for the Eighth Judicial District, Cuyahoga County, affirmed. State v. Terry, 5 Ohio App. 2d 122, 214 N.E. 2d 114 (1966). The Supreme Court of Ohio dismissed their appeal on the ground that no "substantial constitutional question" was involved. We granted certiorari, 387 U.S. 929, 87 S.Ct. 2050, 18 L.Ed.2d 989 (1967), to determine whether the admission of the revolvers in evidence violated petitioner's rights under the Fourth Amendment, made applicable to the States by the Fourteenth. Mapp v. Ohio, 367 U.S. 643, 81 S.Ct. 1684, 6 L.Ed.2d 1081 (1961). We affirm the conviction.

The Fourth Amendment provides that "the right of the people to be secure in their persons, houses, papers, and effects, against

unreasonable searches and seizures, shall not be violated . . . ."
This inestimable right of personal security belongs as much to the
citizen on the streets of our cities as to the homeowner closeted in
his study to dispose of his secret affairs. For, as this Court has always
recognized,

> No right is held more sacred, or is more carefully guarded, by the com-
> mon law, than the right of every individual to the possession and control of his
> own person, free from all restraint or interference of others, unless by clear and
> unquestionable authority of law. Union Pac. R. Co. v. Botsford, 141 U.S. 250,
> 251, 11 S.Ct. 1000, 1001, 35 L.Ed. 734 (1891).

We have recently held that "the Fourth Amendment protects people,
not places," Katz v. United States, 389 U.S. 347, 351, 88 S.Ct. 507,
511, 19 L.Ed.2d 576 (1967), and wherever an individual may harbor
a reasonable "expectation of privacy," id., at 361, 88 S.Ct. at 507,
(Mr. Justice Harlan, concurring), he is entitled to be free from unreasonable governmental intrusion. Of course, the specific content and
incidents of this right must be shaped by the context in which it is
asserted. For "what the Constitution forbids is not all searches and
seizures, but unreasonable searches and seizures." Elkins v. United
States, 364 U.S. 206, 222, 80 S.Ct. 1437, 1446, 4 L.Ed.2d 1669
(1960). Unquestionably petitioner was entitled to the protection of
the Fourth Amendment as he walked down the street in Cleveland.
The question is whether in all the circumstances of this on-the-street
encounter, his right to personal security was violated by an unreasonable search and seizure.

We would be less than candid if we did not acknowledge that
this question thrusts to the fore difficult and troublesome issues
regarding a sensitive area of police activity—issues which have never
before been squarely presented to this Court. Reflective of the
tensions involved are the practical and constitutional arguments
pressed with great vigor on both sides of the public debate over the
power of the police to "stop and frisk"—as it is sometimes euphe-
mistically termed—suspicious persons.

On the one hand, it is frequently argued that in dealing with the
rapidly unfolding and often dangerous situations on city streets the
police are in need of an escalating set of flexible responses, graduated
in relation to the amount of information they possess. For this
purpose it is urged that distinctions should be made between a "stop"
and an "arrest" (or a "seizure" of a person), and between a "frisk"
and a "search." Thus, it is argued, the police should be allowed to
"stop" a person and detain him briefly for questioning upon suspicion

that he may be connected with criminal activity. Upon suspicion that the person may be armed, the police should have the power to "frisk" him for weapons. If the "stop" and the "frisk" give rise to probable cause to believe that the suspect has committed a crime, then the police should be empowered to make a formal "arrest," and a full incident "search" of the person. This scheme is justified in part upon the notion that a "stop" and a "frisk" amount to a mere "minor inconvenience and petty indignity," which can properly be imposed upon the citizen in the interest of effective law enforcement on the basis of a police officer's suspicion.

On the other side the argument is made that the authority of the police must be strictly circumscribed by the law of arrest and search as it has developed to date in the traditional jurisprudence of the Fourth Amendment. It is contended with some force that there is not—and cannot be—a variety of police activity which does not depend solely upon the voluntary cooperation of the citizen and yet which stops short of an arrest based upon probable cause to make such an arrest. The heart of the Fourth Amendment, the argument runs, is a severe requirement of specific justification for any intrusion upon protected personal security, coupled with a highly developed system of judicial controls to enforce upon the agents of the State the commands of the Constitution. Acquiescence by the courts in the compulsion inherent in the field interrogation practices at issue here, it is urged, would constitute an abdication of judicial control over, and indeed an encouragement of, substantial interference with liberty and personal security by police officers whose judgment is necessarily colored by their primary involvement in "the often competitive enterprise of ferreting out crime." Johnson v. United States, 333 U.S. 10, 14, 68 S.Ct. 367, 369, 92 L.Ed. 436 (1948). This, it is argued, can only serve to exacerbate police-community tensions in the crowded centers of our Nation's cities.

In this context we approach the issues in this case mindful of the limitations of the judicial function in controlling the myriad daily situations in which policemen and citizens confront each other on the street. The State has characterized the issue here as "the right of a police officer . . . to make an on-the-street stop, interrogate and pat down for weapons (known in street vernacular as 'stop and frisk')." But this is only partly accurate. For the issue is not the abstract propriety of the police conduct, but the admissibility against petitioner of the evidence uncovered by the search and seizure. Ever since its inception, the rule excluding evidence seized in violation of the Fourth Amendment has been recognized as a principal mode of discouraging lawless police conduct. See Weeks v. United States, 232 U.S. 383, 391-393, 34 S.Ct. 341, 344, 58 L.Ed. 652 (1914). Thus its major thrust is a deterrent one, see Linkletter v. Walker, 381 U.S. 618, 629-635, 85 S.Ct. 1731, 1741, 14 L.Ed.2d 601 (1965), and experience has taught that it is the only effective deterrent to police misconduct in the criminal context, and that without it the constitutional guarantee against unreasonable searches and seizures would be a mere "form of words." Mapp v. Ohio, 367 U.S. 643, 655, 81 S.Ct. 1684, 1692, 6 L.Ed.2d 1081 (1961). The rule also serves another vital function—"the imperative of judicial integrity." Elkins v. United States, 364 U.S. 206, 222, 80 S.Ct. 1437, 1447, 4 L.Ed.2d 1669 (1960). Courts which sit under our Constitution cannot and will not be made party to lawless invasions of the constitutional rights of citizens by permitting unhindered governmental use of the fruits of such invasions. Thus in our system evidentiary rulings provide the context in which the judicial process of inclusion and exclusion approves some conduct as comporting with constitutional guarantees and disapproves other actions by state agents. A ruling admitting evidence in a criminal trial, we recognize, has the necessary effect of legitimizing the conduct which produced the evidence, while an application of the exclusionary rule withholds the constitutional imprimatur.

The exclusionary rule has its limitations, however, as a tool of judicial control. It cannot properly be invoked to exclude the products of legitimate police investigative techniques on the ground that much conduct which is closely similar involves unwarranted intrusions upon constitutional protections. Moreover, in some contexts the rule is ineffective as a deterrent. Street encounters between citizens and police officers are incredibly rich in diversity. They range from wholly friendly exchanges of pleasantries or mutually useful information to hostile confrontations of armed men involving arrests, or injuries, or loss of life. Moreover, hostile confrontations are not all of a piece. Some of them begin in a friendly enough manner, only to take a different turn upon the injection of some unexpected element into the conversation. Encounters are initiated by the police for a wide variety of purposes, some of which are wholly unrelated to a desire to prosecute for crime. Doubtless some police "field interrogation" conduct violates the Fourth Amendment. But a stern refusal by this Court to condone such activity does not necessarily render it responsive to the exclusionary rule. Regardless of how effective the rule may be where obtaining convictions is an important objective of the police, it is powerless to deter invasions of constitutionally guaranteed rights where the police either have no interest in prosecuting or are willing to forgo successful prosecution in the interest of serving some other goal.

Proper adjudication of cases in which the exclusionary rule is invoked demands a constant awareness of these limitations. The wholesale harassment by certain elements of the police community, of which minority groups, particularly Negroes, frequently complain, will not be stopped by the exclusion of any evidence from any criminal trial. Yet a rigid and unthinking application of the exclusionary rule, in futile protest against practices which it can never be used effectively to control, may exact a high toll in human injury and frustration of efforts to prevent crime. No judicial opinion can comprehend the protean variety of the street encounter, and we can only judge the facts of the case before us. Nothing we say today is to be taken as indicating approval of police conduct outside the legitimate investigative sphere. Under our decision, courts still retain their traditional responsibility to guard against police conduct which is overbearing or harassing, or which trenches upon personal security without the objective evidentiary justification which the Constitution requires. When such conduct is identified, it must be condemned by the judiciary and its fruits must be excluded from evidence in criminal trials. And, of course, our approval of legitimate and restrained investigative conduct undertaken on the basis of ample factual justification should in no way discourage the employment of other remedies than the exclusionary rule to curtail abuses for which that sanction may prove inappropriate.

Having thus roughly sketched the perimeters of the constitutional debate over the limits on police investigative conduct in general and the background against which this case presents itself, we turn our attention to the quite narrow question posed by the facts before us: whether it is always unreasonable for a policeman to seize a person and subject him to a limited search for weapons unless there is probable cause for an arrest. Given the narrowness of this question, we have no occasion to canvass in detail the constitutional limitations upon the scope of a policeman's power when he confronts a citizen without probable cause to arrest him.

Our first task is to establish at what point in this encounter the Fourth Amendment becomes relevant. That is, we must decide whether and when Officer McFadden "seized" Terry and whether and when he conducted a "search." There is some suggestion in the use of such terms as "stop" and "frisk" that such police conduct is outside the purview of the Fourth Amendment because neither

action rises to the level of a "search" or "seizure" within the meaning of the Constitution. We emphatically reject this notion. It is quite
plain that the Fourth Amendment governs "seizures" of the person
which do not eventuate in a trip to the station house and prosecution
for crime—"arrests" in traditional terminology. It must be recognized
that whenever a police officer accosts an individual and restrains his
freedom to walk away, he has "seized" that person. And it is nothing
less than sheer torture of the English language to suggest that a
careful exploration of the outer surfaces of a person's clothing all
over his or her body in an attempt to find weapons is not a "search."
Moreover, it is simply fantastic to urge that such a procedure performed in public by a policeman while the citizen stands helpless,
perhaps facing a wall with his hands raised, is a "petty indignity." It
is a serious intrusion upon the sanctity of the person, which may
inflict great indignity and arouse strong resentment, and it is not to
be undertaken lightly.

The danger in the logic which proceeds upon distinctions between a "stop" and an "arrest," or "seizure" of the person, and
between a "frisk" and a "search" is twofold. It seeks to isolate from
constitutional scrutiny the initial stages of the contact between the
policeman and the citizen. And by suggesting a rigid all-or-nothing
model of justification and regulation under the Amendment, it
obscures the utility of limitations upon the scope, as well as the
initiation, of police action as a means of constitutional regulation.
This Court has held in the past that a search which is reasonable at its
inception may violate the Fourth Amendment by virtue of its intolerable intensity and scope. The scope of the search must be
"strictly tied to and justified by" the circumstances which rendered
its initiation permissible.

The distinctions of classical "stop-and-frisk" theory thus serve
to divert attention from the central inquiry under the Fourth Amendment—the reasonableness in all the circumstances of the particular
governmental invasion of a citizen's personal security. "Search" and
"seizure" are not talismans. We therefore reject the notions that the
Fourth Amendment does not come into play at all as a limitation
upon police conduct if the officers stop short of something called a
"technical arrest" or a "full-blown search."

In this case there can be no question, then, that Officer
McFadden "seized" petitioner and subjected him to a "search" when
he took hold of him and patted down the outer surfaces of his
clothing. We must decide whether at that point it was reasonable for
Officer McFadden to have interfered with petitioner's personal

security as he did. And in determining whether the seizure and search were "unreasonable" our inquiry is a dual one—whether the officer's action was justified at its inception, and whether it was reasonably related in scope to the circumstances which justified the interference in the first place . . . .

The crux of this case, however, is not the propriety of Officer McFadden's taking steps to investigate petitioner's suspicious behavior, but rather, whether there was justification for McFadden's invasion of Terry's personal security by searching him for weapons in the course of that investigation. We are now concerned with more than the governmental interest in investigating crime; in addition, there is the more immediate interest of the police officer in taking steps to assure himself that the person with whom he is dealing is not armed with a weapon that could unexpectedly and fatally be used against him. Certainly it would be unreasonable to require that police officers take unnecessary risks in the performance of their duties. American criminals have a long tradition of armed violence, and every year in this country many law enforcement officers are killed in the line of duty, and thousands more are wounded. Virtually all of these deaths and a substantial portion of the injuries are inflicted with guns and knives.

In view of these facts, we cannot blind ourselves to the need for law enforcement officers to protect themselves and other prospective victims of violence in situations where they may lack probable cause for an arrest. When an officer is justified in believing that the individual whose suspicious behavior he is investigating at close range is armed and presently dangerous to the officer or to others, it would appear to be clearly unreasonable to deny the officer the power to take necessary measures to determine whether the person is in fact carrying a weapon and to neutralize the threat of physical harm.

We must still consider, however, the nature and quality of the intrusion on individual rights which must be accepted if police officers are to be conceded the right to search for weapons in situations where probable cause to arrest for crime is lacking. Even a limited search of the outer clothing for weapons constitutes a severe, though brief, intrusion upon cherished personal security, and it must surely be an annoying, frightening, and perhaps humiliating experience . . . .

Our evaluation of the proper balance that has to be struck in this type of case leads us to conclude that there must be a narrowly drawn authority to permit a reasonable search for weapons for the protection of the police officer, where he has reason to believe that he is dealing with an armed and dangerous individual, regardless of whether he has probable cause to arrest the individual for a crime. The officer need not be absolutely certain that the individual is armed; the issue is whether a reasonably prudent man in the circumstances would be warranted in the belief that his safety or that of others was in danger. And in determining whether the officer acted reasonably in such circumstances, due weight must be given, not to his inchoate and unparticularized suspicion or "hunch," but to the specific reasonable inferences which he is entitled to draw from the facts in light of his experience . . . .

The scope of the search in this case presents no serious problem in light of these standards. Officer McFadden patted down the outer clothing of petitioner and his two companions. He did not place his hands in their pockets or under the outer surface of their garments until he had felt weapons, and then he merely reached for and removed the guns. He never did invade Katz' person beyond the outer surfaces of his clothes, since he discovered nothing in his patdown which might have been a weapon. Officer McFadden confined his search strictly to what was minimally necessary to learn whether the men were armed and to disarm them once he discovered the weapons. He did not conduct a general exploratory search for whatever evidence of criminal activity he might find.

We conclude that the revolver seized from Terry was properly admitted in evidence against him. At the time he seized petitioner and searched him for weapons, Officer McFadden had reasonable grounds to believe that petitioner was armed and dangerous, and it was necessary for the protection of himself and others to take swift measures to discover the true facts and neutralize the threat of harm if it materialized. The policeman carefully restricted his search to what was appropriate to the discovery of the particular items which he sought. Each case of this sort will, of course, have to be decided on its own facts. We merely hold today that where a police officer observes unusual conduct which leads him reasonably to conclude in light of his experience that criminal activity may be afoot and that the persons with whom he is dealing may be armed and presently dangerous, where in the course of investigating this behavior he identifies himself as a policeman and makes reasonable inquiries, and where nothing in the initial stages of the encounter serves to dispel his reasonable fear for his own or others' safety, he is entitled for the protection of himself and others in the area to conduct a carefully limited search of the outer clothing of such persons in an attempt to discover weapons which might be used to assault him.

Such a search is a reasonable search under the Fourth Amendment, and any weapons seized may properly be introduced in evidence against the person from whom they were taken.

James Draper v. United States, Supreme Court of the United States, 358 U.S. 307 (1959)

Mr. Justice WHITTAKER delivered the opinion of the Court.

The evidence offered at the hearing on the motion to suppress was not substantially disputed. It established that one Marsh, a federal narcotic agent with twenty-nine years' experience, was stationed at Denver; that one Hereford had been engaged as a "special employee" of the Bureau of Narcotics at Denver for about six months, and from time to time gave information to Marsh regarding violations of the narcotic laws, for which Hereford was paid small sums of money, and that Marsh had always found the information given by Hereford to be accurate and reliable. On September 3, 1956, Hereford told Marsh that James Draper (petitioner) recently had taken up abode at a stated address in Denver and "was peddling narcotics to several addicts" in that city. Four days later, on September 7, Hereford told Marsh "that Draper had gone to Chicago the day before [September 6] by train [and] that he was going to bring back three ounces of heroin [and] that he would return to Denver either on the morning of the 8th of September or the morning of the 9th of September also by train." Hereford also gave Marsh a detailed physical description of Draper and of the clothing he was wearing, and said that he would be carrying "a tan zipper bag," and habitually "walked real fast."

On the morning of September 8, Marsh and a Denver police officer went to the Denver Union Station and kept watch over all incoming trains from Chicago, but they did not see anyone fitting the description that Hereford had given. Repeating the process on the morning of September 9, they saw a person, having the exact physical attributes and wearing the precise clothing described by Hereford, alight from an incoming Chicago train and start walking "fast" toward the exit. He was carrying a tan zipper bag in his right hand and the left was thrust in his raincoat pocket. Marsh, accompanied by the police officer, overtook, stopped and arrested him. They then searched him and found the two "envelopes containing heroin" clutched in his left hand in his raincoat pocket, and found the syringe in the tan zipper bag. Marsh then took him (petitioner) into custody. Hereford died four days after the arrest and therefore did not testify at the hearing on the motion.

26 U.S.C. (Supp. V) § 7607, added by § 104 (a) of the Narcotic Control Act of 1956, 70 Stat. 570, 26 U.S.C.A. § 7607, provides, in pertinent part:

> The Commissioner . . . and agents, of the Bureau of Narcotics . . . may— . . .
>
> (2) Make arrests without warrant for violations of any law of the United States relating to narcotic drugs . . . where the violation is committed in the presence of the person making the arrest or where such person has reasonable grounds to believe that the person to be arrested has committed or is committing such violation.

The crucial question for us then is whether knowledge of the related facts and circumstances gave Marsh "probable cause" within the meaning of the Fourth Amendment, and "reasonable grounds" within the meaning of § 104 (a), supra, to believe that petitioner had committed or was committing a violation of the narcotic laws. If it did, the arrest, though without a warrant, was lawful . . .

Petitioner . . . contends (1) that the information given by Hereford to Marsh was "hearsay" and, because hearsay is not legally competent evidence in a criminal trial, could not legally have been considered, but should have been put out of mind, by Marsh in assessing whether he had "probable cause" and "reasonable grounds" to arrest petitioner without a warrant, and (2) that, even if hearsay could lawfully have been considered, Marsh's information should be held insufficient to show "probable cause" and "reasonable grounds" to believe that petitioner had violated or was violating the narcotic laws and to justify his arrest without a warrant.

Considering the first contention, we find petitioner entirely in error. Brinegar v. United States, 338 U.S. 160, 172-173, 69 S.Ct. 1302, 1309, has settled the question the other way. There, in a similar situation, the convict contended "that the factors relating to inadmissibility of the evidence [for] *purposes of proving guilt at the trial* deprive [d] the evidence as a whole of sufficiency to show probable cause for the search . . . ." (Emphasis added.) But this Court, rejecting that contention, said: "[T]he so-called distinction places a wholly unwarranted emphasis upon the criterion of admissibility in evidence, to prove the accused's guilt, of facts relied upon to show probable cause. The emphasis, we think, goes much too far in confusing and disregarding the difference between what is required to prove guilt in a criminal case and what is required to show probable cause for arrest or search. It approaches requiring (if it does not in practical effect require) proof sufficient to establish guilt in order to substantiate the existence of probable cause. There is a large difference between the two things to be proved [guilt and probable cause], as well as between the tribunals which determine them, and therefore a like difference in the *quanta* and modes of proof required to establish them . . . ."

Nor can we agree with petitioner's second contention that Marsh's information was insufficient to show probable cause and reasonable grounds to believe that petitioner had violated or was violating the narcotic laws and to justify his arrest without a warrant. The information given to narcotic agent Marsh by "special employee" Hereford may have been hearsay to Marsh, but coming from one employed for that purpose and whose information had always been found accurate and reliable, it is clear that Marsh would have been derelict in his duties had he not pursued it. And when, in pursuing that information, he saw a man, having the exact physical attributes and wearing the precise clothing and carrying the tan zipper bag that Hereford had described, alight from one of the very trains from the very place stated by Hereford and start to walk at a "fast" pace toward the station exit, Marsh had personally verified every facet of the information given him by Hereford except whether petitioner had accomplished his mission and had the three ounces of heroin on his person or in his bag. And surely, with every other bit of Hereford's information being thus personally verified, Marsh had "reasonable grounds" to believe that the remaining unverified bit of Hereford's information—that Draper would have the heroin with him—was likewise true.

"In dealing with probable cause . . . as the very name implies, we deal with probabilities. These are not technical; they are the factual and practical considerations of everyday life on which reasonable and prudent men, not legal technicians, act." Brinegar v. United States, supra, 338 U.S. at page 175, 69 S.Ct. at page 1310. Probable cause exists where "the facts and circumstances within their [the arresting officers'] knowledge and of which they had reasonably trustworthy information [are] sufficient in themselves to warrant a man of reasonable caution in the belief that" an offense has been or is being committed. Carroll v. United States, 267 U.S. 132, 162, 45 S.Ct. 280, 288 . . . .

We believe that, under the facts and circumstances here, Marsh had probable cause and reasonable grounds to believe that petitioner was committing a violation of the laws of the United States relating to narcotic drugs at the time he arrested him. The arrest was therefore lawful, and the subsequent search and seizure, having been made incident to that lawful arrest, were likewise valid. It follows that

petitioner's motion to suppress was properly denied and that the seized heroin was competent evidence lawfully received at the trial.
Affirmed.

Chapter 4: Search and Seizure Generally

Dollree Mapp v. *State of Ohio,* Supreme Court of the United States, 367 U.S. 643 (1961)

Mr. Justice CLARK delivered the opinion of the Court.

Appellant stands convicted of knowingly having had in her possession and under her control certain lewd and lascivious books, pictures, and photographs in violation of § 2905.34 of Ohio's Revised Code. As officially stated in the syllabus to its opinion, the Supreme Court of Ohio found that her conviction was valid though "based primarily upon the introduction in evidence of lewd and lascivious books and pictures unlawfully seized during an unlawful search of defendant's home . . . ." 170 Ohio St. 427-428, 166 N.E.2d 387, 388.

On May 23, 1957, three Cleveland police officers arrived at appellant's residence in that city pursuant to information that "a person [was] hiding out in the home, who was wanted for questioning in connection with a recent bombing, and that there was a large amount of policy paraphernalia being hidden in the home." Miss Mapp and her daughter by a former marriage lived on the top floor of the two-family dwelling. Upon their arrival at that house, the officers knocked on the door and demanded entrance but appellant, after telephoning her attorney, refused to admit them without a search warrant. They advised their headquarters of the situation and undertook a surveillance of the house.

The officers again sought entrance some three hours later when four or more additional officers arrived on the scene. When Miss Mapp did not come to the door immediately, at least one of the several doors to the house was forcibly opened and the policemen gained admittance. Meanwhile Miss Mapp's attorney arrived, but the officers, having secured their own entry, and continuing in their defiance of the law, would permit him neither to see Miss Mapp nor to enter the house. It appears that Miss Mapp was halfway down the stairs from the upper floor to the front door when the officers, in this high-handed manner, broke into the hall. She demanded to see the search warrant. A paper, claimed to be a warrant, was held up by one of the officers. She grabbed the "warrant" and placed it in her bosom. A struggle ensued in which the officers recovered the piece of paper and as a result of which they handcuffed appellant because she had been "belligerent" in resisting their official rescue of the "warrant" from her person. Running roughshod over appellant, a policeman "grabbed" her, "twisted [her] hand," and she "yelled [and] pleaded with him" because "it was hurting." Appellant, in handcuffs, was then forcibly taken upstairs to her bedroom where the officers searched a dresser, a chest of drawers, a closet and some suitcases. They also looked into a photo album and through personal papers belonging to the appellant. The search spread to the rest of the second floor including the child's bedroom, the living room, the kitchen and a dinette. The basement of the building and a trunk found therein were also searched. The obscene materials for possession of which she was ultimately convicted were discovered in the course of that widespread search.

At the trial no search warrant was produced by the prosecution, nor was the failure to produce one explained or accounted for. At best, "There is, in the record, considerable doubt as to whether there ever was any warrant for the search of defendant's home." 170 Ohio St. at page 430, 166 N.E.2d at page 389. The Ohio Supreme Court believed a "reasonable argument" could be made that the conviction should be reversed "because the 'methods' employed to obtain the [evidence] were such as to 'offend "a sense of justice," ' " but the court found determinative the fact that the evidence had not been taken "from defendant's person by the use of brutal or offensive physical force against defendant." 170 Ohio St. at page 431, 166 N.E.2d at pages 389-390.

The State says that even if the search were made without authority, or otherwise unreasonably, it is not prevented from using the unconstitutionally seized evidence at trial, citing Wolf v. People of State of Colorado, 1949, 338 U.S. 25, at page 33, 69 S.Ct. 1359, at page 1364, 93 L.Ed. 1782, in which this Court did indeed hold "that in a prosecution in a State court for a State crime the Fourteenth Amendment does not forbid the admission of evidence obtained by an unreasonable search and seizure." On this appeal, of which we have noted probable jurisdiction, 364 U.S. 868, it is urged once again that we review that holding.

Seventy-five years ago, in Boyd v. United States, 1886, 116 U.S. 616, 630, considering the Fourth and Fifth Amendments as running "almost into each other" on the facts before it, this Court held that the doctrines of those Amendments

apply to all invasions on the part of the government and its employes of the sanctity of a man's home and the privacies of life. It is not the breaking of his doors, and the rummaging of his drawers, that constitutes the essence of the offence; but it is the invasion of his indefeasible right of personal security, personal liberty and private property . . . . Breaking into a house and opening boxes and drawers are circumstances of aggravation; but any forcible and compulsory extortion of a man's own testimony or of his private papers to be used as evidence to convict him of crime or to forfeit his goods, is within the condemnation . . . [of those Amendments].

The Court noted that

constitutional provisions for the security of person and property should be liberally construed . . . . It is the duty of courts to be watchful for the constitutional rights of the citizen, and against any stealthy encroachments thereon. At page 635 of 116 U.S., at page 535 of 6 S.Ct.

In this jealous regard for maintaining the integrity of individual rights, the Court gave life to Madison's prediction that "independent tribunals of justice . . . will be naturally led to resist every encroachment upon rights expressly stipulated for in the Constitution by the declaration of rights." I Annals of Cong. 439 (1789). Concluding, the Court specifically referred to the use of the evidence there seized as "unconstitutional."

Less than thirty years after Boyd, this Court, in Weeks v. United States, 1914, 232 U.S. 383, at pages 391-392, stated that:

the 4th Amendment . . . put the courts of the United States and Federal officials, in the exercise of their power and authority, under limitations and restraints [and] . . . forever secure[d] the people, their persons, houses, papers, and effects, against all unreasonable searches and seizures under the guise of law . . . and the duty of giving to it force and effect is obligatory upon all entrusted under our Federal system with the enforcement of the laws.

Specifically dealing with the use of the evidence unconstitutionally seized, the Court concluded:

If letters and private documents can thus be seized and held and used in evidence against a citizen accused of an offense, the protection of the Fourth Amendment declaring his right to be secure against such searches and seizures is of no value, and, so far as those thus placed are concerned, might as well be stricken from the Constitution. The efforts of the courts and their officials to bring the guilty to punishment, praiseworthy as they are, are not to be aided by the sacrifice of those great principles established by years of endeavor and suffering which have resulted in their embodiment in the fundamental law of the land. At page 393 of 232 U.S.

Finally, the Court in that case clearly stated that use of the seized evidence involved "a denial of the constitutional rights of the accused." At page 398 of 232 U.S., at page 346 of 34 S.Ct. Thus, in the year 1914, in the Weeks case, this Court "for the first time" held that "in a federal prosecution the Fourth Amendment barred the use of evidence secured through an illegal search and seizure." Wolf v. People of State of Colorado, supra, 338 U.S. at page 28, 69 S.Ct. at page 1361. This Court has ever since required of federal law officers a strict adherence to that command which this Court has held to be a clear, specific, and constitutionally required—even if judicially implied—deterrent safeguard without insistence upon which the Fourth Amendment would have been reduced to "a form of words." Holmes J., Silverthorne Lumber Co. v. United States, 1920, 251 U.S. 385, 392, 40 S.Ct. 182, 183, 64 L.Ed. 319. It meant, quite simply, that "conviction by means of unlawful seizures and enforced confessions . . . should find no sanction in the judgments of the courts . . .," Weeks v. United States, supra, 232 U.S. at page 392, 34 S.Ct. at page 344, and that such evidence "shall not be used at all." Silverthorne Lumber Co. v. United States, supra, 251 U.S. at page 392, 40 S.Ct. at page 183.

In 1949, thirty-five years after Weeks was announced, this Court, in Wolf v. People of State of Colorado, supra, again for the first time, discussed the effect of the Fourth Amendment upon the States through the operation of the Due Process Clause of the Fourteenth Amendment. It said:

[W]e have no hesitation in saying that were a State affirmatively to sanction such police incursion into privacy it would run counter to the guaranty of the Fourteenth Amendment. At page 28 of 338 U.S.

Nevertheless, after declaring that the "security of one's privacy against arbitrary intrusion by the police" is "implicit in 'the concept of ordered liberty' and as such enforceable against the States through the Due Process Clause," cf. Palko v. State of Connecticut, 1937, 302 U.S. 319, 58 S.Ct. 149, 82 L.Ed. 288, and announcing that it "stoutly adhere[d]" to the Weeks decision, the Court decided that the Weeks exclusionary rule would not then be imposed upon the States as "an essential ingredient of the right." 338 U.S. at pages 27-29, 69 S.Ct. at page 1362. The Court's reasons for not considering essential to the right to privacy, as a curb imposed upon the States by the Due Process Clause, that which decades before had been posited as part and parcel of the Fourth Amendment's limitation upon federal encroachment of individual privacy, were bottomed on factual considerations.

Some five years after Wolf, in answer to a plea made here Term after Term that we overturn its doctrine on applicability of the Weeks exclusionary rule, this Court indicated that such should not be done until the States had "adequate opportunity to adopt or reject the [Weeks] rule." Irvine v. People of State of California, supra, 347 U.S. at page 134, 74 S.Ct. at page 384. There again it was said:

Never until June of 1949 did this Court hold the basic search-and-seizure prohibition in any way applicable to the states under the Fourteenth Amendment. Ibid.

Since the Fourth Amendment's right of privacy has been declared enforceable against the States through the Due Process Clause of the Fourteenth, it is enforceable against them by the same sanction of exclusion as is used against the Federal Government. Were it otherwise, then just as without the Weeks rule the assurance against unreasonable federal searches and seizures would be "a form of words," valueless and undeserving of mention in a perpetual charter of inestimable human liberties, so too, without that rule the freedom from state invasions of privacy would be so ephemeral and so nearly severed from its conceptual nexus with the freedom from all brutish means of coercing evidence as not to merit this Court's high regard as a freedom "implicit in 'the concept of ordered liberty.' " At the time that the Court held in Wolf that the Amendment was applicable to the States through the Due Process Clause, the cases of this Court, as we have seen, had steadfastly held that as to federal officers the Fourth Amendment included the exclusion of the evidence seized in violation of its provisions.

Moreover, our holding that the exclusionary rule is an essential part of both the Fourth and Fourteenth Amendments is not only the logical dictate of prior cases, but it also makes very good sense. There is no war between the Constitution and common sense. Presently, a federal prosecutor may make no use of evidence illegally seized, but a State's attorney across the street may, although he supposedly is operating under the enforceable prohibitions of the same Amendment. Thus the State, by admitting evidence unlawfully seized, serves to encourage disobedience to the Federal Constitution which it is bound to uphold. Moreover, as was said in Elkins, "[t]he very essence of a healthy federalism depends upon the avoidance of needless conflict between state and federal courts." 364 U.S. at page 221, 80 S.Ct. at page 1446. Such a conflict, hereafter needless, arose this very Term, in Wilson v. Schnettler, 1961, 365 U.S. 381, 81 S.Ct. 632, 5 L.Ed.2d 620, in which, and in spite of the promise made by Rea, we gave full recognition to our practice in this regard by refusing to restrain a federal officer from testifying in a state court as to evidence unconstitutionally seized by him in the performance of his duties.

There are those who say, as did Justice (then Judge) Cardozo, that under our constitutional exclusionary doctrine "[t]he criminal is to go free because the constable has blundered." People v. Defore, 242 N.Y. at page 21, 150 N.E. at page 587. In some cases this will undoubtedly be the result. But, as was said in Elkins, "there is another consideration—the imperative of judicial integrity." 364 U.S. at page 222, 80 S.Ct. at page 1447. The criminal goes free, if he must, but it is the law that sets him free. Nothing can destroy a government more quickly than its failure to observe its own laws, or worse, its disregard of the charter of its own existence. As Mr. Justice Brandeis, dissenting, said in Olmstead v. United States, 1928, 277 U.S. 438, 485, 48 S.Ct. 564, 575, 72 L.Ed. 944: "Our government is the potent, the omnipresent teacher. For good or for ill, it teaches the whole people by its example . . . . If the government becomes a lawbreaker, it breeds contempt for law; it invites every man to become a law unto himself; it invites anarchy." Nor can it lightly be assumed that, as a practical matter, adoption of the exclusionary rule fetters law enforcement.

Having once recognized that the right to privacy embodied in the Fourth Amendment is enforceable against the States, and that the right to be secure against rude invasions of privacy by state officers is, therefore, constitutional in origin, we can no longer permit that right to remain an empty promise. Because it is enforceable in the same manner and to like effect as other basic rights secured by the Due Process Clause, we can no longer permit it to be revocable at the whim of any police officer who, in the name of law enforcement itself, chooses to suspend its enjoyment. Our decision, founded on reason and truth, gives to the individual no more than that which the Constitution guarantees him, to the police officer no less than that to which honest law enforcement is entitled, and, to the courts, that judicial integrity so necessary in the true administration of justice.

The judgment of the Supreme Court of Ohio is reversed and the cause remanded for further proceedings not inconsistent with this opinion.

Reversed and remanded.

Chapter 5: Arrest and Search Warrants

William Spinelli v. *United States,* Supreme Court of the United States,
393 U.S. 410 (1969)

Mr. Justice HARLAN delivered the opinion of the Court.

William Spinelli was convicted under 18 U.S.C. § 1952 of traveling to St.Louis, Missouri, from a nearby Illinois suburb with the intention of conducting gambling activities proscribed by Missouri law . . . . At every appropriate stage in the proceedings in the lower courts, the petitioner challenged the constitutionality of the warrant which authorized the FBI search that uncovered the evidence necessary for his conviction . . . .

Believing it desirable that the principles of [Aguilar v. Texas, 378 U.S. 108, 84 S.Ct. 1509 (1964)] should be further explicated, we granted certiorari, our writ being later limited to the question of the constitutional validity of the search and seizure. For reasons that follow we reverse.

In *Aguilar*, a search warrant had issued upon an affidavit of police officers who swore only that they had "received reliable information from a credible person and do believe" that narcotics were being illegally stored on the described premises. While recognizing that the constitutional requirement of probable cause can be satisfied by hearsay information, this Court held the affidavit inadequate for two reasons. First, the application failed to set forth any of the "underlying circumstances" necessary to enable the magistrate independently to judge of the validity of the informant's conclusion that the narcotics were where he said they were. Second, the affiant-officers did not attempt to support their claim that their informant was " 'credible' or his information 'reliable.' " The Government is, however, quite right in saying that the FBI affidavit in the present case is more ample than that in *Aguilar*. Not only does it contain a report from an anonymous informant, but it also contains a report of an independent FBI investigation which is said to corroborate the informant's tip. We are, then, required to delineate the manner in which *Aguilar's* two-pronged test should be applied in these circumstances.

In essence, the affidavit, reproduced in full in the Appendix to this opinion, contained the following allegations:

1. The FBI had kept track of Spinelli's movements on five days during the month of August 1965. On four of these occasions, Spinelli was seen crossing one of two bridges leading from Illinois into St. Louis, Missouri, between 11 a.m. and 12:15 p.m. On four of the five days, Spinelli was also seen parking his car in a lot used by

residents of an apartment house at 1108 Indian Circle Drive in St. Louis, between 3:30 p.m. and 4:45 p.m. On one day, Spinelli was followed further and seen to enter a particular apartment in the building.

2. An FBI check with the telephone company revealed that this apartment contained two telephones listed under the name of Grace P. Hagen, and carrying the numbers WYdown 4-0029 and WYdown 4-0136.

3. The application stated that "William Spinelli is known to this affiant and to federal law enforcement agents and local law enforcement agents as a bookmaker, an associate of bookmakers, a gambler, and an associate of gamblers."

4. Finally it was stated that the FBI "has been informed by a confidential reliable informant that William Spinelli is operating a handbook and accepting wagers and disseminating wagering information by means of the telephones which have been assigned the numbers WYdown 4-0029 and WYdown 4-0136."

There can be no question that the last item mentioned, detailing the informant's tip, has a fundamental place in this warrant application. Without it, probable cause could not be established. The first two items reflect only innocent-seeming activity and data. Spinelli's travels to and from the apartment building and his entry into a particular apartment on one occasion could hardly be taken as bespeaking gambling activity; and there is surely nothing unusual about an apartment containing two separate telephones. Many a householder indulges himself in this petty luxury. Finally, the allegation that Spinelli was "known" to the affiant and to other federal and local law enforcement officers as a gambler and an associate of gamblers is but a bald and unilluminating assertion of suspicion that is entitled to no weight in appraising the magistrate's decision. Nathanson v. United States, 290 U.S. 41, 46, 54 S.Ct. 11, 12 (1933).

So much indeed the Government does not deny. Rather, following the reasoning of the Court of Appeals, the Government claims that the informant's tip gives a suspicious color to the FBI's reports detailing Spinelli's innocent-seeming conduct and that, conversely, the FBI's surveillance corroborates the informant's tip, thereby entitling it to more weight. It is true, of course, that the magistrate is obligated to render a judgment based upon a commonsense reading of the entire affidavit. United States v. Ventresca, 380 U.S. 102, 108, 85 S.Ct. 741, 745 (1964). We believe, however, that the "totality of circumstances" approach taken by the Court of Appeals paints with too broad a brush. Where, as here, the informer's tip is a necessary element in a finding of probable cause its proper weight must be determined by a more precise analysis.

The informer's report must first be measured against *Aguilar's* standards so that its probative value can be assessed. If the tip is found inadequate under *Aguilar*, the other allegations which corroborate the information contained in the hearsay report should then be considered. At this stage as well, however, the standards enunciated in *Aguilar* must inform the magistrate's decision. He must ask: Can it fairly be said that the tip, even when certain parts of it have been corroborated by independent sources, is as trustworthy as a tip which would pass *Aguilar's* tests without independent corroboration? *Aguilar* is relevant at this stage of the inquiry as well because the tests it establishes were designed to implement the longstanding principle that probable cause must be determined by a "neutral and detached magistrate," and not by "the officer engaged in the often competitive enterprise of ferreting out crime." Johnson v. United States, 333 U.S. 10, 14, 68 S.Ct. 367, 369 (1948). A magistrate cannot be said to have properly discharged his constitutional duty if he relies on an informer's tip which—even when partially corroborated—is not as reliable as one which passes *Aguilar's* requirements when standing alone.

Applying these principles to the present case, we first consider the weight to be given the informer's tip when it is considered apart from the rest of the affidavit. It is clear that a Commissioner could not credit it without abdicating his constitutional function. Though the affiant swore that his confidant was "reliable," he offered the magistrate no reason in support of this conclusion. Perhaps even more important is the fact that *Aguilar's* other test has not been satisfied. The tip does not contain a sufficient statement of the underlying circumstances from which the informer concluded that Spinelli was running a bookmaking operation. We are not told how the FBI's source received his information—it is not alleged that the informant personally observed Spinelli at work or that he had ever placed a bet with him. Moreover, if the informant came by the information indirectly, he did not explain why his sources were reliable. Compare Jaben v. United States, 381 U.S. 214, 85 S.Ct. 1365 (1965). In the absence of a statement detailing the manner in which the information was gathered, it is specially important that the tip describe the accused's criminal activity in sufficient detail so that the magistrate may know that he is relying on something more substantial than a casual rumor circulating in the underworld or an accusation based merely on an individual's general reputation.

The detail provided by the informant in Draper v. United States, 358 U.S. 307, 79 S.Ct. 329 (1959), provides a suitable benchmark. While Hereford, the FBI's informer in that case did not state the way in which he had obtained his information he reported that Draper had gone to Chicago the day before by train and that he would return to Denver by train with three ounces of heroin on one of two specified mornings. Moreover Hereford went on to describe with minute particularity the clothes that Draper would be wearing upon his arrival at the Denver station. A magistrate, when confronted with such detail, could reasonably infer that the informant had gained his information in a reliable way. Such an inference cannot be made in the present case. Here, the only facts supplied were that Spinelli was using two specified telephones and that these phones were being used in gambling operations. This meager report could easily have been obtained from an offhand remark heard at a neighborhood bar.

Nor do we believe that the patent doubts *Aguilar* raises as to the report's reliability are adequately resolved by a consideration of the allegations detailing the FBI's independent investigative efforts. At most, these allegations indicated that Spinelli could have used the telephones specified by the informant for some purpose. This cannot by itself be said to support both the inference that the informer was generally trustworthy and that he had made his charge against Spinelli on the basis of information obtained in a reliable way. Once again, *Draper* provides a relevant comparison. Independent police work in that case corroborated much more than one small detail that had been provided by the informant. There, the police, upon greeting the inbound Denver train on the second morning specified by informer Hereford, saw a man whose dress corresponded precisely to Hereford's detailed description. It was then apparent that the informant had not been fabricating his report out of whole cloth; since the report was of the sort which in common experience may be recognized as having been obtained in a reliable way, it was perfectly clear that probable cause had been established.

We conclude, then, that in the present case the informant's tip —even when corroborated to the extent indicated—was not sufficient to provide the basis for a finding of probable cause. This is not to say that the tip was so insubstantial that it could not properly have counted in the magistrate's determination. Rather, it needed some further support. When we look to the other parts of the application, however, we find nothing alleged which would permit the suspicions engendered by the informant's report to ripen into a judgment that a crime was probably being committed. As we have already seen, the allegations detailing the FBI's surveillance of Spinelli and its investigation of the telephone company records contain no suggestion of criminal conduct when taken by themselves—and they are not endowed with an aura of suspicion by virtue of the informer's tip. Nor do we find that the FBI's reports take on a sinister color when read in light of common knowledge that bookmaking is often carried on over the telephone and from premises ostensibly used by others for perfectly normal purposes. Such an argument would carry weight in a situation in which the premises contain an unusual number of telephones or abnormal activity is observed, cf. McCray v. Illinois, 386 U.S. 300, 302, 87 S.Ct. 1056, 1057 (1967), but it does not fit this case where neither of these factors is present. All that remains to be considered is the flat statement that Spinelli was "known" to the FBI and others as a gambler. But just as a simple assertion of police suspicion is not itself a sufficient basis for a magistrate's finding of probable cause, we do not believe it may be used to give additional weight to allegations that would otherwise be insufficient.

The affidavit, then, falls short of the standards set forth in *Aguilar, Draper*, and our other decisions that give content to the notion of probable cause. In holding as we have done, we do not retreat from the established propositions that only the probability, and not a prima facie showing, of criminal activity is the standard of probable cause, Beck v. Ohio, 379 U.S. 89, 96, 85 S.Ct. 223, 228 (1964); that affidavits of probable cause are tested by much less rigorous standards than those governing the admissibility of evidence at trial, McCray v. Illinois, 386 U.S. 300, 311, 87 S.Ct. 1056, 1062 (1967); that in judging probable cause issuing magistrates are not to be confined by niggardly limitations or by restrictions on the use of their common sense. United States v. Ventresca, 380 U.S. 102, 108, 85 S.Ct. 741, 745 (1964); and that their determination of probable cause should be paid great deference by reviewing courts, Jones v. United States, 362 U.S. 257, 270-271, 80 S.Ct. 725, 735-736 (1960). But we cannot sustain this warrant without diluting important safeguards that assure that the judgment of a disinterested judicial officer will interpose itself between the police and the citizenry.

The judgment of the Court of Appeals is reversed and the case is remanded to that court for further proceedings consistent with this opinion.

It is so ordered.

Reversed and remanded.

Mr. Justice MARSHALL took no part in the consideration or decision of this case.

APPENDIX

AFFIDAVIT IN SUPPORT OF SEARCH WARRANT

I, Robert L. Bender, being duly sworn, depose and say that I am a Special Agent of the Federal Bureau of Investigation, and as such am authorized to make searches and seizures.

That on August 6, 1965, at approximately 11:44 a.m., William Spinelli was observed by an Agent of the Federal Bureau of Investigation driving a 1964 Ford convertible, Missouri license HC3-649, onto the Eastern approach of the Veterans Bridge leading from East St. Louis, Illinois, to St. Louis, Missouri.

That on August 11, 1965, at approximately 11:16 a.m., William Spinelli was observed by an Agent of the Federal Bureau of Investigation driving a 1964 Ford convertible, Missouri license HC3-649, onto the Eastern approach of the Eads Bridge leading from East St. Louis, Illinois, to St. Louis, Missouri.

Further, at approximately 11:18 a.m. on August 11, 1965, I observed William Spinelli driving the aforesaid Ford convertible from the Western approach of the Eads Bridge into St. Louis, Missouri.

Further, at approximately 4:40 p.m. on August 11, 1965, I observed the aforesaid Ford convertible, bearing Missouri license HC3-649, parked in a parking lot used by residents of The Chieftain Manor Apartments, approximately one block east of 1108 Indian Circle Drive.

On August 12, 1965, at approximately 12:07 p.m. William Spinelli was observed by an Agent of the Federal Bureau of Investigation driving the aforesaid 1964 Ford convertible onto the Eastern approach of the Veterans Bridge from East St. Louis, Illinois, in the direction of St. Louis, Missouri.

Further, on August 12, 1965, at approximately 3:46 p.m., I observed William Spinelli driving the aforesaid 1964 Ford convertible onto the parking lot used by the residents of The Chieftain Manor Apartments approximately one block east of 1108 Indian Circle Drive.

Further, on August 12, 1965, at approximately 3:49 p.m., William Spinelli was observed by an Agent of the Federal Bureau of Investigation entering the front entrance of the two-story apartment building located at 1108 Indian Circle Drive, this building being one of The Chieftain Manor Apartments.

On August 13, 1965, at approximately 11:08 a.m., William Spinelli was observed by an Agent of the Federal Bureau of Investigation driving the aforesaid Ford convertible onto the Eastern approach of the Eads Bridge from East St. Louis, Illinois, heading towards St. Louis, Missouri.

Further, on August 13, 1965, at approximately 11:11 a.m., I observed William Spinelli driving the aforesaid Ford convertible from the Western approach of the Eads Bridge into St. Louis, Missouri.

Further, on August 13, 1965, at approximately 3:45 p.m., I observed William Spinelli driving the aforesaid 1964 Ford convertible onto the parking area used by residents of The Chieftain Manor Apartments, said parking area being approximately one block from 1108 Indian Circle Drive.

Further, on August 13, 1965, at approximately 3:55 p.m., William Spinelli was observed by an Agent of the Federal Bureau of Investigation entering the corner apartment located on the second floor in the southwest corner, known as Apartment F, of the two-story apartment building known and numbered as 1108 Indian Circle Drive.

On August 16, 1965, at approximately 3:22 p.m., I observed William Spinelli driving the aforesaid Ford convertible onto the parking lot used by the residents of The Chieftain Manor Apartments approximately one block east of 1108 Indian Circle Drive.

Further, an Agent of the F.B.I. observed William Spinelli alight from the aforesaid Ford convertible and walk toward the apartment building located at 1108 Indian Circle Drive.

The records of the Southwestern Bell Telephone Company reflect that there are two telephones located in the southwest corner apartment on the second floor of the apartment building located at 1108 Indian Circle Drive under the name of Grace P. Hagen. The numbers listed in the Southwestern Bell Telephone Company records for the aforesaid telephones are WYdown 4-0029 and WYdown 4-0136.

William Spinelli is known to this affiant and to federal law enforcement agents and local law enforcement agents as a bookmaker, an associate of bookmakers, a gambler, and an associate of gamblers.

The Federal Bureau of Investigation has been informed by a confidential reliable informant that William Spinelli is operating a handbook and accepting wagers and disseminating wagering information by means of the telephones which have been assigned the numbers WYdown 4-0029 and WYdown 4-0136.

/s/ Robert L. Bender,
Robert L. Bender,
Special Agent Federal Bureau of Investigation.

410

Appendix E

Subscribed and sworn to before me this 18th day of August, 1965, at St. Louis, Missouri.

/s/ William R. O'Toole.

Chapter 6: Interrogations, Confessions, and Nontestimonial Evidence

Ernesto Miranda v. *State of Arizona,* Supreme Court of the United States, 384 U.S. 436 (1966)

Mr. Chief Justice WARREN delivered the opinion of the Court.

The cases before us raise questions which go to the roots of our concepts of American criminal jurisprudence: the restraints society must observe consistent with the Federal Constitution in prosecuting individuals for crime. More specifically, we deal with the admissibility of statements obtained from an individual who is subjected to custodial police interrogation and the necessity for procedures which assure that the individual is accorded his privilege under the Fifth Amendment to the Constitution not to be compelled to incriminate himself . . . .

The constitutional issue we decide in each of these cases is the admissibility of statements obtained from a defendant questioned while in custody or otherwise deprived of his freedom of action in any significant way. In each, the defendant was questioned by police officers, detectives, or a prosecuting attorney in a room in which he was cut off from the outside world. In none of these cases was the defendant given a full and effective warning of his rights at the outset of the interrogation process. In all the cases, the questioning elicited oral admissions, and in three of them, signed statements as well which were admitted at their trials. They all thus share salient features—incommunicado interrogation of individuals in a police-dominated atmosphere, resulting in self-incriminating statements without full warning of constitutional rights.

An understanding of the nature and setting of this in-custody interrogation is essential to our decisions today. The difficulty in depicting what transpires at such interrogations stems from the fact that in this country they have largely taken place incommunicado. From extensive factual studies undertaken in the early 1930's, including the famous Wickersham Report to Congress by a Presidential Commission, it is clear that police violence and the "third degree" flourished at that time. In a series of cases decided by this Court long after these studies, the police resorted to physical brutality—beating, hanging, whipping—and to sustained and protracted questioning incommunicado in order to extort confessions. The Commission on

Civil Rights in 1961 found much evidence to indicate that "some policemen still resort to physical force to obtain confessions," 1961 Comm'n on Civil Rights Rep, Justice, pt 5, 17. The use of physical brutality and violence is not, unfortunately, relegated to the past or to any part of the country. Only recently in Kings County, New York, the police brutally beat, kicked and placed lighted cigarette butts on the back of a potential witness under interrogation for the purpose of securing a statement incriminating a third party. People v Portelli, 15 NY2d 235, 205 NE2d 857, 257 NYS2d 931 (1965).

The examples given above are undoubtedly the exception now, but they are sufficiently widespread to be the object of concern. Unless a proper limitation upon custodial interrogation is achieved— such as these decisions will advance—there can be no assurance that practices of this nature will be eradicated in the foreseeable future.

. . . we stress that the modern practice of in-custody interrogation is psychologically rather than physically oriented.

In the cases before us today, given this background, we concern ourselves primarily with this interrogation atmosphere and the evils it can bring. In No. 759, Miranda v Arizona, the police arrested the defendant and took him to a special interrogation room where they secured a confession. In No. 760, Vignera v New York, the defendant made oral admissions to the police after interrogation in the afternoon, and then signed an inculpatory statement upon being questioned by an assistant district attorney later the same evening. In No. 761, Westover v United States, the defendant was handed over to the Federal Bureau of Investigation by local authorities after they had detained and interrogated him for a lengthy period, both at night and the following morning. After some two hours of questioning, the federal officers had obtained signed statements from the defendant. Lastly, in No. 584, California v Stewart, the local police held the defendant five days in the station and interrogated him on nine separate occasions before they secured his inculpatory statement.

In these cases, we might not find the defendants' statements to have been involuntary in traditional terms. Our concern for adequate safeguards to protect precious Fifth Amendment rights is, of course, not lessened in the slightest. In each of the cases, the defendant was thrust into an unfamiliar atmosphere and run through menacing police interrogation procedures. The potentiality for compulsion is forcefully apparent, for example, in Miranda, where the indigent Mexican defendant was a seriously disturbed individual with pronounced sexual fantasies, and in Stewart, in which the defendant was an indigent Los Angeles Negro who had dropped out of school in the sixth grade. To be sure, the records do not evince overt physical coercion or patent psychological ploys. The fact remains that in none of these cases did the officers undertake to afford appropriate safeguards at the outset of the interrogation to insure that the statements were truly the product of free choice.

It is obvious that such an interrogation environment is created for no purpose other than to subjugate the individual to the will of his examiner. This atmosphere carries its own badge of intimidation. To be sure, this is not physical intimidation, but it is equally destructive of human dignity. The current practice of incommunicado interrogation is at odds with one of our Nation's most cherished principles—that the individual may not be compelled to incriminate himself. Unless adequate protective devices are employed to dispel the compulsion inherent in custodial surroundings, no statement obtained from the defendant can truly be the product of his free choice . . . .

Today, then, there can be no doubt that the Fifth Amendment privilege is available outside of criminal court proceedings and serves to protect persons in all settings in which their freedom of action is curtailed in any significant way from being compelled to incriminate themselves. We have concluded that without proper safeguards the process of in-custody interrogation of persons suspected or accused of crime contains inherently compelling pressures which work to undermine the individual's will to resist and to compel him to speak where he would not otherwise do so freely. In order to combat these pressures and to permit a full opportunity to exercise the privilege against self-incrimination, the accused must be adequately and effectively apprised of his rights and the exercise of those rights must be fully honored.

At the outset, if a person in custody is to be subjected to interrogation, he must first be informed in clear and unequivocal terms that he has the right to remain silent. For those unaware of the privilege, the warning is needed simply to make them aware of it—the threshold requirement for an intelligent decision as to its exercise. More important, such a warning is an absolute prerequisite in overcoming the inherent pressures of the interrogation atmosphere. It is not just the subnormal or woefully ignorant who succumb to an interrogator's imprecations, whether implied or expressly stated . . . .

The warning of the right to remain silent must be accompanied by the explanation that anything said can and will be used against the individual in court. This warning is needed in order to make him aware not only of the privilege, but also of the consequences of forgoing it. It is only through an awareness of these consequences that there can be any assurance of real understanding and intelligent exercise of the privilege. Moreover, this warning may serve to make the individual more acutely aware that he is faced with a phase of the adversary system—that he is not in the presence of persons acting solely in his interest.

The circumstances surrounding in-custody interrogation can operate very quickly to overbear the will of one merely made aware of his privilege by his interrogators. Therefore, the right to have counsel present at the interrogation is indispensable to the protection of the Fifth Amendment privilege under the system we delineate today. Our aim is to assure that the individual's right to choose between silence and speech remains unfettered throughout the interrogation process. A once-stated warning, delivered by those who will conduct the interrogation, cannot itself suffice to that end among those who most require knowledge of their rights. A mere warning given by the interrogators is not alone sufficient to accomplish that end. Thus, the need for counsel to protect the Fifth Amendment privilege comprehends not merely a right to consult with counsel prior to questioning, but also to have counsel present during any questioning if the defendant so desires.

The presence of counsel at the interrogation may serve several significant subsidiary functions as well. If the accused decides to talk to his interrogators, the assistance of counsel can mitigate the dangers of untrustworthiness. With a lawyer present the likelihood that the police will practice coercion is reduced, and if coercion is nevertheless exercised the lawyer can testify to it in court. The presence of a lawyer can also help to guarantee that the accused gives a fully accurate statement to the police and that the statement is rightly reported by the prosecution at trial. See Crooker v California, 357 US 433, 443-448, 2 L ed 2d 1448, 1456-1459, 78 S Ct 1287 (1958) (Douglas, J., dissenting).

An individual need not make a pre-interrogation request for a lawyer. While such request affirmatively secures his right to have one, his failure to ask for a lawyer does not constitute a waiver. No effective waiver of the right to counsel during interrogation can be recognized unless specifically made after the warnings we here delineate have been given. The accused who does not know his rights and therefore does not make a request may be the person who most needs counsel. As the California Supreme Court has aptly put it:

Finally, we must recognize that the imposition of the requirement for the request would discriminate against the defendant who does not know his rights. The defendant who does not ask for counsel is the very defendant who most needs counsel. We cannot penalize a defendant who, not understanding his constitutional rights, does not make the formal request and by such failure demonstrates his helplessness. To require the request would be to favor the defendant whose sophistication or status had fortuitously prompted him to make it. People v Dorado, 62 Cal 2d 338, 351, 398 P 2d 361, 369-370, 42 Cal Rptr 169, 177-178 (1965) (Tobriner, J.).

Accordingly we hold that an individual held for interrogation must be clearly informed that he has the right to consult with a lawyer and to have the lawyer with him during interrogation under the system for protecting the privilege we delineate today. As with the warnings of the right to remain silent and that anything stated can be used in evidence against him, this warning is an absolute prerequisite to interrogation. No amount of circumstantial evidence that the person may have been aware of this right will suffice to stand in its stead. Only through such a warning is there ascertainable assurance that the accused was aware of this right.

If an individual indicates that he wishes the assistance of counsel before any interrogation occurs, the authorities cannot rationally ignore or deny his request on the basis that the individual does not have or cannot afford a retained attorney. The financial ability of the individual has no relationship to the scope of the rights involved here. The privilege against self-incrimination secured by the Constitution applies to all individuals. The need for counsel in order to protect the privilege exists for the indigent as well as the affluent. In fact, were we to limit these constitutional rights to those who can retain an attorney, our decisions today would be of little significance. The cases before us as well as the vast majority of confession cases with which we have dealt in the past involve those unable to retain counsel. While authorities are not required to relieve the accused of his poverty, they have the obligation not to take advantage of indigence in the administration of justice. Denial of counsel to the indigent at the time of interrogation while allowing an attorney to those who can afford one would be no more supportable by reason or logic than the similar situation at trial and on appeal struck down in Gideon v Wainwright, 372 US 335, 9 L ed 2d 799, 83 S Ct 792 (1963), and Douglas v California, 372 US 353, 9 L ed 2d 811, 83 S Ct 814 (1963).

In order fully to apprise a person interrogated of the extent of his rights under this system then, it is necessary to warn him not only that he has the right to consult with an attorney, but also that if he is indigent a lawyer will be appointed to represent him. Without this additional warning, the admonition of the right to consult with counsel would often be understood as meaning only that he can consult with a lawyer if he has one or has the funds to obtain one. The warning of a right to counsel would be hollow if not couched in terms that would convey to the indigent—the person most often subjected to interrogation—the knowledge that he too has a right to have counsel present. As with the warnings of the right to remain silent and of the general right to counsel, only by effective and express explanation to the indigent of this right can there be assurance that he was truly in a position to exercise it.

Once warnings have been given, the subsequent procedure is clear. If the individual indicates in any manner, at any time prior to or during questioning, that he wishes to remain silent, the interrogation must cease. At this point he has shown that he intends to exercise his Fifth Amendment privilege; any statement taken after the person invokes his privilege cannot be other than the product of compulsion, subtle or otherwise. Without the right to cut off questioning, the setting of in-custody interrogation operates on the individual to overcome free choice in producing a statement after the privilege has been once invoked. If the individual states that he wants an attorney, the interrogation must cease until an attorney is present. At that time, the individual must have an opportunity to confer with the attorney and to have him present during any subsequent questioning. If the individual cannot obtain an attorney and he indicates that he wants one before speaking to police, they must respect his decision to remain silent . . . .

To summarize, we hold that when an individual is taken into custody or otherwise deprived of his freedom by the authorities in any significant way and is subjected to questioning, the privilege against self-incrimination is jeopardized. Procedural safeguards must be employed to protect the privilege, and unless other fully effective means are adopted to notify the person of his right of silence and to assure that the exercise of the right will be scrupulously honored, the following measures are required. He must be warned prior to any questioning that he has the right to remain silent, that anything he says can be used against him in a court of law, that he has the right to the presence of an attorney, and that if he cannot afford an attorney one will be appointed for him prior to any questioning if he so desires. Opportunity to exercise these rights must be afforded to him throughout the interrogation. After such warnings have been given, and such opportunity afforded him, the individual may knowingly and intelligently waive these rights and agree to answer questions or make a statement. But unless and until such warnings and waiver are demonstrated by the prosecution at trial, no evidence obtained as a result of interrogation can be used against him.

Chapter 7: Discovery

Clinton E. Jencks v. United States of America,
Supreme Court of the United States, 353 U.S. 657, 77 S. Ct. 1007 (1957)

Mr. Justice BRENNAN delivered the opinion of the Court.

On April 28, 1950, the petitioner, as president of Amalgamated Bayard District Union, Local 890, International Union of Mine, Mill & Smelter Workers, filed an "Affidavit of Non-Communist Union Officer" with the National Labor Relations Board, pursuant to § 9 (h) of the National Labor Relations Act. He has been convicted under a two-count indictment charging that he violated 18 USC § 1001 by falsely swearing in that affidavit that he was not on April 28, 1950, a member of the Communist Party or affiliated with such Party. The Court of Appeals for the Fifth Circuit affirmed the conviction, and also an order of the District Court denying the petitioner's motion for a new trial. This Court granted certiorari.

Two alleged trial errors are presented for our review. Harvey F. Matusow and J. W. Ford, the Government's principal witnesses, were Communist Party members paid by the Federal Bureau of Investigation contemporaneously to make oral or written reports of Communist Party activities in which they participated. They made such reports to the F. B. I. of activities allegedly participated in by the petitioner, about which they testified at the trial. Error is asserted in the denial by the trial judge of the petitioner's motions to direct the Government to produce these reports for inspection and use in cross-examining Matusow and Ford ....

Former Party members testified that they and the petitioner, as members of the Communist Party of New Mexico, had been expressly instructed to conceal their membership and not to carry membership cards. They also testified that the Party kept no membership records or minutes of membership meetings, and that such meetings were secretly arranged and clandestinely held. One of the witnesses said that special care was taken to conceal the Party membership of members, like the petitioner, "occupying strategic and important positions in labor unions and other organizations where public knowledge of their membership to non-Communists would jeopardize their position in the organization." Accordingly the Government did

not attempt to prove the petitioner's alleged membership in the
Communist Party on April 28, 1950, with any direct admissions by
the petitioner of membership, by proof of his compliance with Party
membership requirements, or that his name appeared upon a membership roster, or that he carried a membership card.

The evidence relied upon by the Government was entirely
circumstantial. It consisted of testimony of conduct of the petitioner
from early 1946 through October 15, 1949, and of Matusow's testimony concerning alleged conversations between him and the petitioner
at a vacation ranch in July or August 1950, and concerning a lecture
delivered by the petitioner at the ranch. The Government also
attached probative weight to the action of the petitioner in executing
and filing an Affidavit of Non-Communist Union Officer on October
15, 1949, because of the event surrounding the filing of that affidavit . . . .

J. W. Ford was a member of the Communist Party of New Mexico
from 1946 to September 1950 and, from 1948, was a member of the
State Board and a Party security officer. He said that in 1948 he
became a paid undercover agent for the F. B. I. and reported regularly
upon Party activities and meetings. He testified that the petitioner
was also a Party and a State Board member, and he related in detail
occurrences at five closed Party meetings which he said the petitioner
attended.

Ford's duties as a Party security officer were to keep watch on
all Party members and to report "any particular defections from the
Communist philosophy or any peculiar actions, statements or associations, which would endanger the security of the Communist Party of
the state." If any defection reported by a security officer were considered important, the member "would be called in and would be
either severely reprimanded or criticized, or disciplined. If he refused
to accept such discipline he would either be suspended or expelled."
Ford testified that between August 1949 and September 1950, when
Ford ceased his activities with the New Mexico Party, there was no
disciplinary action taken against the petitioner and, to his knowledge,
the petitioner was not replaced in his position on the State Board of
the Communist Party.

The events leading up to the petitioner's execution and filing,
on October 15, 1949, of an Affidavit of Non-Communist Union
Officer were testified to by a former International Union representative, a Communist Party member during 1947 to 1949. He said that,
about 17 months before, in May or June 1948, a meeting of Party
members, holding offices in locals of the International Union of Mine,

Mill & Smelter Workers, was held in Denver to formulate plans for combatting a movement, led by non-Communists, to secede from the International Union. He said that the Party members, including the petitioner, were informed of Party policy not to sign affidavits required by § 9 (h) of the then recently enacted Taft-Hartley Act. There was no testimony that that policy changed before October 15, 1949.

The affidavit was filed shortly before a C. I. O. convention was scheduled to expel the Mine-Mill International and other unions from its membership. After filing the affidavit, the petitioner and other Local 890 officers published an article in "The Union Worker" charging that the contemplated C. I. O. action was part of a program of "right-wing unions . . . gobbling up chunks of militant unions . . . . Our International Union and its officers have swallowed a lot of guff, a lot of insults. But that is not the point . . . . Now that our Union has signed the phony affidavits we can defend ourselves . . . in case of raids. We do not fear attack from that quarter any longer."

Matusow was a member of the Communist Party of New York and was a paid undercover agent for the F. B. I. before he went to New Mexico. In July or August 1950, he spent a 10-day vacation on a ranch near Taos, New Mexico, with the petitioner and a number of other people. He testified to several conversations with the petitioner there. He said he twice told the petitioner of his desire to transfer his membership from the New York to the New Mexico Party, and that on both occasions the petitioner applauded the idea and told him, "we can use you out here, we need more active Party members." On one of these occasions, Matusow said, the petitioner asked him for suggestions for a lecture the petitioner was preparing for delivery at the ranch, particularly as to what the New York Communists were doing about the Stockholm Peace Appeal . . . .

Matusow testified that the petitioner delivered his planned lecture, informed his audience of the "do-day" idea, praised the Soviet Union's disarmament plan, referred to the United States as the aggressor in Korea, and urged all to read the "Daily People's World," identified by Matusow as the "West Coast Communist Party newspaper."

Matusow also testified that, in one of their conversations, the petitioner told him of a program he was developing with leaders of the Mexican Miners Union to negotiate simultaneous expiration dates of collective bargaining agreements, to further a joint action of Mexican and American workers to cut off production to slow down the Korean War effort. Matusow also testified that when he told the petitioner that he had joined the Taos Chapter of the Mexican-

American Association, the petitioner told him that this was proper Communist work because the Association was a key organization, controlled by the Party, for Communist activities in New Mexico and that he, the petitioner, was active in the Association in the Silver City area.

Ford and Matusow were subjected to vigorous cross-examination about their employment as informers for the F. B. I. Ford testified that in 1948 he went to the F. B. I. and offered his services, which were accepted. He thereafter regularly submitted reports to the F. B. I., "sometimes once a week, sometimes once a month, and at various other times; maybe three or four times a week, depending on the number of meetings . . . [he] attended and the distance between the meetings." He said that his reports were made immediately following each meeting, while the events were still fresh in his memory. He could not recall, however, which reports were oral and which in writing.

The petitioner moved "for an order directing an inspection of reports of the witness Ford to the Federal Bureau of Investigation dealing with each of the meetings which he said that he attended with the defendant Jencks in the years 1948 and 1949." The trial judge, without stating reasons, denied the motion.

Matusow, on his cross-examination, testified that he made both oral and written reports to the F. B. I. on events at the ranch, including his conversations with the petitioner. The trial judge, again without reasons, denied the motion to require "the prosecution to produce in Court the report submitted to the F. B. I. by this witness [Matusow] concerning matters which he saw or heard at the . . . Ranch during the period that he was a guest there . . ." on the sole ground that a preliminary foundation was not laid of inconsistency between the contents of the reports and the testimony of Matusow and Ford. The Court of Appeals rested the affirmance primarily upon that ground.

Both the trial court and the Court of Appeals erred. We hold that the petitioner was not required to lay a preliminary foundation of inconsistency, because a sufficient foundation was established by the testimony of Matusow and Ford that their reports were of the events and activities related in their testimony.

The reliance of the Court of Appeals upon Gordon v United States, 344 US 414, 97 L ed 447, 73 S Ct 369, is misplaced. It is true that one fact mentioned in this Court's opinion was that the witness admitted that the documents involved contradicted his testimony. However, to say that Gordon held a preliminary showing of inconsistency a prerequisite to an accused's right to the production for inspection of documents in the Government's possession, is to misinterpret the Court's opinion. The necessary essentials of a foundation, emphasized in that opinion, and present here, are that "[t]he demand was for production of . . . *specific documents and did not propose any broad or blind fishing expedition* among documents possessed by the Government on the chance that something impeaching might turn up. Nor was this a demand for statements taken from persons or informants not offered as witnesses." (Emphasis added.) 344 US at 419. We reaffirm and re-emphasize these essentials. "For production purposes, it need only appear that the evidence is relevant, competent, and outside of any exclusionary rule . . . ." 344 US at 420.

The crucial nature of the testimony of Ford and Matusow to the Government's case is conspicuously apparent. The impeachment of that testimony was singularly important to the petitioner. The value of the reports for impeachment purposes was highlighted by the admissions of both witnesses that they could not remember what reports were oral and what written, and by Matusow's admission: "I don't recall what I put in my reports two or three years ago, written or oral I don't know what they were."

Every experienced trial judge and trial lawyer knows the value for impeaching purposes of statements of the witness recording the events before time dulls treacherous memory. Flat contradiction between the witness's testimony and the version of the events given in his reports is not the only test of inconsistency. The omission from the reports of facts related at the trial, or a contrast in emphasis upon the same facts, even a different order of treatment, are also relevant to the cross-examining process of testing the credibility of a witness' trial testimony.

Requiring the accused first to show conflict between the reports and the testimony is actually to deny the accused evidence relevant and material to his defense. The occasion for determining a conflict cannot arise until after the witness has testified, and unless he admits conflict, as in Gordon, the accused is helpless to know or discover conflict without inspecting the reports. A requirement of a showing of conflict would be clearly incompatible with our standards for the administration of criminal justice in the federal courts and must therefore be rejected. For the interest of the United States in a criminal prosecution ". . . is not that it shall win a case, but that justice shall be done . . . ." Berger v United States, 295 US 78, 88, 79 L ed 1314, 1321, 55 S Ct 629.

We now hold that the petitioner was entitled to an order directing the Government to produce for inspection all reports of Matusow and Ford in its possession, written and, when orally made, as recorded by the F. B. I., touching the events and activities as to which they testified at the trial. We hold, further, that the petitioner is entitled to inspect the reports to decide whether to use them in his defense. Because only the defense is adequately equipped to determine the effective use for purpose of discrediting the Government's witness and thereby furthering the accused's defense, the defense must initially be entitled to see them to determine what use may be made of them. Justice requires no less.

The practice of producing government documents to the trial judge for his determination of relevancy and materiality without hearing the accused, is disapproved. Relevancy and materiality for the purposes of government to suppress documents, even when they will help determine controversies between third persons, we cannot agree that this should include their suppression in a criminal prosecution, founded upon those very dealings to which the documents relate, and whose criminality they will, or may, tend to exculpate. So far as they directly touch the criminal dealings, the prosecution necessarily ends any confidential character the documents may possess; it must be conducted in the open, and will lay bare their subject matter. The government must choose; either it must leave the transactions in the obscurity from which a trial will draw them, or it must expose them fully. Nor does it seem to us possible to draw any line between documents whose contents bears directly upon the criminal transactions, and those which may be only indirectly relevant. "Not only would such a distinction be extremely difficult to apply in practice, but the same reasons which forbid suppression in one case forbid it in the other, though not, perhaps, quite so imperatively . . . ."

We hold that the criminal action must be dismissed when the Government, on the ground of privilege, elects not to comply with an order to produce, for the accused's inspection and for admission in evidence, relevant statements or reports in its possession of government witnesses touching the subject matter of their testimony at the trial. Accord, Roviaro v United States, 353 US 53, 60, 61, 1 L ed 2d 639, 644, 645, 77 S Ct 623. The burden is the Government's, not to be shifted to the trial judge, to decide whether the public prejudice of allowing the crime to go unpunished is greater than that attendant upon the possible disclosure of state secrets and other confidential information in the Government's possession.

Reversed.

United States v. *Richard M. Nixon,* Supreme Court of the United States,
418 U.S. 683, 94 S.Ct. 3090 (1974)

Mr. Chief Justice BURGER delivered the opinion of the Court.

This litigation presents for review the denial of a motion, filed in the District Court on behalf of the President of the United States, in the case of United States v Mitchell (DC Crim No. 74-110), to quash a third-party subpoena duces tecum issued by the United States District Court for the District of Columbia, pursuant to Fed Rul Crim Proc 17(c). The subpoena directed the President to produce certain tape recordings and documents relating to his conversations with aides and advisers. The court rejected the President's claims of absolute executive privilege, of lack of jurisdiction, and of failure to satisfy the requirements of Rule 17(c). The President appealed to the Court of Appeals. We granted both the United States' petition for certiorari before judgment (No. 73-1766) and also the President's cross-petition for certiorari before judgment (No. 73-1834), because of the public importance of the issues presented and the need for their prompt resolution, 417 US 927 and 960, 41 L Ed 2d 231, and 1134, 94 S Ct 2637, and 3162 (1974).

On March 1, 1974, a grand jury of the United States District Court for the District of Columbia returned an indictment charging seven named individuals with various offenses, including conspiracy to defraud the United States and to obstruct justice. Although he was not designated as such in the indictment, the grand jury named the President, among others, as an unindicted coconspirator. On April 18, 1974, upon motion of the Special Prosecutor, infra, a subpoena duces tecum was issued pursuant to Rule 17(c) to the President by the United States District Court and made returnable on May 2, 1974. This subpoena required the production, in advance of the September 9 trial date, of certain tapes, memoranda, papers, transcripts, or other writings relating to certain precisely identified meetings between the President and others. The Special Prosecutor was able to fix the time, place, and persons present at these discussions because the White House daily logs and appointment records had been delivered to him. On April 30, the President publicly released edited transcripts of 43 conversations; portions of 20 conversations subject to subpoena in the present case were included. On May 1, 1974, the President's counsel filed a "special appearance" and a motion to quash the subpoena under Rule 17(c). This motion was accompanied by a formal claim of privilege. At a subsequent hearing, further motions to expunge the grand jury's action naming the President as an unindicted coconspirator and for protective orders against the disclosure of that information were filed or raised orally by counsel for the President.

On May 20, 1974, the District Court denied the motion to quash and the motions to expunge and for protective orders. 377 F Supp 1326. It further ordered "the President or any subordinate officer, official, or employee with custody or control of the documents or objects subpoenaed," id., at 1331, to deliver to the District Court, on or before May 31, 1974, the originals of all subpoenaed items, as well as an index and analysis of those items, together with tape copies of those portions of the subpoenaed recordings for which transcripts had been released to the public by the President on April 30. The District Court rejected jurisdictional challenges based on a contention that the dispute was nonjusticiable because it was between the Special Prosecutor and the Chief Executive and hence "intra-executive" in character; it also rejected the contention that the judiciary was without authority to review an assertion of executive privilege by the President. The court's rejection of the first challenge was based on the authority and powers vested in the Special Prosecutor by the regulation promulgated by the Attorney General; the court concluded that a justiciable controversy was presented. The second challenge was held to be foreclosed by the decision in Nixon v Sirica, 159 US App DC 58, 487 F2d 700 (1973).

The District Court held that the judiciary, not the President, was the final arbiter of a claim of executive privilege. The court concluded that, under the circumstances of this case, the presumptive privilege was overcome by the Special Prosecutor's prima facie "demonstration of need sufficiently compelling to warrant judicial examination in chambers . . . ." 377 F Supp, at 1330. The court held, finally, that the Special Prosecutor had satisfied the requirements of Rule 17(c). The District Court stayed its order pending appellate review on condition that review was sought before 4 p.m., May 24. The court further provided that matters filed under seal remain under seal when transmitted as part of the record.

On May 24, 1974, the President filed a timely notice of appeal from the District Court order, and the certified record from the District Court was docketed in the United States Court of Appeals for the District of Columbia Circuit. On the same day, the President also filed a petition for writ of mandamus in the Court of Appeals seeking review of the District Court order.

Later on May 24, the Special Prosecutor also filed, in this Court, a petition for a writ of certiorari before judgment. On May 31, the petition was granted with an expedited briefing schedule.

417 US 927, 41 L Ed 2d 231, 94 S Ct 2637. On June 6, the President
filed, under seal, a cross-petition for writ of certiorari before judgment. This cross-petition was granted June 15, 1974, 417 US 960,
41 L Ed 2d 1134, 94 S Ct 3162, and the case was set for argument
on July 8, 1974

THE CLAIM OF PRIVILEGE

A

Having determined that the requirements of Rule 17(c) were
satisfied, we turn to the claim that the subpoena should be quashed
because it demands "confidential conversations between a President
and his close advisors that it would be inconsistent with the public
interest to produce." App 48a. The first contention is a broad claim
that the separation of powers doctrine precludes judicial review of a
President's claim of privilege. The second contention is that if he
does not prevail on the claim of absolute privilege, the court should
hold as a matter of constitutional law that the privilege prevails over
the subpoena duces tecum.

In the performance of assigned constitutional duties each branch
of the Government must initially interpret the Constitution, and the
interpretation of its powers by any branch is due great respect from
the others. The President's counsel, as we have noted, reads the
Constitution as providing an absolute privilege of confidentiality for
all Presidential communications. Many decisions of this Court, however, have unequivocally reaffirmed the holding of Marbury v Madison,
1 Cranch 137, 2 L Ed 60 (1803), that "[i]t is emphatically the
province and duty of the judicial department to say what the law
is." Id., at 177, 2 L Ed 60.

No holding of the Court has defined the scope of judicial power
specifically relating to the enforcement of a subpoena for confidential
Presidential communications for use in a criminal prosecution, but
other exercises of power by the Executive Branch and the Legislative
Branch have been found invalid as in conflict with the Constitution.
Powell v McCormack, 395 US 486, 23 L Ed 2d 491, 89 S Ct 1944
(1969); Youngstown Sheet & Tube Co. v Sawyer, 343 US 579, 96 L
Ed 1153, 72 S Ct 863, 26 ALR2d 1378 (1952). In a series of cases,
the Court interpreted the explicit immunity conferred by express
provisions of the Constitution on Members of the House and Senate
by the Speech or Debate Clause, US Const Art I, § 6. Doe v McMillan,
412 US 306, 36 L Ed 2d 912, 93 S Ct 2018 (1973); Gravel v United
States, 408 US 606, 33 L Ed 2d 583, 92 S Ct 2614 (1972); United
States v Brewster, 408 US 501, 33 L Ed 2d 507, 92 S Ct 2531 (1972);

United States v Johnson, 383 US 169, 15 L Ed 2d 681, 86 S Ct 749 (1966). Since this Court has consistently exercised the power to construe and delineate claims arising under express powers, it must follow that the Court has authority to interpret claims with respect to powers alleged to derive from enumerated powers.

Our system of government "requires that federal courts on occasion interpret the Constitution in a manner at variance with the construction given the document by another branch." Powell v McCormack, supra, at 549, 23 L Ed 2d 491. And in Baker v Carr, 369 US, at 211, 7 L Ed 2d 663, the Court stated:

> Deciding whether a matter has in any measure been committed by the Constitution to another branch of government, or whether the action of that branch exceeds whatever authority has been committed, is itself a delicate exercise in constitutional interpretation, and is a responsibility of this Court as ultimate interpreter of the Constitution.

Notwithstanding the deference each branch must accord the others, the "judicial Power of the United States" vested in the federal courts by Art III, § 1, of the Constitution can no more be shared with the Executive Branch than the Chief Executive, for example, can share with the Judiciary the veto power, or the Congress share with the Judiciary the power to override a Presidential veto. Any other conclusion would be contrary to the basic concept of separation of powers and the checks and balances that flow from the scheme of a tripartite government. The Federalist, No. 47, p 313 (S. Mittell ed 1938). We therefore reaffirm that it is the province and duty of this Court "to say what the law is" with respect to the claim of privilege presented in this case. Marbury v Madison, supra, at 177, 2 L Ed 60.

B

In support of his claim of absolute privilege, the President's counsel urges two grounds, one of which is common to all governments and one of which is peculiar to our system of separation of powers. The first ground is the valid need for protection of communications between high Government officials and those who advise and assist them in the performance of their manifold duties; the importance of this confidentiality is too plain to require further discussion. Human experience teaches that those who expect public dissemination of their remarks may well temper candor with a concern for appearances and for their own interests to the detriment of the decisionmaking process. Whatever the nature of the privilege of confidentiality of Presidential communications in the exercise of Art II powers, the privilege can be said to derive from the supremacy of each branch within its own assigned area of constitutional duties. Certain powers and privileges flow from the nature of enumerated powers; the protection of the confidentiality of Presidential communications has similar constitutional underpinnings.

The second ground asserted by the President's counsel in support of the claim of absolute privilege rests on the doctrine of separation of powers. Here it is argued that the independence of the Executive Branch within its own sphere, Humphrey's Executor v United States, 295 US 602, 629-630, 79 L Ed 1611, 55 S Ct 869 (1935); Kilbourn v Thompson, 103 US 168, 190-191, 26 L Ed 377 (1881), insulates a President from a judicial subpoena in an ongoing criminal prosecution, and thereby protects confidential Presidential communications.

However, neither the doctrine of separation of powers, nor the need for confidentiality of high-level communications, without more, can sustain an absolute, unqualified Presidential privilege of immunity from judicial process under all circumstances. The President's need for complete candor and objectivity from advisers calls for great deference from the courts. However, when the privilege depends solely on the broad, undifferentiated claim of public interest in the confidentiality of such conversations, a confrontation with other values arises. Absent a claim of need to protect military, diplomatic, or sensitive national security secrets, we find it difficult to accept the argument that even the very important interest in confidentiality of Presidential communications is significantly diminished by production of such material for in camera inspection with all the protection that a district court will be obliged to provide.

The impediment that an absolute, unqualified privilege would place in the way of the primary constitutional duty of the Judicial Branch to do justice in criminal prosecutions would plainly conflict with the function of the courts under Art III. In designing the structure of our Government and dividing and allocating the sovereign power among three co-equal branches, the Framers of the Constitution sought to provide a comprehensive system, but the separate powers were not intended to operate with absolute independence.

> While the Constitution diffuses power the better to secure liberty, it also contemplates that practice will integrate the dispersed powers into a workable government. It enjoins upon its branches separateness but interdependence, autonomy but reciprocity. Youngstown Sheet & Tube Co. v Sawyer, 343 US, at 635, 96 L Ed 1153, 26 ALR2d 1378 (Jackson, J., concurring).

To read the Art II powers of the President as providing an absolute privilege as against a subpoena essential to enforcement of criminal statutes on no more than a generalized claim of the public interest in confidentiality of nonmilitary and nondiplomatic discussions would upset the constitutional balance of "a workable government" and gravely impair the role of the courts under Art III.

C

Since we conclude that the legitimate needs of the judicial process may outweigh Presidential privilege, it is necessary to resolve those competing interests in a manner that preserves the essential functions of each branch. The right and indeed the duty to resolve that question does not free the judiciary from according high respect to the representations made on behalf of the President. United States v Burr, 25 F Cas 187, 190, 191-192 (No. 14,694) (CC Va 1807).

The expectation of a President to the confidentiality of his conversations and correspondence, like the claim of confidentiality of judicial deliberations, for example, has all the values to which we accord deference for the privacy of all citizens and added to those values the necessity for protection of the public interest in candid, objective, and even blunt or harsh opinions in Presidential decision making. A President and those who assist him must be free to explore alternatives in the process of shaping policies and making decisions and to do so in a way many would be unwilling to express except privately. These are the considerations justifying a presumptive privilege for Presidential communications. The privilege is fundamental to the operation of government and inextricably rooted in the separation of powers under the Constitution. In Nixon v Sirica, 159 US App DC 58, 487 F2d 700 (1973), the Court of Appeals held that such Presidential communications are "presumptively privileged," id., at 75, 487 F2d, at 717, and this position is accepted by both parties in the present litigation. We agree with Mr. Chief Justice Marshall's observation, therefore, that "[i]n no case of this kind would a court be required to proceed against the President as against an ordinary individual." United States v Burr, 25 F Cas, at 192.

But this presumptive privilege must be considered in light of our historic commitment to the rule of law. This is nowhere more profoundly manifest than in our view that "the twofold aim [of criminal justice] is that guilt shall not escape or innocence suffer." Berger v United States, 295 US, at 88, 79 L Ed 1314. We have elected to employ an adversary system of criminal justice in which the parties contest all issues before a court of law. The need to develop all relevant facts in the adversary system is both fundamental and comprehensive. The ends of criminal justice would be defeated if judgments were to be founded on a partial or speculative presentation of the facts. The very integrity of the judicial system and public confidence in the system depend on full disclosure of all the facts, within the framework of the rules of evidence. To ensure that justice is done, it is imperative to the function of courts that compulsory process be available for the production of evidence needed either by the prosecution or by the defense.

Only recently the Court restated the ancient proposition of law, albeit in the context of a grand jury inquiry rather than a trial,

that "the public . . . has a right to every man's evidence," except for those persons protected by a constitutional, common-law, or statutory privilege, United States v Bryan, 339 US, [323, 331] (94 L Ed 884, 70 S Ct 724) [(1950)]; Blackmer v United States, 284 US 421, 438, [76 L Ed 375, 52 S Ct 252] (1932) . . . Branzburg v Hayes, 408 US 665, 688, [33 L Ed 2d 626, 92 S Ct 2646] (1972).

The privileges referred to by the Court are designed to protect weighty and legitimate competing interests. Thus, the Fifth Amendment to the Constitution provides that no man "shall be compelled in any criminal case to be a witness against himself." And, generally, an attorney or a priest may not be required to disclose what has been revealed in professional confidence. These and other interests are recognized in law by privileges against forced disclosure, established in the Constitution, by statute, or at common law. Whatever their origins, these exceptions to the demand for every man's evidence are not lightly created nor expansively construed, for they are in derogation of the search for truth.

In this case the President challenges a subpoena served on him as a third party requiring the production of materials for use in a criminal prosecution; he does so on the claim that he has a privilege against disclosure of confidential communications. He does not place his claim of privilege on the ground they are military or diplomatic secrets. As to these areas of Art II duties the courts have traditionally shown the utmost deference to Presidential responsibilities. In C. & S. Air Lines v Waterman S. S. Corp. 333 US 103, 111, 92 L Ed 568, 68 S Ct 431 (1948), dealing with Presidential authority involving foreign policy considerations, the Court said:

The President, both as Commander-in-Chief and as the Nation's organ for foreign affairs, has available intelligence services whose reports are not and ought not to be published to the world. It would be intolerable that courts, without the relevant information, should review and perhaps nullify actions of the Executive taken on information properly held secret.

In United States v Reynolds, 345 US 1, 97 L Ed 727, 73 S Ct 528, 32 ALR 2d 382 (1953), dealing with a claimant's demand for evidence in a damage case against the Government the Court said:

> It may be possible to satisfy the court, from all the circumstances of the case, that there is a reasonable danger that compulsion of the evidence will expose military matters which, in the interest of national security, should not be divulged. When this is the case, the occasion for the privilege is appropriate, and the court should not jeopardize the security which the privilege is meant to protect by insisting upon an examination of the evidence, even by the judge alone, in chambers. Id., at 10, 97 L Ed 727.

No case of the Court, however, has extended this high degree of deference to a President's generalized interest in confidentiality. Nowhere in the Constitution, as we have noted earlier, is there any explicit reference to a privilege of confidentiality, yet to the extent this interest relates to the effective discharge of a President's powers, it is constitutionally based.

The right to the production of all evidence at a criminal trial similarly has constitutional dimensions. The Sixth Amendment explicitly confers upon every defendant in a criminal trial the right "to be confronted with the witnesses against him" and "to have compulsory process for obtaining witnesses in his favor." Moreover, the Fifth Amendment also guarantees that no person shall be deprived of liberty without due process of law. It is the manifest duty of the courts to vindicate those guarantees, and to accomplish that it is essential that all relevant and admissible evidence be produced.

In this case we must weigh the importance of the general privilege of confidentiality of Presidential communications in performance of his responsibilities against the inroads of such a privilege on the fair administration of criminal justice. The interest in preserving confidentiality is weighty indeed and entitled to great respect. However, we cannot conclude that advisers will be moved to temper the candor of their remarks by the infrequent occasions of disclosure because of the possibility that such conversations will be called for in the context of a criminal prosecution.

On the other hand, the allowance of the privilege to withhold evidence that is demonstrably relevant in a criminal trial would cut deeply into the guarantee of due process of law and gravely impair the basic function of the courts. A President's acknowledged need for confidentiality in the communications of his office is general in nature, whereas the constitutional need for production of relevant evidence in a criminal proceeding is specific and central to the fair adjudication of a particular criminal case in the administration of justice. Without access to specific facts a criminal prosecution may be totally frustrated. The President's broad interest in confidentiality of communications will not be vitiated by disclosure of a limited number of conversations preliminarily shown to have some bearing on the pending criminal cases.

We conclude that when the ground for asserting privilege as to subpoenaed materials sought for use in a criminal trial is based only on the generalized interest in confidentiality, it cannot prevail over the fundamental demands of due process of law in the fair administration of criminal justice. The generalized assertion of privilege must yield to the demonstrated, specific need for evidence in a pending criminal trial.

Chapter 8: Privileged Communications

People of the State of New York v. Francis R. Belge,
Onondaga County Court, 372 N.Y.S. 2d 798 (1975)

ORMAND N. GALE, Judge.

In the summer of 1973 Robert F. Garrow, Jr. stood charged in Hamilton County with the crime of MURDER. The Defendant was assigned two attorneys, Frank M. Armani and Francis R. Belge. A defense of insanity had been interposed by counsel for Mr. Garrow. During the course of the discussions between Garrow and his two counsel, three other murders were admitted by Garrow, one being in Onondaga County. On or about September of 1973 Mr. Belge conducted his own investigation based upon what his client had told him and with the assistance of a friend the location of the body of Alicia Hauck was found in Oakwood Cemetery in Syracuse. Mr. Belge personally inspected the body and was satisfied, presumably, that this was the Alicia Hauck that his client had told him that he murdered.

This discovery was not disclosed to the authorities, but became public during the trial of Mr. Garrow in June of 1974, when to affirmatively establish the defense of insanity, these three other murders were brought before the jury by the defense in the Hamilton County trial. Public indignation reached the fever pitch; statements were made by the District Attorney of Onondaga County relative to the situation and he caused the Grand Jury of Onondaga County, then sitting, to conduct a thorough investigation. As a result of this investigation Frank Armani was No Billed by the Grand Jury but Indictment No. 75-55 was returned as against Francis R. Belge, Esq., accusing him of having violated § 4200(1) of the Public Health Law, which, in essence, requires that a decent burial be accorded the dead, and § 4143 of the Public Health Law, which, in essence, requires anyone knowing of the death of a person without medical attendance, to report the same to the proper authorities. Defense counsel moves for a dismissal of the Indictment on the grounds that a confidential, privileged communication existed between him and Mr. Garrow, which should excuse the attorney from making full disclosure to the authorities.

The National Association of Criminal Defense Lawyers, as Amicus Curiae, citing *Times Publishing Co.* v. *Williams,* 222 So.2d 470, 475 (Fla.App.1970) succinctly state the issue in the following language:

> If this indictment stands,
> The attorney-client privilege will be effectively destroyed. No defendant will be able to freely discuss the facts of his case with his attorney. No attorney will be able to listen to those facts without being faced with the Hobson's choice of violating the law or violating his professional code of Ethics.

Initially in England the practice of law was not recognized as a profession, and certainly some people are skeptics today. However, the practice of learned and capable men appearing before the Court on behalf of a friend or an acquaintance became more and more demanding. Consequently, the King granted a privilege to certain of these men to engage in such practice. There had to be rules governing their duties. These came to be known as "Canons." The King has, in this country, been substituted by a democracy, but the "Canons" are with us today, having been honed and refined over the years to meet the changes of time . . . .

Our system of criminal justice is an adversary system and the interests of the state are not absolute, or even paramount.

> The dignity of the individual is respected to the point that even when the citizen is known by the state to have committed a heinous offense, the individual is nevertheless accorded such rights as counsel, trial by jury, due process, and the privilege against self incrimination.

A trial is in part a search for truth, but it is only partly a search for truth. The mantle of innocence is flung over the defendant to such an extent that he is safeguarded by rules of evidence which frequently keep out absolute truth, much to the chagrin of juries. Nevertheless, this has been a part of our system since our laws were taken from the laws of England and over these many years has been found to best protect a balance between the rights of the individual and the rights of society.

The concept of the right to counsel has again been with us for a long time, but since the decision of *Gideon* v. *Wainwright*, 372 U.S. 335, 83 S.Ct. 792, 9 L.Ed.2d 799, it has been extended more and more so that at the present time a defendant is entitled to have counsel at a parole hearing or a probation violation hearing.

The effectiveness of counsel is only as great as the confidentiality of its client-attorney relationship. If the lawyer cannot get all the facts about the case, he can only give his client half of a defense. This, of necessity, involves the client telling his attorney everything remotely connected with the crime.

Apparently, in the instant case, after analyzing all the evidence, and after hearing of the bizarre episodes in the life of their client, they decided that the only possibility of salvation was in a defense of insanity. For the client to disclose not only everything about this particular crime but also everything about other crimes which might have a bearing upon his defense, requires the strictest confidence in, and on the part of, the attorney.

When the facts of the other homicides became public, as a result of the defendant's testimony to substantiate his claim of insanity, "Members of the public were shocked at the apparent callousness of these lawyers, whose conduct was seen as typifying the unhealthy lack of concern of most lawyers with the public interest and with simple decency." A hue and cry went up from the press and other news media suggesting that the attorneys should be found guilty of such crimes as obstruction of justice or becoming an accomplice after the fact. From a layman's standpoint, this certainly was a logical conclusion. However, the constitution of the United States of America attempts to preserve the dignity of the individual and to do that guarantees him the services of an attorney who will bring to the bar and to the bench every conceivable protection to the inroads of the state against such rights as are vested in the constitution for one accused of crime. Among those substantial constitutional rights is that a defendant does not have to incriminate himself. His attorneys were bound to uphold that concept and maintain what has been called a sacred trust of confidentiality . . . .

In the recent and landmark case of *United States* v. *Nixon*, 418 U.S. 683, at page 713, 94 S.Ct. 3090, at page 3110, 41 L.Ed. 1039, at page 1061 the Court stated:

The constitutional need for production of relevant evidence in a criminal proceeding is specific and neutral to the fair adjudication of a particular criminal case in the administration of justice. Without access to specific facts a criminal prosecution may be totally frustrated.

In the case at bar we must weigh the importance of the general privilege of confidentiality in the performance of the defendant's duties as an attorney, against the inroads of such a privilege, on the fair administration of criminal justice as well as the heart tearing that went on in the victim's family by reason of their uncertainty as to the whereabouts of Alicia Hauck. In this type situation the Court must balance the rights of the individual against the rights of society as a whole. There is no question but Attorney Belge's failure to bring to the attention of the authorities the whereabouts of Alicia Hauck when he first verified it, prevented bringing Garrow to the immediate bar of justice for this particular murder. This was in a sense, obstruction of justice. This duty, I am sure, loomed large in the mind of Attorney Belge. However, against this was the Fifth Amendment right of his client, Garrow, not to incriminate himself. If the Grand Jury had returned an indictment charging Mr. Belge with obstruction of justice under a proper statute, the work of this Court would have been much more difficult than it is.

There must always be a conflict between the obstruction of the administration of criminal justice and the preservation of the right against self-incrimination which permeates the mind of the attorney as the alter ego of his client. But that is not the situation before this Court. We have the Fifth Amendment right, derived from the constitution, on the one hand, as against the trivia of a pseudo-criminal statute on the other, which has seldom been brought into play. Clearly the latter is completely out of focus when placed alongside the client-attorney privilege. An examination of the Grand Jury testimony sheds little light on their reasoning. The testimony of Mr. Armani added nothing new to the facts as already presented to the Grand Jury. He and Mr. Belge were co-counsel. Both were answerable to the Canons of professional ethics. The Grand Jury chose to indict one and not the other. It appears as if that body were grasping at straws.

It is the decision of this Court that Francis R. Belge conducted himself as an officer of the Court with all the zeal at his command to protect the constitutional rights of his client. Both on the grounds of a privileged communication and in the interests of justice the Indictment is dismissed.

People of the State of New York v. *Gene Squitieri,*
Supreme Court of N.Y., Appellate Division, 375 N.Y.S. 2d 124 (1975)

CAPOZZOLI, Justice:

This is an appeal by the defendant from a judgment of conviction upon his plea of guilty to the crime of an attempt to receive a bribe. Although a plea of guilty was entered, the question presented on this appeal was preserved and is before us for review.

It is the contention of the defendant that the prosecution violated his Fifth and Sixth Amendment rights of access to and advice from counsel, as provided in the Federal Constitution. He bases this on the claim that the prosecuting authorities deliberately arranged for one, Richard Curro, a correction officer under arrest, to surreptitiously record a conference with an attorney, at the attorney's office, which ostensibly was being held for the purpose of securing advice and general counselling from the lawyer for the defendant and Curro who were both involved in the same crime . . . .

Of course, we recognize the importance to the prosecution of the incriminating statements made by the defendant, Squitieri, during this conference, for, without them, there would have been no corroboration of the testimony of Curro, the confessed accomplice. Nevertheless, it does not justify the conduct of the authorities under the circumstances. Their behavior, as disclosed by the evidence, was not only illegal and contrary to precedent, but also a clear deprivation of the defendant's constitutional rights to counsel, as provided in the Federal Constitution.

In *Lanza* v. *N. Y. State Joint Leg. Comm.*, 5 Misc.2d 324, 164 N.Y.S.2d 531, rev'd 3 A.D.2d 531, at p. 533, 162 N.Y.S.2d 467, at p. 470, this Court said:

> Of course, communication between an attorney and his client, especially where the client is a defendant in a criminal matter, involves much more than a mere privilege. Also involved is the right to counsel, which carries with it the corollary right to communicate with counsel in secrecy and confidence, and without intrusion, especially by public officials. In this case that constitutional right was violated, and, indeed, violated in an atrocious and inexcusable manner.

All in all, the conduct of the authorities in this case was contrary to law and cannot be condoned. The language of Presiding Justice Stevens, sitting at Special Term, in *Lanza* v. *N. Y. State Joint Leg. Comm.*, 5 Misc.2d 324, at p. 328, 164 N.Y.S.2d 531, at p. 534, is particularly applicable.

> The use of such a subterfuge is unworthy of the sovereign.

Therefore, the judgment should be reversed, on the law and on the facts, the motion to suppress granted and the case remanded for further proceedings.

Chapter 9: Questions, Answers, Impeachment, and Cross-Examination of Witnesses

State of Utah v. *Fay Ward Jr.*, Supreme Court of Utah, 347 P. 2d 865 (1959)

CROCKETT, Chief Justice.

Fay Ward, Jr. appeals from a conviction by a jury of the crime of rape. He charges that the evidence is not sufficient to sustain the verdict and that prejudicial errors were committed in rulings on evidence . . . .

One assignment of error relating to the admission of evidence also relates to the question of identification: the prosecutor was permitted to ask what the defense characterizes as a leading question. In examining the prosecutrix he elicited from her a description of her assailant, but she failed to mention his eyes as she had done at the preliminary hearing, whereupon the following occurred:

"Mr. Newey: Did you notice anything about his eyes at this particular time?

"Mr. Bingham: Your Honor, I'll object. I believe that it's leading.

"The Court: * * * I'm going to permit the answer * * *

"A. Yes, I do remember his eyes. They were kind of—I don't really know how to described it—just starey eyed. They would kind of glare at you."

We do not think this question should be characterized as leading. The vice in a leading question is that it in effect puts words in the witness's mouth so the testimony is really that of the questioner and not the witness. This usually occurs in so framing a question that it assumes a fact to be true, or in reciting a fact and merely seeking affirmation from the witness, or in so phrasing the question as to suggest the desired answer. However, to simply direct the attention of the witness to a subject or some phase thereof, as was done here, does not render the question objectionable as leading. It is not only proper, but desirable to do so in order to confine the testimony to matters material to the issues and avoid the difficulty of turning a witness loose to ramble in the hope that he will touch upon the pertinent matter.

This further may be said: even if it should be assumed that the question under discussion was leading or suggestive of the desired answer, as the defendant contends, it is well settled that the trial judge should be allowed considerable latitude of discretion as to the extent counsel may lead or suggest to a witness. Generally, due to his advantaged position, he can and will sense whether the testimony being elicited is that of the witness or is merely an echo of counsel's ideas. Permitting such a question would not be prejudicial error upon which to predicate a reversal unless it appeared that the court had abused its discretion in allowing examination from which it could reasonably be assumed that the question provided the answer on a material issue adverse to the defendant's interest.

Judgment affirmed.

Martha P. Martyn v. *Robert Donlin,* Supreme Court of Connecticut, 198 A. 2d 700 (1964)

This was an action for the recovery of damages for the wrongful death of the plaintiff's decedent, who was shot, on April 20, 1958, just after midnight, by the defendant Robert Donlin, a regular police officer of the defendant city of Hartford, in the course of an attempt to effect the decedent's arrest . . . .

We turn first to certain rulings on evidence. The plaintiff called Donlin as a witness. Since Donlin was an adverse party, the plaintiff, under § 52-178 of the General Statutes, was entitled to a statutory examination which would permit the use of leading questions "which, * * [prior to the statute], had ordinarily been permitted only in the case of a witness whom the court had found to be hostile or to have so testified as to have worked a surprise or deceit on the examining party." Mendez v. Dorman, 151 Conn. 193, 197, 195 A.2d 561, 564. There is no claim that the plaintiff was not accorded this statutory examination. Thereafter, counsel for Donlin proceeded to cross-examine him, and in the course of the cross-examination counsel was permitted, over the plaintiff's objection, to ask leading questions. The plaintiff claims this should not have been allowed since Donlin was not hostile to himself. Since our statute removes the requirement of a finding of hostility in fact as a condition precedent to the allowance of leading questions on the statutory (direct) examination to an adverse party, the claim that such a finding is nonetheless a prerequisite to the right to ask leading questions on cross-examination by the adverse party's own counsel would be wholly unfair and is obviously without merit . . . .

Cases on this point are collected in an annotation in 38 A.L.R.2d 952. There is nothing in the wording of our statute which, except for the elimination of the question of hostility in fact, is even suggestive of any legislative intent either to abridge or to enlarge the usual scope and manner of cross-examination even though it is conducted by counsel for an adverse party who had been called as a witness under the statute. See Bushnell v. Bushnell, 103 Conn. 583, 596, 131 A. 432, 44 A.L.R. 785; Mendez v. Dorman, supra. There was no error in permitting the use of leading questions in Donlin's cross-examination by his own counsel.

Chapter 10: Opinion Evidence

People of the State of Illinois v. *George H. Miller,* Appellate Court of Illinois, 243 N. E. 2d 277 (1968)

BURKE, Presiding Justice.

George H. Miller was convicted of the offense of driving a motor vehicle while under the influence of intoxicating liquor and fined $100 and $5.00 costs. As a result, his driver's license was revoked for one year in accordance with statutory provisions. He appeals.

The sole evidence presented by the People was the testimony of arresting Officer Max Steel. He testified that on the evening of March 11, 1967, he was in a squad car driving north along Kimball Avenue when he approached the intersection of that street with Armitage Avenue in Chicago. As he did so he noticed the automobile being driven by George Miller, which was stopped in the right-hand traffic lane waiting for the stop light to change. The officer also observed that there was another automobile stopped for the light directly to the left of that occupied by Miller. When the light changed to green Miller immediately accelerated his automobile and while still in the intersection swerved over to the left cutting off the automobile which was proceeding north to the left of and slightly behind the Miller car. Since this action constituted a traffic violation, Officer Steel pursued Miller's car and brought it to a halt one and one-half to two blocks north of the intersection.

Officer Steel alighted and went to Miller's automobile but as he began to engage the defendant in conversation he noted the odor of alcohol on the defendant's breath. He asked the defendant to get out of his car and noticed that he swayed as he did so and that he stood leaning against or holding onto the car. The witness stated that defendant's eyes were bloodshot, that his face was flushed and that he spoke in a manner described as "mush mouthed." The witness testified defendant swayed as he walked and turned and had difficulty in maintaining his balance. On the basis of his experience of 12 years as a police officer, the witness concluded that the defendant was under

the influence of alcohol and unfit to drive his automobile. He, therefore, transported the defendant to a district police station where the
defendant refused to answer questions or take any tests without the
assistance of counsel. Officer Steel testified on cross-examination that
he did not know why defendant held onto or leaned against his car
during their conversation at the scene and that at no time did the
defendant require any assistance or support. He further stated that
defendant never tripped, slipped, staggered, stumbled or fell, and
that he walked up the stairs at the police station in a proper manner.

The defendant testified that he arrived at work on the day in
question at approximately 10:30 or 11:00 A.M. and worked until
approximately 4:45 P.M.; that he went to lunch about 3:00 P.M. and
with his lunch consumed two bottles of beer; and that he had nothing
else to drink on this day. He further testifed that he usually has a
drink with his lunch. He stated that upon leaving work he went to a
friend's house to leave a package. He stayed at his friend's house for
half an hour and was proceeding on his way when he was arrested. He
testified that the alcohol had no "effect" on him, and that on this day
he was walking and talking in his normal manner. He testified that he
had no physical defects that would cause him to sway when he
walked.

Following the finding of guilty (on a motion for a new trial) the
court heard the testimony of two defense witnesses, Phillip F. George
and Raymond Wilson. Mr. George testified he had worked with the
defendant from 11:00 A.M. to approximately 5:00 P.M.; that they
had lunch together during which each consumed two bottles of beer.
It was Mr. George's opinion that the defendant was not under the
influence of alcohol on the day in question. Mr. Raymond Wilson
testified that the defendant delivered a package to his home about
5:30 P.M. and remained about 15 minutes. The witness stated that
he had occasion to talk to the defendant and that defendant did not
sway when he walked. In the witness' opinion the defendant was not
under the influence of alcohol.

The defendant, in arguing that the People did not prove him
guilty beyond a reasonable doubt says that he was arrested for a
minor traffic violation; that there was no testimony of erratic driving;
that there had been no accident; that there were no unusual actions
on his part; that he cooperated with the police and that he availed
himself of his constitutional right to refuse to answer any questions or
to take any tests. He further states that he gave account of his whereabouts during the hours preceding his arrest, including when, where
and how much alcohol he had consumed and that he had done

everything that a normal, rational person would have done in a similar situation. Defendant also calls attention to the testimony of two witnesses introduced on the hearing of his motion for a new trial and urges that they substantiate his testimony that he was not under the influence of intoxicating liquor while driving his car on that date. Defendant cites People v. Mundorf, 85 Ill.App.2d 244, 229 N.E.2d 313, for the proposition that while the trial judge is the sole judge of credibility of witnesses, if the evidence is so unsatisfactory as to raise a reasonable doubt of guilt, the Appellate Court will reverse.

In our opinion the evidence of Officer Steel was sufficient to support the conviction. The question presented to the trial judge was one of credibility of the witnesses. The determination of the trial court will not be lightly disturbed by a court of review. Whether the evidence is sufficient to show that the defendant was driving a motor vehicle while under the influence of intoxicating liquor is for the determination of the trier of fact who has the advantage of seeing and hearing the witnesses and observing their demeanor while on the witness stand. People v. Buzinski, 64 Ill.App.2d 194, 212 N.E.2d 270; People v. Raddle, 39 Ill.App.2d 265, 188 N.E.2d 101; People v. Krueger, Ill.App., 241 N.E.2d 707 (1st Dist., 9/23/68).

The testimony of the police officer that he observed the defendant's eyes to be bloodshot, his color flushed, his speech slurred, his walk unbalanced, when coupled with the officer's opinion that the defendant was under the influence of intoxicants at the time, supports the conviction. There is nothing about the testimony of the officer which would warrant the court in substituting its judgment for that of the trial judge. Officer Steel stopped the defendant for a routine traffic violation, noticed the odor of alcohol on defendant's breath, then went further in his investigation, which revealed that the defendant's speech was "mush mouthed," that his eyes were bloodshot, that his face was flushed and that he swayed when he walked or attempted to turn.

The introduction of the additional testimony was permitted by the trial court over the objection of the State's Attorney. There was no showing that these two witnesses could not have been produced at the trial. The trial judge decided to hear the testimony of the two witnesses and after listening to this testimony, the trial judge denied the motion for a new trial. The evidence presented by defendant was not newly discovered since the persons who gave it and what they would say was known to him before the trial began. Nevertheless the trial judge gave the defendant the benefit of the testimony of the two witnesses. It cannot be said that in doing this he committed error.

We find that there is sufficient evidence in the record to establish the guilt of the defendant beyond a reasonable doubt; therefore, the judgment is affirmed.

Judgment affirmed.

Chapter 11: Hearsay Evidence

Leon Chambers v. State of Mississippi, Supreme Court of the United States, 410 U.S. 284, 93 S. Ct. 1038 (1973)

Mr. Justice POWELL delivered the opinion of the Court.

Petitioner, Leon Chambers, was tried by a jury in a Mississippi trial court and convicted of murdering a policeman. The jury assessed punishment at life imprisonment, and the Mississippi Supreme Court affirmed, one justice dissenting. 252 So 2d 217 (1971) . . . .

The events that led to petitioner's prosecution for murder occurred in the small town of Woodville in southern Mississippi. On Saturday evening, June 14, 1969, two Woodville policemen, James Forman and Aaron "Sonny" Liberty, entered a local bar and pool hall to execute a warrant for the arrest of a youth named C. C. Jackson. Jackson resisted and a hostile crowd of some 50 or 60 persons gathered. The officers' first attempt to handcuff Jackson was frustrated when 20 or 25 men in the crowd intervened and wrestled him free. Forman then radioed for assistance and Liberty removed his riot gun, a 12-gauge sawed-off shotgun, from the car. Three deputy sheriffs arrived shortly thereafter and the officers again attempted to make their arrest. Once more, the officers were attacked by the onlookers and during the commotion five or six pistol shots were fired. Forman was looking in a different direction when the shooting began, but immediately saw that Liberty had been shot several times in the back. Before Liberty died, he turned around and fired both barrels of his riot gun into an alley in the area from which the shots appeared to have come. The first shot was wild and high and scattered the crowd standing at the face of the alley. Liberty appeared, however, to take more deliberate aim before the second shot and hit one of the men in the crowd in the back of the head and neck as he ran down the alley. That man was Leon Chambers.

Officer Forman could not see from his vantage point who shot Liberty or whether Liberty's shots hit anyone. One of the deputy sheriffs testified at trial that he was standing several feet from Liberty and that he saw Chambers shoot him. Another deputy sheriff stated that, although he could not see whether Chambers had a gun in his hand, he did see Chambers "break his arm down" shortly before the shots were fired. The officers who saw Chambers fall testified that they thought he was dead but they made no effort at that time either to examine him or to search for the murder weapon.

The story of Leon Chambers is intertwined with the story of another man, Gable McDonald. McDonald, a lifelong resident of Woodville, was in the crowd on the evening of Liberty's death. Sometime shortly after that day, he left his wife in Woodville and moved to Louisiana and found a job at a sugar mill. In November of that same year, he returned to Woodville when his wife informed him that an acquaintance of his, known as Reverend Stokes, wanted to see him. Stokes owned a gas station in Natchez, Mississippi, several miles north of Woodville, and upon his return McDonald went to see him. After talking to Stokes, McDonald agreed to make a statement to Chambers' attorneys, who maintained offices in Natchez. Two days later, he appeared at the attorneys' offices and gave a sworn confession that he shot Officer Liberty. He also stated that he had already told a friend of his, James Williams, that he shot Liberty. He said that he used his own pistol, a nine-shot .22-caliber revolver, which he had discarded shortly after the shooting. In response to questions from Chambers' attorneys, McDonald affirmed that his confession was voluntary and that no one had compelled him to come to them. Once the confession had been transcribed, signed, and witnessed, McDonald was turned over to the local police authorities and was placed in jail.

One month later, at a preliminary hearing, McDonald repudiated his prior sworn confession. He testified that Stokes had persuaded him to confess that he shot Liberty. He claimed that Stokes had promised that he would not go to jail and that he would share in the proceeds of a lawsuit that Chambers would bring against the town of Woodville . . . .

The local justice of the peace accepted McDonald's repudiation and released him from custody. The local authorities undertook no further investigation of his possible involvement.

Chambers' case came on for trial in October of the next year. At trial, he endeavored to develop two grounds of defense . . . . Chambers attempted to prove that McDonald had admitted responsibility for the murder on four separate occasions, once when he gave the sworn statement to Chambers' counsel and three other times prior to that occasion in private conversations with friends.

In large measure, he was thwarted in his attempt to present this portion of his defense by the strict application of certain Mississippi rules of evidence . . . . The trial court refused to allow him to introduce the testimony of Hardin, Turner, and Carter. Each would have testified to the statements purportedly made by McDonald, on three separate occasions shortly after the crime, naming himself as the murderer. The State Supreme Court approved the exclusion of this evidence on the ground that it was hearsay.

The hearsay rule, which has long been recognized and respected by virtually every State, is based on experience and grounded in the notion that untrustworthy evidence should not be presented to the triers of fact. Out-of-court statements are traditionally excluded because they lack the conventional indicia of reliability: they are ''sually not made under oath or other circumstances that impress the .peaker with the solemnity of his statements; the declarant's word is not subject to cross-examination; and he is not available in order that his demeanor and credibility may be assessed by the jury. California v Green, 399 US 149, 158, 26 L Ed 2d 489, 90 S Ct 1930 (1970). A number of exceptions have developed over the years to allow admission of hearsay statements made under circumstances that tend to assure reliability and thereby compensate for the absence of the oath and opportunity for cross-examination. Among the most prevalent of these exceptions is the one applicable to declarations against interest—an exception founded on the assumption that a person is unlikely to fabricate a statement against his own interest at the time it is made. Mississippi recognizes this exception but applies it only to declarations against pecuniary interest. It recognizes no such exception for declarations, like McDonald's in this case, that are against the penal interest of the declarant. Brown v State, 99 Miss 719, 55 So 961 (1911).

This materialistic limitation on the declaration-against-interest hearsay exception appears to be accepted by most States in their criminal trial processes, although a number of States have discarded it. Declarations against penal interest have also been excluded in federal courts under the authority of Donnelly v United States, 228 US 243, 272-273, 57 L Ed 820, 33 S Ct 449 (1913), although exclusion would not be required under the newly proposed Federal Rules of Evidence. Exclusion, where the limitation prevails, is usually premised on the view that admission would lead to the frequent presentation of perjured testimony to the jury. It is believed that confessions of criminal activity are often motivated by extraneous considerations and, therefore, are not as inherently reliable as statements against pecuniary or proprietary interest. While that rationale has been the subject of considerable scholarly criticism, we need not decide in this case whether, under other circumstances, it might serve some valid state purpose by excluding untrustworthy testimony.

The hearsay statements involved in this case were originally made and subsequently offered at trial under circumstances that provided considerable assurance of their reliability. First, each of McDonald's confessions was made spontaneously to a close acquaintance shortly after the murder had occurred. Second, each one was corroborated by some other evidence in the case—McDonald's sworn confession, the testimony of an eyewitness to the shooting, the testimony that McDonald was seen with a gun immediately after the shooting, and proof of his prior ownership of a .22-caliber revolver and subsequent purchase of a new weapon. The sheer number of independent confessions provided additional corroboration for each. Third, whatever may be the parameters of the penal-interest rationale, each confession here was in a very real sense self-incriminatory and unquestionably against interest. See United States v Harris, 403 US 573, 584, 29 L Ed 2d 723, 91 S Ct 2075 (1971); Dutton v Evans, 400 US, at 89, 27 L Ed 2d 213. McDonald stood to benefit nothing by disclosing his role in the shooting to any of his three friends and he must have been aware of the possibility that disclosure would lead to criminal prosecution. Indeed, after telling Turner of his involvement, he subsequently urged Turner not to "mess him up." Finally, if there was any question about the truthfulness of the extra-judicial statements, McDonald was present in the courtroom and had been under oath. He could have been cross-examined by the State, and his demeanor and responses weighed by the jury. See California v Green, 399 US 149, 26 L Ed 2d 489, 90 S Ct 1930 (1970). The availability of McDonald significantly distinguishes this case from the prior Mississippi precedent, Brown v State, supra, and from the Donnelly-type situation, since in both cases the declarant was unavailable at the time of trial.

Few rights are more fundamental than that of an accused to present witnesses in his own defense. E. g., Webb v Texas, 409 US 95, 34. In the exercise of this right, the accused, as is required of the State, must comply with established rules of procedure and evidence designed to assure both fairness and reliability in the ascertainment of guilt and innocence. Although perhaps no rule of evidence has been more respected or more frequently applied in jury trials than that applicable to the exclusion of hearsay, exceptions tailored to allow the introduction of evidence which in fact is likely to be trustworthy have long existed. The testimony rejected by the trial court here bore persuasive assurances of trustworthiness and thus was well within the basic rationale of the exception for declarations against interest. That testimony also was critical to Chambers' defense. In these circumstances, where constitutional rights directly affecting the ascertainment of guilt are implicated, the hearsay rule may not be applied mechanistically to defeat the ends of justice.

We conclude that the exclusion of this critical evidence . . . denied him a trial in accord with traditional and fundamental standards of due process. In reaching this judgment, we establish no new principles of constitutional law. Nor does our holding signal any diminution in the respect traditionally accorded to the States in the establishment and implementation of their own criminal trial rules and procedures. Rather, we hold quite simply that under the facts and circumstances of this case the rulings of the trial court deprived Chambers of a fair trial.

The judgment is reversed and the case is remanded to the Supreme Court of Mississippi for further proceedings not inconsistent with this opinion.

It is so ordered.

Waller v. State of Georgia, Georgia Court of Appeals, 56 S.E. 2d 491 (1949)

GARDNER, Judge.

The defendant was found guilty in the City Court of Decatur upon two counts in an accusation. The first count of the accusation charged the defendant with operating a motor vehicle at a greater speed than 55 miles per hour. Regarding this first count of the accusation, the jury was authorized to find, under the evidence, that the defendant operated his motor vehicle on the highway named in the accusation at a speed of approximately 100 miles per hour . . . .

The peace officers of DeKalb County began chasing the defendant on the Buford Highway between Clairmont Road and the DeKalb County-Fulton County line . . . .

During the chase the DeKalb County officers (there were two of them in the car) wrote down the name of the defendant and his license tag number. The officers by means of a radio, broadcasted the chase of the defendant, giving the defendant's name, his license tag number, and the description of the motor vehicle. This radio message was received and logged by the operator on duty of the Radio Department of the DeKalb Department of Public Safety, at 4:07 o'clock A.M. on the morning of the chase. From there the message was telephoned to the Atlanta police department, and the defendant was thus apprehended and arrested. When arrested, he was in possession of the same car, bearing the same license tag number. The

State offered a photostatic copy of the log made by the operator on duty in the Radio Department of the DeKalb County Department of Public Safety. The defendant objected to the introduction of it on the ground that it was hearsay evidence and that it was not made in the presence of the defendant. The court overruled the objection and admitted the photostatic copy hereinabove described. It is our opinion that this contention is not meritorious for two reasons: First, the same facts had already been admitted in evidence without objection when DeKalb County officers who chased the defendant testified that it was the defendant, the motor vehicle in which he was riding, bearing the described tag number as shown by the log, and at the same time of the morning. There are many decisions to this effect . . . .

In the second place, after considering this question carefully, we have come to the conclusion that the broadcast in the circumstances of this case was a part of the res gestae and for that reason was admissible. It must be kept in mind that this evidence shows beyond peradventure that at the time the DeKalb County officers were chasing this defendant over hills and dales, the defendant was in the very act of committing the crime for which he was convicted. There is a Code section which covers this, i. e., § 38-305, as follows: "Declarations accompanying an act, or so nearly connected therewith in time as to be free from all suspicion of device or afterthought, shall be admissible in evidence as part of the res gestae." This court in Alvaton Mercantile Company v. Caldwell, et al., 34 Ga.App. 151, 128 S.E. 781, said: "Circumstances, acts, and declarations growing out of main fact, and contemporaneous with it, and which serve to illustrate it, are part of res gestae."

It is apparent that this comparatively modern device of radio broadcasting is largely used by our peace officers in alerting other peace officers on duty and guard, is effective in apprehending criminals on the highways, and other places, and is of great service and benefit to the general public. It would therefore seem to be unthinkable that the communication of these officers, one with the other, should be excluded as hearsay testimony while a criminal is at the very time committing a crime or escaping from the commission of a crime at the time the communications are in progress. We will not so exclude such testimony as hearsay, but will extend such, if need be and we think soundly so, to assist in the apprehension and arrest of criminals. We are making no new law, but merely applying the principles which exist to the means and methods of modern science.

The court did not err in overruling the motion for a new trial for any of the reasons assigned.

Judgment affirmed.

Chapter 12: Documentary Evidence, Photographs, Demonstrations, and the Best Evidence Rule

People of the State of California v. *Alexander Robillard XIV,*
Supreme Court of California (In Bank), 358 P. 2d 295 (1960)

McCOMB, Justice.

This is an automatic appeal from a judgment of guilty of murder in the first degree . . . .

These questions are presented for determination:

. . . Third. *Did the trial court commit prejudicial error in receiving in evidence (a) a manikin, which was used to illustrate the path of the bullets fired into Officer Doran's body by defendant, (b) photographs of the deceased officer* . . . .

[In] the present case the questioned evidence was properly admitted.

(a) The manikin was a perfectly proper method of introducing highly relevant evidence. It was extremely important in this case to present the manner in which defendant had shot the officer. No one saw the shooting. Therefore, the prosecution was entitled to demonstrate the position of the wounds in the officer's body in order to substantiate its theory that defendant had literally executed the officer in order to escape detection.

Dr. Lack, the county pathologist, testified that he found six bullet wounds in Officer Doran's body and that he had established the trajectory of the bullets into the body. He then described these various wounds and trajectories in the appropriate medical terms. Thereafter, he identified a group of photographs which illustrated the trajectories and explained that he had also prepared the manikin to demonstrate further his previous testimony.

The use of a dummy under such circumstances in a homicide case to show the type and placement of the wounds received by the victim is proper. (Ford v. State, 257, S.W.2d 30, 33.)

The rule is settled in California that the use of demonstrative evidence, even though it may have some prejudicial effect, is admissible as long as it "tends to prove a material issue or clarify the circumstances of the crime." (People v. Cavanaugh, 282 P.2d 53, 61; People v. Brubaker, 346 P.2d 8.)

Defendant claimed that he had shot Officer Doran six times in rapid succession when the officer tried to draw his gun. Placement and trajectories of the bullets in the officer's body tended to belie this story. Dr. Lack, in answer to questions put to him by defendant, testified that in his opinion the wounds in the body could not have been inflicted in the manner described by defendant. The criminologist, Mr. Grodsky, also testified that two of the bullets fired into the officer's body had been fired at extremely close range, which would indicate that the shots had not all been fired at the same time.

The district attorney properly used the manikin in his argument in support of his theory as to how the crime was committed, particularly that it tended to show that the murder was a cold-blooded killing. (Cf. People v. Jones, supra, 343 P.2d at page 588.)

(b) The photographs of the deceased officer's body taken at the scene of the murder were properly received in evidence. (People v. Love, 53 Cal.2d 843, 3 Cal.Rptr. 665, 350 P.2d 705; People v. Brubaker, 53 Cal.2d 37.)

Defendant complains about the photographs of the deceased's body taken during the autopsy. These photographs were merely marked for identification and were never received in evidence. Therefore, there is no merit to defendant's contention that they were improperly received in evidence . . . .

The judgment is affirmed.

Chapter 13: Physical and Scientific Evidence: Preservation and Custody

State of New Jersey v. *Dominick Dantonio*, Supreme Court of New Jersey,
115 A. 2d 35 (1955)

JACOBS, J.

State Troopers operating radar speedmeter equipment along the New Jersey Turnpike charged the defendant with having violated its 60-mile speed limit. The defendant was found guilty in the Municipal Court of Milltown and, after trial *de novo* in the Middlesex County Court, he was again found guilty. See State v. Dantonio, 31 N.J.Super. 105, 105 A.2d 918 (Cty.Ct.1954). He appealed to the Appellate Division and we certified under R.R. 1:10-1.

On February 2, 1954 Troopers Armstrong, Trainor and Trpisovsky, as members of a radar team, set up their equipment along the New Jersey Turnpike. The radar equipment, which included transmitting and receiving devices as well as a calibrated speedmeter needle and a permanent graph indicating the speed of cars passing within range of the waves being transmitted, was placed on a station wagon alongside the road. Trooper Trpisovsky testified that he hooked up the power supply, tested the machinery after a warmup period to see that it was operating properly, and observed that both the meter and the graph were at zero when no cars were within range. Troopers Armstrong and Trainor testified that after the machinery was tested they drove their cars within range and, by radio communication, notified Trooper Trpisovsky of their respective speeds; when Trooper Armstrong's car was traveling at 75 miles per hour as evidenced by his own speedometer the radar device recorded 75 miles per hour; when Trooper Trainor's car was traveling at 89 miles per hour as evidenced by his own speedometer the radar device recorded 86 miles per hour. Dr. Kopper, a qualified electrical engineer associated with Johns Hopkins University, testified that in his opinion the Troopers' radar equipment "was properly and carefully used and that it would give an accurate indication of speed." He testified further that there would be tolerances for errors of "two miles plus or minus" and that any inaccuracies resulting from the placing of the equipment at the side rather than in the center of the road or from the weakening of the machinery or its power would produce lower rather than higher speed readings. See Kopper, The Scientific Reliability of Radar Speedmeters, 33 N.C.L.Rev. 343, 352 (1955). He expressed the view that it was not necessary that the operator of the radar equipment "be an electrical engineer or have other special technical skills"; Trooper Armstrong had been operating it since February 1953 and Trooper Trpisovsky had been operating it since August 1953. Cf. Kopper, supra at 353, where the author states that "the average person engaged in traffic control work can learn to use the radar speedmeter after about one and one-half to two hours of instruction . . . ."

The County Court expressly determined (1) that the radar equipment "was properly set up and tested for accuracy and was functioning properly and was a correct recorder of speed"; (2) that the defendant "was exceeding the speed limit of the New Jersey Turnpike and was traveling at 66 miles per hour, as charged"; and (3) that the State had "established the guilt of the defendant beyond a reasonable doubt." Our function on appeal ordinarily is not to make new factual findings but simply to decide whether there was adequate evidence before the County Court to justify its finding of guilt . . . .

Although there have been no appellate decisions in our own State there have been several decisions in courts of other states and numerous articles in legal publications which have dealt comprehensively with the evidential problems presented by the use of radar speedmeters . . . .

Through the years our courts have properly been called upon to recognize scientific discoveries and pass upon their effects in judicial proceedings. When fingerprint evidence was not accepted as universally as it is now, the Court of Errors and Appeals was required to deal with the contention that the trial court had erred in permitting an expert to testify as to the art of fingerprinting and its use as a means of identification; in holding that the testimony had properly been admitted justice Minturn in State v. Cerciello, 86 N.J.L. 309, 314, 90 A. 1112, 1114, 52 L.R.A.,N.S., 1010 (E. & A. 1914), aptly said:

> In principle its admission as legal evidence is based upon the theory that the evolution in practical affairs of life, whereby the progressive and scientific tendencies of the age are manifest in every other department of human endeavor, cannot be ignored in legal procedure, but that the law, in its efforts to enforce justice by demonstrating a fact in issue, will allow evidence of those scientific processes which are the work of educated and skillful men in their various departments, and apply them to the demonstration of a fact, leaving the weight and effect to be given to the effort and its results entirely to the consideration of the jury. Stephen Dig. Ev. 267; 2 Best on Ev. 514 . . . .

Since World War II members of the public have become generally aware of the widespread use of radar methods in detecting the presence of objects and their distance and speed; and while they may not fully understand their intricacies they do not question their general accuracy and effectiveness. Dr. Kopper has pointed out that, in contrast to other radar methods, the method actually used in the speedmeter is rather simple and has been adopted by many law enforcement bodies; a recent tabulation indicates that speedmeters are being used in 43 states by almost 500 police departments. See Radar Traffic Controls, 23 Tenn.L.Rev. 784 (1955). The writings on the subject assert that when properly operated they accurately record speed (within reasonable tolerances of perhaps two or three miles per hour) and nothing to the contrary has been brought to our attention; under the circumstances it would seem that evidence of radar speedmeter readings should be received in evidence upon a showing that the speedmeter was properly set up and tested by the police officers without any need for independent expert testimony by electrical engineers as to its general nature and trustworthiness . . . .

In the instant matter the State Troopers were sufficiently qualified to set up their radar speedmeter and the evidence indicated that they duly tested it before its use. They had then been operating it for many months and could readily observe whether it was in regular working order. They had no difficulty in reading the calibrated needle and the permanent graph and it was no more necessary that they actually understand the intricate electrical workings of the device than that they understand how their car speedometers work. They tested the speedmeter to see that it registered "zero" when nothing was in range and they pushed a designated switch to "test" position to observe that the needle reacted properly; then they compared radar readings with speedometer readings on their cars which were driven within range. In one instance these readings were identical and in the other they favored the car; it may be noted, as Dr. Kopper testified below, that all types of error actually suggested during the trial would result in lower radar readings thus favoring the car . . . .

The defendant points out that there was no affirmative evidence introduced by the State to establish that the speedometers in the Troopers' cars had been recently tested. It would, perhaps, have been the better course for the State to have introduced such testimony and presumably it would have done so if the defendant had raised the point in due time before the close of the trial. However, he did not in anywise question the Troopers on the subject and made no mention of it until the testimony had been fully completed and summations were taking place. Under these circumstances the defendant is hardly in any just position to attack the accuracy of the speedometers . . . .

The number of highway accidents is appalling and speed is generally recognized as a factor particularly where fatalities and serious injuries are involved . . . . In dealing with this as well as other law enforcement problems, enlightened officials properly avail themselves of scientific discoveries as soon as their reliability appears and modern courts of justice may not rightly lag far behind. We are satisfied that readings on radar speedometers which have been set up and operated in the manner established by the evidence in the instant matter constitute legally admissible evidence which may readily support a finding of guilt by the trier of the facts.

Affirmed.

State of Ohio v. *Minnix,* Court of Appeals of Ohio, 137 N.E. 2d 572 (1956)

COLLIER, Judge.

The defendant, appellant herein, was convicted on May 13, 1955, in the Municipal Court of Chillicothe, Ross County, Ohio, on a charge of operating a motor vehicle while under the influence of intoxicating liquor. The four assignments of error raise two principal questions of law, to wit, error in the admission of evidence and error in charging the jury.

During the trial, Fred Bouillion, police captain, was called as a witness on behalf of the state and was interrogated in regard to an alcoometer test made on the defendant. Over objection of the defendant he was permitted to testify as follows:

"Q. What was the result of the test? A. Twenty-five.

"Q. Are you familiar with the National Safety Council standards, Captain Bouillion? A. Yes, Sir.

"Q. Using the result of the defendant's test in relation to the National Safety Council standards, what would that indicate as to the defendant's condition? A. He was intoxicated."

On cross-examination, the witness was asked the following question and gave the following answer:

"Q. Do you know anything at all about this machine? A. No, I don't know a thing about it."

The testimony of persons skilled in the mechanics and use of modern machines and equipment to test or determine bodily conditions is generally accepted in courts as proper evidence. However, this rule does not extend to permitting an unskilled person who admits he knows nothing about such an instrument to give expert testimony upon the result of a test made with it. Such evidence is clearly in the class of expert testimony and, in order to be competent, the witness must be skilled, learned or experienced in the mechanics and use of such machines, so as to qualify as an expert witness. To hold otherwise would deny a party the right to cross-examine such witness as to the truth and accuracy of the reading of the instrument. See 3 Wigmore on Evidence (3 Ed.), 189, 195, Sections 795 and 795a.

We have examined the record and find the other assignments of error not well taken. For error in the admission of evidence and the erroneous instructions to the jury above set forth, the judgment is reversed and the cause remanded for further proceedings as provided by law.

Judgment reversed.

Chapter 14: Special Problems of Proof

People ex rel. Hegeman v. *Corrigan*, New York Court of Appeals, 87 N.E. 792 (1909)

CULLEN, Ch. J. The perjury with which the relator is charged is the verification under oath of a report to the insurance department of the state in which, in answer to a question calling for a statement of the loans held by the company secured by the pledge of bonds, stock or other collateral, it was stated that there were none . . . .

Doubtless, to constitute perjury there must be criminal intent, but intent must be distinguished from motive and from ultimate object. As was said by Judge Werner in People v. Molineux (168 N.Y. 264, 297, 61 N.E. 286): "In the popular mind intent and motive are not infrequently regarded as one and the same thing. In law there is a clear distinction between them. Motive is the moving power which impels to action for a definite result. Intent is the purpose to use a particular means to effect such result." (See, also, Burrill's Law Dictionary, vol. 1.) "Motive is that which incites or stimulates a person to do an act . . . . Motive is never an essential element of a crime. A good motive does not prevent an act from being a crime." (Clark's Crim.Law, sec. 14.) There runs through the criminal law a distinction between offenses that are *mala prohibita* in which no intent to do wrong is necessary to constitute the offense, and offenses that are *mala in se* in which a criminal intent is a necessary ingredient of the crime. While there are to be found both in judicial decisions and in text books elaborate discussions of what is a criminal intent, no attempt has been made to accurately define the term. Very possibly the attempt to make a definition so comprehensive as to be applicable to all cases would be futile, and it has often been doubted whether the term "intent" is an accurate one. However this may be, it is very apparent that the innocence or criminality of the intent in a particular act generally depends on the knowledge or belief of the actor at the time. An honest and reasonable belief in the existence of circumstances which, if true, would make the act for which the defendant is prosecuted innocent, would be a good defense. Thus, if a man killed another under such circumstances as gave proper and reasonable grounds for the belief that the person killed was about to take the life of the slayer, although the person killed was only playing a practical joke, no crime would be committed. But if the facts and circumstances which the person believed to exist were not such as in law to justify his act, then there would be no defense to the act. In other words, it is the knowledge or belief of the actor at the time that stamps identically the same intent as either criminal or innocent, for the intent to take life, unless under circumstances that the law regards as sufficient to justify the taking, is the criminal intent and the only criminal intent that can exist in case of murder (excepting where the killing is done in the commission of an independant felony). So, ordinarily, a criminal intent is an intent to do knowingly and willfully that which is condemned as wrong by the law and common morality of the country, and if such an intent exists, it is neither justification nor excuse that the actor intended by its commission to accomplish some ultimate good. (1 Bishop's Crim.Law, § 341.)

To constitute perjury under our law it is not necessary to establish any other intent than that specified in the statute, for by its terms it is not sufficient that the affiant testifies as to what is false, but the testimony must be given willfully and knowingly, and the affiant must know that the testimony is false; if it be given in the honest belief that it is true, or by mistake or inadvertence, the case does not fall within the statute. Therefore, if a person willfully testifies to what he knows to be false, this is the criminal intent and the only criminal intent that can exist in the crime. That the ultimate object to be attained by the perjury may be beneficent or indifferent in no way absolves or qualifies the criminality of the act. One may not commit a crime because he hopes or expects that good will come of it. It is no defense to a charge of intentionally committing an act prohibited by law even that the dictates of his religious belief require one to do the act. In Reynolds v. United States, 98 U.S. 145, 25 L.Ed. 244, the prisoner was indicted for having committed bigamy in Utah, and contended in his defense that polygamy was a duty enjoined on him by his religious belief. The court there said: "This (defense) would be introducing a new element into criminal law. Laws are made for the government of actions, and while they cannot interfere with mere religious belief and opinions, they may with practices. Suppose one believed that human sacrifices were a necessary part of religious worship, would it be seriously contended that the civil government under which he lived could not interfere to prevent a sacrifice?" In People v. Pierson (176 N.Y. 201, 68 N.E. 243) this court upheld a conviction for misdemeanor where the father, acting under the dictates of his religious faith, failed to call a physician to attend his sick child. (To the same effect, see Regina v. Morby, L.R. [8 Q.B.Div.] 571, and Regina v. Downes, 13 Cox Crim.Cas. 111.) In that case the defendant, far from intending to injure his child, sought by his conduct to preserve it, and believed that his action would most conduce to that result . . . .

If one may not violate the law with impunity in obedience to the requirements of his religious faith, much less can he justify such violation merely to escape personal inconvenience or annoyance. Therefore, the explanation offered by the relator that his act was impelled solely by the desire to escape the importunities of "Wall street," if true (and the truth of this statement was plainly a question of fact), is entirely immaterial to the charge against him. The sole questions in this prosecution are: 1st. Were the facts stated by the relator in the report true or false? 2nd. If false, did the relator know them to be false when he verified the report? Though the statements made in the return may have been incorrect, if the relator made them in good faith either by inadvertence or mistake, or in the honest belief that the statements were true, then, of course, he did not commit the offense. We think the evidence contained in the affidavits was sufficient to present a question of fact on these issues.

The order of the Appellate Division should be reversed, that of the Special Term affirmed, and the relator remanded to custody . . . .

George William Bruton v. *United States,* Supreme Court of the United States, 391 U.S. 123, 88 S. Ct. 1620 (1968)

Mr. Justice BRENNAN delivered the opinion of the Court.

This case presents the question, last considered in Delli Paoli v United States, 352 US 232, 1 L Ed 2d 278, 77 S Ct 294, whether the conviction of a defendant at a joint trial should be set aside although the jury was instructed that a codefendant's confession inculpating the defendant had to be disregarded in determining his guilt or innocence.

A joint trial of petitioner and one Evans in the District Court for the Eastern District of Missouri resulted in the conviction of both by a jury on a federal charge of armed postal robbery, 18 USC § 2114. A postal inspector testified that Evans orally confessed to him that Evans and petitioner committed the armed robbery. The postal inspector obtained the oral confession, and another in which Evans admitted he had an accomplice whom he would not name, in the course of two interrogations of Evans at the city jail in St. Louis, Missouri, where Evans was held in custody on state criminal charges. Both petitioner and Evans appealed their convictions to the Court of Appeals for the Eighth Circuit. That court set aside Evans' conviction on the ground that his oral confessions to the postal inspector should not have been received in evidence against him. 375 F2d 355, 361. However, the court, replying upon Delli Paoli, affirmed petitioner's conviction because the trial judge instructed the jury that although Evans' confession was competent evidence against Evans it was inadmissible hearsay against petitioner and therefore had to be disregarded in determining petitioner's guilt or innocence. 375 F2d at 361-363. We granted certiorari to reconsider Delli Paoli. 389 US 818, 19 L Ed 2d 70, 88 S Ct 126. The Solicitor General has since submitted a memorandum stating that "in the light of the record in this particular case and in the interests of justice, the judgment below should be reversed and the cause remanded for a new trial." The Solicitor General states that this disposition is urged in part because "[h]ere it has been determined that the confession was wrongly admitted against [Evans] and his conviction has been reversed, leading to a new trial at which he was acquitted. To argue, in this situation, that [petitioner's] conviction should nevertheless stand may be to place too great a strain upon the [Delli Paoli] rule—at least, where, as here, the other evidence against [petitioner] is not strong." We have concluded, however, that Delli Paoli should be overruled. We hold that, because of the substantial risk that the jury, despite instructions to the contrary, looked to the incriminating extrajudicial statements in determining petitioner's guilt, admission of Evans' confession in this joint trial violated petitioner's right of cross-examination secured by the Confrontation Clause of the Sixth Amendment. We therefore overrule Delli Paoli and reverse.

Mr. Justice Stewart, concurring.

I join the opinion and judgment of the Court. Although I did not agree with the decision in Jackson v Denno, 378 US 368, 12 L Ed 2d 908, 84 S Ct 1774, 1 ALR3d 1205 (see id., at 427, 12 L Ed 2d at 945, 1 ALR3d 1205), I accept its holding and share the Court's conclusion that it compels the overruling of Delli Paoli v United States, 352 US 232, 1 L Ed 2d 278, 77 S Ct 294.

Quite apart from Jackson v Denno, however, I think it clear that the underlying rationale of the Sixth Amendment's Confrontation Clause precludes reliance upon cautionary instructions when the highly damaging out-of-court statement of a co-defendant, who is not subject to cross-examination, is deliberately placed before the jury at a joint trial. A basic premise of the Confrontation Clause, it seems to me, is that certain kinds of hearsay (see, e.g., Pointer v Texas, 380 US 400, 13 L Ed 2d 923, 85 S Ct 1065; Douglas v Alabama, 380 US 415, 13 L Ed 2d 934, 85 S Ct 1074) are at once so damaging, so suspect, and yet so difficult to discount, that jurors cannot be trusted to give such evidence the minimal weight it logically deserves, *whatever* instructions the trial judge might give . . . . It is for this very reason that an out-of-court accusation is universally conceded to be constitutionally *inadmissible* against the accused, rather than admissible for the little it may be worth. Even if I did not consider Jackson v Denno controlling, therefore, I would still agree that Delli Paoli must be overruled.

Chapter 15: Grand Juries, Suppression Hearings, Appeals, and Forfeiture Proceedings

United States v. *John P. Calandra,* Supreme Court of the United States, 414 U.S. 338, 94 S. Ct. 613 (1974)

Mr. Justice POWELL delivered the opinion of the Court.

This case presents the question whether a witness summoned

to appear and testify before a grand jury may refuse to answer questions on the ground that they are based on evidence obtained from an unlawful search and seizure. The issue is of considerable importance to the administration of criminal justice . . . .

The institution of the grand jury is deeply rooted in Anglo-American history. In England, the grand jury served for centuries both as a body of accusers sworn to discover and present for trial persons suspected of criminal wrongdoing and as a protector of citizens against arbitrary and oppressive governmental action. In this country the Founders thought the grand jury so essential to basic liberties that they provided in the Fifth Amendment that federal prosecution for serious crimes can only be instituted by "a presentment or indictment of a Grand Jury." The grand jury's historic functions survive to this day. Its responsibilities continue to include both the determination whether there is probable cause to believe a crime has been committed and the protection of citizens against unfounded criminal prosecutions. . . .

Traditionally the grand jury has been accorded wide latitude to inquire into violations of criminal law. No judge presides to monitor its proceedings. It deliberates in secret and may determine alone the course of its inquiry. The grand jury may compel the production of evidence or the testimony of witnesses as it considers appropriate, and its operation generally is unrestrained by the technical procedural and evidentiary rules governing the conduct of criminal trials. "It is a grand inquest, a body with powers of investigation and inquisition, the scope of whose inquiries is not to be limited narrowly by questions of propriety or forecasts of the probable result of the investigation, or by doubts whether any particular individual will be found properly subject to an accusation of crime." Blair v. United States, 250 U.S. 273, 282, 39 S.Ct. 468, 471, 63 L.Ed. 979 (1919).

The scope of the grand jury's powers reflects its special role in insuring fair and effective law enforcement. A grand jury proceeding is not an adversary hearing in which the guilt or innocence of the accused is adjudicated. Rather, it is an *ex parte* investigation to determine whether a crime has been committed and whether criminal proceedings should be instituted against any person. The grand jury's investigative power must be broad if its public responsibility is adequately to be discharged . . . .

The grand jury's sources of information are widely drawn, and the validity of an indictment is not affected by the character of the evidence considered. Thus, an indictment valid on its face is not subject to challenge on the ground that the grand jury acted on the basis of inadequate or incompetent evidence, Costello v. United States, *supra*; Holt v. United States, 218, U.S. 245, 31 S.Ct. 2, 54 L.Ed. 1021 (1910); or even on the basis of information obtained in violation of a defendant's Fifth Amendment privilege against self-incrimination.

In the instant case, the Court of Appeals held that the exclusionary rule of the Fourth Amendment limits the grand jury's power to compel a witness to answer questions based on evidence obtained from a prior unlawful search and seizure. The exclusionary rule was adopted to effectuate the Fourth Amendment right of all citizens "to be secure in their persons, houses, papers, and effects, against unreasonable search and seizures . . . ." Under this rule, evidence obtained in violation of the Fourth Amendment cannot be used in a criminal proceeding against the victim of the illegal search and seizure. Weeks v. United States, 232 U.S. 383, 34 S.Ct. 341, 58 L.Ed. 652 (1914); Mapp v. Ohio, 367 U.S. 643, 81 S.Ct. 1684, 6 L.Ed.2d 1081 (1961). This prohibition applies as well to the fruits of the illegally seized evidence. Wong Sun v. United States, 371 U.S. 471, 83 S.Ct. 407, 9 L.Ed.2d 441 (1963); Silverthorne Lumber Co. v. United States, 251 U.S. 385, 40 S.Ct. 182, 64 L.Ed. 319 (1920).

The purpose of the exclusionary rule is not to redress the injury to the privacy of the search victim:

> [T]he ruptured privacy of the victims' homes and effects cannot be restored. Reparation comes too late. Linkletter v. Walker, 381 U.S. 618, 637, 85 S.Ct. 1731, 1742, 14 L.Ed.2d 601 (1965).

Instead, the rule's prime purpose is to deter future unlawful police conduct and thereby effectuate the guarantee of the Fourth Amendment against unreasonable search and seizures:

> The rule is calculated to prevent, not to repair. Its purpose is to deter—to compel respect for the constitutional guaranty in the only effectively available way—by removing the incentive to disregard it. Elkins v. United States, 364 U.S. 206, 217, 80 S.Ct. 1437, 1444, 4 L.Ed.2d 1669 (1960).

Accord, Mapp v. Ohio, *supra*, 367 U.S., at 656, 81 S.Ct., at 1692; Tehan v. United States ex rel. Shott, 382 U.S. 406, 416, 86 S.Ct. 459, 465, 15 L.Ed.2d 453 (1966); Terry v. Ohio, 392 U.S. 1, 29, 88 S.Ct. 1868, 1884, 20 L.Ed.2d 889 (1968). In sum, the rule is a judicially created remedy designed to safeguard Fourth Amendment rights generally through its deterrent effect, rather than a personal constitutional right of the party aggrieved.

Despite its broad deterrent purpose, the exclusionary rule has never been interpreted to proscribe the use of illegally seized evidence in all proceedings or against all persons. As with any remedial device, the application of the rule has been restricted to those areas where its remedial objectives are thought most efficaciously served. The balancing process implicit in this approach is expressed in the contours of the standing requirement. Thus, standing to invoke the exclusionary rule has been confined to situations where the Government seeks to use such evidence to incriminate the victim of the unlawful search. Brown v. United States, 411 U.S. 223, 93 S.Ct. 1565, 36 L.Ed.2d 208 (1973); Alderman v. United States, 394 U.S. 165, 89 S.Ct. 961, 22 L.Ed.2d 176 (1969); Wong Sun v. United States, *supra*; Jones v. United States, 362 U.S. 257, 80 S.Ct. 725, 4 L.Ed.2d 697 (1960). This standing rule is premised on a recognition that the need for deterrence and hence the rationale for excluding the evidence are strongest where the Government's unlawful conduct would result in imposition of a criminal sanction on the victim of the search.

In deciding whether to extend the exclusionary rule to grand jury proceedings, we must weigh the potential injury to the historic role and functions of the grand jury against the potential benefits of the rule as applied in this context. It is evident that this extension of the exclusionary rule would seriously impede the grand jury. Because the grand jury does not finally adjudicate guilt or innocence, it has traditionally been allowed to pursue its investigative and accusatorial functions unimpeded by the evidentiary and procedural restrictions applicable to a criminal trial. Permitting witnesses to invoke the exclusionary rule before a grand jury would precipitate adjudication of issues hitherto reserved for the trial on the merits and would delay and disrupt grand jury proceedings. Suppression hearings would halt the orderly progress of an investigation and might necessitate extended litigation of issues only tangentially related to the grand jury's primary objective. The probable result would be "protracted interruption of grand jury proceedings," Gelbard v. United States, 408 U.S. 41, 70, 92 S.Ct. 2357, 2372, 33 L.Ed.2d 179 (1972) (White, J., concurring), effectively transforming them into preliminary trials on the merits. In some cases the delay might be fatal to the enforcement of the criminal law. Just last Term we reaffirmed our disinclination to allow litigious interference with grand jury proceedings:

Any holding that would saddle a grand jury with minitrials and preliminary showings would assuredly impede its investigation and frustrate the public's interest in the fair and expeditious administration of the criminal laws.

United States v. Dionisio, 410 U.S. 1, 17, 93 S.Ct. 764, 773, 35 L.Ed.2d 67 (1973).

Cf. United States v. Ryan, 402 U.S. 530, 91 S.Ct. 1580, 29 L.Ed.2d 85 (1971); Cobbledick v. United States, 309 U.S. 323, 60 S.Ct. 540, 84 L.Ed. 783 (1940). In sum, we believe that allowing a grand jury witness to invoke the exclusionary rule would unduly interfere with the effective and expeditious discharge of the grand jury's duties.

Against this potential damage to the role and functions of the grand jury, we must weigh the benefits to be derived from this proposed extension of the exclusionary rule. Suppression of the use of illegally seized evidence against the search victim in a criminal trial is thought to be an important method of effectuating the Fourth Amendment. But it does not follow that the Fourth Amendment requires adoption of every proposal that might deter police misconduct . . . .

Any incremental deterrent effect which might be achieved by extending the rule to grand jury proceedings is uncertain at best. Whatever deterrence of police misconduct may result from the exclusion of illegally seized evidence from criminal trials, it is unrealistic to assume that application of the rule to grand jury proceedings would significantly further that goal. Such an extension would deter only police investigation consciously directed toward the discovery of evidence solely for use in a grand jury investigation. The incentive to disregard the requirement of the Fourth Amendment solely to obtain an indictment from a grand jury is substantially negated by the inadmissibility of the illegally seized evidence in a subsequent criminal prosecution of the search victim. For the most part, a prosecutor would be unlikely to request an indictment where a conviction could not be obtained. We therefore decline to embrace a view that would achieve a speculative and undoubtedly minimal advance in the deterrence of police misconduct at the expense of substantially impeding the role of the grand jury.

Astol Calero-Toledo, Supt. of Police v. Pearson Yacht Leasing Co., Supreme Court of the United States, 416 U.S. 663, 94 S. Ct. 2080 (1974)

Mr. Justice BRENNAN delivered the opinion of the Court.

The question presented is whether the Constitution is violated by application to appellee, the lessor of a yacht, of Puerto Rican statutes providing for seizure and forfeiture of vessels used for unlawful purposes when (1) the yacht was seized without prior notice or hearing after allegedly being used by a lessee for an unlawful purpose, and (2) the appellee was neither involved in nor aware of the act of the lessee which resulted in the forfeiture . . . .

Appellants challenge the District Court's holding that the appellee was denied due process of law by the omission from § 2512(b), as it incorporates § 1722, of provisions for preseizure notice and hearing. They argue that seizure for purposes of forfeiture is one of those "'extraordinary situations' that justify postponing notice and opportunity for a hearing." Fuentes v. Shevin, 407 U.S., at 90, 92 S.Ct., at 1999 . . . .

Fuentes reaffirmed, however, that, in limited circumstances, immediate seizure of a property interest, without an opportunity for prior hearing, is constitutionally permissible. Such circumstances are those in which

the seizure has been directly necessary to secure an important governmental or general public interest. Second, there has been a special need for very prompt action. Third, the State has kept strict control over its monopoly of legitimate force: the person initiating the seizure has been a government official responsible for determining, under the standards of a narrowly drawn statute, that it was necessary and justified in the particular instance. *Id.*, at 91, 92 S.Ct., at 2000.

The considerations that justified postponement of notice and hearing in those cases are present here. First, seizure under the Puerto Rican statutes serves significant governmental purposes: Seizure permits Puerto Rico to assert *in rem* jurisdiction over the property in order to conduct forfeiture proceedings, thereby fostering the public interest in preventing continued illicit use of the property and in enforcing criminal sanctions. Second, preseizure notice and hearing might frustrate the interests served by the statutes, since the property seized—as here, a yacht—will often be of a sort that could be removed to another jurisdiction, destroyed, or concealed, if advance warning of confiscation were given. And finally, unlike the situation in *Fuentes,* seizure is not initiated by self-interested private parties; rather, Commonwealth officials determine whether seizure is appropriate under the provisions of the Puerto Rican statutes. In these circumstances, we hold that this case presents an "extraordinary" situation in which postponement of notice and hearing until after seizure did not deny due process.

Appellants next argue that the District Court erred in holding that the forfeiture statutes unconstitutionally authorized the taking for government use of innocent parties' property without just compensation. They urge that a long line of prior decisions of this Court establish the principle that statutory forfeiture schemes are not rendered unconstitutional because of their applicability to the property interests of innocents, and further that United States v. United States Coin & Currency, 401 U.S. 715, 91 S.Ct. 1041, 28 L.Ed.2d 434 (1971), did not—contrary to the opinion of the District Court—overrule those prior precedents *sub silentio*. We agree. The historical background of forfeiture statutes in this country and this Court's prior decisions sustaining their constitutionality lead to that conclusion . . . .

Plainly, the Puerto Rican forfeiture statutes further the punitive and deterrent purposes that have been found sufficient to uphold, against constitutional challenge, the application of other forfeiture statutes to the property of innocents. Forfeiture of conveyances that have been used—and may be used again—in violation of the narcotics laws fosters the purposes served by the underlying criminal statutes, both by preventing further illicit use of the conveyance and by imposing an economic penalty, thereby rendering illegal behavior unprofitable . . . . To the extent that such forfeiture provisions are applied to lessors, bailors, or secured creditors who are innocent of any wrongdoing, confiscation may have the desirable effect of inducing them to exercise greater care in transferring possession of their property.

[In] this case appellee voluntarily entrusted the lessees with possession of the yacht, and no allegation has been made or proof offered that the company did all that it reasonably could to avoid having its property put to an unlawful use. The judgment of the District Court is reversed.

Appendix F. Rules of Evidence for United States Courts and Magistrates

Article I. General Provisions

Rule 101. Scope

These rules govern proceedings in the courts of the United States and before United States magistrates, to the extent and with the exceptions stated in Rule 1101.

Rule 102. Purpose and Construction

These rules shall be construed to secure fairness in administration, elimination of unjustifiable expense and delay, and promotion of growth and development of the law of evidence to the end that the truth may be ascertained and proceedings justly determined.

Rule 103. Rulings on Evidence

(a) Effect of erroneous ruling. Error may not be predicated upon a ruling which admits or excludes evidence unless a substantial right of the party is affected, and

(1) Objection. In case the ruling is one admitting evidence a timely objection or motion to strike appears of record, stating the specific ground of objection, if the specific ground was not apparent from the context; or

(2) Offer of proof. In case the ruling is one excluding evidence, the substance of the evidence was made known to the judge by offer or was apparent from the context within which questions were asked.

(b) Record of offer and ruling. The court may add any other or further statement which shows the character of the evidence, the

463

form in which it was offered, the objection made, and the ruling thereon. It may direct the making of an offer in question and answer form.

(c) Hearing of jury. In jury cases, proceedings shall be conducted, to the extent practicable, so as to prevent inadmissible evidence from being suggested to the jury by any means, such as making statements or offers of proof or asking questions in the hearing of the jury.

(d) Plain error. Nothing in this rule precludes taking notice of plain errors affecting substantial rights although they were not brought to the attention of the court.

Rule 104. Preliminary Questions

(a) Questions of admissibility generally. Preliminary questions concerning the qualification of a person to be a witness, the existence of a privilege, or the admissibility of evidence shall be determined by the court, subject to the provisions of subdivision (b). In making its determination it is not bound by the rules of evidence except those with respect to privileges.

(b) Relevancy conditioned on fact. When the relevancy of evidence depends upon the fulfillment of a condition of fact, the judge shall admit it upon, or subject to the introduction of evidence sufficient to support a finding of the fulfillment of the condition.

(c) Hearing of jury. Hearings on the admissibility of confessions shall in all cases be conducted out of the hearing of the jury. Hearings on other preliminary matters shall be so conducted when the interests of justice require or, when an accused is a witness, if he so requests.

(d) Testimony by accused. The accused does not, by testifying upon a preliminary matter, subject himself to cross-examination as to other issues in the case.

(e) Weight and credibility. This rule does not limit the right of of a party to introduce before the jury evidence relevant to weight or credibility.

Rule 105. Limited Admissibility

When evidence which is admissible as to one party or for one purpose but not admissible as to another party or for another purpose is admitted, the court, upon request, shall restrict the evidence to its proper scope and instruct the jury accordingly.

Rule 106. Remainder of or Related Writings or Recorded Statements

When a writing or recorded statement or part thereof is introduced by a party, an adverse party may require him at that time to introduce any other part or any other writing or recorded statement which ought in fairness to be considered contemporaneously with it.

Article II. Judicial Notice

Rule 201. Judicial Notice of Adjudicative Facts

(a) Scope of rule. This rule governs only judicial notice of adjudicative facts.

(b) Kinds of facts. A judicially noticed fact must be one not subject to reasonable dispute in that it is either (1) generally known within the territorial jurisdiction of the trial court or (2) capable of accurate and ready determination by resort to sources whose accuracy cannot reasonably be questioned.

(c) When discretionary. A court may take judicial notice, whether requested or not.

(d) When mandatory. A court shall take judicial notice if requested by a party and supplied with the necessary information.

(e) Opportunity to be heard. A party is entitled upon timely request to an opportunity to be heard as to the propriety of taking judicial notice and the tenor of the matter noticed. In the absence of prior notification, the request may be made after judicial notice has been taken.

(f) Time of taking notice. Judicial notice may be taken at any stage of the proceeding.

(g) Instructing jury. In a civil action or proceeding, the court shall instruct the jury to accept as conclusive any fact judicially noticed. In a criminal case, the court shall instruct the jury that it may, but is not required to, accept as conclusive any fact judicially noticed.

Article III. Presumptions in Civil Actions and Proceedings

Rule 301. Presumptions in General in Civil Actions and Proceedings

In all civil actions and proceedings not otherwise provided for by Act of Congress or by these rules, a presumption imposes on the party against whom it is directed the burden of going forward with evidence to rebut or meet the presumption, but does not shift to such party the burden of proof in the sense of the risk of non-persuasion, which remains throughout the trial upon the party on whom it was originally cast.

Rule 302. Applicability of State Law in Civil Actions and Proceedings

In civil actions and proceedings, the effect of a presumption respecting a fact which is an element of a claim or defense as to which state law supplies the rule of decision is determined in accordance with state law.

Article IV. Relevancy and Its Limits

Rule 401. Definition of "Relevant Evidence"

"Relevant evidence" means evidence having any tendency to make the existence of any fact that is of consequence to the determination of the action more probable or less probable than it would be without the evidence.

Rule 402. Relevant Evidence Generally Admissible;
Irrelevant Evidence Inadmissible

All relevant evidence is admissible, except as otherwise provided by the Constitution of the United States, by Act of Congress, by these rules, or by other rules prescribed by the Supreme Court pursuant to statutory authority. Evidence which is not relevant is not admissible.

Rule 403. Exclusion of Relevant Evidence on Grounds of Prejudice,
Confusion, or Waste of Time

Although relevant, evidence may be excluded if its probative value is substantially outweighed by the danger of unfair prejudice, confusion of the issues, or misleading the jury, or by considerations of undue delay, waste of time, or needless presentation of cumulative evidence.

Rule 404. Character Evidence Not Admissible to Prove Conduct;
Exceptions; Other Crimes

(a) Character evidence generally. Evidence of a person's character or a trait of his character is not admissible for the purpose of proving that he acted in conformity therewith on a particular occasion, except:

(1) Character of accused. Evidence of a pertinent trait of his character offered by an accused, or by the prosecution to rebut the same;

(2) Character of victim. Evidence of a pertinent trait of character of the victim of the crime offered by an accused, or by the prosecution to rebut the same, or evidence of a character trait of

peacefulness of the victim offered by the prosecution in a homicide case to rebut evidence that the victim was the first aggressor;

(3) Character of witness. Evidence of the character of a witness, as provided in Rules 607, 608, and 609.

(b) Other crimes, wrongs, or acts. Evidence of other crimes, wrongs, or acts is not admissible to prove the character of a person in order to show that he acted in conformity therewith. It may, however, be admissible for other purposes, such as proof of motive, opportunity, intent, preparation, plan, knowledge, identity, or absence of mistake or accident.

Rule 405. Methods of Proving Character

(a) Reputation or opinion. In all cases in which evidence of character or a trait of character of a person is admissible, proof may be made by testimony as to reputation or by testimony in the form of an opinion. On cross-examination, inquiry is allowable into relevant specific instances of conduct.

(b) Specific instances of conduct. In cases in which character or a trait of character of a person is an essential element of a charge, claim, or defense, proof may also be made of specific instances of his conduct.

Rule 406. Habit; Routine Practice

Evidence of the habit of a person or of the routine practice of an organization, whether corroborated or not and regardless of the presence of eyewitnesses, is relevant to prove that the conduct of the person or organization on a particular occasion was in conformity with the habit or routine practice.

Rule 407. Subsequent Remedial Measures

When, after an event, measures are taken which if taken previously, would have made the event less likely to occur, evidence of the subsequent measures is not admissible to prove negligence or culpable conduct in connection with the event. This rule does not require the exclusion of evidence of subsequent measures when offered for another purpose, such as proving ownership, control, or feasibility of precautionary measures, if controverted, or impeachment.

Rule 408. Compromise and Offers to Compromise

Evidence of (1) furnishing or offering or promising to furnish, or (2) accepting or offering or promising to accept a valuable consideration in compromising or attempting to compromise a claim which was disputed as to either validity or amount, is not admissible to prove liability for or invalidity of the claim or its amount. Evidence of conduct or statements made in compromise negotiations is likewise not admissible. This rule does not require the exclusion of any evidence otherwise discoverable merely because it is presented in the course of compromise negotiations. This rule also does not require exclusion when the evidence is offered for another purpose, such as proving bias or prejudice of a witness, negativing a contention of undue delay, or proving an effort to obstruct a criminal investigation or prosecution.

Rule 409. Payment of Medical and Similar Expenses

Evidence of furnishing or offering or promising to pay medical, hospital, or similar expenses occasioned by an injury is not admissible to prove liability for the injury.

Rule 410. Offer to Plead Guilty; Nolo Contendere; Withdrawn Plea of Guilty

Except as otherwise provided by Act of Congress, evidence of a plea of guilty, later withdrawn, or a plea of nolo contendere, or of an offer to plead guilty or nolo contendere to the crime charged or any other crime, or of statements made in connection with any of the foregoing pleas or offers, is not admissible in any civil or criminal action, case, or proceeding against the person who made the plea or offer. This rule shall not apply to the introduction of voluntary and reliable statements made in court on the record in connection with any of the foregoing pleas or offers where offered for impeachment purposes or in a subsequent prosecution of the declarant for perjury or false statement.

This rule shall not take effect until August 1, 1976, and shall be superseded by any amendment to the Federal Rules of Criminal Procedure which is inconsistent with this rule, and which takes effect after the date of the enactment of the Act establishing these Federal Rules of Evidence.

Rule 411. Liability Insurance

Evidence that a person was or was not insured against liability is not admissible upon the issue whether he acted negligently or otherwise wrongfully. This rule does not require the exclusion of evidence of insurance against liability when offered for another purpose, such as proof of agency, ownership, or control, or bias or prejudice of a witness.

Article V. Privileges

Rule 501. General Rule

Except as otherwise required by the Constitution of the United States or provided by Act of Congress or in rules prescribed by the Supreme Court pursuant to statutory authority, the privilege of a witness, person, government, State, or political subdivision thereof shall be governed by the principles of the common law as they may be interpreted by the courts of the United States in the light of reason and experience. However, in civil actions and proceedings, with respect to an element of a claim or defense as to which State law supplies the rule of decision, the privilege of a witness, person, government, State, or political subdivision thereof shall be determined in accordance with State law.

Article VI. Witnesses

Rule 601. General Rule of Competency

Every person is competent to be a witness except as otherwise provided in these rules. However, in civil actions and proceedings, with respect to an element of a claim or defense as to which State law supplies the rule of decision, the competency of a witness shall be determined in accordance with State law.

Rule 602. Lack of Personal Knowledge

A witness may not testify to a matter unless evidence is introduced sufficient to support a finding that he has personal knowledge of the matter. Evidence to prove personal knowledge may, but need not, consist of the testimony of the witness himself. This rule is subject to the provisions of Rule 703, relating to opinion testimony by expert witnesses.

Rule 603. Oath or Affirmation

Before testifying, every witness shall be required to declare that he will testify truthfully, by oath or affirmation administered in a form calculated to awaken his conscience and impress his mind with his duty to do so.

Rule 604. Interpreters

An interpreter is subject to the provisions of these rules relating to qualification as an expert and the administration of an oath or affirmation that he will make a true translation.

Rule 605. Competency of Judge as Witness

The judge presiding at the trial may not testify in that trial as a witness. No objection need be made in order to preserve the point.

Rule 606. Competency of Juror as Witness

(a) At the trial. A member of the jury may not testify as a witness before that jury in the trial of the case in which he is sitting as a juror. If he is called so to testify, the opposing party shall be afforded an opportunity to object out of the presence of the jury.

(b) Inquiry into validity of verdict or indictment. Upon an inquiry into the validity of a verdict or indictment, a juror may not testify as to any matter or statement occurring during the course of the jury's deliberations or to the effect of anything upon his or any other juror's mind or emotions as influencing him to assent to or dissent from the verdict or indictment or concerning his mental processes in connection therewith, except that a juror may testify on the question whether extraneous prejudicial information was improperly brought to the jury's attention or whether any outside influence was improperly brought to bear upon any juror. Nor may his affidavit or evidence of any statement by him concerning a matter about what he would be precluded from testifying be received for these purposes.

Rule 607. Who May Impeach

The credibility of a witness may be attacked by any party, including the party calling him.

Rule 608. Evidence of Character and Conduct of Witness

(a) Opinion and reputation evidence of character. The credibility of a witness may be attacked or supported by evidence in the form of opinion or reputation, but subject to these limitations: (1) the evidence may refer only to character for truthfulness or untruthfulness, and (2) evidence of truthful character is admissible only after the character of the witness for truthfulness has been attacked by opinion or reputation evidence or otherwise.

(b) Specific instances of conduct. Specific instances of the conduct of a witness, for the purpose of attacking or supporting his credibility, other than conviction of crime as provided in Rule 609, may not be proved by extrinsic evidence. They may, however, in the discretion of the court, if probative of truthfulness or untruthfulness, be inquired into on cross-examination of the witness (1) concerning the character for truthfulness or untruthfulness of another witness as to which character the witness being cross-examined has testified.

The giving of testimony, whether by an accused or by any other witness, does not operate as a waiver of his privilege against self-incrimination when examined with respect to matters which relate only to credibility.

Rule 609. Impeachment by Evidence of Conviction of Crime

(a) General rule. For the purpose of attacking the credibility of a witness, evidence that he has been convicted of a crime shall be admitted if elicited from him or established by public record during cross-examination but only if the crime (1) was punishable by death or imprisonment in excess of one year under the law under which he was convicted, and the court determines that the probative value of admitting this evidence outweighs its prejudicial effect to the defendant, or (2) involved dishonesty or false statement, regardless of the punishment.

(b) Time limit. Evidence of a conviction under this rule is not admissible if a period of more than ten years has elapsed since the date of the conviction or of the release of the witness from the confinement imposed for that conviction, whichever is the later date, unless the court determines, in the interests of justice, that the probative value of the conviction supported by specific facts and circumstances substantially outweighs its prejudicial effect. However, evidence of a conviction more than 10 years old as calculated herein, is not admissible unless the proponent gives to the adverse party sufficient advance written notice of intent to use such evidence to provide the adverse party with a fair opportunity to contest the use of such evidence.

(c) Effect of pardon, annulment, or certificate of rehabilitation. Evidence of a conviction is not admissible under this rule if (1) the conviction has been the subject of a pardon, annulment, certificate of rehabilitation, or other equivalent procedure based on a finding of the rehabilitation of the person convicted, and that person has not been convicted of a subsequent crime which was punishable by death or imprisonment in excess of one year, or (2) the conviction has been the subject of a pardon, annulment, or other equivalent procedure based on a finding of innocence.

(d) Juvenile adjudications. Evidence of juvenile adjudications is generally not admissible under this rule. The court may, however, in a criminal case allow evidence of a juvenile adjudication of a witness other than the accused if conviction of the offense would be admissible to attack the credibility of an adult and the court is satisfied that admission in evidence is necessary for a fair determination of the issue of guilt or innocence.

(e) Pendency of appeal. The pendency of an appeal therefrom does not render evidence of a conviction inadmissible. Evidence of the pendency of an appeal is admissible.

Rule 610. Religious Beliefs or Opinions

Evidence of the beliefs or opinions of a witness on matters of religion is not admissible for the purpose of showing that by reason of their nature his credibility is impaired or enhanced.

Rule 611. Mode and Order of Interrogation and Presentation

(a) Control by court. The court shall exercise reasonable control over the mode and order of interrogating witnesses and presenting evidence so as to (1) make the interrogation and presentation effective for the ascertainment of the truth, (2) avoid needless consumption of time, and (3) protect witnesses from harassment or undue embarrassment.

(b) Scope of cross-examination. Cross-examination should be limited to the subject matter of the direct examination and matters affecting the credibility of the witness. The court may, in the exercise of discretion, permit inquiry into additional matters as if on direct examination.

(c) Leading questions. Leading questions should not be used on the direct examination of a witness except as may be necessary to develop his testimony. Ordinarily leading questions should be permitted on cross-examination. When a party calls a hostile witness, an adverse party, or a witness identified with an adverse party, interrogation may be by leading questions.

Rule 612. Writing Used to Refresh Memory

Except as otherwise provided in criminal proceedings by section 3500 of title 18, United States Code, if a witness uses a writing to refresh his memory for the purpose of testifying, either—

(1) while testifying, or
(2) before testifying, if the court in its discretion determines it is necessary in the interests of justice,

an adverse party is entitled to have the writing produced at the hearing, to inspect it, to cross-examine the witness thereon, and to introduce in evidence those portions which relate to the testimony of the witness. If it is claimed that the writing contains matters not related to the subject matter of the testimony the court shall examine the writing in camera, excise any portions not so related, and order delivery of the remainder to the party entitled thereto. Any portion withheld over objections shall be preserved and made available to the appellate court in the event of an appeal. If a writing is not produced or delivered pursuant to order under this rule, the court shall make any order justice requires, except that in criminal cases when the prosecution elects not to comply, the order shall be one striking the testimony or, if the court in its discretion determines that the interests of justice so require, declaring a mistrial.

Rule 613. Prior Statements of Witnesses

(a) *Examining witness concerning prior statement.* In examining a witness concerning a prior statement made by him, whether written or not, the statement need not be shown nor its contents disclosed to him at that time, but on request the same shall be shown or disclosed to opposing counsel.

(b) *Extrinsic evidence of prior inconsistent statement of witness.* Extrinsic evidence of a prior inconsistent statement by a witness is not admissible unless the witness is afforded an opportunity to explain or deny the same and the opposite party is afforded an opportunity to interrogate him thereon, or the interests of justice otherwise require. This provision does not apply to admissions of a party-opponent as defined in Rule 801 (d) (2).

Rule 614. Calling and Interrogation of Witnesses by Court

(a) *Calling by court.* The court may, on its own motion or at the suggestion of a party, call witnesses, and all parties are entitled to cross-examine witnesses thus called.

(b) *Interrogation by court.* The court may interrogate witnesses, whether called by itself or by a party.

(c) *Objections.* Objections to the calling of witnesses by the court or to interrogation by it may be made at the time or at the next available opportunity when the jury is not present.

Rule 615. Exclusion of Witnesses

At the request of a party the court shall order witnesses excluded so that they cannot hear the testimony of other witnesses, and it may make the order of its own motion. This rule does not authorize exclusion of (1) a party who is a natural person, or (2) an officer or employee of a party which is not a natural person designated as its representative by its attorney, or (3) a person whose presence is shown by a party to be essential to the presentation of his cause.

Article VII. Opinions and Expert Testimony

Rule 701. Opinion Testimony by Lay Witnesses

If the witness is not testifying as an expert, his testimony in the form of opinions or inferences is limited to those opinions or inferences which are (a) rationally based on the perception of the witness and (b) helpful to a clear understanding of his testimony or the determination of a fact in issue.

Rule 702. Testimony by Experts

If scientific, technical, or other specialized knowledge will assist the trier of fact to understand the evidence or to determine a fact in issue, a witness qualified as an expert by knowledge, skill, experience, training, or education, may testify thereto in the form of an opinion or otherwise.

Rule 703. Bases of Opinion Testimony by Experts

The facts or data in the particular case upon which an expert bases an opinion or inference may be those perceived by or made known to him at or before the hearing. If of a type reasonably relied upon by experts in the particular field in forming opinions or inferences upon the subject, the facts or data need not be admissible in evidence.

Rule 704. Opinion on Ultimate Issue

Testimony in the form of an opinion or inference otherwise admissible is not objectionable because it embraces an ultimate issue to be decided by the trier of fact.

Rule 705. Disclosure of Facts or Data Underlying Expert Opinion

The expert may testify in terms of opinion or inference and give his reasons therefor without prior disclosure of the underlying facts or data, unless the judge requires otherwise. The expert may in any event be required to disclose the underlying facts or data on cross-examination.

Rule 706. Court Appointed Experts

(a) *Appointment.* The court may on its own motion or on the motion of any party enter an order to show cause why expert witnesses should not be appointed, and may request the parties to submit nominations. The court may appoint any expert witnesses agreed upon by the parties, and may appoint witnesses of its own selection.

An expert witness shall not be appointed by the court unless he consents to act. A witness so appointed shall be informed of his duties by the court in writing, a copy of which shall be filed with the clerk, or at a conference in which the parties shall have opportunity to participate. A witness so appointed shall advise the parties of his findings, if any; his deposition may be taken by any party; and he may be called to testify by the court or any party. He shall be subject to cross-examination by each party, including a party calling him as a witness.

(b) Compensation. Expert witnesses so appointed are entitled to reasonable compensation in whatever sum the court may allow. The compensation thus fixed is payable from funds which may be provided by law in criminal cases and civil actions and proceedings involving just compensation under the Fifth Amendment. In other civil actions and proceedings the compensation shall be paid by the parties in such proportion and at such time as the court directs, and thereafter charged in like manner as other costs.

(c) Disclosure of appointment. In the exercise of its discretion, the court may authorize disclosure to the jury of the fact that the court appointed the expert witness.

(d) Parties' experts of own selection. Nothing in this rule limits the parties in calling expert witnesses of their own selection.

Article VIII. Hearsay

Rule 801. Definitions

The following definitions apply under this Article:

(a) Statement. A "statement" is (1) an oral or written assertion or (2) nonverbal conduct of a person, if it is intended by him as an assertion.

(b) Declarant. A "declarant" is a person who makes a statement.

(c) Hearsay. "Hearsay" is a statement, other than one made by the declarant while testifying at the trial or hearing, offered in evidence to prove the truth of the matter asserted.

(d) Statements which are not hearsay. A statement is not hearsay if—

(1) Prior statement by witness. The declarant testifies at the trial or hearing and is subject to cross-examination concerning the statement, and the statement is (A) inconsistent with his testimony, and was given under oath subject to the penalty of perjury at a trial, hearing, or other proceeding, or in a deposition, or (B) consistent

with his testimony and is offered to rebut an express or implied charge against him of recent fabrication or improper influence or motive, or

(2) *Admission by party-opponent.* The statement is offered against a party and is (A) his own statement, in either his individual or a representative capacity or (B) a statement of which he has manifested his adoption or belief in its truth, or (C) a statement by a person authorized by him to make a statement concerning the subject, or (D) a statement by his agent or servant concerning a matter within the scope of his agency or employment, made during the existence of the relationship, or (E) a statement by a co-conspirator of a party during the course and in furtherance of the conspiracy.

Rule 802. Hearsay Rule

Hearsay is not admissible except as provided by these rules or by other rules prescribed by the Supreme Court pursuant to statutory authority or by Act of Congress.

Rule 803. Hearsay Exceptions: Availability of Declarant Immaterial

The following are not excluded by the hearsay rule, even though the declarant is available as a witness:

(1) *Present sense impression.* A statement describing or explaining an event or condition made while the declarant was perceiving the event or condition, or immediately thereafter.

(2) *Excited utterance.* A statement relating to a startling event or condition made while the declarant was under the stress of excitement caused by the event or condition.

(3) *Then existing mental, emotional, or physical condition.* A statement of the declarant's then existing state of mind, emotion, sensation, or physical condition (such as intent, plan, motive, design, mental feeling, pain, and bodily health), but not including a statement of memory or belief to prove the fact remembered or believed unless it relates to the execution, revocation, identification, or terms of declarant's will.

(4) *Statements for purposes of medical diagnosis or treatment.* Statements made for purposes of medical diagnosis or treatment and describing medical history, or past or present symptoms, pain, or sensations, or the inception or general character of the cause or external source thereof insofar as reasonably pertinent to diagnosis or treatment.

(5) *Recorded recollection.* A memorandum or record concerning a matter about which a witness once had knowledge but now has

insufficient recollection to enable him to testify fully and accurately, shown to have been made or adopted by the witness when the matter was fresh in his memory and to reflect that knowledge correctly. If admitted, the memorandum or record may be read into evidence but may not itself be received as an exhibit unless offered by an adverse party.

(6) Records of regularly conducted activity. A memorandum, report, record, or data compilation, in any form, of acts, events, conditions, opinions, or diagnoses, made at or near the time by, or from information transmitted by, a person with knowledge, if kept in the course of a regularly conducted business activity, and if it was the regular practice of that business activity to make the memorandum, report, record, or data compilation, all as shown by the testimony of the custodian or other qualified witness, unless the source of information or the method or circumstances of preparation indicate lack of trustworthiness. The term "business" as used in this paragraph includes business, institution, association, profession, occupation, and calling of every kind, whether or not conducted for profit.

(7) Absence of entry in records kept in accordance with the provisions of paragraph (6). Evidence that a matter is not included in the memoranda, reports, records, or data compilations, in any form, kept in accordance with the provisions of paragraph (6), to prove the nonoccurrence or nonexistence of the matter, if the matter was of a kind of which a memorandum, report, record, or data compilation was regularly made and preserved, unless the sources of information or other circumstances indicate lack of trustworthiness.

(8) Public records and reports. Records, reports, statements, or data compilations, in any form, of public offices or agencies, setting forth (A) the activities of the office or agency, or (B) matters observed pursuant to duty imposed by law as to which matters there was a duty to report, excluding, however, in criminal cases matters observed by police officers and other law enforcement personnel, or (C) in civil actions and proceedings and against the Government in criminal cases, factual findings resulting from an investigation made pursuant to authority granted by law, unless the sources of information or other circumstances indicate lack of trustworthiness.

(9) Records of vital statistics. Records or data compilations, in any form, of births, fetal deaths, deaths, or marriages, if the report thereof was made to a public office pursuant to requirements of law.

(10) Absence of public record or entry. To prove the absence of a record, report, statement, or data compilation, in any form, or the nonoccurrence or nonexistence of a matter of which a record, report,

statement, or data compilation, in any form, was regularly made and preserved by a public office or agency, evidence in the form of a certification in accordance with Rule 902, or testimony, that diligent search failed to disclose the record, report, statement, or data compilation, or entry.

(11) Records of religious organizations. Statements of births, marriages, divorces, deaths, legitimacy, ancestry, relationship by blood or marriage, or other similar facts of personal or family history, contained in a regularly kept record of a religious organization.

(12) Marriage, baptismal, and similar certificates. Statements of fact contained in a certificate that the maker performed a marriage or other ceremony or administered a sacrament, made by a clergyman, public official, or other person authorized by the rules or practices of a religious organization or by law to perform the act certified, and purporting to have been issued at the time of the act or within a reasonable time thereafter.

(13) Family records. Statements of fact concerning personal or family history contained in family Bibles, genealogies, charts, engravings on rings, inscription on family portraits, engravings on urns, crypts, or tombstones, or the like.

(14) Records of documents affecting an interest in property. The record of a document purporting to establish or affect an interest in property, as proof of the content of the original recorded document and its execution and delivery by each person by whom it purports to have been executed, if the record is a record of a public office and an applicable statute authorized the recording of documents of that kind in that office.

(15) Statements in documents affecting an interest in property. A statement contained in a document purporting to establish or affect an interest in property if the matter stated was relevant to the purpose of the document, unless dealings with the property since the document was made have been inconsistent with the truth of the statement or the purport of the document.

(16) Statements in ancient documents. Statements in a document in existence 20 years or more whose authenticity is established.

(17) Market reports, commercial publications. Market quotations, tabulations, lists, directories, or other published compilations, generally used and relied upon by the public or by persons in particular occupations.

(18) Learned treatises. To the extent called to the attention of an expert witness upon cross-examination or relied upon by him in

direct examination, statements contained in published treatises, periodicals, or pamphlets on a subject of history, medicine, or other science or art, established as a reliable authority by the testimony or admission of the witness or by other expert testimony or by judicial notice. If admitted, the statements may be read into evidence but may not be received as exhibits.

(19) Reputation concerning personal or family history. Reputation among members of his family by blood, adoption, or marriage, or among his associates, or in the community, concerning a person's birth, adoption, marriage, divorce, death, legitimacy, relationship by blood, adoption, or marriage, ancestry, or other similar fact of his personal or family history.

(20) Reputation concerning boundaries or general history. Reputation in a community, arising before the controversy, as to boundaries of or customs affecting lands in the community, and reputation as to events of general history important to the community or state or nation in which located.

(21) Reputation as to character. Reputation of a person's character among his associates or in the community.

(22) Judgment of previous conviction. Evidence of a final judgment, entered after a trial or upon a plea of guilty (but not upon a plea of *nolo contendere*), adjudging a person guilty of a crime punishable by death or imprisonment in excess of one year, to prove any fact essential to sustain the judgment, but not including, when offered by the government in a criminal prosecution for purposes other than impeachment, judgments against persons other than the accused. The pendency of an appeal may be shown but does not affect admissibility.

(23) Judgment as to personal, family or general history, or boundaries. Judgments as proof of matters of personal, family or general history, or boundaries, essential to the judgment, if the same would be provable by evidence of reputation.

(24) Other exceptions. A statement not specifically covered by any of the foregoing exceptions but having equivalent circumstantial guarantees of trustworthiness, if the court determines that (A) the statement is offered as evidence of a material fact; (B) the statement is more probative on the point for which it is offered than any other evidence which the proponent can procure through reasonable efforts; and (C) the general purposes of these rules and the interests of justice will best be served by admission of the statement into evidence. However, a statement may not be admitted under this exception unless the proponent of it makes known to the adverse party

sufficiently in advance of the trial or hearing to provide the adverse party with a fair opportunity to prepare to meet it, his intention to offer the statement and the particulars of it, including the name and address of the declarant.

Rule 804. Hearsay Exceptions: Declarant Unavailable

(a) Definition of unavailability. "Unavailability as a witness" includes situations in which the declarant:

(1) Is exempted by ruling of the court on the ground of privilege from testifying concerning the subject matter of his statement; or

(2) Persists in refusing to testify concerning the subject matter of his statement despite an order of the court to do so; or

(3) Testifies to a lack of memory of the subject matter of his statement; or

(4) Is unable to be present or to testify at the hearing because of death or then existing physical or mental illness or infirmity; or

(5) Is absent from the hearing and the proponent of his statement has been unable to procure his attendance (or in the case of a hearsay exception under subdivision (b) (2), (3), or (4), his attendance or testimony) by process or other reasonable means.

A declarant is not unavailable as a witness if his exemption, refusal, claim of lack of memory, inability, or absence is due to the procurement or wrongdoing of the proponent of his statement for the purpose of preventing the witness from attending or testifying.

(b) Hearsay exceptions. The following are not excluded by the hearsay rule if the declarant is unavailable as a witness:

(1) Former testimony. Testimony given as a witness at another hearing of the same or a different proceeding, or in a deposition taken in compliance with law in the course of the same or another proceeding, if the party against whom the testimony is now offered, or, in a civil action or proceeding, a predecessor in interest, had an opportunity and similar motive to develop the testimony by direct, cross, or redirect examination.

(2) Statement under belief of impending death. In a prosecution for homicide or in a civil action or proceeding, a statement made by a declarant while believing that his death was imminent, concerning the cause or circumstances of what he believed to be his impending death.

(3) Statement against interest. A statement which was at the time of its making so far contrary to the declarant's pecuniary

or proprietary interest, or so far tended to subject him to civil or criminal liability, or to render invalid a claim by him against another, that a reasonable man in his position would not have made the statement unless he believed it to be true. A statement tending to expose the declarant to criminal liability and offered to exculpate the accused is not admissible unless corroborating circumstances clearly indicate the trustworthiness of the statement.

(4) Statement of personal or family history. (A) A statement concerning the declarant's own birth, adoption, marriage, divorce, legitimacy, relationship by blood, adoption, or marriage, ancestry, or other similar fact of personal or family history, even though declarant had no means of acquiring personal knowledge of the matter stated; or (B) a statement concerning the foregoing matters, and death also, of another person, if the declarant was related to the other by blood, adoption, or marriage or was so intimately associated with the other's family as to be likely to have accurate information concerning the matter declared.

(5) Other exceptions. A statement not specifically covered by any of the foregoing exceptions but having equivalent circumstantial guarantees of trustworthiness, if the court determines that (A) the statement is offered as evidence of a material fact; (B) the statement is more probative on the point for which it is offered than any other evidence which the proponent can procure through reasonable efforts; and (C) the general purposes of these rules and the interests of justice will best be served by admission of the statement into evidence. However, a statement may not be admitted under this exception unless the proponent of it makes known to the adverse party sufficiently in advance of the trial or hearing to provide the adverse party with a fair opportunity to prepare to meet it, his intention to offer the statement and the particulars of it, including the name and address of the declarant.

Rule 805. Hearsay within Hearsay

Hearsay included within hearsay is not excluded under the hearsay rule if each part of the combined statements conforms with an exception to the hearsay rule provided in these rules.

Rule 806. Attacking and Supporting Credibility of Declarant

When a hearsay statement, or a statement defined in Rule 801 (d) (2), (C), (D), or (E), has been admitted in evidence, the credibility of the declarant may be attacked, and if attacked may be supported, by any evidence which would be admissible for those purposes if declarant had testified as a witness. Evidence of a statement or conduct by the declarant at any time, inconsistent with his hearsay statement, is not subject to any requirement that he may have been afforded an opportunity to deny or explain. If the party against whom a hearsay statement has been admitted calls the declarant as a witness, the party is entitled to examine him on the statement as if under cross-examination.

Article IX. Authentication and Identification

Rule 901. Requirement of Authentication or Identification

(a) General provision. The requirement of authentication or identification as a condition precedent to admissibility is satisfied by evidence sufficient to support a finding that the matter in question is what its proponent claims.

(b) Illustrations. By way of illustration only, and not by way of limitation, the following are examples of authentication or identification conforming with the requirements of this rule:

(1) Testimony of witness with knowledge. Testimony that a matter is what it is claimed to be.

(2) Nonexpert opinion on handwriting. Nonexpert opinion as to the genuineness of handwriting, based upon familiarity not acquired for purposes of the litigation.

(3) Comparison by trier or expert witness. Comparison by the trier of fact or by expert witnesses with specimens which have been authenticated.

(4) Distinctive characteristics and the like. Appearance, contents, substance, internal patterns, or other distinctive characteristics, taken in conjunction with circumstances.

(5) Voice identification. Identification of a voice, whether heard firsthand or through mechanical or electronic transmission or recording, by opinion based upon hearing the voice at any time under circumstances connecting it with the alleged speaker.

(6) Telephone conversations. Telephone conversations, by evidence that a call was made to the number assigned at the time by the telephone company to a particular person or business, if (A) in the case of a person, circumstances, including self-identification, show the person answering to be the one called, or (B) in the case of a business, the call was made to a place of business and the conversation related to business reasonably transacted over the telephone.

(7) Public records or reports. Evidence that a writing authorized by law to be recorded or filed and in fact recorded or filed in a public office, or a purported public record, report, statement, or data compilation, in any form, is from the public office where items of this nature are kept.

(8) Ancient documents or data compilations. Evidence that a document or data compilation, in any form, (A) is in such condition as to create no suspicion concerning its authenticity, (B) was in a place where it, if authentic, would likely be, and (C) has been in existence 20 years or more at the time it is offered.

(9) Process or system. Evidence describing a process or system used to produce a result and showing that the process or system produces an accurate result.

(10) Methods provided by statute or rule. Any method of authentication or identification provided by Act of Congress or by other rules prescribed by the Supreme Court pursuant to statutory authority.

Rule 902. Self-Authentication

Extrinsic evidence of authenticity as a condition precedent to admissibility is not required with respect to the following:

(1) Domestic public documents under seal. A document bearing a seal purporting to be that of the United States, or of any state, district, commonwealth, territory, or insular possession thereof, or the Panama Canal Zone, or the Trust Territory of the Pacific Islands, or of a political subdivision, department, officer, or agency thereof, and a signature purporting to be an attestation or execution.

(2) Domestic public documents not under seal. A document purporting to bear the signature in his official capacity of an officer or employee or any entity included in paragraph (1) hereof, having no seal, if a public officer having a seal and having official duties in the district or political subdivision of the officer or employee certifies under seal that the signer has the official capacity and that the signature is genuine.

(3) Foreign public documents. A document purporting to be executed or attested in his official capacity by a person authorized by the laws of a foreign country to make the execution or attestation, and accompanied by a final certification as to the genuineness of the signature and official position (A) of the executing or attesting person, or (B) of any foreign official whose certificate of genuineness of signature and official position relates to the execution or attestation or is in a chain of certificates of genuineness of signature and

official position relating to the execution or attestation. A final certification may be made by a secretary of embassy or legation, consul general, consul, vice consul, or consular agent of the United States, or a diplomatic or consular official of the foreign country assigned or accredited to the United States. If reasonable opportunity has been given to all parties to investigate the authenticity and accuracy of official documents, the court may, for good cause shown, order that they be treated as presumptively authentic without final certification or permit them to be evidenced by an attested summary with or without final certification.

(4) Certified copies of public records. A copy of an official record or report or entry therein, or of a document authorized by law to be recorded or filed and actually recorded or filed in a public office, including data compilations in any form, certified as correct by the custodian or other person authorized to make the certification, by certificate complying with paragraph (1), (2) or (3) of this Rule or complying with any Act of Congress or rule prescribed by the Supreme Court pursuant to statutory authority.

(5) Official publications. Books, pamphlets, or other publications purporting to be issued by public authority.

(6) Newspapers and periodicals. Printed materials purporting to be newspapers or periodicals.

(7) Trade inscriptions and the like. Inscriptions, signs, tags, or labels purporting to have been affixed in the course of business and indicating ownership, control, or origin.

(8) Acknowledged documents. Documents accompanied by a certificate of acknowledgment executed in the manner provided by law by a notary public or other officer authorized by law to take acknowledgments.

(9) Commercial paper and related documents. Commercial paper, signatures thereon, and documents relating thereto to the extent provided by general commercial law.

(10) Presumptions under acts of Congress. Any signature, document, or other matter declared by Act of Congress to be presumptively or prima facie genuine or authentic.

Rule 903. Subscribing Witness' Testimony Unnecessary

The testimony of a subscribing witness is not necessary to authenticate a writing unless required by the laws of the jurisdiction whose laws govern the validity of the writing.

Article X. Contents of Writings, Recordings, and Photographs

Rule 1001. Definitions

For purposes of this article the following definitions are applicable.

(1) Writings and recordings. "Writings" and "recordings" consist of letters, words, or numbers, or their equivalent, set down by handwriting, typewriting, printing, photostating, photographing, magnetic impulse, mechanical or electronic recording, or other form of data compilation.

(2) Photographs. "Photographs" include still photographs, X-ray films, and motion pictures.

(3) Original. An "original" of a writing or recording is the writing or recording itself or any counterpart intended to have the same effect by a person executing or issuing it. An "original" of a photograph includes the negative or any print therefrom. If data are stored in a computer or similar device, any printout or other output readable by sight, shown to reflect the data accurately, is an "original."

(4) Duplicate. A "duplicate" is a counterpart produced by the same impression as the original, or from the same matrix, or by means of photography, including enlargements and miniatures, or by mechanical or electronic re-recording, or by chemical reproduction, or by other equivalent techniques which accurately reproduce the original.

Rule 1002. Requirement of Original

To prove the content of a writing, recording, or photograph, the original writing, recording, or photograph is required, except as otherwise provided in these rules or by Act of Congress.

Rule 1003. Admissibility of Duplicates

A duplicate is admissible to the same extent as an original unless (1) a genuine question is raised as to the authenticity of the original or (2) in the circumstances it would be unfair to admit the duplicate in lieu of the original.

Rule 1004. Admissibility of Other Evidence of Contents

The original is not required, and other evidence of the contents of a writing, recording, or photograph is admissible if—

(1) Originals lost or destroyed. All originals are lost or have been destroyed, unless the proponent lost or destroyed them in bad faith; or

(2) Original not obtainable. No original can be obtained by any available judicial process or procedure; or

(3) Original in possession of opponent. At a time when an original was under the control of the party against whom offered, he was put on notice, by the pleadings or otherwise, that the contents would be a subject of proof at the hearing, and he does not produce the original at the hearing; or

(4) Collateral matters. The writing, recording, or photograph is not closely related to a controlling issue.

Rule 1005. Public Records

The contents of an official record, or of a document authorized to be recorded or filed and actually recorded or filed, including data compilations in any form, if otherwise admissible, may be proved by copy, certified as correct in accordance with Rule 902 or testified to be correct by a witness who has compared it with the original. If a copy which complies with the foregoing cannot be obtained by the exercise of reasonable diligence, then other evidence of the contents may be given.

Rule 1006. Summaries

The contents of voluminous writings, recordings, or photographs which cannot conveniently be examined in court may be presented in the form of a chart, summary, or calculation. The originals, or duplicates, shall be made available for examination or copying, or both, by other parties at reasonable time and place. The court may order that they be produced in court.

Rule 1007. Testimony or Written Admission of Party

Contents of writings, recordings, or photographs may be proved by the testimony or deposition of the party against whom offered or by his written admission, without accounting for the nonproduction of the original.

Rule 1008. Functions of Court and Jury

When the admissibility of other evidence of contents of writings, recordings, or photographs under these rules depends upon the fulfillment of a condition of fact, the question whether the condition has been fulfilled is ordinarily for the court to determine in accordance with the provisions of Rule 104. However, when an issue is raised (a) whether the asserted writing ever existed, or (b) whether another writing, recording, or photograph produced at the trial is the original, or (c) whether other evidence of contents correctly reflects the contents, the issue is for the trier of fact to determine as in the case of other issues of fact.

Article XI. Miscellaneous Rules

Rule 1101. Applicability of Rules

(a) *Courts and magistrates.* These rules apply to the United States district courts, the District Court of Guam, the District Court of the Virgin Islands, the District Court for the District of the Canal Zone, the United States courts of appeals, the Court of Claims, and to United States magistrates, in the actions, cases, and proceedings and to the extent hereinafter set forth. The terms "judge" and "court" in these rules include United States magistrates, referees in bankruptcy, and commissioners of the Court of Claims.

(b) *Proceedings generally.* These rules apply generally to civil actions and proceedings, including admiralty and maritime cases, to criminal cases and proceedings, to contempt proceedings except those in which the court may act summarily, and to proceedings and cases under the Bankruptcy Act.

(c) *Rule of privilege.* The rule with respect to privileges applies at all stages of all actions, cases, and proceedings.

(d) *Rules inapplicable.* The rules (other than with respect to privileges) do not apply in the following situations:

(1) *Preliminary questions of fact.* The determination of questions of fact preliminary to admissibility of evidence when the issue is to be determined by the court under rule 104.

(2) *Grand jury.* Proceedings before grand juries.

(3) *Miscellaneous proceedings.* Proceedings for extradition or rendition; preliminary examinations in criminal cases; sentencing, or granting or revoking probation; issuance of warrants for arrest, criminal summonses, and search warrants; and proceedings with respect to release on bail or otherwise.

(e) *Rules applicable in part.* In the following proceedings these rules apply to the extent that matters of evidence are not provided for in the statutes which govern procedure therein or in other rules prescribed by the Supreme Court pursuant to statutory authority; the trial of minor and petty offenses by United States magistrates; review of agency actions when the facts are subject to trial de novo under section 706(2)(F) of title 5, United States Code; review of orders of the Secretary of Agriculture under section 2 of the Act entitled "An Act to authorize association of producers of agricultural products" approved February 18, 1922 (7 U.S.C. 292), and under sections 6 and 7(c) of the Perishable Agricultural Commodities Act, 1930 (7 U.S.C. 499f, 499g(c)); naturalization and revocation of naturalization under sections 310-318 of the Immigration and Nationality Act (8 U.S.C. 1421-1429); prize proceedings in admiralty under sections 7651-7681 of title 10, United States Code; review of orders of the Secretary of the Interior under section 2 of the Act entitled "An Act authorizing associations of producers of aquatic products" approved June 25, 1931 (15 U.S.C. 522); review of orders of petroleum control boards under section 5 of the Act entitled "An Act to regulate interstate and foreign commerce in petroleum and its products by prohibiting the shipment in such commerce of petroleum and its products produced in violation of State law, and for other purposes," approved February 22, 1935 (15 U.S.C. 715d); actions for fines, penalties, or forfeitures under part V of title IV of the Tariff Act of 1930 (19 U.S.C. 1581-1624), or under the Anti-Smuggling Act (19 U.S.C. 1701-1711); criminal libel for condemnation, exclusion of imports, or other proceedings under the Federal Food, Drug, and Cosmetic Act (21 U.S.C. 301-392); disputes between seamen under sections 4079, 4080, and 4081 of the Revised Statutes (22 U.S.C. 256-258); habeas corpus under sections 2241-2254 of title 28, United States Code; motions to vacate, set aside or correct sentence under section 2255 of title 28, United States Code; actions for penalties for refusal to transport destitute seamen under section 4578 of the Revised Statutes (46 U.S.C. 679); actions against the United States under the Act entitled "An Act authorizing suits against the United States in admiralty for damage caused by and salvage service rendered to public vessels belonging to the United States, and for other purposes," approved March 3, 1925 (46 U.S.C. 781-790), as implemented by section 7730 of title 10, United States Code.

Rule 1102. Amendments

Amendments to the Federal Rules of Evidence may be made as provided in section 2076 of title 28 of the United States Code.

Rule 1103. Title

These rules may be known and cited as the Federal Rules of Evidence.

Effective date: July 1, 1975

Glossary

Abandoned property. Property that has been abandoned and belongs to no one. The voluntary relinquishment of possession, right, and claim to something, accompanied by an apparent intention of not reclaiming it.

Accessory. A person who has aided, abetted, or assisted the principal offender, or who has counseled and encouraged the perpetration of a crime.

Accessory after the fact. A person who has knowledge of the crime and assists the perpetrator in avoiding arrest or in an escape.

Accessory before the fact. A person who has aided or encouraged the offense before its commission, but who did not, either actually or constructively, physically participate in its commission.

Accomplice. A person who knowingly, voluntarily, and with the common intent with the principal offender unites in the commission of a crime. The cooperation must be real, not apparent; mere presence coupled with knowledge that a crime is about to be committed, without some contribution, does not raise the liability of an accomplice.

Acquittal. A verdict of not guilty. The certification by a court or jury of the innocence of a defendant during or after trial.

Ad hoc. Specially pertaining to, or for the sake of, this case alone.

Adjudicate. To hear, try, and determine the claims of litigants before the court.

Admissibility. Determination of whether testimony, exhibits, or evidence will be allowed in trial.

Advocacy. The act of defending, assisting, or pleading for another; to defend by argument.

Advocate. One who renders legal advice and pleads the cause of another before a court or tribunal; one who speaks in favor of another. A lawyer.

Affidavit. A voluntary, sworn written statement.

Alibi. A plea by a suspect of having been elsewhere at the time of the commission of the crime.

Ancient document rule. A document is "ancient" if it is twenty or more years old, and the proof of its age suffices as authentication. An ancient document, if relevant to the inquiry and free from suspicion, can be admissible in evidence without the ordinary requirements of proof of execution.

Answer. Defendant's written response to a civil complaint, containing his admission or denial of each of the allegations in the complaint. Cf. Plea.

Appeal. The judicial review of a decision of a trial court by a higher court with no new testimony taken or issue raised. A post-conviction step in judicial proceedings.

Appointed attorney. Legal counsel provided by a court for defendants who are without funds to hire private counsel.

Arm's reach doctrine. Officers can only search without a warrant the arrestee and the area immediately around him where the arrestee can reach or jump over to. This curtailment of the scope of searches evident to a legal arrest was ruled by the Supreme Court in *Chimel* v. *California*, 395 U.S. 752 (1969).

Arrest. To take a person into custody for the purpose of answering to the court. To consummate an arrest an officer must have the authority to make an arrest and an intention to arrest the suspect. There must be some restraint of the suspect, either physical or mental, and the suspect must understand that he is arrested.

Authenticating witness. One who establishes that a writing or document is what it purports to be and that it was made by the party to whom it was attributed.

Authentication. A legal process of proof that is designed to establish the genuineness, not the truth, of the contents of a writing or document.

Bail. To procure the release of a defendant from legal custody by guaranteeing his future appearance in court and compelling him to remain within jurisdiction of the court. Cash or other security may be required.

Ballistics. The identification of the firing characteristics of a firearm or cartridge; the scientific examination of evidence found at crime scenes and connected with firearms; firearms, spent bullets, empty cartridge or shell cases, cartridges, and shells.

Bench. The presiding judge (and his position at the front of the courtroom).

Best evidence rule. The contents of any writing must be proven by the writing itself or the failure to do so must be adequately explained. In addition to documents in writing, the rule is also applicable to recordings, X rays, photographs, and films.

Bill of particulars. A written statement of the facts upon which a charge is brought, that is more specific than the complaint of information, and is produced on the demand of a defendant.

Burden of proof. The duty of establishing the truth of the issue at trial by such a quantum of evidence as the law requires.

Capias. A writ used to seize the property or person of the defendant; sometimes used to bring in a person for a mental examination.

Circumstantial evidence. Facts and circumstances concerning a trans-action from which the jury may infer other connected facts that reasonably follow according to common human experience.

Citation. Reference to an authority for a point of law, as a case by title, volume, and page of the report or reports in which the opinion appears and the year it was decided.

Citizen's arrest. Citizens are authorized to make arrests in felonies or breach of the peace without a warrant, when the offense is committed in their presence.

Compensatory damages. Damages assessed for the pain or suffering, humiliation, and defamation of the plaintiff.

Complaint. The pleading that initiates a criminal proceeding; some-times called a criminal affidavit.

Consensual search. The party in possession of what is to be searched validly consents to a search by police. The suspect voluntarily, without coercion or deceit, relinquishes the right under the Fourth and Fourteenth Amendments to demand a search warrant.

Conspiracy. An agreement between two or more people to commit a criminal act, coupled with an overt act in furtherance.

Contraband. Things that are illegally possessed and that cannot be lawfully owned.

Coram nobis. Writ of error. A petition to fight a criminal conviction to the original court that seeks to set aside a conviction on some alleged error that does not appear on the record.

Corpus delicti. Body of crime.

Corroborating evidence. Evidence that supports and supplements previously offered evidence. It is directed at the same issue as the initial evidence, but it comes from a separate source and is designed to enhance the credibility of the prior testimony.

Criminal act. Any act or omission that is punishable as a crime.

Criminal intent. A guilty or evil state of mind to do an act prohibited as a crime by law.

Cross-examination. The interrogation of a witness by counsel for the opposing party by questions to test the truthfulness and accuracy of his testimony.

Curtilage. The area immediately surrounding a person's home and all attached structures that has the same constitutional protections as the home.

Declarant. A person who makes a statement.

Declarations against interest. Out-of-court statements by a person that are in conflict with his pecuniary interests.

Declarations against penal interest. Out-of-court statements by a person that are in conflict with his innocence.

Demonstrative evidence. A model, an illustration, a chart, or an experiment offered as proof; real evidence.

Deposition. The testimony of a witness, compelled by subpoena, at a proceeding where counsel, but not the judge, attend. It is a pretrial discovery device.

Detention. A stop of a suspect by an officer; a temporary curtailment of personal freedoms. An officer may detain a suspicious individual to ask him questions about his conduct.

Dictum, dicta. A judicial opinion on some aspect of a case not essential to a court's decision on the issue under review.

Direct evidence. Evidence that comes from any of the witness' five senses and is in itself proof or disproof of a fact in issue.

Discovery. The compelled disclosure of facts, statements, or the production of documents, through subpoena duces tecum, interrogatories, or deposition, prior to trial.

Diversion. Finding alternatives to formal action in the criminal justice system.

Documentary evidence. Tangible objects that can express a fact or that tend to clarify the truth or untruth of the issues in question. Broad category includes private writings, documents, official records, newspapers, maps, or any other objects on which symbols have been placed with the intention of preserving a record of events or impressions.

Double jeopardy. Being tried more than once for the same crime.

Duress. An affirmative defense by a suspect that he was forced or coerced to commit a crime.

Dying declaration. A statement made by a homicide victim about to die without any hope of recovery concerning the facts and circumstances under which the fatal injury was inflicted. This declaration is offered in evidence at the trial of the person charged with having caused the speaker's death.

En banc. All the qualified judges of a court (particularly an appellate court) sitting and hearing a case.

Entrapment. The procurement of a person to commit a crime that he did not contemplate or would not have committed, for the sole purpose of prosecuting that person.

Evidence. Anything offered in court to prove the truth or falsity of a fact in issue.

Exclusionary rule. A rule of evidence that suppresses and rejects otherwise admissible evidence because it was obtained in violation of the Fourth or Fifth Amendment; applies to direct and derivative evidence, seized as a result of an illegal arrest or search.

Exemplar. A sample of handwriting; a specimen; a model.

Exigent circumstances. An emergency situation. If a true emergency exists, or is reasonably believed to exist, police officers may enter the premises without a warrant. In most jurisdictions anything seen inside in plain view may be seized without a warrant.

Expert witness. A person who must appear to the trial judge to have such knowledge, skill, or experience within the particular subject of inquiry that his opinion will be of some aid to the trier of fact in arriving at the true facts.

Facts. Findings as to what particular occurrences did or did not take place, which must be proved by evidence.

False arrest. The unlawful physical retainment of a citizen. An arrest of a civil plaintiff by an officer without probable cause.

False imprisonment. The unlawful incarceration of a person.

Field interrogation. Questioning of a suspect by the police outside of a police station.

Forensic. Pertaining to or belonging to the courts of justice.

Forensic science. The use of scientific knowledge to investigate and solve crimes.

Foundation. The preliminary basis required for the admission of certain evidence.

Fresh pursuit. See Hot pursuit doctrine.

Frisk. A limited form of searching; a pat-down of a person's outer clothing for a weapon.

Fruit of the crime. An object directly obtained by criminal means.

Fruit of the Poisoned Tree doctrine. The application of the exclusionary rule to evidence *derived* from an illegal search.
Grand jury. An accusatory body that inquires into felonies committed
  within a particular district.
Guilty. A defendant's plea in a criminal prosecution; admission of
  having committed the crime with which he is charged.
Habeas corpus. A writ seeking to bring a person already in custody
  before a court or judge to challenge the lawfulness of the
  imprisonment.
Habeas corpus ad testificandum. A writ directed to the person having
  legal custody of an inmate in a jail or prison that orders him to
  bring the prisoner to court to testify.
Hearsay. An out-of-court statement offered to prove the truth of the
  matter contained in the statement. It is only hearsay if it is
  offered to prove that the statement itself is true.
Hot pursuit doctrine. An officer who chases a fugitive, or is in fresh
  pursuit, does not need a search warrant to continue his chase
  into homes or offices, and anything found in the course of the
  pursuit and is incident to it is an admissible item.
Impeachment. The act of discrediting a person or a thing. Questioning the credibility of a witness.
In camera. In judicial chambers. A hearing in which all but counsel
  are excluded from the courtroom.
Indictment. A written accusation, provided by a grand jury, charging
  a person with the commission of a crime.
Information. An affidavit, filed by the prosecutor, that initiates a
  criminal proceeding.
Informer's privilege. Right of the police *not* to disclose the identity
  of informants to protect them from retaliation and to maintain
  a confidential source of information about crime.
Inquest. An examination of the cause and circumstances of a violent
  or suspicious death.
Instructions to jury. A final charge given to the jury by the trial
  judge. An explanation of the law of the case being tried to
  furnish guidance to the jury in their deliberations.
Instrumentality. A thing used to facilitate a crime such as a tool or
  weapon.
Intent. The mental purpose to do a specific thing.
Interrogation. Any questioning likely or expected to yield incriminating statements.
Interrogatories. Written questions by one party to a proceeding sent
  to the opposing party, which are to be answered under oath; a
  discovery device.

Inventory. A check of the contents of an impounded vehicle by officers pursuant to departmental regulations or standing custom. It is conducted for the purpose of safeguarding any valuables found in the vehicle, and it protects the officers from liability from mysterious disappearance of the valuables.

Judicial notice. The recognition by the court that a given fact is true without requiring formal proof. The fact must be one that is certain and indisputable, or the fact must be one of common, everyday knowledge in that jurisdiction, which everyone of average intelligence and knowledge can be presumed to know.

Juvenile. A child up to the age of eighteen who is tried in a special court on the issues of neglect and delinquency.

Latent (fingerprint). Present but not visible. A latent fingerprint must be searched for and developed by evidence technicians with special skill and equipment and preserved as evidence.

Lay witness. A nonexpert person who must be able to base his testimony upon his ability to observe, recollect, and explain to others. He may testify only to facts that he has acquired through his own senses.

Leading question. A question that suggests the desired answer to the witness.

Malicious prosecution. The actual prosecution of criminal charges against an accused person when there is no probable cause and when the charges were brought for malicious reasons.

Mens rea. An evil intent; criminal state of mind.

Modus operandi (m.o.). Method of operation; the characteristics of a particular criminal conduct or technique.

Motion. An application made to a court or judge to obtain an order.

Motion to suppress. A motion made by the defendant prior to the actual start of his trial to exclude evidence under the theory that it has been "tainted" by being seized or obtained in violation of the Fourth or Fifth Amendment.

Motive. The moving power, the reason for doing something.

Ne exeat. A writ ordering the detention of a person until he posts an appearance bond in a civil case that will "guarantee" his appearance.

Nolle prosequi. A formal entry on the record, by the prosecutor, that he will no longer prosecute the case.

Nolo contendere. A plea of "no contest" having the same effect as a plea of guilty.

Objection. A protest against a determination by the court, especially a ruling upon the admissibility of evidence.

Open field doctrine. Officers may enter private outdoor property to look for evidence, without a warrant or other justification, and anything seen in the course of their expedition falls within the plain view rule.

Peace officer. A public officer such as a policeman, sheriff, deputy sheriff, marshal, constable, or state investigator; a "sworn" officer.

Per se. By or through itself.

Physical evidence. Items, things, and traces found at a crime scene; suspects or other persons or places concerned with a criminal investigation.

Plain view rule. Readily observable things seen by an officer (in a place where he has a right to be) that are not the product of a search and are not subject to exclusion from evidence.

Plea. In criminal cases, the official answer to the charge brought against him. The usual pleas are guilty, not guilty, and nolo contendere.

Plea bargaining. The process whereby a defendant and the state bargain a plea of guilty for a reduced sentence. The "agreement" is supervised by the court prior to approval.

Posse comitatus. Male, and in some jurisdictions female, adults whom a sheriff or other officers may summon to their assistance. Citizens who may be deputized to assist officers in making an arrest.

Preliminary hearing. A judicial examination of witnesses to determine whether or not a crime has been committed and if the evidence presented against the accused is sufficient to warrant bail or commitment pending trial.

Presentence report. A report compiled under court direction by a probation officer on the social and criminal history of a convicted defendant with a recommendation to the sentencing judge of the best corrections program for the offender.

Presumption. The drawing of a particular inference of one fact from the existence of a related known or proven fact.

Prima facie. First view. Evidence in a criminal case that on its surface is sufficient to prove the charge.

Privileged communication. A communication between persons in a confidential relationship, such as husband and wife, attorney and client, confessor and penitent, or doctor and patient. Under public policy the court will not allow such information to be disclosed or inquired into.

Probable cause. A conclusion of law that an offense probably was committed and the suspect probably is guilty thereof.

Public place. A place exposed to the public where people gather together and pass to and fro and where whatever occurs would be seen by a number of persons.

Punitive damages. Damages awarded by a jury to "teach and punish" the civil defendant. In most jurisdictions neither cities nor insurance companies will indemnify an officer for punitive damages, and they cannot be discharged through the bankruptcy courts.

Real evidence. Tangible objects presented in the courtroom for the trier of fact to view. Something directly connected with the incident out of which the cause of action arose.

Rebuttal. The answer of the prosecution to the defense case in chief.

Rebuttal evidence. Evidence disputing or answering that given by the opposite side. Evidence that denies any affirmative fact that the adverse party has endeavored in any matter to prove.

Rejoinder (surrebuttal). The answer of the defense to the prosecutor's rebuttal.

Relevancy. Relevant evidence is that evidence which "advances the inquiry"; that is, it proves something.

Replevin. A civil action to recover things wrongfully possessed by another, such as stolen goods. Also brought by acquitted defendants for return of property illegally seized.

Res gestae. Exclamations and statements made by the participants, victims, or spectators of a crime immediately before, during, or after the commission of the crime, where such statements were made as a reaction to, or utterance inspired by, the occasion and where there was no opportunity for the declarant to deliberate or fabricate a false statement.

Return (search warrant). A statement in writing of police action taken while executing a search warrant, including a description of the place searched and an inventory of property seized.

Rules of evidence. The laws that determine what evidence may be used to prove facts. These laws are not concerned with what the outcome will be once the facts are finally decided (as most laws are), but instead are only concerned with the admissibility of various evidence that is offered to prove facts.

Rules of law. Once the facts are determined from evidence presented, certain rules are then applied to those facts that determine the outcome of the case.

Search. The seeking of something not in plain sight, in places where the object (or person) sought might be concealed.

Search warrant. A legal process, issued by a judge upon a supporting affidavit, that authorizes a peace officer to search a person or place for evidence of an offense, contraband, instrumentalities, and fruits of a crime.

Secondary evidence. See Circumstantial evidence.

Special damages. See Punitive damages.

Stare decisis. To abide by, or adhere to, decided cases. Policy of courts to stand by precedent and not to disturb a settled point.

Statement. Oral, written, or even nonverbal conduct that conveys a message.

Stipulation. The admittance of proof by agreement of the opposing attorneys.

Stop and frisk. The right of a police officer to detain suspicious individuals temporarily and to frisk (pat-down search) those who appear dangerous. Upheld by the landmark case *Terry* v. *Ohio,* 392 U.S. 1 (1968).

Subpoena. A process to cause a witness to appear and give testimony, commanding him to lay aside all pretenses and excuses, and appear before a court or magistrate therein named at a time therein mentioned to testify.

Subpoena ad testificandum. A technical and descriptive term for the ordinary subpoena.

Subpoena duces tecum. A process by which the court, at the request of a party, commands a witness who has in his possession or control some document or paper that is pertinent to the issues of a pending controversy to produce it at the trial.

Suppression hearing. A formal motion by a defendant's lawyer to suppress and reject either tangible or intangible evidence that was allegedly illegally obtained.

Testimony. Spoken evidence given by a competent witness, under oath or affirmation; as distinguished from evidence derived from writings and other sources.

Tort. A civil wrong committed to the person or property of another and resulting in some damage or injury.

True bill. A grand jury indictment.

Venue. A neighborhood, place, or county in which an injury is declared to have been done, or fact declared to have happened. Also, the county (or geographical division) in which an action or prosecution is brought for trial, and which is to furnish the panel of jurors. In a criminal case the defendant has a constitutional right, which he can waive, to be tried in the district in which the crime was committed.

Verbal act. An action by words. A statement that shows the motive, character, and object of an act.

Vital statistics. Data relating primarily to health, such as the registration of births, marriages, and deaths, which have been compiled under public authority.

Voir dire. The examination of prospective jurors or witnesses before the trial begins to determine if they have the necessary qualifications to be fair and impartial.

Voluntary statement. A statement that is free of duress and coercion, but is usually elicited by questioning.

Volunteered statement. An utterance made without elicitation, frequently a spontaneous statement.

Weight of evidence. The believability of evidence. Evidence may be technically legal and, thus, admissible in court, but the question remains as to whether or not it should be given any value or weight.

Witness. One who, being present, personally sees or perceives a thing; a beholder, spectator, or eyewitness.

Index